Violent Intermediaries

NEW AFRICAN HISTORIES

SERIES EDITORS: JEAN ALLMAN, ALLEN ISAACMAN, AND DEREK R. PETERSON

*Books in this series are published with support from the
Ohio University National Resource Center for African Studies.*

David William Cohen and E. S. Atieno Odhiambo, *The Risks of Knowledge: Investigations into the Death of the Hon. Minister John Robert Ouko in Kenya, 1990*

Belinda Bozzoli, *Theatres of Struggle and the End of Apartheid*

Gary Kynoch, *We Are Fighting the World: A History of the Marashea Gangs in South Africa, 1947–1999*

Stephanie Newell, *The Forger's Tale: The Search for Odeziaku*

Jacob A. Tropp, *Natures of Colonial Change: Environmental Relations in the Making of the Transkei*

Jan Bender Shetler, *Imag^ining Serengeti: A History of Landscape Memory in Tanzania from Earliest Times to the Present*

Cheikh Anta Babou, *Fighting the Greater Jihad: Amadu Bamba and the Founding of the Muridiyya in Senegal, 1853–1913*

Marc Epprecht, *Heterosexual Africa? The History of an Idea from the Age of Exploration to the Age of AIDS*

Marissa J. Moorman, *Intonations: A Social History of Music and Nation in Luanda, Angola, from 1945 to Recent Times*

Karen E. Flint, *Healing Traditions: African Medicine, Cultural Exchange, and Competition in South Africa, 1820–1948*

Derek R. Peterson and Giacomo Macola, editors, *Recasting the Past: History Writing and Political Work in Modern Africa*

Moses E. Ochonu, *Colonial Meltdown: Northern Nigeria in the Great Depression*

Emily S. Burrill, Richard L. Roberts, and Elizabeth Thornberry, editors, *Domestic Violence and the Law in Colonial and Postcolonial Africa*

Daniel R. Magaziner, *The Law and the Prophets: Black Consciousness in South Africa, 1968–1977*

Emily Lynn Osborn, *Our New Husbands Are Here: Households, Gender, and Politics in a West African State from the Slave Trade to Colonial Rule*

Robert Trent Vinson, *The Americans Are Coming! Dreams of African American Liberation in Segregationist South Africa*

James R. Brennan, *Taifa: Making Nation and Race in Urban Tanzania*

Benjamin N. Lawrance and Richard L. Roberts, editors, *Trafficking in Slavery's Wake: Law and the Experience of Women and Children*

David M. Gordon, *Invisible Agents: Spirits in a Central African History*

Allen F. Isaacman and Barbara S. Isaacman, *Dams, Displacement, and the Delusion of Development: Cahora Bassa and Its Legacies in Mozambique, 1965–2007*

Stephanie Newell, *The Power to Name: A History of Anonymity in Colonial West Africa*

Gibril R. Cole, *The Krio of West Africa: Islam, Culture, Creolization, and Colonialism in the Nineteenth Century*

Meredith Terretta, *Nation of Outlaws, State of Violence: Nationalism, Grassfields Tradition, and State Building in Cameroon*

Paolo Israel, *In Step with the Times: Mapiko Masquerades of Mozambique*

Michelle R. Moyd, *Violent Intermediaries: African Soldiers, Conquest, and Everyday Colonialism in German East Africa*

Violent Intermediaries

African Soldiers, Conquest, and Everyday
Colonialism in German East Africa

⤳

Michelle R. Moyd

OHIO UNIVERSITY PRESS ⤳ ATHENS, OHIO

Ohio University Press, Athens, Ohio 45701
ohioswallow.com
© 2014 by Ohio University Press

To obtain permission to quote, reprint, or otherwise reproduce or distribute
material from Ohio University Press publications, please contact our rights
and permissions department at (740) 593-1154 or (740) 593-4536 (fax).

Printed in the United States of America
Ohio University Press books are printed on acid-free paper ⊗ ™

24 23 22 21 20 19 18 17 16 15 14   5 4 3 2 1

Library of Congress Cataloging-in-Publication Data

Moyd, Michelle R., 1968– author.
 Violent intermediaries : African soldiers, conquest, and everyday colonialism
in German East Africa / Michelle R. Moyd.
    pages cm. — (New African histories)
Includes bibliographical references and index.
 ISBN 978-0-8214-2089-8 (pb : alk. paper) — ISBN 978-0-8214-4487-0 (pdf)
 1. German East Africa—History, Military. 2. Mercenary troops—German
East Africa. 3. German East Africa—History. 4. German East Africa—
Colonization. 5. Germany—Colonies—Africa, East. I. Title. II. Series: New
African histories series.
 DT447.M69 2014
 967.802—dc23

2014012487

For my parents, Ann and Henry Moyd

Contents

Illustrations

Preface

This book began as an effort to answer what seemed a simple question: who were the *askari*, the African men who fought for the German colonial army during the East African campaign of World War I? Having stumbled across descriptions of them as "loyal askari" who followed their German commanders to the bitter end of a long and taxing military campaign, I became curious about their origins and motivations. Laboring under some rather simplistic assumptions about German racism and militarism in the twentieth century, I found the question of why African men would have fought for the Germans at all an intriguing, yet vexing, one. My preconceived and sometimes naïve notions about what constituted a professional military, based on my own experiences of growing up in a military household and later as an Air Force officer, also complicated my first attempts to understand the askari.

The photograph on the front cover of this book encapsulates much of what I hope this book conveys about the soldiers of the German colonial army in East Africa. The image reflects German priorities in representing their colonial soldiers. At the same time, however, it reveals askari priorities in representing themselves. In the photograph, an askari is dressed in full military kit, rifle over his shoulder. With his gaze directed slightly downward, he faces his wife, and they hold hands lightly. Surrounded by children, she too looks slightly downward and to the side. The older children reach toward their parents' hands. The photograph's message seems clear—the askari is leaving his family to go to war. The photograph's formal and formulaic arrangement plays to German understandings of family and soldiering, evoking a sentimental response from the viewer. At the same time though, the photograph reveals something of what the askari himself may have valued. While the askari and his family are the focal point of the image, in the background we also see his thatched home and objects suggestive of domestic labor and leisure activities—a chair, clothing, and cooking accessories. The photograph thus also provides a glimpse into what motivated this soldier to fight—his household, a primary marker of his status as a respectable man.

Explaining askari willingness to fight for the Germans without taking into account either the social and economic rewards they received for doing so or the meanings they attributed to their work produces a hollow understanding of why they fought for the Germans. This book attempts to counter such understandings by explaining the askari as men whose aspirations for respectability tied them and those around them to the colonial state's inherently violent governance practices. During the colonial era, representations like those on this book's cover helped divert attention away from the everyday violence of colonialism. One hundred years later, I submit that such evidence should be used to better understand these agents of colonial violence as men, soldiers, and intermediaries, so that we might also better understand how empires work.

Acknowledgments

When I undertook my first research trip related to this book's topic fifteen years ago, I had little sense that I could write a book that people might want to read. I had even less sense of how books get written. That I now am nearing the end of this particular sojourn is due in great measure to the many family, friends, colleagues, administrators, and institutions who kept reminding me of the project's value, and who helped me put it together piece by piece. I would like to express my heartfelt gratitude to all of those on three continents who made this book possible. I hope anyone I have inadvertently omitted will also accept my thanks.

At Ohio University Press, Gillian Berchowitz expressed enthusiasm for my manuscript right away, and handled the process with admirable efficiency and patience, accommodating many delays caused by professional and family obligations. Series editors Jean Allman and Allen Isaacman, as well as two anonymous reviewers, read the manuscript with great care. Their suggestions tightened the book's argument, rescued me from interpretive mistakes, and challenged me to be bold in my assertions. Nancy Basmajian oversaw the last stages of the book's production, saving me from a number of mistakes, big and small, and providing valuable editorial advice. Beth Pratt created the book's eye-catching cover, and John Pratt helped me straighten out permissions. Copyeditor Bob Furnish was meticulous and thorough, sharpening the book's presentation. Brian Balsley produced the wonderful maps. I learned a great deal from working with the press. I feel fortunate that they took on my first book project with such gusto.

I would also like to thank Heather Roberts for her masterful indexing skills. Her reputation rightly precedes her.

Cambridge University Press granted permission to use portions of my article "'We don't want to die for nothing': *Askari* at War in German

East Africa, 1914–1918" in the introduction. University of Michigan Press granted permission to use portions of my piece "Bomani: African Soldiers as Colonial Intermediaries in German East Africa, 1890–1914," in chapters 4 and 5. Hartmut Bergenthum granted permission to use images from the image collection of the German Colonial Society, held at the University of Frankfurt's Johann Christian Senckenberg Library. Martina Caspers helped me gain permission to use images from the Bundesarchiv-Bildarchiv. I am most grateful to all who helped me with these permissions.

At Cornell University, a number of History Department faculty members took an interest in my project and offered constructive criticism through all stages of its development. My dissertation advisers Sandra Greene, Isabel Hull, and Barry Strauss not only pushed me to become a better researcher, writer, and thinker but also modeled excellent mentorship, teaching, and leadership skills. I cannot thank them enough for their years of guidance and enthusiasm about my work. I would also like to thank Edward Baptist, Daniel Baugh, Vicki Caron, Holly Case, Duane Corpis, Peter Dear, Oren Falk, Durba Ghosh, TJ Hinrichs, Peter Holquist, Dominick Lacapra, Daniel Magaziner, Suman Seth, Robert Travers, and Rachel Weil, who all offered valuable interventions at critical stages of my project. In German Studies, Leslie Adelson helped me think more carefully about connections between my work and German colonial and postcolonial history. Salah Hassan (Art History/Africana), Dagmawi Woubshet (English), and Fouad Makki (Development Sociology) encouraged me to rethink significant threads of my argument. I could not have asked for a richer intellectual and collegial environment within which to embark on this project.

I must also acknowledge my colleagues in the Department of History at the United States Air Force Academy (USAFA), where I taught from 1996 to 2000. They were the first to encourage me to pursue this project. I am especially grateful to Deborah Schmitt, Michael Neiberg, and William Astore. They have all moved on to other institutions, but they will forever remain linked to "the Springs" in my mind. The USAFA Dean of Faculty provided funds for exploratory archival research in Freiburg and Berlin in 1999. Dennis Showalter at Colorado College also provided early mentorship and encouragement.

Over the years I have enjoyed generous research support, which came from numerous institutions and foundations. Fulbright IIE funded seven months of archival and library research in Tanzania in 2003–4. The Berlin Program for Advanced German and European Studies, adeptly administered by Karin Goihl, supported fifteen months (2004–5) of research in Germany, and a Cornell University Mellon Dissertation Fellowship allowed me to stay in Berlin for an additional year (2005–6) to research and write. A Cornell University Women's Studies Program Beatrice Brown Award provided funding for research-related costs, as did an Einaudi Center International Travel Grant. Also at Cornell, a Seymour Bluestone Fellowship from the Peace Studies Program and a Provost's Diversity Fellowship supported two semesters of dissertating. In 2009, a Summer Faculty Fellowship from Indiana University (IU), and a Richard M. Hunt Fellowship from the American Council on Germany allowed me to spend a month in Germany conducting further research. I spent 2010–11 as a residential fellow at the Institute for Historical Studies at the University of Texas, Austin, where I benefited from uninterrupted writing time, as well as energetic collegial exchange with other fellows and faculty members. I undertook further revisions to the manuscript while a residential fellow at the International Research Center for Work and Human Lifecycle in Global History (Re: Work), Humboldt University, Berlin, in 2012–13. Andreas Eckert, Felicitas Hentschke, Maïté Kersaint, and the entire Re: Work staff ensured a productive and pleasant year in Berlin. Indiana University's Office of the Vice Provost for Research awarded me Research Leave Supplements to support each of the two residential fellowships, as well as a Grant-in-Aid to help defray indexing costs. The IU History Department and the African Studies Program funded travel to several annual conferences where I presented chapters-in-progress. To all of these agencies and those who make them work, I am most thankful.

Numerous archives, libraries, museums, and institutes facilitated access to the materials used in writing this book. At Cornell University, librarians at Olin Library agreed to purchase items based on my recommendations, and anticipated my needs on more than one occasion. Interlibrary services also came through with materials I never dreamed would be available to me in the United States. In Tanzania, I would like to thank COSTECH for granting me permission to conduct research in Tanzania. The librarians at the University of Dar es Salaam's (UDSM) East Africana collection granted access to materials held there, and provided a friendly environment in which to read them.

The archivists at the Tanzania National Archives were most helpful in locating files and photocopying items. At the Benedictine abbey in Peramiho (near Songea), Abbott Engelbert entrusted me to use materials on short notice. In Germany, I am thankful to archivists, librarians, and staff at the Bundesarchiv branches in Berlin-Lichterfelde, Freiburg, and Koblenz; the Geheimes Staatsarchiv in Berlin-Dahlem; the Bayerisches Hauptstaatsarchiv in Munich; the Leibniz Institut für Länderkunde in Leipzig (especially Franz Peter Brogiato); the Berlin Mission archive; the Leipzig Mission archive; the Moravian Mission archive at Herrnhut; the Ethnographic Museum in Berlin; the Auswärtiges Amt archive in Berlin; and the Franckesche Stiftungen archives in Halle. In England, I would like to thank the archivists and staff at the Rhodes House in Oxford; the National Archives at Kew; and the Imperial War Museum in London. At IU, I would like to thank African Studies librarian Marion Frank-Wilson and Interlibrary Services for supporting my many research requests.

A number of colleagues in Tanzania, Europe, and the United States offered their wisdom and kindly shared sources and ideas with me over the years. At the UDSM Department of History and Archaeology, Professors Nestor Luanda, Yusufu Lawi, Bertram Mapunda, Anselm Tambila, and Fred Kaijage sponsored my research and offered tips for maximizing my time in Tanzania. Felicitas Becker shared research tips and sources with me. In Germany, Tanja Bührer, Pascal Grosse, Susann Lewerenz, Stefanie Michels, Thomas Morlang, and Michael Pesek shared their work and sources with me without reservation. Conversations with Ulrike Lindner have helped me better understand how my work fits with the study of empires, and she gave me a place to stay on three different research trips to Munich and Cambridge. In England, Jan-Georg Deutsch, John Iliffe, and Eckard Michels all dispensed valuable research advice. The Tanzanian studies communities have also been a tremendous resource for me. I would especially like to thank Jan Bender-Shetler, Steven Fabian, James Giblin, Lorne Larson, Juhani Koponen, and Thaddeus Sunseri for their support and advice over the years. Special thanks goes to Jamie Monson for her mentorship, and for reading my entire manuscript and providing first-rate comments that helped me improve it. Holly Hanson has been a reliable mentor and friend for many years. John Lamphear read an early version of what became chapters 2 and 5, and we spent a lovely afternoon discussing it at his home outside Austin, Texas, in 2011. Shortly after my arrival in Bloomington in 2008, Phyllis Martin read my dissertation and offered much-needed clarity on how to proceed with revisions. Timothy Parsons also read the entire manuscript, and a number of his critical interventions made this book far stronger than it would have been without his perspective.

Graduate student friends and colleagues also helped me shape and reshape arguments during our years together at Cornell. The members of my writing group, Tze May Loo, Michelle Smith, Guillaume Ratel, Sean Franzel, Ryan Plumley, and Marie Muschalek, consistently pushed me to sharpen my arguments and writing. Ryan and Marie merit special thanks for allowing me to share their kitchen table as writing space, and for being great friends and colleagues over the long haul. Successive members of Cornell's European History Colloquium, including Mary Gayne, Tracie Matysik, Benjamin Brower, Camille Robcis, Peter Staudenmaier, Emma Kuby, and Adelheid Voskuhl, also offered suggestions that sometimes took me ages to process, but that turned out to be among the most productive I have ever received.

Different parts of the manuscript benefited from feedback received from colleagues who took the time to read my work or to attend talks at various institutions. I presented early versions of what became chapters 2 and 5 at IU's African Studies Program Noon Talk and at the Wednesday Seminar. I am grateful to Maria Grosz-Ngaté and Ruth Stone, respectively, for inviting me to present my work in these venues. At the Institute for Historical Studies at UT–Austin in 2010, I presented a draft chapter. In addition, the IHS organized a manuscript workshop in which I benefited from a careful reading of the entire draft manuscript by IHS Director Julie Hardwick, as well as David Crew, Tiffany Gill, Benjamin Brower, and Tracie Matysik. This session helped me decide how to proceed with revisions, and energized me to get on with it. I extend heartfelt thanks to the IHS staff—especially Courtney Meador—for pulling this workshop together. In 2011 I presented an early version of chapter 2 at the Triangle Seminar in the History of the Military, War, and Society at Duke University in January 2011. Wayne Lee, Karen Hagemann, Anna Krylova, Bruce Hall, and others offered criticisms and suggestions that redirected my thinking. I am especially thankful to Dirk Bönker for inviting me to present in this exceptional series, and to Willeke Sandler for guiding me through part of my visit.

Shortly thereafter, a talk at Texas Southern University (TSU) in Houston helped me organize my thinking at a messy juncture in the writing process. Gregory Maddox deserves special thanks for inviting me to TSU, and Kerry Ward (Rice University) made astute observations that stayed with me long after I left Houston. In 2011, a German Studies Association conference panel on the "German Alltag" helped me sort out "everyday colonialism" as a concept. Thanks to Paul Steege for his insightful comments on the paper, and to Monica Black and Molly Loberg for a fantastic panel. Monica Black also facilitated a visit to the University of Tennessee–Knoxville, where I presented an overview of my book's arguments. I am most grateful for her friendship and collegiality over the last decade. I also wish to thank Oliver Janz and Sebastian Conrad for inviting me to present a draft version of chapter 3 to a combined meeting of their graduate seminars at the Freie Universität in Berlin. I am humbled by the realization of how many people contributed to the intellectual development of this book.

At Indiana University–Bloomington, I received a warm welcome from colleagues across campus. They helped improve my research and teaching in ways large and small, and also helped me build a fulfilling life in Bloomington. I am especially grateful to John Hanson and Marissa Moorman for helping me feel at home as an Africanist in the department, for sharing their strategies for success in research and teaching, and for their friendship. Jeannine Bell, Nick Cullather, Konstantin Dierks, Michael Dodson, Carl Ipsen, Padraic Kenney, Sarah Knott, Kevin Martin, Khalil Muhammad, Julia Roos, Mark Roseman, Robert Schneider, and Sara Scalenghe made me feel at home in Bloomington. My mentor Wendy Gamber graciously shared with me her experiences and perspectives on how to navigate the institutional and everyday demands of our profession. Judith Allen's enthusiasm for my work and sense of humor lifted my spirits on many occasions. Claudia Breger, Stephanie DeBoer, Matthew Guterl, Karen Inouye, Lara Kriegel, Rebecca Lave, Alex Lichtenstein, Pedro Machado, Krista Maglen, Amrita Chakrabarti Myers, John Nieto-Phillips, Roberta Pergher, Micol Siegel, Rebecca Spang, and Brigitta Wagner all helped me feel part of a vibrant and fun intellectual community. I am thankful to Claude Clegg and Peter Guardino who, in their roles as chairs of the Department of History, expertly guided my professional development. Both have also been excellent mentors. In the African Studies

Program, Samuel Obeng and Maria Grosz-Ngaté have provided research support whenever they could, for which I am most grateful.

I owe special thanks to IU Department of History administrators Becky Bryant, Nancy Ashley, Blake Harvey, Deana Hutchins, and Sara Skinner for the consummate professionalism they bring to all their work, from which I have benefited on multiple occasions.

Faith Hawkins, Jacob Lee, Jason McGraw, Glenda Schulz, Christina Snyder, and Ellen Wu have gone above and beyond as friends and colleagues in more ways than I can list here. I cannot thank them enough for their generous spirits and the many kindnesses they have shown me over the years. I look forward to many more years of friendship with all of them.

Jeanette Gorgas, whom I have known since eighth grade, allowed me to stay in her lovely Kensington apartment while I conducted a month of research at Kew, London. I am thankful for her hospitality and friendship.

Despite the geographic distances that separate us, my friends Lee Ann Fujii, Elizabeth Otto, and Carina Ray have always been there to celebrate my professional accomplishments and personal triumphs, and to buoy my spirits when I needed it. I thank each of them for their compassion, directness, and friendship.

My family in England—Graham and Lynne Verney, Natalie Verney and Tim Bendall, and Fay Camerling-Verney and Mike Camerling—have shared with me celebrations, housing, rides, home-cooked meals, and technological advice that helped keep my research going. I am most grateful to them all.

Thanks to Janine Harris for her longstanding friendship with my family, and for her excitement about this book's publication.

The writing of this book took place alongside some of the most significant events in my adult life—marriage and becoming a mother. My husband, Scot Wright, believed in my abilities, relocated twice in furtherance of this project, and always demonstrated patience and strength. He has been my biggest fan, but he has also never let me off the hook. To him, my love and gratitude. Thanks to Shirley and Paul Wright, Sr.; Lisa, Palmer, Esmaude, and Preston Jason; and Melanie and Paul Wright, Jr., and daughter Jasmine for welcoming me to the family. I am sorry that my father-in-law was not here to see this book published. I thank Samantha McCormick for accepting me as her stepmom, and for her ability to imagine a year in Berlin as an opportunity and adventure. I am also thankful to Elyssia McCormick for her trust and willingness to share her daughter with me.

Evren Moyd-Wright arrived while I was finishing this book. It is tempting to joke about one gestation period's duration in relation to the other, but I will refrain. Nothing can compare with the experience of being Evren's mother. I look forward to the day when she will understand that I finished this book in her first few months of life, and I thank her in advance for her understanding and patience as I write more.

How do I adequately thank my parents, Ann and Henry Moyd, for a lifetime of love and support? I think the best way is to dedicate this book to them, for it grew out of the life experiences they made available to me. I thank them for creating the opportunities and nurturing the skills required to finish a project like this, and for trusting that I knew what I was doing, even when I did not.

Despite all the help I have received along the way to publishing this book, I take full responsibility for any factual and interpretive errors and omissions that remain.

A Note on Spellings, Currency, and Measurements

In most cases, this book uses spellings or transliterations of words as they appear in the original texts from which they are drawn. For German East African/Tanzanian place names however, I use the standard current Kiswahili spellings (example: Aruscha [German] = Arusha [Kiswahili]). I have similarly altered German spellings of Kiswahili words (example: *Schauri* [German] = *shauri* [Kiswahili]). I have not attempted to standardize the transliteration of Arabic terms or names, opting instead to leave such words as they appear in the original texts.

↜

Between 1890 and 1916, the rupee was the main currency used in German East Africa. Its value fluctuated until 1905, when officials established a fixed exchange rate of 15 rupees = 20 German marks.

↜

All weights and measures referenced in this book have been left as rendered in the original source materials. Although German colonizers used the metric system most frequently, they sometimes used the German pound (*Pfund*) as well. During the imperial period, a German pound equaled 500 grams. In addition, officials sometimes used the German mile (equal to 7.5 kilometers) to measure distance.

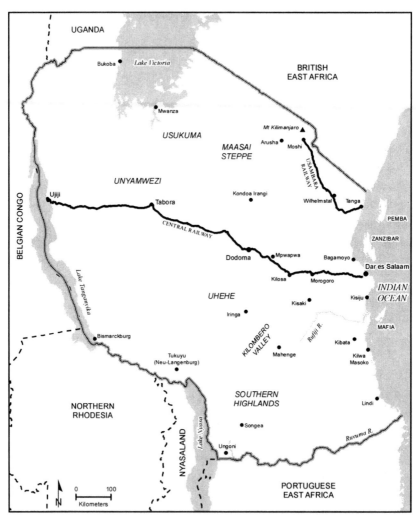

MAP 1. German East Africa Overview. *Map by Brian Edward Balsley, GISP*

Reconstructing Askari Realities

IN LATE September 1917 a company of African colonial soldiers operating behind Allied lines in the northern part of German East Africa
reached the limit of their willingness to continue fighting under their
commander, a German naval engineer named Bockmann.[1] Weeks of
successive forced marches through the arid Maasai Steppe had left
the soldiers, known as *askari*, undernourished, ill, and "at the end
of their strength."[2] Indiscipline began to manifest among the troops,
with soldiers and porters deserting in large numbers as the company
continued to march. At some point, Bockmann promised his remaining exhausted soldiers rest, but with dwindling numbers of porters on
hand, he instead ordered his soldiers to help move the company's matériel to an overnight campsite.[3] Indignant over this perceived slight,
the soldiers then leveled a series of complaints against Bockmann
and the German colonial army, the *Schutztruppe*.[4] They complained
that he lacked *nguvu*—Kiswahili for strength or hardness. They were
incredulous that they would ever receive long-overdue back pay from
their German employers, who appeared to the askari to be in disarray.
At the same time, they seemed convinced that transferring their loyalty to the British colonial army, the King's African Rifles (KAR),
would automatically bring them higher rank and lighter work. They
summed up their feelings of anger, hopelessness, and fear in one simple, but remarkable sentence: "We don't want to die for nothing."[5]
A bewildered Bockmann dismissed his soldiers' concerns as "inane"

and instead offered them what he called a "genuinely well-meaning speech" as a salve. But the damage was done. The following night, four more askari deserted the company.[6]

Not long after these desertions, Bockmann surrendered the remainder of his company to the British, and they all became prisoners of war. His British captors separated him from his troops and transported him to the town of Arusha to receive medical treatment. The next day, he looked out the window of his room and became "an eyewitness to how [his] askari, without exception, enlisted as English askari." Only his old senior askari, Majaliwa—a Schutztruppe member since the organization's founding, in 1889—refused to sign on with the British. Disabused of any naive ideas about his former soldiers' loyalty to the German Empire, Bockmann spent the rest of the war in captivity in Tanga, Dar es Salaam, and Alexandria, while his remaining askari went to Nairobi as "uniformed KAR."[7]

The simple but powerful declaration "we don't want to die for nothing" might easily have come from any number of wartime contexts in history. Certainly the notion that soldiers volunteer for military service, thereby risking injury or death, for patriotic, nationalistic, or civic reasons is commonplace in the United States and Great Britain, for example. Even nation-states that use conscription to populate their armies use the language of shared sacrifice for the common good to justify recruitment of young men and women to the military. Bockmann's askari, however, linked their continued willingness to risk their lives in the Schutztruppe to their immediate social and material circumstances. Thus, in criticizing Bockmann's lack of nguvu and inability to protect their status as African colonial elites, they articulated their perception that the Schutztruppe, and German colonial rule itself, had become feeble. One historian aptly labels this aspect of askari experience in World War I "the loss of the aura of the big man."[8] The soldiers' disbelief that Germany would ever make restitution to them underlined this point further, as did the idea that the KAR would offer them much better opportunities. At the heart of these complaints, and inherent in the decisions of Bockmann's askari to desert the company, lay an assessment that the Germans had proven themselves irresponsible as patrons to their askari clients by not caring for their needs and not respecting their status vis-à-vis those the askari perceived as beneath them, such as porters.[9] In short, Bockmann's askari viewed their commander's masculinity and abilities as an effective patron—his nguvu—as compromised. They therefore looked to the new regional power brokers, the British, for patronage in the rapidly shifting political and military environment World War I unleashed in East Africa.

This example would be far less remarkable had the Schutztruppe's askari previously shown tendencies to acts of collective indiscipline, strikes, or mutinies. Far more serious acts of indiscipline, strikes, or mutinies occurred in British and French contexts, for example, than in the German East African case.[10] These can be explained by variations in conditions of colonial soldiers' employment, which directly affected soldiers' willingness to fight in various contexts. Such conditions included rates and frequency of pay; recruitment terms or lack thereof; the presence or absence of women; soldiers' assessments of risk during combat and other violent confrontations; and the extent to which officers recognized the boundaries between appropriate and inappropriate treatment of their soldiers. In many ways, then, how officers treated their soldiers had much to do with whether or not the soldiers rebelled.

But apart from a few notable incidents in the Schutztruppe's formative years (1890–95), when inexperienced or reckless Schutztruppe officers made errors in judgment that cost them unit discipline and obedience, askari lived up to their reputations as dedicated Schutztruppe soldiers.[11] The absence of significant acts of mass indiscipline sets the Schutztruppe's experience apart from the experiences of other colonial armies, and especially from other British colonial forces operating in East Africa during the same period.[12] The hardships of the latter half of the East African campaign of World War I revealed, however, the fragility of this apparent dedication to duty. More pointedly, it revealed the extent to which askari loyalty was tied to the ability of the Schutztruppe to maintain its soldiers' status as respectable men, or at least the ability to restore them to that status once the war ended. Bockmann's askari recognized their precarious future far earlier than others whose circumstances, while still harsh, had not yet caused them to abandon their commanders for lacking nguvu. Most notably, the approximately twelve hundred askari who surrendered alongside Schutztruppe commander General Paul von Lettow-Vorbeck in late November 1918 seem not to have expected defeat, at least in part because they perceived the general as a strong leader and patron until the very end.[13] They believed, in short, that Lettow-Vorbeck would take care of them. Although it took many years, he ultimately did convince the German government to pay the ex-askari what they were owed for their wartime service, thus at least fiscally acknowledging what Germans who had worked in the colonies already knew—that German colonialism in East Africa could not have existed without the askari.[14]

This book tells the story of how the askari helped make the colonial state in German East Africa. They did so not just as soldiers who carried out the violent conquest of German East Africa, but in their everyday activities as tax collectors, messengers, escorts, guards, and executioners that shaped the character of colonialism in German East Africa between 1890 and 1918. In these acts of everyday colonialism, askari routinely interfaced with East African colonial subjects and European colonizers. Such interactions placed them in the category of "intermediaries" that historians have recently used to describe other kinds of African colonial employees, such as clerks, interpreters, and teachers.[15] This book thus illuminates the microprocesses involved in the making of colonialism and empire from the vantage point of the African soldiers and agents of colonialism who carried them out.

The askari enabled state making in German East Africa through their efforts to fashion themselves as local "big men"[16] (see fig. 1). They aspired to and pursued a kind of respectability, or "a right to respect that individuals believed they possessed but could enjoy only if it was admitted by others."[17] The askari version of respectability was characterized by the accumulation of large households, herds of livestock, and the ability to act as wealthy patrons and power brokers to others. In the process of becoming big men, they helped tie increasing numbers of East Africans to German colonial state-making projects. On one hand, these pursuits provided some measure of domestic security, kinship, and belonging to vulnerable, opportunistic, or aspirational individuals who became dependents in askari households and communities.[18] On the other hand, the askari took advantage of their positions of authority to benefit themselves, most notably through the capture of women and children and the expropriation of livestock and goods.[19] Some of these actions they carried out in the course of warfare, but many others were integral to the quotidian interactions that characterized German colonial administration. As the sizes of their households increased, they also had the potential to attract new dependents in need of the security afforded by kinship or clients in need of economic resources. The

FIGURE 1. This photo, taken sometime between 1907 and 1914 by Schutztruppe lieutenant colonel Kurt von Schleinitz, bears the caption "Sultan Moham. Achmed with his wives." The title "Sultan" perhaps indicates that at the time Schleinitz took the photo, Mohammed Achmed was a veteran askari, and that he had assumed a local leadership role in the colonial administration. His uniform shows that he had achieved the rank of sol, the highest possible for rank-and-file askari, and that he was highly decorated. His rank and decorations suggest that he was Sudanese. Women dressed in brightly colored cloth wraps known as *kanga* surround him, providing visible markers of his household's size, its ability to acquire prestige goods, and its cosmopolitanism. In this photograph, Mohammed Achmed exudes the status of "big man" that aligned askari household interests with those of the colonial state. *Used with permission of the Photo Archive of the German Colonial Society, University Library, Frankfurt am Main.*

soldiers' aspirations to become big men through colonial military service led to their participation in coercive and violent activities that simultaneously served their own interests and those of the German colonial state.[20] This mutually beneficial relationship between the askari and the German colonial state, as mediated by German Schutztruppe officers and noncommissioned officers (NCOs), facilitated colonial rule throughout most of the German period in East Africa. Following the askari through their everyday lives as soldiers, colonial agents, householders, and community members shows the "working of the colonial state" from the perspective of those who performed its most mundane bureaucratic tasks, its most spectacular acts of violence, and a range of state-making activities that fell somewhere between these two poles on a spectrum of tactics used to secure and maintain colonial rule.[21]

THE ASKARI BETWEEN MYTH AND HISTORY

German colonialism in East Africa, like other European colonial projects on the continent in the late nineteenth century, formally began with the violence of military conquest. In May 1889 a small and hastily assembled provisional army of African soldiers under German officers' leadership stormed and overwhelmed a fort located outside the East African town of Bagamoyo, on the coast of what is today mainland Tanzania. The fort belonged to the prominent planter and caravan trader Bushiri bin Salim, whose allies and followers had been at war with the German East Africa Company (DOAG), the dominant European commercial and protocolonial concern in the area, since December 1888.[22] The defeat of Bushiri's fort gave the German army, called the *Wissmanntruppe* after its founder, Major Hermann von Wissmann, its first victory over the coastal leaders, and marked the beginning of the German Empire's intention to effectively occupy this portion of East Africa in order to establish formal colonial rule.[23] It took until March 1891 for all the coastal leaders to submit to German authority. Meanwhile, the German colonial army received the designation Imperial Protectorate Force for German East Africa (Kaiserliche Schutztruppe für Deutsch-Ostafrika) from the Reichstag in 1889.[24] The Schutztruppe eventually conquered the coastal strongholds and then pressed into the territory's interior, where it spent most of the 1890s trying to establish military and administrative control over the territory.[25] The Schutztruppe's use of extreme violence against East African polities existed alongside negotiated settlements and alliances with local leaders and decision makers who opted for these tactics as the best hope for securing "the greatest possible independence and power" in the face of the Schutztruppe's encroachment in the region in the 1890s.[26] Violence—understood here both as physical infliction of pain or death as well as "assaults on the personhood, dignity, sense of worth or value of the victim"—existed in many forms and to varying degrees of intensity throughout the entire period of German colonial rule in East Africa.[27] During the Maji Maji war (1905–7), the Schutztruppe responded to what it imagined as a widespread coordinated anticolonial rebellion with scorched earth tactics that took the familiar methods and effects of the colonial warfare of the 1890s to shocking new levels of devastation, especially for the inhabitants of Tanzania's southern highlands.[28]

German rule in East Africa also came to its formal conclusion following sustained violence, this time deployed by European colonial armies against one other, but with many of the same deadly effects on East African peoples as Maji Maji had wrought just over a decade earlier. Two weeks after the armistice that ended World War I in Europe, Lettow-Vorbeck surrendered to the Allies at Abercorn, Northern Rhodesia. German East Africa was the last of Germany's four African colonies to fall to Allied armed forces during World War I.[29] The official Schutztruppe historian of the East African campaign, Lieutenant Ludwig Boell, described the East African campaign as "a wrestling match that held the whole world in shock and disbelief."[30] Boell's hyperbole notwithstanding, the campaign indeed featured elements that lent themselves easily to future popular constructions as a rollicking adventure story, in which Lettow-Vorbeck and his loyal askari overcame all manner of hardship to remain "undefeated" on the battlefield.[31] Lettow-Vorbeck's strategy from the war's outset had been to engage as many Allied troops as possible in East Africa so that they could not fight in Europe or elsewhere. Surrounded on all sides by colonies belonging to Allied nations, and their armies of askari, the Schutztruppe found itself in a difficult position. Because of its inability to receive reinforcements, supplies, or provisions from outside, Lettow-Vorbeck's army undertook a mobile "hit-and-run" campaign that destroyed lives and livelihoods across parts of eastern and southeastern Africa.[32] "Lettow-Vorbeck's brilliant campaign," John Iliffe pointedly observed, "was the climax of Africa's exploitation: its use as a mere battlefield."[33] Some three hundred thousand civilians died in German East Africa "as a direct result of the German authorities' conduct of the war," and that number does not include those conscripted as porters, whose mortality rates were notoriously high.[34]

Despite these sobering statistics, until quite recently accounts of the campaign tended to emphasize not the destruction it caused but the exploits of Lettow-Vorbeck and his "loyal askari." At the beginning of World War I, there were approximately 4,700 askari (2,540 in the Schutztruppe, 2,160 in the *Polizeitruppe*).[35] During the war, the Schutztruppe's numbers swelled to about 14,600. Only some twelve hundred askari and three thousand others, including dependents and porters, attended Lettow-Vorbeck's surrender in November 1918.[36] Out of that event, colorfully described by witnesses to the scene, a persistent myth about Lettow-Vorbeck's "loyal askari" gathered strength, taking on a life of its own through the 1920s, 1930s, and beyond.[37] Lettow-Vorbeck himself fueled the myth in his numerous publications, which began appearing almost immediately after the war ended.[38] Heinrich Schnee, the last colonial governor of German East Africa, also published a number of texts after the war that lauded the askari, and by extension all Tanzanians, for their ostensible loyalty to the German cause.[39]

Lettow-Vorbeck's army of askari, having held out against the numerically superior and better-equipped Allied forces for more than four years despite their ultimate defeat, thus became enduring symbols of past German military prowess and imperial power. Representations of the askari in their khaki uniforms and imperial German military insignia circulated widely in post–World War I German popular culture, seemingly needing little introduction or explanation to the German reading, viewing, and consuming publics.[40]

Until recently, secondary literature about the askari has tended to mirror two kinds of historical writing that emerged after German colonial rule ended, in 1918. In the interwar period a small but vociferous group of German colonial apologists advocated steadily for the return of Germany's former African colonies, which the 1919 Versailles settlement had turned into League of Nations mandate territories administered by former Allied nations.[41] Colonial advocates used the idea of the loyal askari in their propaganda campaigns against what they called the *Kolonialschuldlüge* (colonial guilt lie), a subset of the broader *Kriegsschuldlüge* (war guilt lie), which foregrounded Germany's postwar victimization at the hands of the Allies. They used the loyal-askari image to stand in for all Africans living in the former German colonies, arguing that they all eagerly awaited the return of German colonial rule.[42] The absurdity of this kind of claim, which relied on self-representations of Germany as a "model colonizer" that deserved to remain part of the community of empires, did nothing to prevent the loyal-askari myth from flavoring anglophone military historiography. This historiography painted askari's service as uncomplicated, loyal, and even heroic.[43] Such representations often featured alongside the almost uniformly heroic ones of General Lettow-Vorbeck, who was hailed in Germany and elsewhere as a brilliant strategist, tactician, leader of men, and gentleman.[44] For many years, these depictions of the askari as doggedly loyal soldiers of German colonialism received surprisingly little scrutiny, even though ample evidence pointed to a more complicated story. More recently scholars have offered subtler explanations for how and why less than 15 percent of Schutztruppe askari (2,000 of 14,600) managed to stay with Lettow-Vorbeck until he surrendered.[45] Still, the question of what motivated the askari to fight for Germany has remained largely unexplored.

Additionally, colonial-apologist and military-history narratives that celebrated the askari as skillful, brave, and dedicated soldiers of the German Empire obscured their involvement in the everyday and extraordinary violence that occurred in German East Africa. Colonial apologists, often former administrators or soldiers who had lived in East Africa, promulgated this narrative as a way of upholding the image of Germany as a model colonizer.[46] Their publications became source material for future military historians, who focused on the East African campaign of World War I to the exclusion of the history of other colonial wars in German East Africa. The askari emerged from this historiography with uncomplicated reputations as good soldiers who executed their duties in exemplary fashion, despite the terrible destruction they caused in East Africa during the entire colonial period.

Tanzanian nationalist scholarship of the 1960s and 1970s used the askari to make quite a different point about the colonial past. Nationalist historians from Tanzania and Europe (especially Great Britain and, strikingly, the German Democratic Republic, where many colonial archival documents were held) set about the task of creating a "usable past" for the newly independent nation-state. On the canvas representing Tanzania's historical path to independence, they painted the askari and other colonial employees as collaborators, a category that almost spoke for itself. In this historiography, the askari figured as "bands of mercenaries" who fought for the Germans simply because they paid well.[47] They were the perpetrators of countless acts of coercion and violence against East Africans, and thus the categorical enemies of the protonational heroes who had resisted German colonial rule during the Maji Maji war and other anticolonial conflicts. They featured as faceless menaces who, like locusts, consumed or destroyed everything in their paths. Nationalist historians prioritized research on

East African resistance to colonial authority, and virtually ignored the histories of African agents of colonialism like the askari, who were so obviously situated on the wrong side of history.[48] While their emphasis on creating a usable past is certainly understandable, it has also meant that historians who came after them tended to view the German colonial period in East Africa through the prisms of African independence and the Cold War. Neither of these perspectives left much room for studying colonial agents like the askari beyond stereotypes.

Between these two modes of viewing the askari, however, lie valuable insights into the relationship between soldiering, violence, everyday colonialism, and empire, as well as the relationships between Germans and East Africans that molded colonialism's local histories and metropolitan reverberations.[49] This book sits at the intersection of a few distinct historiographies and, through the askari, brings these fields into conversation in order to suggest new critical and methodological paths to understanding how colonialisms worked in practice.

AFRICAN COLONIAL SOLDIERS: HISTORIES AND HISTORIOGRAPHIES

Primarily a work of African history, this book engages the extensive research done by social and cultural historians of Africa that has dramatically expanded the state of knowledge about African colonial militaries over the last two decades.[50] A number of striking commonalities among recruits emerge from the historiography on African colonial armies, and my findings on the Schutztruppe askari largely coincide with other scholars' research in this area. First, colonial officers' recruitment practices were infused with, and shaped by, a variant of racial thought that ranked different ethnic groups as "martial" or "warlike" based on characteristics that generally had far more to do with how colonizers viewed themselves as soldiers than they did with any objective truths about one or another group's actual suitability for soldiering. These "martial race" theories often had significant effects on how young men came to understand themselves in relationship to colonial regimes, and the theories sometimes instantiated self-fulfilling cycles by which young men of certain ethnic groups came to elevate "martial" identities over preexisting ones.[51] This is not to argue that colonial officers' and African soldiers' ideas about what it meant to be a martial race coincided. To the contrary, Timothy Parsons has convincingly argued for British

East Africa that British and Kamba notions of "what constituted a martial race" differed quite dramatically: "To British officers, soldiers from a martial race were masculine, tough, and above all, obedient. Most Kamba askaris, however, believed that their status as a martial race enhanced their status in colonial society." And most important, "they expected specific considerations from the colonial government in return for their service."[52] Such tensions between how colonial officers and African troops interpreted soldiering and its value within colonial society had meaningful consequences for how these armies were built and maintained.

Second, in conjunction with martial race ideologies, colonizers employed a spectrum of recruitment practices, ranging from forced conscription to the use of incipient market forces to attract soldiers to colonial armies. These patterns affected how colonial armies developed in different parts of Africa, under different colonialisms, and in different periods. Diverse recruitment practices sometimes even existed side by side during the conquest phase, as Myron Echenberg's seminal work has shown for French West Africa.[53] French recruitment in western Africa, and British recruitment practices in northeast and eastern Africa, also highlight the degree to which early colonial armies relied on the conscription of soldiers with slave or otherwise "unfree" backgrounds.[54] In other cases, like German East Africa, colonial officers attracted pools of men to the Schutztruppe through the promise of regular and substantial pay, prestige, and opportunities for upward mobility provided by allying with German colonizers. Still, many of the men they recruited in 1889 to fight the coastal war in German East Africa also had "slave soldier" or otherwise unfree backgrounds, even if their subsequent employment and good treatment in the Schutztruppe somewhat dissipated their associations with these past histories.

Third, most colonial officers ultimately conceded, however grudgingly, that soldiers' household members had to be included in garrison, and often enough, campaign life.[55] In so doing, they acknowledged two vital facts of colonial army life that also reveal much about the nature of the colonial state. To begin with, the presence of soldiers' dependents in army communities helped increase the ability of local colonial administrations to cheaply mobilize labor, since they performed much of the intensive day-to-day physical labor that kept soldiers' households and military stations functional.[56] Moreover, in many African contexts, the size of a man's household was one of the most visible and recognizable markers of his social rank. For colonial officers to deny their troops the ability to display their socioeconomic standing would also have been to undercut the ties that bound African troops to colonial armies. This was a risk that most European officers would have judged imprudent in light of the fragility of most colonial undertakings, especially in the formative years of European imperial rule in Africa.[57] Finally, there was a direct link between soldiers' morale and the extent to which they could access the "comforts of home"—including prepared food, companionship, and sex—whether in garrison or on the march.[58]

The processes by which colonial authorities came to include soldiers' household members—that is, women, children, and other dependents of colonial soldiers—in their administrative and spatial arrangements unfolded gradually, and in response to their troops' demands for the "flavor of domesticity" in army life.[59] These processes developed in conjunction with those of the colonial armies themselves, with armies of African auxiliaries or company retainers being replaced by formal, state-supported colonial armies. For example, French colonial officers established the *tirailleurs sénégalais* in 1857 in French West Africa, and between about 1860 and 1880, they came to view the women with whom the soldiers established domestic and sexual relationships increasingly as integral and vital to the garrison communities.[60] For the Wissmanntruppe in German East Africa, on the other hand, the process happened with great rapidity. In 1889, when they undertook the conquest of German East Africa, they were latecomers to the imperial enterprise, and establishing a reliable colonial military posthaste was essential. By allowing their Sudanese recruits to bring their families with them to German East Africa right away, they gestured their recognition of the value of allowing the soldiers' families to accompany them. In so doing, the Wissmanntruppe established a precedent that informed Schutztruppe practices for the rest of the organization's existence.

Fourth, existing historiography reveals that soldiers had limits to their willingness to fight for colonial goals.[61] Although European officers routinely labeled their soldiers loyal in public discourses, a closer look reveals that African soldiers' loyalties had far more to do with their own understandings of social hierarchies and relationships of mutual obligation than with any abstract loyalties to European causes or governments, especially in the formative stages of colonial rule.[62] By interpreting the histories of colonial militaries through the lens of African social relations, this scholarship, as well as my own, demonstrates that African colonial soldiers actively participated in local sociocultural hierarchies, networks, and practices alongside their roles as the blunt instruments of the colonial state's violent practices.

But in other ways, *Violent Intermediaries* probes distinct and new directions in the social and cultural history of African colonial armies. By and large, existing studies have not included extended discussion of colonial soldiers' precolonial histories and how those histories produced the men that officers recruited to their ranks.[63] There are good reasons for these lacunae, including source limitations and the understandable desire to circumscribe research projects to keep them manageable and intellectually coherent. But Richard Reid sees this trend as part of a problematic "privileging of the modern" and "presentism" in African historiography.[64] One consequence of what he considers an overwhelming focus on the twentieth century as it pertains to Africa's history of warfare is that "the era of partition and 'pacification' . . . placed precolonial war in a historical cul-de-sac, with spear-wielding savages firmly bricked up in the basement of the colonial edifice."[65] In chapter 1 of this book I take up the challenge of "writing on war in the deep past," and this approach diverges somewhat from existing historiography in its attention to tracing the social and cultural histories of the Schutztruppe askari from their disparate geographic origins in northeastern, eastern, and southeastern Africa.[66] A productive side effect of this approach is that the book locates the askari as actors within some broad historical trends and events of late-nineteenth- and early-twentieth-century African and colonial history. In outlining their origins and paths into the Schutztruppe, the book highlights mobility as a theme in understanding how colonial cultures developed, and traverses colonial, national, and regional boundaries that have discouraged *longue durée* histories of colonial armies.

By crossing these boundaries, *Violent Intermediaries* points up how patterns of warfare, enslavement practices, and colonial military incursions that occurred across mid-to-late-nineteenth-century Africa configured African masculinities in ways that influenced recruitment patterns for colonial armies all over the continent. The performance of these militarized masculinities—through uniform wear, drill and ceremony, and the corporeal embodiment of authority they enabled—filtered into other colonial subcultures and helped shape expressive cultures in novel ways. The most telling example from Schutztruppe askari history is the interplay between the askari and the East African dance form, *ngoma*. Evidence suggests that the askari's activities on the Schutztruppe's *Exerzierplätze* likely inspired new forms of ngoma, which spread across East Africa during the latter stages of German colonial rule. Other historians (most notably Terence Ranger and Michael Pesek) have written about this relationship between the askari and a particular variant of ngoma, the *beni*, which incorporated significant military elements in its performance.[67] *Violent Intermediaries* engages and extends these analyses by illustrating how the soldiers' everyday activities around the military and administrative stations known as *maboma* [sing. *boma*] may have helped shape local colonial cultures.[68]

Another difference in how this book approaches the history of colonial troops is that it presents the askari as men who passed through several stages on their way to becoming colonial soldiers. It traces their experiences through the different sociocultural contexts that molded them. Here, the book's most important historiographical contribution comes through its focus on military training as a socialization process. It explores the quintessential military elements of soldiers' lives and the meanings they produced for soldiers as well as for those around them.[69] Thus askari uniforms, training, drill and ceremony, and combat experiences are a focal point. My interest in engaging broader military historiographies coincides with military historians' recent assessments of the state of their field, particularly regarding the need for "more comparative work and more international perspectives." They see these aspects as vital to the work of countering underlying "cultural assumptions" that impede more complex analyses of the similarities and differences between various military cultures and histories.[70] Military historians also increasingly acknowledge cultural history's value in formulating "more holistic questions of the evidence" and in helping scholars "probe more deeply the context of the landscape of choices" that soldiers have made in different historical contexts.[71] Cultural history thus provides common ground on which Africanists and military historians might fruitfully engage questions in colonial African military history that have attracted the attention of anthropologists but less so Africanist historians.[72]

While there are now many histories of African soldiers, and histories of African wars, there are surprisingly few histories of African colonial soldiers *at war*.[73] By focusing on how askari fought and then made meaning out of their combat experiences, this book brings colonial military historiographies into closer conversation with the social histories of East African wars, most notably the Maji Maji war (1905–7) and the East African campaign of World War I (1914–18). It embeds soldiers' combat experiences within the East African "warscapes" that they helped create as a result of Schutztruppe military actions against many African peoples, only some of whom considered themselves to be in a state of war with the Germans at any given time.[74] Studying soldiers as military actors as well as social actors within wartime contexts furthers the process of folding Africa's military history into global histories of soldiering and warfare and contributes to the development of comparative work across temporal and regional boundaries.

If the elucidation of askari soldierly contexts in training and combat form one major area of divergence from existing historiography, my focus on their roles as state-making agents is another. Thinking of the askari as both soldiers and agents of colonialism expands the category of intermediary to include those who used not literacy but instead violence or the threat of violence—implicit or explicit—as methods of colonial governance.[75] By this logic, the askari are best understood as integral parts of the diverse African and colonial histories they helped construct, and not as alien mercenaries kept isolated from East African colonial subjects. The specificity of the German case, in which the Schutztruppe's evolution was cut off by its defeat in 1918, in some ways enables my analysis of the askari as intermediaries. Most important, it has led me to question the notion that colonial armies, at least during the earliest stages of colonial rule, were isolated from surrounding populations. Such isolation developed in other colonial armies later on as part of military modernization processes that never played out in German East Africa because of the German defeat in World War I. Had the German East African colonial enterprise continued beyond 1918, perhaps the Schutztruppe also would have moved in the direction of trying to physically isolate its troops by moving them into barracks.[76] But there is little evidence to support the idea that that isolation occurred between 1890 and 1918 in German East Africa, Schutztruppe officer protestations to the contrary notwithstanding.

European colonial armies in Africa tended to follow similar trajectories in their organizational development patterns. The pace at which those patterns transpired, however, varied according to the local constraints and opportunities colonizers encountered when they arrived, as well as the military histories and imperial imaginations that shaped their expectations of how conquest and consolidation of authority would progress.[77] In most cases, formal colonialism was preceded first by European explorers and missionaries. As these colonial forerunners traveled through various parts of Africa, often with significant amounts of trade goods, scientific equipment, and personal items, they used small groups of soldiers, either hired directly or negotiated through allies, to provide security for their expeditions. Commercial companies like the German East Africa Company also usually preceded the formalization of colonialism. Like explorers and missionaries before them, these companies also employed military retainers to secure their interests and to escort them from place to place. In the decade following the Berlin Conference of 1884–85, at which the major European powers negotiated and confirmed spheres of influence on the African continent, efforts to establish effective occupation over African territories accelerated.[78] At first relying on company and other locally recruited retainers that we might think of as protocolonial armies, by the 1890s most colonial powers had formalized standing armies composed mainly of African recruits.[79] These were the armies that conquered and consolidated colonial rule for each respective European empire. The story of the Schutztruppe askari fits squarely within this larger set of late-nineteenth- and early-twentieth-century historical developments.

In the early stages of conquest, colonial armies set up outposts or garrisons at strategic and trading sites, or at places where allied military concentrations already existed. These military stations, often built quickly with whatever labor and materials could be locally sourced, or taken over from previous occupants, served as launch points for future military expeditions. As more and more of these outposts were established, they formed networks that linked often far-flung colonial strongholds to each other, establishing the spatial arrangements that evolved into colonial administrative structures. From these stations, colonizers and their African employees, including askari, attempted to establish authority and control over the vast territories they claimed as their colonial possessions.

The process of "conquest" involved far more than the military aspects that most readily jump to mind, and it is here that *Violent Intermediaries* makes another intervention into existing historiography on colonial armies. I argue that the askari played a critical role in making the colonial state. Askari personal aspirations to become respectable men and householders worked in conjunction with state-making processes designed to convince vast numbers of disparate East African peoples of the German colonial state's might and authority.

Generally speaking, the askari served in two state-making capacities. First, they were soldiers, responsible for the conquest of German East Africa. They secured colonial territorial and material gains and backed up colonial claims to power. In addition, however, they acted as a constabulary force, assisting in the day-to-day policing and administration of the colony. There are likely two reasons that this second capacity has not been treated within existing historiography. First, different colonies handled constabulary or policing work in different ways. In German East Africa, askari performed both soldiering and policing functions, despite the nominal existence of two separate organizations (Schutztruppe and *Polizeitruppe*). In German Southwest Africa, by contrast, police and soldiers belonged to separate organizations with distinct identities and divisions of labor. The same held for British East Africa, although the differentiation occurred later in the 1900s, again pointing up the need for attention to periodization in narrating histories of colonial armies.[80] Second, and related to the first point, the particular constabulary role that the Schutztruppe askari filled was directly related to the specificities of the German East African case. In short, it was not a classical settler colony that required a substantial white police force to uphold "the prestige of race" in the maintenance of law and order.[81] Moreover, Germany's defeat during World War I stunted German East Africa's colonial trajectory, so that the kinds of differentiations that played out over time in other colonial contexts never occurred there.[82] The critical point here is that askari constabulary roles featured centrally in their abilities to act as colonial intermediaries, which also supports the larger point—that they helped, from the very beginning, to make the colonial state. The praise leveled by their officers on the one hand, and the dread they produced among East Africans on the other, suggest a degree of effectiveness in carrying out the colonial state's goals. In the process, they solidified ties to families, communities, and wider networks that at times reinforced, and at times complicated, their positions as the primary African agents of state authority.

State making refers to the colonizers' "conscious effort at creating an apparatus of control" over German East Africa—the processes by which German colonizers and their African agents performed their claims to authority, and by which they attempted to negotiate with, convince, or force East Africans to submit to that authority.[83] This is not to argue that colonial control was total, for it was not.[84] Rather, the colonizers' keen awareness of their manpower and resource deficiencies led them to pursue particular strategies of state making that were designed to mask these problems.[85] Pesek has argued convincingly that "insufficient resources meant an insufficient presence of the colonial state and its agents," and that in turn this condition caused the colonizers to use spectacular and often devastating displays of military power to "redouble their presence in the consciousness of the colonized."[86] Performances of power undoubtedly figured prominently in colonial efforts to exert a semblance of control over the vast territory of German East Africa and its peoples. Yet it was precisely that insufficient presence, and the compensatory state-making practices necessitated by it, which helped individual askari become big men. During the conquest and policing of German East Africa, askari accumulated war spoils, including goods and livestock. They also captured women and children, enslaving or otherwise incorporating them into their households as dependents. Insufficient presence, then, was in the eye of the beholder during most of the period of German colonial rule over East Africa.

The highly destructive and spectacular military operations of the Schutztruppe's conquest of German East Africa constituted only one part of colonial state-making practices, however. As the Schutztruppe pressed into the German East African interior, it established maboma as military garrisons and nodes of colonial administration. In order to enact an image of a strong colonial state, officials undertook periodic expeditions to conduct official business and "show the flag." In these "choreographies" of colonial rule, the askari played central roles as escorts, guards, and messengers.[87] They conducted patrols, collected taxes, summoned people to judicial proceedings, and searched for fugitives. In all these capacities, the askari acted as primary state-making agents. At the same time, these roles gave them a largely unchecked ability to coerce and expropriate resources from the peoples they encountered in their day-to-day movements and encounters around the stations. Such duties also put them in intermediary positions between colonial state interests and those of the East African peoples who lived within the "concentric circles of influence and control" that surrounded the maboma.[88] Positioned between colonizers and colonized, askari enabled both state authority and practices of power while simultaneously opening up opportunities for their own upward mobility and wealth accumulation, as well as for outsiders to become incorporated into their households and communities. Thus ever-larger numbers of East Africans became tied to the maboma through the askari. Moreover, increasing numbers of East Africans developed boma connections through family, religious networks, and other communities of belonging, such as the competitive dance associations known as ngoma. These networks sometimes extended over great distances and encompassed disparate groups who might not otherwise have been connected to the colonial centers. In contrast to later colonial experiences in which soldiers were kept largely separate from other populations, in this early phase askari were part and parcel of the colonial political, social, and economic landscape, and they were at the heart of the production of the nascent colonial state.

Askari relationships to the colonial state elevated their status vis-à-vis other colonized subjects of German East Africa, and thus proved profitable to the soldiers. Yet paradoxically, askari desires for recognition as big men collided with racist and civilizationist colonial ideologies that positioned the soldiers as less than fully adult men in European imaginations. The Schutztruppe military hierarchy consisted of two separate rank structures (one white/German, one black/African) and thus bolstered a form of colonial racism by foreclosing the possibility that African soldiers would ever command white men. Colonial officers and administrators viewed the soldiers through paternalist lenses, partly a feature of German military rank hierarchies and paradigms, and partly a strain of racist thought that cast Africans as eternal children. European settlers contributed yet another strain of racist thought and practice to everyday colonial life in their vehement disapproval of colonial administrators' placement of askari in authority positions, especially in policing roles. Colonial racisms certainly constrained the soldiers' range of possibilities, but the inconsistencies between the different kinds of racist thought and practice that featured in colonial life also exposed spaces within which askari asserted their self-understandings—their "situated subjectivities"—as respectable men by opposing what they considered disrespectful or abusive treatment from Europeans.[89] As Lisa Lindsay and Stephan Miescher put it, "colonial racism denigrated African men, but it did not prevent assertions of powerful masculinity outside of its gaze."[90] The soldiers' positions thus exposed contradictions within colonial governance.

The khaki-clad askari embodied some of these very contradictions. Their uniformed bodies were supposed to represent colonial ideals of order and obedience. Their uniforms, insignia, and weapons marked them as soldiers and agents of the colonial state, clearly displaying their rank and status among themselves, as well as to those they encountered in battle and in the course of carrying out colonial administrative and disciplinary work. In part as a result of their outward uniformity, which presented an image of political and military might, many people feared the askari and minimized contact with them. But uniforms could be worn improperly; missing pieces or misplaced insignia potentially signaled the incompleteness of colonial control over their soldiers. Uniforms also connoted prestige and relative wealth, which attracted people into askari communities, for employment or membership in askari or other colonial households.[91] By becoming connected to askari households, individuals who otherwise would have been without kin or community found a sort of domestic security, thereby decreasing their socioeconomic vulnerability during times when being without kin could have dire consequences.[92] As more people became integrated into the boma communities through the askari and other colonial employees, the colonial state shifted to accommodate their presence.

Askari communities appeared orderly on the surface, but that superficial calm masked messy household dynamics that often disrupted the troops' good order and discipline.[93] Colonial officers and administrators found themselves negotiating all manner of household and community-level disputes—a role they endlessly complained about but that also allowed self-congratulatory reflections on their self-defined roles as civilizing agents. As askari and their family members turned to colonial authorities to help them resolve disputes, they also helped shape a colonial political culture that challenged German efforts to impose order on not just their African colonial employees but all the peoples they considered subject to their authority.[94] Yet because the families and communities that lived around the maboma were indispensable to maintaining their troops' morale and to colonial labor needs more generally, they made concessions that tacitly acknowledged the incomplete capacity of the colonial state to control African lives, social relations, and economies.

Askari, their families, and the communities that developed around them in the vicinities of the maboma contributed directly to new local economies that similarly exemplified the inability of the colonial state to control the outcomes of the processes it had set in motion. Boma economies centered on providing goods and services especially to the soldiers, as well as others who lived at or near the stations and to those passing through surrounding areas. Askari spending habits infused cash into local economies, thus likely reshaping socioeconomic relationships beyond the maboma. Traders of all types took advantage of the concentrations of people around the stations to set up businesses. These traders included women who set up small businesses near the maboma, where they sold beer, surplus produce, and handcrafted items to community members and passersby. Askari "wives" and daughters also ran small businesses that added to household wealth.[95] Although the maboma served first and foremost as military forts and administrative spaces, they were also multipurpose sites that included markets, livestock pens, gardens, and storage areas. Laborers reported to the maboma for assignment to colonial building, upkeep, and transportation projects. This mix of soldiers, traders, workers, and others animated the maboma, making them into centers of economic exchange.

At the same time, askari involvement in everyday boma life laid bare the most exploitative features of colonialism, including the predatory features of a nascent capitalist economy. For example, askari supervised and guarded chain gang prisoners and other unfree persons who performed unpaid labor over extended periods and who thus directly experienced the askari as practitioners of the everyday violence of colonialism. Askari actively participated in the boma economies that made a wide range of goods and services available to them, but many of them failed to grasp, or ignored, the consequences of their spending habits. They notoriously owed great amounts of money to the traders who sold them goods on credit. The appearance of markets around the maboma stimulated local economies that served colonial goals by bringing pools of laborers to the stations. Askari certainly benefited from these opportunities to perform their authority, and perhaps even to forcibly incorporate vulnerable prisoner-laborers into their households. Yet reckless use of their relative cash wealth in the colonial economy made them vulnerable to creditors' claims, which in turn made them subject to punishments administered by the colonial government, including chain-gang labor. Viewing the colonial state from the soldiers' vantage point exposes some contradictions within colonialism, but with a twist. That is, the askari, as both wielders and subjects of colonial power, serve as an analytical pivot around which to consider the contradictions inherent in the colonial state's reliance on African soldiers and their community members as their key agents of conquest and administration.[96]

In telling a story of colonial conquest, state making, and empire building from the bottom up, this book also intervenes critically in modern German historiography. It pinpoints and explicates some of the local African histories that gave rise to German discursive practices around its colonial past in the interwar period. These narrative and visual practices used the celebratory image of the loyal askari to stand in for the violence that German Schutztruppe officers ordered and oversaw in the colonies.[97] At the same time, images of the askari represented a stoic military masculinity that appealed to certain audiences within the defeated nation. *Violent Intermediaries* argues that postwar German discourses about colonialism make real sense only when they are linked with the soldiers' local histories. These very histories were used as plot devices in the construction of potent narratives about Germany's colonial past, in which that country appeared as the exemplar of the European civilizing mission. These "colonial fantasies" shaped how most Germans remembered and forgot their colonial past until the 1990s, when scholars reignited interest in German colonialism as a field of historical inquiry, demanding that it be taken seriously as an integral piece in understanding modern German history, particularly its intertwined histories of violence and racism.[98]

Exploring how German and African military cultures interacted with each other in the Schutztruppe, especially through military training, drill, and ceremony, also ties Germany's military history and its colonial history together in textured ways. *Violent Intermediaries* argues for thinking of colonialism as more than a top-down process, whereby

German military ideals and practices reshaped African men into pseudo-German soldiers.[99] Instead, it argues that making the Schutztruppe required an interactive sociocultural process between Africans and Germans and that it yielded an army and style of warfare that, more often than not, served Germany's colonial aspirations to deadly effect.

SOURCES AND METHODS

Recovering the sociocultural history of the askari requires the use of sources and interpretive techniques that differ somewhat from those employed in other histories of colonial armies in Africa. While historiographies on the francophone and anglophone African colonial armies developed out of historians' extensive collections of oral interviews documenting African colonial soldiers' and veterans' life histories, no such effort was ever undertaken for the Schutztruppe askari. Allied bombing of Germany during World War II also destroyed many Schutztruppe files that might have provided additional written official documents on the askari's lives. In reconstructing their lives and communities, I have thus used a mosaic of sources including government, missionary, and personal archival materials from Germany, Great Britain, and Tanzania; photography; newspapers; military manuals, guides, and phrasebooks; and published memoirs and reports. Published life histories of askari and other Africans who observed and wrote about them, as well as the transcribed oral histories from the Maji Maji Research Project (MMRP), and Kiswahili epic poetry, all contribute to the construction of a multifaceted representation of the askari that accounts for their various subjectivities as colonial agents, soldiers, householders, and community members.

But how exactly does one read, interpret and use such sources to render a useful representation of the askari? The European provenance of most of the sources and the lack of available oral histories presented me with a research challenge: how could I situate the askari within their overlapping and diverse African history contexts without access to their "voices"?[100] A multipronged solution emerged. First, I layered different kinds of sources to help me gain an impression about the questions at hand. To whatever extent possible, I also situated the sources within the contexts of their production. For example, I used Schutztruppe training manuals, translation guides, and military handbooks as sources for understanding askari military lives. These sources offer idealized visions of Schutztruppe operations, or described situations that might be used as models for how to manage troops under various circumstances. Most of them were not published until quite late in the Schutztruppe's history, and it is unclear to what extent officers used them. Still, when paired with other sources, such as newspaper articles, diaries, anecdotes in memoirs, and photography, these documents offer us a glimpse of the Schutztruppe's accumulated knowledge base regarding its soldiers. They provide instructive and sometimes unexpected insights into officers' expectations, soldiers' reception of the rules and regimens that ordered parts of their lives, and the presence of a wider askari community that the Schutztruppe tried to regulate. In addition—perhaps an obvious point that nonetheless bears reiterating—these military documents were indispensable in reconstructing the soldiers' military context, an area thus far largely neglected in the English-language historiography, but a central focus of this book.[101]

A second way of addressing the problem of the lack of sources where askari might have revealed aspects of their self-understandings and interpretations of their experiences, is to read the available sources in two directions—against the grain and along the grain. Reading against the grain reveals evidence that the authors may not have intended to produce, but which nevertheless helps us see otherwise invisible aspects of the soldiers' history. On the other hand, reading materials along the grain exposes what German officers, administrators, missionaries, and other European representatives of colonialism thought they were doing as they built German East Africa, and how their practices of governance grew out of these logics.[102] Taken together, these two ways of reading sources show the askari operating through a range of power relations and social settings, adding substance and refinement to how we understand African intermediaries in everyday colonialism. Reading against and along the grain also shows how askari roles in everyday colonial state projects generated new communities of belonging, political alignments, enmities, and abuses.

In addition to conventional archival materials, this book draws heavily on life histories, biographies, and anecdotes found in colonial memoirs as evidence from which "to begin considering what is said or not said, done or not done, in the universe of possibilities that constitutes the lifeworld of the past."[103] This genre of colonial text, usually written by the European explorers, missionaries, officials, and officers whom Marcia Wright calls "intimate outsiders," has been underutilized in the historiography of German East Africa. Wright cautions that "colonial literature in this genre often verges on fiction in that it enters imaginatively into the life circumstances of Africans . . . and transgresses boundaries between the observer and the observed."[104] The authors of these texts employed contemporary racist stereotypes of African peoples with abandon in support of their overt agendas of fostering German imperial expansion and colonial enterprises. Yet precisely because of their overt agendas, these authors also provided rich, unvarnished, and otherwise unavailable details on everyday life in the colony. Askari featured prominently in these texts because of their central roles in the routines of colonial life, as well as in the mechanics of colonial administration. Because the askari were so central to the German East African colonial project, authors of such texts represented their troops in subtler terms than typical racist renditions of Africans in circulation during the *Kaiserreich*. By paying attention to the genre's characteristics and quirks, and using other sources to critique and contextualize them, these memoirs have proven indispensable to the work of recovering askari self-understandings. Perhaps more important, however, these texts show that the askari created their own narratives about the past to help them live in their immediate circumstances.[105] The narratives also provide insights into how askari, and sometimes those close to them, such as their "wives," positioned themselves in relation to the intimate outsiders who recorded their stories.[106]

A bit more explanation of my interpretive method in using these "intimate outsider" texts is warranted here. In particular, the published life histories of the Sudanese askari Abdulcher Farrag, and the Nyamwezi askari Ali Kalikilima, raised troubling questions about how to responsibly use such fraught sources in a reconstructive historical project such as mine.[107] There is no question that these narratives, as highly mediated texts, present a welter of methodological problems. Questions of translation, transcription, genre conventions, and memory abound. For example, the texts were published in European languages, but we know little about the translation and transcription processes involved in producing them. And how did Europeans record these stories in the first place? Without a doubt, these narratives reflect the editorial, stylistic, and genre preferences of the intimate outsiders who recorded the soldiers' stories—their amanuenses.[108] So what is the historian to do? Is it possible to "disentangle the voice" of the African soldier from that of his amanuensis?[109] Perhaps not fully. Yet as Sandra Greene has recently shown in her work on African slave narratives, by paying attention to the "identities and concerns of both the narrators and the recorders,"[110] we might glimpse how the soldiers understood and represented their experiences, as well as how they used their interlocutors to aid in the pursuit of their own "projects" and politics.[111]

Reading the source materials ethnographically — by which I mean using a combination of primary and secondary materials to reconstruct the sociocultural historical contexts of the peoples under consideration — is a first step in the direction of discerning the range of interests of the historical actors treated in these problematic materials. This method aids in the task of discerning askari interpretations of life experiences and choices within their locally informed yet malleable self-understandings.[112] Regardless of their geographic origins, the men who became askari were shaped by distinctive socioeconomic and often racialized structures and hierarchies; gendered notions of authority, prestige, and work; as well as local and cosmopolitan outlooks and cosmologies that actively influenced how they made sense of the world and their places in it.[113]

In addition to devoting careful attention to the historical contexts within which African men came of age and became candidates for the Schutztruppe, however, I have tried to keep in mind that both the askari narrators and their amanuenses played roles in shaping the texts. In Abdulcher Farrag's and other similar narratives, at least two layers of shaping occurred — first by the African narrators in explaining their pasts to their recorders, and second by the recorders in conveying their stories to wider, mostly European, readerships.[114] It is hardly surprising that doing this work is far easier for the European interlocutors than it is for the African men who told their stories to them. Thus alongside the ethnographic readings of sources described above, I have also compared and analyzed available narratives for any commonalities in life experiences and trajectories that led to the men becoming colonial soldiers. For example, a comparison of Farrag's narrative to those of two other Sudanese men who lived through soldiering experiences in the late nineteenth century, Salim C. Wilson and Ali Effendi Gifoon, reveals his breathtaking story of serving in first the Anglo-Egyptian army, then the Mahdi's army, then the Schutztruppe, as plausible. Indeed,

Schutztruppe major Georg von Prittwitz und Gaffron claimed that in 1898 he met an old Sudanese askari, Effendi Murgan, whose experiences mirror those of Farrag. Murgan, a survivor of the 1891 Zelewski catastrophe,[115] had been a Schutztruppe askari since the organization's founding. He retired from the Schutztruppe sometime around 1897, returning to Cairo. But he found it not to his liking and asked to return to the Schutztruppe. The officer gushed about Murgan in his journal: "Murgan Effendi is a soldier who has become old and gray in military service, who fought in Sudan, Khartoum and Kassala. He is the model of a professional Sudanese lansquenet. He is 'Effendi,' which means [he is a] black officer and an exceptionally capable, responsible soldier. He was already 'Effendi' [when he was] taken over from the Egyptian army."[116] Prittwitz's encounter with Murgan confirms the possibility of Farrag's existence, however much Farrag's amanuensis, August Leue, may have shaped the narrative for publication.

In addition, I identify common or recurring narrative strategies regarding masculinities, social hierarchies, the trappings of modernity that expressed the narrators' aspirations and affinities for soldiering in colonial armies, and the constraints that forced some of them onto a soldiering path. Ali Kalikilima's life history, for instance, highlights his memory of the moment when he transitioned from boyhood to manhood, recalling the significance of learning to fire a muzzleloader under his father's tutelage, as well as the pride of independently supervising his first long-distance caravan and slave raid.[117] In a similar way, Farrag's narrative returns over and over to attributes like "steadfastness" that Schutztruppe officers most appreciated, emphasizing this and similar themes while downplaying others. The narrative's fabric interweaves several such thematic threads that reinforce the notion that askari perceived themselves as men with martial aptitudes with aspirations to becoming big men. They threw in their lot with an alien authority, the Schutztruppe, expecting to receive privileges and rewards that would help them secure respectable futures.

And what of the amanuenses' roles in shaping these narratives? The prefatory pages of their texts often purport having goals similar to those stated in Leue's text, namely, to provide "a collection of modest sketches and pictures" while at the same time "contribut[ing] to the general advancement of interest for our often unrecognized colony German East Africa."[118] This genre of colonial writing offers intriguing information on the nature of day-to-day colonialism, but it presents numerous analytical problems for the historian. After all, how did these authors recall the vivid life-history details they conveyed? What were their particular interests in relating these stories, and what were their purposes in conveying these stories in such meticulous detail? How do we interpret the layers of translation embedded in the text? Farrag's narrative, as conveyed by Leue, accurately reflects what occurred in Egypt and Sudan in the early 1880s. Leue provided considerable historical context to his readers, noting key dates and explanations of events throughout, and interjecting his own voice into the narrative by way of posing questions to Farrag that are clearly meant to help clarify both the story line and the historical context of the period of the Mahdi wars in Sudan. Numerous sources on the Mahdi wars, including captivity narratives, were available at the time Leue wrote his memoir, and it seems that he had familiarized himself with the region's history. His role in applying context to Farrag's story emerges clearly in his attention to historical detail.

Most authors of these kinds of texts had authorized or participated in devastating violence in German East Africa as Schutztruppe officers or colonial officials. They therefore were invested in presenting themselves to their readerships as men who could respect a fellow soldier, regardless of racial difference, if they fit into German conceptions of who constituted soldierly material. These narratives thus often diverge from other contemporary racist representations, which tended to show Africans as childlike or irresponsible, an image in keeping with imperial German and wider European print and visual cultures.[119] Leue, for example, represents himself as being genuinely interested in Farrag, questioning him directly about his traumatic experiences of soldiering in three different armies, and as a prisoner-of-war. His attitude toward Farrag stands in stark contrast to his expressed racist attitudes toward other Africans—that "the African must first feel the clenched fist before he will become accustomed to the easy yoke."[120] His recounting of Farrag's story is that of "a recollected relationship" presented from his position as an intimate outsider to African life.[121] Although Marcia Wright uses this term to highlight men's ability to gain ethnographic insights through their physically intimate relationships with African women, it is also a useful way of thinking about the masculine intimacy, or comradeship, that inhered in Schutztruppe officers' relationships with their askari.[122] Through Farrag, Leue expressed his thoughts on the "human dimensions" of warfare and comradeship in the colonies while still remaining within the genre framework his readership preferred.[123] Working within the conventions of the memoir, he expressed professional respect and even fondness for Farrag and the askari. At the time of publication, in 1903, German interest in the colonies was on the upswing because of the activities of patriotic organizations such as the Pan-German League and the Navy League. Leue's sympathetic portrait of one askari's life served the purposes of German colonialism by providing a humane, intimate portrait of a colonial subject who voluntarily participated in the furtherance of German colonial objectives. Perhaps Leue wanted to assure readers back home in Germany that reliance on African troops in the colonies was the best solution to the colonies' security problems, even if they were not seen as suitable for service in Europe.[124]

The blend of sources used here, coupled with my interpretive methods — layering, reading in multiple directions, using memoirs and anecdotes, and working toward thick description — have resulted in what can aptly be described as a history of everyday colonialism. Everyday colonialism, like the everyday more generally, is both a category of human experience and a category of analysis.[125] On one level, this book focuses on practice by using *everyday colonialism* to refer to the routinized processes by which colonial representatives, whether German or African, sought to establish (or perform a vision of) dominance and control over German East Africa and its peoples. It also considers the range of ways that these peoples engaged, opposed, or perhaps just ignored these state-making efforts.[126] The soldiers' self-understandings, socially embedded practices, and the local outcomes they produced support more general conclusions about the roles of soldiers, police, and their families in state making.[127] If the "history of everyday life" genre has been criticized for eliding the "big issues" in history, one goal of this book is to show that a fuller understanding of the processes behind the big issues — such as how colonial states came to exert a measure of control over African peoples, economies, and territories — can result from closely studying how individuals like the askari participated in those processes.[128] Delineating these microprocesses within the larger histories of colonial "conquest" and "governance" underlines the point that the idea of an inevitable European conquest of Africa is a luxury of hindsight — a point already made by other historians but one that bears repeating.[129]

"Everyday colonialism" also functions as a category of analysis — a kind of frame within which to discern the micropolitics involved in colonial state-making processes. Like other historians of everyday life, I treat daily life in German East Africa as "problematic," context-driven, and fluid, and try to avoid casting it as unproblematic, "self-evident," or static.[130] In this sense, the notion that the askari routinized certain processes of conquest and administration also accommodates the fact that their routines changed unpredictably according to events, contexts, and their own "willfulness."[131] Following the day-to-day activities of African agents of colonialism — their movements in, around, and between the maboma — reveals that local geographies are very useful vantage points from which to think about the workings of colonialism and empire from the ground up. In addition, a focus on the movements of African colonial agents brings their families, social networks, and hierarchies into the analytic frame, enabling a view of how colonial state making relied on ordinary people and their everyday activities around the maboma.

Violent Intermediaries treats the askari as practitioners of everyday colonialism in several ways. First, it examines their ordinary experiences across the scope of the Schutztruppe's organizational history, highlighting the activities that made them (in)famous, including their involvement in colonial brutalities and their seemingly exceptional performance during the East African campaign of World War I. It does so, however, with an eye toward the meanings they associated with these activities.[132] At the same time, the book shows the soldier's entanglements in diverse household, community, and state-level encounters that blur the boundaries between colonizers and colonized, revealing the askari as intermediaries of a different sort than the better studied "interpreters and clerks" who also acted as colonial intermediaries.[133]

Second, I regard individual "agency" as laden with political potential, even when it must operate "in the shadow of massive, and culturally (as well as physically) hostile, forms of power," such as colonialism.[134] As Sherry Ortner has argued, agency can be understood as operating in two fluid fields of meaning — one that relates to "domination and resistance," and one that relates to "ideas of intention, to people's (culturally constituted) projects in the world and their ability to engage and enact them."[135] The askari moved back and forth between these modes, deploying power for the state, as well as for themselves, in the "projects" that helped turn them into men of influence in their local settings. The power they exercised was "double-edged," functioning at times as domination, at times as resistance, and often somewhere on the continuum between the two. The incident cited at the beginning of this chapter, in which askari expressed disdain for their German commander's leadership, and for the Schutztruppe as a whole, before deserting to the British, exemplifies "resistance," even as their soldierly roles firmly ensconced them in the mechanics of colonial domination.

Third, this book foregrounds locality and mobility, using the maboma and askari movement between and around them to highlight some of the ways that various kinds of communities, including militarized ones, "are ultimately social in nature: the product of human labor, gestures, and interactions."[136] This emphasis on the local also points up the "larger consequences of daily activities" in shaping the "structures of cultural regulation and political expropriation" of colonial life in German East Africa.[137] In these ways, *Violent Intermediaries* argues for interpreting the past through the lens of "the everyday" in order to show how quotidian actions and complicities produce the institutions and practices that often discipline societies in diverse historical contexts.

HOW THIS BOOK IS ORGANIZED

How did recruits become soldiers? What parts did they play in making the state, and how did their lives around the stations contribute to the making of new colonial cultures? *Violent Intermediaries* addresses these questions by examining the askari's experiences, or "processes of identity production," in different contexts.[138] This approach reveals the askari as makers of colonialism in multiple circumstances, and also locates them as actors in different registers of "the colonial encounter."

Before the recent burst of scholarship on the Schutztruppe askari that grew out of parallel historiographical movements to understand the social history of African militaries on the one hand, and the cultural history of Germany's colonial past on the other, historians tended either to vilify the askari for their coercive and violent actions or to valorize their military exploits and loyalty, especially during World War I. This book tries to avoid either of these poles of categorizing the askari. Instead, it treats them as social beings engaged in projects that directly and simultaneously served their personal aspirations and needs, as well as those of the colonial state.[139] They undertook these projects seemingly without regard to the steep costs borne by those many East Africans who could not somehow avoid, or defend themselves against, the extractive and often murderous power the askari commanded as soldiers and colonial agents.

Each of the chapters that follow offers a distinct vantage point on askari lives. Looking at them within multiple contexts, and situated within various social networks, provides insights into the processes behind conquest and the making of a colonial military culture. It also uncovers the mechanisms by which the colonial state insinuated itself into the lives of East Africans.[140]

To illustrate how particular military cultures and moral economies aided in the creation of the Schutztruppe, I begin by tracing the sociocultural histories and geographical origins of men who became askari to their sites of recruitment in disparate African locations. Chapter 1 begins with the sociocultural histories of men recruited mainly from Egyptian Sudan ("Sudanese") who formed the core of the Schutztruppe in its initial years (1889–92), and continues with the histories of men recruited later from the central steppe and Great Lakes regions of German East Africa and Belgian Congo.[141] Identifying the ethnographic contours of the earliest stage of the Schutztruppe's formation reveals the kinds of masculinities, military aptitudes, and relationships to authority that askari and their officers valued.[142] These ideals shaped what it meant to be askari throughout the rest of the period of German rule over East Africa.

Chapter 2 considers the Schutztruppe training process and combat as the factors that turned these recruits, who came from far and wide, into Schutztruppe askari. This chapter describes the mechanics of the training process, emphasizing its role in socializing recruits. It understands colonial military training as a cultural encounter between different, and sometimes competing, visions of military masculinity.[143]

Chapter 3 examines how askari, under German officers' and NCOs' tutelage, developed a way of war reflective of their training as well as the aptitudes and sensibilities they brought with them into the Schutztruppe. Colonial conquest might thus be imagined as a series of violent "cross-cultural encounters" between Schutztruppe soldiers and those they sought to defeat militarily or otherwise bring into political submission.[144] The basic styles of warfare employed during the conquest phase of the 1890s remained in place through Maji Maji (1905–7) and World War I (1914–18), but the scale of these later military confrontations led the Schutztruppe to intensify these tactics in ways that caused massive loss of life, especially in the southern highlands, the epicenter of destruction in both wars.

Chapter 4 analyzes the askari in their everyday capacities as colonial intermediaries, state makers, and big men. The "askari villages," where soldiers lived with their families and dependents, provided them with all the comforts of home, as well as spaces for conviviality, cultural expression, and economic exchange. It also explores askari involvement in religious communities around the maboma and traces how veterans continued to embody colonial authority in their post-Schutztruppe lives.

Chapters 3 and 4 also call attention to the prominent roles played by women and other askari dependents as the "constitutive other" of the men known as askari.[145] *Violent Intermediaries* is, first and foremost, a history of the men who became askari. But to fully comprehend what made them men, we also must consider that their maleness was a "social category that derive[d] its meaning from being counterposed against that which it [was] not—the female."[146] Moreover, women's presence in the military columns and the maboma were not only essential to the askari's abilities to fulfill their maleness as heads of households, but also central to the Schutztruppe's ability to accomplish the logistical and labor tasks that kept it functional. Women also appear throughout the book, reflective of their omnipresence in the making of the Schutztruppe.

Chapter 5 links the everyday of station life with the colonial state's efforts to perform its vision of authority and mastery over German East Africa through the askari. First, it analyzes the askari in their roles as colonial intermediaries, carrying out the everyday business of the colonial state. Thus, the chapter highlights the "larger consequences of daily activities" for the expression and enactment of colonial authority and the building of colonial communities, especially around the stations.[147] Second, it shows that military drill and other ceremonial performances were at the heart of colonial state-making performances. For those living around the maboma, these events provided opportunities to imbibe and reinterpret colonial symbols, imagery, and bodily expression within both local and wider modes of expressive culture. The most visible instantiations of such reinterpretations of colonial symbols of authority occurred in the competitive dance societies and group dances known as ngoma, which often followed Schutztruppe parades during festive colonial occasions. The relationship between formal Schutztruppe parades and the ngoma points up the fallacy of imagining the askari as living in isolation from surrounding populations, especially during its formative years. Instead, their entanglements in localities and networks linked them to East African cultural, social, and religious networks, placing them in the middle of discursive debates about the present that unfolded "in terms of ideas and beliefs drawn from the past."[148] Colonial expressions of authority intertwined with local cultural practices, echoing back to the colonizers in certain ways, while at the same time generating new social ties and potentials that reached beyond what colonial officials imagined they could mold or control.

The Conclusion traces what happened to the askari following the dismantling of the Schutztruppe in late 1918 when Lettow-Vorbeck surrendered to the Allies. This can at best be only a sketch, since evidence to support a fuller history of the ex-askari does not exist. Yet even these sketchy details point up the extent to which their abilities to carry off the roles of respectable men depended on active and viable ties to the German colonial state. It speculates on how the case of the Schutztruppe askari might illuminate contemporary debates around the meanings of soldiering; the nature of soldiers' involvement in the performance of state and imperial power; and the transformations in relationships between soldiers and states as soldiers progress through the ranks and into the status of veterans. With questions about the nature of military professionalism so prominent in public discourse over the last decade, it seems apt to pose probing questions about the full range of historical conditions that produce men who become soldiers, and what consequences result from these recruitment processes.

⤙

Some may wonder why it makes sense to study men who fought in an alien, marauding European power's army in order to improve their circumstances—men who would seem to epitomize membership in the categories of collaborators, perpetrators, and mercenaries. As Daniel Branch astutely notes in explaining why historians have failed to properly analyze Kikuyu "loyalists" during Mau Mau, "historians are noticeably less than eager to describe those in the past that in all likelihood most resemble us."[149] This observation holds true for our current state of knowledge about the askari as well—their "agency in tight corners" disconcerts because it reminds us of our own conscious and unconscious imbrications and complicities in the various state structures and institutions endowed with responsibilities for protecting law and order and national security in our societies.[150] But I submit that it is of some ethical importance to attempt to understand the trends and processes that lead people to join organizations like the Schutz-truppe. In short, attractive incentives, as well as visible and less visible coercive factors that limit, or make impossible, other kinds of opportunities, lead people to negotiate their circumstantial tight corners by working for organizations and institutions that, as a matter of course, employ violent and coercive methods. At its heart, then, this book asks how and why people become part of such institutions and what outcomes these commitments produce for them, for those around them, and for the states that employ them.

1 ⌐ Becoming Askari

Narratives of Early Schutztruppe Recruitment in Context

IN MAY 1889 a small army of African soldiers, led by Wissmanntruppe founder Hermann von Wissmann and other German officers, stormed a boma five miles outside the East African coastal trading town of Baga-moyo. The boma, the stronghold for "charismatic planter and caravan merchant" Bushiri bin Salim and his followers, threatened German military efforts to use Bagamoyo as a base against Bushiri and other local elites, whose attacks against Deutsch-Ostafrika Gesellschaft (DOAG) personnel and property had ignited an all-out war for control of the East African coast. Wissmann ordered his troops to attack the well-defended and "unusually solid" boma after their poor discipline scuttled his plan to rely on artillery to breach the fort before the sol-diers' advance.[1] Once committed to the assault, the soldiers found a hole in the boma's wall and streamed into its interior, killing as many of Bushiri's men as they could, seizing a substantial number of weapons left behind by the fleeing defenders, and laying waste to the fort. It was the first of many military engagements between the Wissmanntruppe (after 1891, the Schutztruppe) in the protracted process of conquering German East Africa.

Twenty years later, the Schutztruppe's official history described the soldiers' performance in the battle against Bushiri as "splendid." A total of seven African units—five "Sudanese," one "Zulu," one "askari" (mean-ing locally recruited)—participated in the operation, along with an all-white sharpshooter unit and a naval landing detachment.[2] According to the official history, the Sudanese troops "had earned nothing but praise" in the battle against Bushiri. On the other hand, Shangaan recruits from Portuguese East Africa, referred to as Zulus, had fought bravely up to the storming of the fort, "but after that they behaved as savages."[3] The official historian, Major Ernst Nigmann, added that their mere six days of German-style military training accounted for their uncontrollability.[4] Finally, the locally recruited DOAG "Swahili" retainers (the "askari") had, with "some minor exceptions," behaved well in battle.[5]

The traits ascribed to these three categories of African soldiers—Sudanese, Zulu, and locally recruited—formed the basis of a racial framework around which German officers' thoughts and actions regarding each group's supposed soldierly aptitudes took shape during German colonial rule in East Africa. In the early years of the Schutz-truppe, officers organized their recruits into separate units based on vague understandings of the soldiers' geographic origins. "Sudanese" soldiers (sometimes also referred to as Nubi) came mainly from southern Sudan, but for German officers the label seemed to cover anyone from northeastern Africa. German officers recruited the Sudanese soldiers from Cairo, where they were living in squalor following their release from Anglo-Egyptian army service. Having already served in one colonial army, they were familiar with European styles of training and warfare. British colonial armies in Kenya and Uganda also recruited "Nubi" in large numbers.[6] From the very beginning of the Schutztruppe, Sudanese soldiers occupied the top position in German officers' visions of the ideal African soldier. On the other hand, the Shangaan ("Zulu") recruits tended to occupy the lowest positions in German officers' assessments of their soldiers' abilities. Finally, locally recruited soldiers, or askari (referred to by the name that would eventually be applied to all African soldiers in the Schutztruppe), fell somewhere between the Sudanese and Shangaan contingents in this nascent martial race ranking.

The fact that *askari* became the label for all African soldiers recruited into the Schutztruppe points to a leveling effect that occurred as the conquest phase wore on, whereby Schutztruppe units began to include a mix of soldiers from the different geocultural groups. By 1892 most of the Shangaan soldiers had left Schutztruppe service and returned to Portuguese East Africa. Around the same time, owing to their own manpower needs in the lead-up to the "reconquest" of Sudan, the British began prohibiting further recruitment of Sudanese soldiers from areas within their sphere of influence. To fill this void, Schutz-truppe officers began recruiting more heavily from within and imme-diately around German East Africa, drawing specifically on Nyamwezi, Sukuma, and Manyema men from the central steppe and lake regions. Officers continued to attach ethnic labels to individual askari (e.g., "Sudanese-askari") in their written practice throughout the period of German colonial rule. They further differentiated individual askari in everyday speech, referring to soldiers by their ranks and names. Still, by the mid-1890s *askari* had become the common term for all uniformed African soldiers in the Schutztruppe.

Understanding the background of askari recruitment and the ter-minologies associated with its patterns provides helpful insights into the making of the Schutztruppe, as well as what meanings these re-cruits from vastly different geographical, social, and cultural back-grounds attached to becoming askari. Scant availability of sources for recovering the histories of soldiers recruited to the Schutztruppe limits what can be known about their individual backgrounds and motiva-tions.[7] Yet existing sources do suggest some of the ways they positioned themselves in their various late-nineteenth-century African social and political contexts. Reconstructing the historical contexts of Schutz-truppe recruits from disparate locations shows how individual paths from different parts of Africa to German East Africa became possible or desirable to some men in the mid- to late nineteenth century. The overview begins with the Sudanese background, then offers a brief dis-cussion of the short-lived Shangaan presence in the Schutztruppe, and concludes with a historical reconstruction of the East African context that produced askari recruits. Without denying the specific historical trajectories that distinguished northeastern, eastern, and southeastern African histories from one another, I argue that young men coming of age in these different regions participated in a range of historical pro-cesses that steered them toward becoming askari. Theirs were worlds marked by profound shifts in socioeconomic power relations, changing military and technological practices, accelerating European encroach-ment, and encounters with changing gender norms. Their navigation of these shifts, when examined as part of the regional histories they lived through, helps us put faces on the men who became Schutz-truppe askari.

"As long as I've been an adult, I've led a life of war, and I am often surprised that I still exist."[8] So begins one of the few available life histories of a senior Sudanese soldier of the Schutztruppe, Abdulcher Farrag. His narrative appeared in the memoir of Captain August Leue, a Schutztruppe officer stationed in German East Africa in the early 1890s, when the conquest of the territory was still in its early phase. Farrag had served with Leue during the 1890 coastal war, during which time he was promoted to *ombasha*, a rank imported from the Turco-Egyptian army's rank structure, and equivalent to that of lance corporal, or *Gefreiter*, in the Prussian army. In 1894, Farrag served under Leue as part of an escort accompanying the German officer from the coast to the interior trading town and German stronghold, Tabora. Leue found him to be "as bright as he was a good fellow," and, having enjoyed their conversations, Leue encouraged the ombasha to share his life story.[9]

Farrag had indeed lived his adult life in the shadow of war. In the 1880s he fought in the Egyptian army during a military coup against Khedive Tawfiq (the 'Urabi Revolt, 1879–82), and then as part of the Egyptian army against the millenarian Islamic movement known as the Mahdiyya in Sudan.[10] He joined the Wissmanntruppe in 1889 and traveled to East Africa, where he fought in the coastal war and other "small wars" of the early 1890s.[11] In 1891 he survived a disastrous expedition against the Hehe, in which nearly 300 askari (of 362 on the expedition) died in battle, along with the expedition's German commander, Emil von Zelewski.[12] Farrag met his end sometime after accompanying Leue on his trek to Tabora, in 1894, "the only one to die in a small bush battle in East Africa."[13]

In the historical patterns it emphasizes, Farrag's story might stand in for those of many other askari from northeast Africa who fought for the Schutztruppe. Farrag was part of the rapidly assembled initial contingent of troops recruited to fight the coastal elites at war with Germany in 1889 and 1890. The urgency of the situation, which threatened German claims to the territory as defined at the Berlin Conference of 1884–85, demanded immediate action. Wissmann and his compatriots were charged with building an ad hoc force made up of suitable recruits from distant lands, using expertise gathered in their previous experiences as explorers of Africa. The 768 soldiers they located came from disparate areas with distinct military histories, including north-east Africa (Sudan, Egypt, and Eritrea), Portuguese East Africa (Mozambique), the Swahili coast, and Somalia.[14] By 1891 the number of askari had grown to fifteen hundred, and their numbers remained approximately at this level until the outbreak of World War I. In 1892, after finally defeating Bushiri, most of the 350-man contingent from Portuguese East Africa ended their contracts and returned home.[15] The numbers of Sudanese troops dwindled over the years as the effects of British recruitment prohibitions took their toll. In order to replenish the army's ranks, German officers began recruiting soldiers from within the boundaries of German East Africa.[16]

Thus the army's makeup changed considerably in the mid-1890s. One might expect that such drastic changes in personnel makeup, which involved new languages, cultural practices, and group affiliations, would have had a negative impact on the Germans' ability to maintain a cohesive force. Yet the askari remained reliable troops who enabled control of German East Africa until 1914. How was that possible? In what ways did these soldiers' circumstances, interests, and aspirations merge with those of the new colonial rulers to support the building of a colonial state?

Historical accounts indicate some constancy in the Schutztruppe's organizational ethos, but this narrative smoothness masks major changes that occurred in the force's personnel composition over time. The process of becoming askari was tied to the steady development of the Schutztruppe into a force that relied, in theory, on its soldiers' interchangeability. This askari identity undergirded organizational continuity despite demographic changes in the Schutztruppe over time.

First, the iconic status of the askari recruited from the territory known as Sudan, as fostered by Schutztruppe officers, propelled particular "Sudanese" qualities to the forefront of being askari.[17] Even though the numbers of soldiers recruited from Egypt and Sudan dwindled over the years due to political circumstances, they remained, in German eyes, their most valuable soldiers. Their seniority and previous experiences in other European-style armies lent them authority and composure under stress that German officers identified with, admired, and hoped younger recruits would emulate. As the Schutztruppe revised its recruitment strategies in the mid-1890s, bringing in more soldiers from within German East Africa, it also accommodated the different range of military sensibilities that these men brought with them. But these qualities never reached the same lofty position in the Schutztruppe martial race paradigm as the Sudanese.

Second, Schutztruppe officers chose their new recruits from groups with identifiable military traditions but, crucially, also from groups whose young men had lost out in the course of imperial conquest, whether Turco-Egyptian, Anglo-Egyptian, or German. For Sudanese men, many of whom had spent their childhoods or young adulthoods as military slaves in Egypt and Sudan, or who had been let go by the Anglo-Egyptian army, the Schutztruppe presented an opportunity to submerge the ignominy of slave origins or impoverishment beneath new roles soldiering for a new distant patron and regime.[18] This path opened possibilities for reestablishing themselves in new contexts where their origins would, in theory, be known only among themselves. Even if in practice their slave origins could not be hidden, soldiers like those recruited in Cairo may have hoped for a fresh start.[19] It was similar for groups recruited from within the colony's boundaries, such as the Nyamwezi, whose livelihoods and masculinities were shaped by mid-nineteenth-century East African socioeconomic and political dynamics, including the consolidation of powerful new states with standing armies, the intensification of violence driven by competition over control of long-distance caravan trade routes, and European imperial incursions. Young men from these regions grew up learning to value certain occupations—such as working as porters and guards in the caravans, or as retainers in regional potentates' armies—as appropriate sites for proving one's manhood and maturity.[20] For some, serving in the Schutztruppe offered a chance to surmount the political and military upheaval of the German conquest, to benefit from the colonial cash economy, and to take steps toward a new variant of respectability within an emergent and fluid sociopolitical context that favored their positions as salaried employees. The end effect was the creation of military communities whose members helped reproduce the Schutztruppe and, in turn, to make the German colonial state.

In 1889, when Wissmann began building his colonial army, he drew from a wide category of African men from disparate locations, including Sudan (by way of Cairo), who were available and perhaps eager for soldierly work, and whom he and other German officers found desirable as recruits. Even if many of these men experienced some forms of coercion—whether economic, social, punitive, or outright enslavement—that led to their becoming Schutztruppe soldiers, evidence suggests that they often came to identify primarily as soldiers, not slaves, over the course of their military lives. Although only a few life histories of African men who experienced military slavery in nineteenth-century Sudan exist, when read closely, these sources suggest more complicated and textured ways of understanding the Sudanese soldiers' commitment to the Schutztruppe than currently exist in scholarship.[21] These narratives provide glimpses into different nineteenth-century southern Sudanese political and cultural entities that produced men who made their ways into the Schutztruppe as "Sudanese" recruits. They also highlight the complexities of nineteenth-century Sudan's social and political history, especially its regional slaving processes and patterns of enslavement.[22] By tracing the connections between the economics of slavery and the expansion of Egyptian military power in Sudan in the nineteenth century, it is possible to show how enslaved men, cut off from their communities because of the violence and disruption caused by slave-raiding practices, could ultimately come to see themselves as professional soldiers allied to a new and completely foreign power, in this case Germany. They worked for their employers so long as those employers, or patrons, met their responsibilities in providing for them and their families. For most of the Sudanese soldiers who joined the Schutztruppe, the Germans were the last in a string of different military patrons. German officers convinced their recruits that fighting for the Schutztruppe made sense by paying them high wages, granting them exceptional privileges and the authority to assert those privileges, and respecting the soldiers' particular skills and aptitudes. Or, as Juhani Koponen puts it, "During German rule the trustworthiness of the askari was never taken for granted. It was conceived as an acquired trait to be fostered with care and a generous salary."[23] In return, these troops carried out the most devastating elements of conquest and everyday colonial rule in German East Africa. At the same time, they aspired to create a kind of respectability for themselves and their families.

RACE, PATRONAGE, AND THE SOCIOLOGY OF SCHUTZTRUPPE RECRUITMENT

Before going further, some explanation of the conceptual frameworks and sociological understandings that informed Schutztruppe officers' decisions about who should serve as askari is warranted. German perceptions of Sudanese characteristics operated discursively to elevate Sudanese soldiers to the top of the askari hierarchy. Recruits came to understand themselves as askari at least in part through the eyes of others, such as their German officers and NCOs, other Europeans in German East Africa, and East African civilians. East Africans encountered the askari as uniformed and powerful colonial employees in a variety of settings, including in daily life around the military stations called maboma, on patrols and expeditions throughout the territory, on guard duty for prison and forced labor details, and of course, in wars. Europeans identified the askari as "Negroes" (German, *Neger*), thus locating them in a particular place in the colonial racial hierarchy, irrespective of their relatively privileged status in comparison to other Africans in the territory. German officials' ambivalent discourses opened a space for the askari to perform their own understandings of how they fit into colonial society. At once construed by their officers as racial inferiors, but also as superior to most other East Africans, askari bolstered their claims to big-man status through their everyday soldiering and policing activities.[24] While Schutztruppe officers understood the need for treating the askari with a degree of respect that corresponded to their relatively privileged place in the colonial racial hierarchy (relative to other Africans), European settlers tended to see things quite differently. Their refusal to regard the askari as legitimate representatives of the colonial state sometimes provoked violent confrontations with the African soldiers. These encounters, which occasionally reveal themselves in fragments of archival materials, afford a glimpse of how the askari sometimes refused to accept their designated place in the colonial racial hierarchy.[25] Colonial authorities allowed the askari to use the fledgling colonial legal system to deal with their complaints of poor treatment at the hands of European settlers. Such moments revealed the flaws in the system as it operated on the ground and laid bare the unattainability of an idealized colonial legal system as envisioned by German legal experts. In addition, and perhaps more important for my argument, these sources show that the askari accepted portions of what their German employers thought of them, but rejected others, particularly when racist attitudes and actions provoked askari to defend their claims to respectability within colonial society.

German officers also viewed potential recruits' suitability as soldiers through a variant of contemporary racial thought known as martial race theory. This practice of racial categorization resembled the more clearly articulated British version that played such a definitive role in the Indian colonial military.[26] Martial race theories posited that certain groups were better suited than others to serve as (colonial) soldiers. Schutztruppe officers did not start out in 1889 with a well-developed or fully articulated martial race theory, but as they built the Schutztruppe into a standing army, a de facto paradigm emerged. Assessments of any given group's martial characteristics, and thus its suitability for colonial military service, "tended to coincide with the positive ethnic preferences of the typical colonial administrator."[27] German officers and NCOs identified and categorized their troops through a fixed military rank structure, but also through a system of ethnic ranking that elevated "Sudanese" traits as the model for all askari to strive toward regardless of their particular regional origins.[28] In their Sudanese askari, German officers saw the traits they believed to be intrinsic to good soldiers of the kaiser, including stoic resolve, unwavering dependability, steadfast loyalty, and iron discipline.[29] These values of "reliability, loyalty, and discipline" often trumped "valour, fearlessness, and fighting skills" in German officers' assessments of good soldiers, although of course they also hoped their soldiers would possess the latter qualities as well.[30] Notably, groups who had held their own against the Europeans before being defeated were thought to make good soldierly candidates.[31] One such case was the Hehe, whom the Schutztruppe defeated in 1899 following nearly a decade of war. After their defeat and reduction to a state of "dependence" on the colonial regime, the Schutztruppe recruited Hehe men in "strong" numbers.[32] For men who had suffered defeat at the hands of colonial armies, and who sought new outlets for their soldierly energies, the prospect of good compensation and upward mobility in colonial armies held some appeal.

To be sure, an economic calculus informed Schutztruppe officers' thinking on how best to ensure their soldiers' loyalty. As a 1911 professional manual insisted, "The strongest tie that connects the colored soldier to German rule is—naturally for a mercenary force—ample pay upon which he can fully count to be paid punctually."[33] Moreover, colonial officers viewed such groups in essentialist terms as sharing certain "tribal" attributes in which "bonds of personal allegiance and reciprocity play[ed] basic roles in locating authority and distributing power."[34] In many African societies at the time of colonial interventions, this kind of dependence or mutual obligation structured a variety of social relations among unequals.[35] Sudanese recruits to the Schutztruppe were dependent on their German officer-patrons in this way, but they also gained standing by fighting for Germany's imperial causes. The Schutztruppe made possible the prospect of starting new lives far away from their lands of origin and the socioeconomic constraints that stifled possibilities for upward mobility.

This emphasis on socioeconomic dependence and vulnerability as key factors in securing soldiers' allegiance highlights another defining element in the relationship between officer and askari. The askari depended on their officers and NCOs for their wages, and also because they were the source of their authority as they carried out everyday colonial duties as constabularies. This relationship also produced opportunities for the askari, along with a range of other people such as traders and laborers, who benefited from their presence in the areas affected most directly by colonial rule. The maboma attracted people to their gates because of the employment opportunities they generated, the possibilities for incorporation into askari or German households they offered, and the business and trading opportunities they enabled. Askari themselves often became patrons, thus helping create new constellations of social and economic relationships that stretched far beyond the walls of the maboma. Soldiers who reached senior ranks incurred more of their own patronage responsibilities. As a former British captain in the Anglo-Egyptian army wrote of a high-ranking Sudanese soldier he had known, "in sickness and in want his purse is open to every one of his 'children,' and there is not a poorer man in the battalion than the adjutant-major."[36] Such dynamics reproduced the hierarchies and sensibilities that helped sustain colonial militaries over time and across wide expanses of territory.

Men recruited into the Schutztruppe joined with an understanding that the Germans, as their new patrons, would provide them with certain material and "intangible" benefits in return for their allegiance and willingness to fight in causes that had little if anything to do with any prior allegiances they might have had.[37] In other words, they identified with the German colonial state because its agents could assure them status of their own, in the form of wages, war spoils, land grants, professional rank, and social prestige.[38] The Schutztruppe provided a path to respectability during a time of dwindling opportunities. German colonial causes did not necessarily serve as motivating factors for the askari, but participation in the exercise of colonial power served their purposes too. The economic element was part of it, but equally important was the possibility of creating for oneself a space within which to perform the role of military professional and big man under changing socioeconomic circumstances.

Sudanese soldiers' availability to join the Wissmanntruppe in 1889 also reflected their geographic and sociocultural origins in areas where military slavery and ties to strong patrons, or big men, had been long-standing practice. Military slavery shaped social relations and state formations in large swathes of Africa in the nineteenth century.[39] The geographic scope of Sudanese military slavery, along with sensitivities surrounding questions of social identity in the region, have worked against full comprehension of the extent to which military slavery shaped colonial state formations in northeastern and eastern Africa.[40] In order to function smoothly, armies of slave soldiers required strong patrons who both symbolically and concretely provided soldiers a clear sense of the sources of their derivative authority, as well as who could ensure their—and their families'—welfare.[41] Soldiers cycled their allegiance from one patron to another with a striking facility. As a British officer in Sudan in the 1880s remarked about the pool of men from which British colonial recruits came, "a man was a Dervish one day; the next day he was in the ranks [of the Egyptian army] and probably went out to fight against his late emir without training of any sort, his neighbours in the ranks putting him in [to the formation] the way he should go."[42] Such soldiers' military professionalism thus had little to do with modern North American and European views of what constitutes military professionalism, which emphasizes civilian control, formal military education, and dedication to "the highest standards of military effectiveness, principally in combat."[43] If a patron failed to live up to the responsibility of protecting the soldiers' statuses, families, and working or living conditions, a soldier might move on to another. In other words, "their loyalty was not the spiritualized, romantic, European concept of loyalty recognized in the medieval courts of chivalry. It was rather a conditional, contractual concept."[44]

Nor was it a loyalty to an overarching concept or ideology, such as nationalism or patriotism. Instead, their allegiance to any given army had to do with how well those in the position of patron—NCOs, officers, traders, political and religious leaders—provided incentives for them to remain loyal.

This dynamic helps explain why groups from Sudan were available to fight for the Germans following careers with the British, the Egyptians, and in some cases, the Mahdiyya, "tracing their professional descent not through one army, but many."[45] With few exceptions, Schutztruppe askari seemed satisfied with their terms of service. They had little reason to seek employment elsewhere, for example with other colonial powers in the region.[46] The practical issue of being far away from their original homes and kinship networks also certainly played a role in keeping soldiers in German East Africa. The Schutztruppe's early recognition of the importance of being good patrons helps explain why most Sudanese askari remained loyal over extended periods of military service, and even into retirement.[47] They recognized their German officers as effective patrons who understood what it would take to make them stay. But askari also challenged their officers and NCOs when they felt mistreated, or when their work conditions failed to meet their expectations. For example, in 1895 an askari company on an expedition near Kilosa refused to continue following their officer "because he was too strict" and because he had treated a disobedient askari disrespectfully by placing him in chains along with common criminals.[48] The Schutztruppe professional manual *Anleitung zum Felddienst in Deutsch-Ostafrika* condemned this practice in recognition of the soldiers' sensitivities concerning questions of status.[49] Askari also did not always conform to German ideals of soldierly discipline or battlefield conduct. Like other askari, Sudanese soldiers sometimes received harsh public punishments, including the infamous *hamsa ishirini*—twenty-five lashes with a hide whip (*kiboko*)—for all manner of infractions.[50] Still, by the mid-1890s something like a consensus on the question of which soldiers should serve as the models for future recruits had emerged. This understanding remained in place throughout the period of German rule in East Africa, despite new waves of recruitment that brought in soldiers from many other locations. This hierarchy formed part of the habitus of German colonial rule in East Africa.

GERMAN OFFICERS, SUDANESE MEN, AND
MARTIAL RACE THEORIES IN PRACTICE

With few exceptions, German officers celebrated their Sudanese askari as the epitome of good soldiering despite their "not exactly excellent achievements in exercises and shooting."[51] Although there are a surprising number of references to Sudanese indiscipline and failings in the records, in the end most commentators on the soldiers agreed that "the Sudanese [were] the bravest blacks" they had ever known.[52] As Magdalena von Prince, the wife of Schutztruppe officer Tom von Prince, wrote in 1897, "the Sudanese are our best askaris and [therefore] must go on every expedition."[53] Schutztruppe officers sometimes drew racial distinctions between "unmixed," darker-skinned Sudanese from the southern regions of Sudan, whom they thought of as "decidedly excellent soldier material" with "no desire or ability to do any other occupation," and lighter-skinned men considered phenotypically and culturally "Arabic."[54] While the former were supposedly born soldiers from "warlike tribes," the latter were considered to come from "less warlike tribes," and to be of low social standing.[55] German officers thus preferred the "dark" Sudanese as recruits. They referred to the Sudanese askari frequently as "black lansquenets," thus drawing a favorable and romantic comparison with Germanic soldiers of the fifteenth and sixteenth centuries, "men who perceived limited opportunities at home but felt that they were as good as anyone else with weapons in their hands."[56] Not surprisingly, German officers valued attributes that mirrored those valued in imperial Germany's "manly-military habitus."[57] A Schutztruppe officer who undertook a number of cartographic expeditions in East Africa in the late 1890s described in his journal a grim situation in which his party encountered provisioning problems. He recorded his admiration of the Sudanese soldiers' calm attitude in responding to the crisis. They "obeyed without complaint," comforting themselves with the words "amri ya mungu," or "it is God's will." He continued,

> When I expressed to my old shaush, Ali Koli, my regrets that there was now nothing to eat, he said: "hai zuru," which means, "It doesn't matter." And when I now said to him "amri ya mungu," he responded calmly, "ndiyo bwana yes, Sir!" That evening I received his special thanks, [because] I gave him and the other shaush each a handful of rice, which I had taken from the very small supply of rice I had brought along with me.[58]

Such observations on the senior Sudanese soldiers' composure appeared frequently in officers' diaries and memoirs. Some, like Prittwitz, explained it in terms of a fatalism they imagined to be characteristic of Muslim spirituality. Yet the exchange above also suggests a moment of recognition between the shaush and Prittwitz, a moment in which the two men communicated through military comradeship about their present circumstances. Prittwitz's journal entry also reveals a face-to-face, locally based paternal relationship between officer and askari, with Prittwitz boasting of his willingness to share his food with his two senior African troops and signaling his role as patron, as well as his awareness that the two soldiers were indispensable to his ability to keep his caravan under control during a hunger crisis.[59]

The position of Sudanese troops at the "apex" of the Schutztruppe martial race ranking remained intact throughout the period of German rule over East Africa, upheld by German military ideals and askari's participation in the ideals.[60] Because of their experience in the Egyptian army, the Germans gave the Sudanese recruits the senior ranks among the askari, with correspondingly higher rates of pay and, in the early years of the Schutztruppe, different uniforms from the other recruits. They also acceded to the soldiers' requests that their families be allowed to accompany them to East Africa, thus setting a precedent for family life in the military garrisons that subsequent generations of askari reproduced.[61] Some officers reported that non-Sudanese askari marked themselves with "Sudanese" facial scarifications and added bits of Arabic to their speech in order to emulate their superiors.[62] Through a constant back-and-forth interplay between German soldierly ideals and Sudanese seniority, dependability, and leadership abilities, Sudanese soldiers secured their place at the top of both the Schutztruppe organization and the martial race hierarchy and thus became the model askari for the rest of the German colonial period.

ABDULCHER FARRAG'S LIFE HISTORY IN CONTEXT: FROM SUDAN TO THE SCHUTZTRUPPE

Tracing the military backgrounds of the soldiers the Germans referred to as Sudanese requires identifying the particular groups from the region today known as Sudan that Europeans lumped into the category Sudanese, a manifestation of the classificatory impetus behind European colonialism. These groups included Dinka, Shilluk, Zande,

Baggara, and others, but German references in the sources to specific linguistic groups, peoples, or polities are sporadic and partial at best.[63] British and Egyptian officers had similar disregard for the specifics of their recruits' geographic or cultural backgrounds, referring to them, as did the Germans, simply as Sudanese or Nubi. Their backgrounds as slave-soldiers further complicates our ability to reconstruct their pre-Schutztruppe histories, requiring consideration of at least three distinct phases of Egyptian/Sudanese/British colonial history. These include Mehmed Ali Pasha's army modernization project (ca. 1821–41); the disastrous regimes and military forays of his successors Said (1855–63), Ismail (1863–79), and Tawfiq (1879–92); and the era of the 'Urabi Revolt, the Mahdiyya, and British and Egyptian efforts to defeat them (1881–98). Mehmed Ali's army began raiding Sudan for boys and young men to fill its ranks as slave soldiers in the 1820s, and similar practices continued throughout the 1800s, at least until the end of the Mahdiyya.

In addition, merchant companies operating in the southern Sudan used slave soldiers in their private armies. Their activities were another driver of instability in the region. According to Douglas Johnson, "There was a frequent interchange of personnel between the army and the merchant companies, many a soldier finding employment in a private army, and many a slave-soldier from the companies would often be absorbed into the Egyptian army."[64] Many men's lives were directly affected by this general pattern of conscription into the region's military institutions, which often started out as enslavement but transformed into a more ambiguous status of military clientage. Slave-soldiers were a feature of life throughout the whole region and provided a ready pool of soldierly candidates for protocolonial and colonial armies. As regional political, economic, and military power relations shifted in late-nineteenth-century northeast Africa, slave-soldiers also shifted their allegiances to reflect changing personal fortunes.

Men from the groups referred to as Dinka and Shilluk ended up in the Schutztruppe in relatively large numbers. Regional slave-raiding patterns—most notably, northern horsemen conducting regular raids against southern peoples—brought large numbers of southern Sudanese men into regional markets, where they were sold into slavery or used as levies paid to local rulers.[65] In twentieth-century ethnographies, Dinkas remembered this period of "Arab" slave-raiding as "the time when the world was spoiled," a time of massive upheaval, fear, and destruction.[66] *Turkiyya* and Mahdiyya military seizures of boys and men for conscription as soldiers, as well as the widespread use of captives to pay annual tribute to regional potentates, shaped southern Sudanese identities and memories far into the twentieth century.[67]

A typical pattern for young men unfortunate enough to end up as captives was to first be forced to work as soldiers' servants ("gunboys"). Later, they became soldiers themselves. This pool of men thus reproduced the ranks of the Egyptian and private armies described above.[68] Salim Wilson (born Hatashil Masha Kathish), a self-identified Dinka,[69] was one such man who, in his youth, experienced military slavery at the hands of slave raiders whom he described as Arabs. Another was Ali Effendi Gifoon, a Shilluk man born around 1836 in Fashoda, who similarly endured harsh captivity and then became a career soldier, first in the Turkiyya, then in the Anglo-Egyptian army. Gifoon's narrative thus traces his life history from youth, to enslavement, to military service, through a succession of different armies.[70] In both cases, forcible separation from their homes and kinship ties created conditions under which military organizations became their new families. Although neither Wilson nor Gifoon became Schutztruppe askari, their narratives provide rich contextual support for Farrag's narrative, to be discussed below, which is the only existing life history of a Sudanese Schutztruppe askari currently available. Along with Farrag's narrative, Wilson's and Gifoon's narratives highlight the qualities that Schutztruppe officers appreciated in southern Sudanese men as askari candidates.[71]

These narratives point up a complex of traits with which boys from this region were socialized. Their communities valued traits like those both Wilson and Gifoon described—courage and composure in dangerous situations, willingness to defend one's honor against insult, and determination to prove oneself braver and more dignified than one's peers.[72] In an extensive socialization and training process, southern Sudanese boys and young men learned how to become fearless hunters and soldiers. Livestock raiding parties occurred routinely, contributing to the development of confidence, daring, and a willingness to use measured violence among young men.[73] For Dinka and Shilluk men, the display of cowardice was unacceptable. Recklessness was discouraged, but young men were tacitly expected to test the boundaries of masculine strength and bravado. Wilson eventually made his way out of this military complex in Sudan, becoming a Christian missionary in England and eschewing the violence of the age. Gifoon's narrative, on the other hand, vividly illustrates that soldier's involvement in violent military engagements and predatory practices across northeastern Africa and beyond. It offers a chilling account of how the everyday violence of military slavery produced professional soldiers whose socioeconomic well-being was connected directly to their willingness to carry out the violence of military conquest and subjugation of local peoples across northeastern Africa.[74]

Such values and experiences were welcome in the Schutztruppe, where officers and NCOs looked for recruits who would not hesitate to use violence in battle or in day-to-day colonial contexts. They also sought to instill fearlessness in their recruits through repetitive marksmanship and combat exercises.[75] Hunting skills were also valued since hunting was part of expeditionary provisioning practices. German officers' military masculine sensibilities gave them a basis for identifying with southern Sudanese men, who seemed to share a reverence for courage, calmness, and self-mastery under stressful conditions.[76] Such was also the case with Schutztruppe officer August Leue's 1893 encounter with Abdulcher Farrag, whose narrative, "Kismet," appeared in Leue's 1903 memoir, *Dar-es-Salaam*.

Unlike Salim Wilson and Ali Effendi Gifoon, Farrag acknowledged no background of enslavement. Instead, he claimed to be Habbaniyya, known as one of the slave-raiding, cattle-herding, "Arab" groups from northeastern Sudan that featured so prominently in southern Sudanese memories of the "spoiled" time in their past.[77] In telling his story to Leue, he emphasized his status as a free man, a man who would not countenance the idea of being enslaved. He also thought of himself as a "civilized" man based on a professed admiration for Egypt's political and technological achievements. Farrag's narrative distances him from certain aspects of his Sudanese background, but emphasizes the qualities he believed made him worthy of respect. Having left behind his past and cultural ties to a slave-raiding group in order to pursue a life he considered more civilized, he presented himself as a skilled professional soldier, a dependable comrade, and a man who appreciated the features of Egyptian modernity.[78] Farrag used his experiences during the Mahdiyya to emphasize personal characteristics that underscored his suitability for membership in the Schutztruppe organization. In the process, he also expressed what it meant to be askari and signaled his willingness to serve the Schutztruppe in East Africa.

Born in Darfur in the early 1860s, Farrag moved as a youth to the Nile River town of Dongola, not far from the birthplace of Sheikh Mohamed Ahmed, the man who would become known as the Mahdi. When he had "ripened" to manhood he traveled with his friend Daut down the river to Cairo to earn money. He took employment as a domestic servant with a European businessman, while Daut, "who was opposed to manual labor," became a soldier in the Egyptian army. Daut regaled Farrag with descriptions of the soldiering life "in such tempting colors, that he thought it not a bad idea to apply [for a position as a soldier himself]."[79] Farrag eventually left his employer, reported to Daut's unit, and became a soldier in the Egyptian army, beginning a colorful military career that exemplifies the historical dynamics that brought men to the Wissmanntruppe in 1889.[80]

Between 1881 and 1885, Farrag claimed to have fought for three different armies—the Egyptian army under Khedive Tawfiq; the Egyptian army under British leadership; and the Mahdist army. His narrative recounts the details of his experiences first as a soldier in the Egyptian army under British leadership on campaign against the Mahdi; then as a prisoner of the Mahdist army, the Ansar; and finally his escape and return to Egyptian lines at Khartoum in 1884.[81]

Farrag's narrative references several key events in the early phase of the Mahdi wars, thereby providing useful firsthand descriptions of the everyday practices of expeditionary warfare.[82] More important, however, he offers a rare non-European (albeit European-mediated) perspective on the qualities the Schutztruppe valued in its soldiers. Woven throughout the narrative are reflections on the trials of day-to-day soldiering, the violence of colonial warfare, and the attractions of colonial modernity, including freedom, as well as access to its trappings, such as modern military technologies. Although the bulk of Farrag's narrative covers his pre-Schutztruppe life, his reflections on these years call attention to the ways in which Sudanese and other soldiers made themselves valuable to their German officer-patrons after 1889.

For one thing, Farrag emphasizes his own resoluteness in overcoming the everyday dangers of warfare, the breadth of his experiences in the war, and the particular skills he brought to bear as a soldier, all of which impressed Leue greatly. In a sense, his narrative unfolds as the story of a learning process in which his military experiences allowed him to gather to himself more and more soldierly acumen and character. Several places in the text illustrate this point. For example, in describing his experience in the Battle of Tel el-Kebir in September 1882, he noted how much better his regiment would have fared against the British if only they had received some training on how to properly aim and fire their Remington rifles:

> Oh *Bwana Mkubwa*, we did what we could. . . . The British marched on us at night, and undertook the attack on our camp at daybreak. When we were alerted, they were already right outside our works. We jumped into the firing trenches and fired everything we had. But always too high, because we didn't know our Remington rifles very well. Had we been better trained on the weapon and most importantly, had we just once had target practice, the situation would have turned out completely differently. In this case, our steadfastness served us little; and there was nothing left for us [to do] but yield.[83]

Here, although describing an experience from his time with the Egyptian army, Farrag underlines two characteristics central to Schutztruppe professional ideals. First, field training instilled in the askari combat skills that would hold up under the stresses of battle.[84] Second, "steadfastness" glued the force together, ensuring that soldiers would not lose their composure in the chaos of battle. In playing up his dedication, and acknowledging his weak shooting skills, Farrag gestured his grasp of the centrality of loyalty, bravery, and tough training as Schutztruppe ideals.

Farrag also accentuated his resourcefulness, hardiness, and trustworthiness as a soldier. His skills of observation showed him to be a capable scout, a skill that Schutztruppe officers appreciated since they operated almost exclusively in small units that relied on surprise attacks and feint.[85] From his vantage point as a camel corpsman, he observed what average foot soldiers could not, such as Ansar scouting practices that proved them to be masters of the art of camouflage.[86] He described living through extreme hardships as the Egyptian army traversed barren landscapes. Having witnessing the march's devastating toll on human and animal alike, Farrag remarked, "little can be expected of people who for weeks have had nothing else to eat but the meat of collapsed camels."[87] Pointing out the consequences of a failure in leadership, he noted that among the men, there were "mutterings" of "disunity" between Egyptian and European officers leading the expedition. Their public disagreements undermined discipline among the exhausted troops, exacerbating already fragile conditions. Thus, even in relating these seemingly mundane details of warfare in Sudan, he was in fact positioning himself as knowledgeable of the characteristics Schutztruppe officers found essential in making good soldiers and leaders.

The violence of expeditionary warfare and the costs of military defeat also appear in Farrag's recollections. Farrag survived the ill-fated Egyptian expedition to recapture El-Obeid from the Mahdists, led by Hicks Pasha, in November 1883. Unlike Gifoon's relatively unemotional descriptions of the effects of the violence he experienced as a soldier, Farrag expressed deep sorrow over the "bloodbath" that occurred at El-Obeid, in which Hicks and ninety-seven hundred (of ten thousand) of his Egyptian soldiers were killed by the Ansar.[88] His dramatic description of the attack and its aftermath is worth quoting at length:

> As we marched we were gravely attacked by huge rebel hordes populated by thousands of warriors. We stopped, built a thorn-boma, and set up our artillery. We were actually successful in fending off the attacking enemy; but we ourselves suffered such losses, that any prospect of victory was out of the question. — It was a terrible night that now followed. We nearly died from hunger and thirst, and additionally we were exposed to the bullets of the enemy, these last of whom crept [up to the boma] again under cover of darkness, and from their hidden positions shot at us from all sides. Because in our boma everything was forced tightly together, almost none of the enemy shots missed [hitting something] — The groaning of the wounded animals, along with the whimpering and screaming of the wounded men, was dreadful.[89]

At daybreak, they were forced to leave behind the "dead, wounded, and artillery pieces" in order to move out quickly to find water. But after marching only a short way, they were attacked again. Farrag's friend Daut died in this attack, and Farrag was severely wounded. This became a defining moment in Farrag's narrative, for when he awoke some time later, he found himself a prisoner of the Ansar.

Farrag equated this moment to entering a state of slavery. At this point, he began to more clearly articulate his self-identification as a Habbaniyya. In invoking his Habbaniyya identity, he emphasized his status as a free man, and his disdain for slavery, the Mahdiyya, and its followers. Farrag's experience as a prisoner ironically allowed him to *be* Habbaniyya in specific ways. Regaining consciousness after the battle, he realized that he was on a stretcher, being cared for and carried by people he did not know. When he awoke, he discovered that his caretakers were Ansar soldiers who had come to plunder the dead bodies. They did not kill Farrag because they recognized from the scarification on his cheeks "that [he] was of their tribe."[90] Farrag spent the next year as a prisoner, during which he and the other Egyptian soldiers were beaten, mistreated, and called "unbelieving dogs." This insult he found bewildering, because to his mind, "we soldiers were at least as good Muslims as the Dervishes."[91] Under these dire circumstances, Farrag turned to his Habbaniyya captors for "protection and refuge," and his treatment improved dramatically. Having been initiated into a Habbaniyya "warrior-society" by his captors, Farrag participated in at least one Ansar campaign in southern Kordofan in the spring of 1884. Tellingly, Farrag elaborated no further on his experiences as an Ansar soldier.

Escaping captivity became his preoccupation. His captors made him wear the patched white smock known as the *jibba*, "a kind of uniform" for the Ansar, which disgusted him.[92] He perceived major differences between himself and followers of the Mahdi, including his Habbaniyya captors: "Those who, like my tribesmen, had only ever lived under the half-wild conditions of the Sudan let themselves be impressed by the teachings of the Dongolani [the Mahdi]; for us others who had gotten to know the culture of Egypt, it was easy to see through the false game of the Mahdi and his khalifs."[93] Presenting himself as more worldly and savvy than the masses of Sudanese who became Mahdists, he elevated his relatively short experience in Egypt to a prominent position in his narration. Given that his experiences there included domestic servitude in a European household and enlistment in the Egyptian army, Farrag's narrative suggests that membership in a defined hierarchy held some value for him. He also valued what he considered "Egyptian" culture, which had been shaped in part by modernization projects directed by European imperial powers.[94] Farrag's narrative indicated conscious movement away from a typical Habbaniyya existence as a "cattle nomad" and what he called the "half-wild" culture of Sudan.[95] His realization that he had become fundamentally different from other Habbaniyya also drove his desire to escape captivity and return to a "familiar" context, the Egyptian army.[96] His narrative thus signaled approval of British imperial methods, in turn tacitly signaling his support for the German imperial mission. He had left behind his "tribesmen" and their culture in favor of his patron, Leue, and the Schutztruppe organization.

Desperate to escape what he considered slave status, Farrag seized the first chance he had to cross back to Anglo-Egyptian lines. In October 1884 he was encamped with the Ansar at the Mahdi's headquarters in Omdurman, just across the Nile from Khartoum, where the Egyptian force under General Charles Gordon had its headquarters. The Habbaniyya who had provided him protection from the worst effects of captivity suspected he might try to escape, and warned him against it, but in the end did nothing to stop him.[97] His escape narrative is especially interesting because it "graphs the process by which a man comes to recognize himself" as a particular kind of subject:[98]

> Destiny willed it that one day I was sent along with a crowd of warriors to the Gesireh peninsula, where Khartoum lay, to reinforce the siege troops. Familiar with the terrain there, the next night I slipped out of our camp and turned toward the city. Fearing that I would be shot at from the ramparts [by Egyptian guards], I took off my jibba and threw it away. My concern was, however, unnecessary because in the dark night my approach went totally unnoticed. It was only when I stood right before the works that I was called to [by the guards]. When I had given myself to be recognized, I was allowed into the fortress, and was greeted in a comradely fashion by the guards.[99]

Farrag thus marked the passage out of his debased status as an Ansar prisoner back to his preferred status as an Egyptian soldier by throwing off the jibba, which he found so shameful. He was accepted back into his "family" of military comrades, headed up by one of the most famous officer-patrons in colonial history, General Gordon.[100]

Farrag reentered Egyptian service, but he found his new duties as a guard uninteresting. Moreover, the Ansar siege of Khartoum was having its effect: if there had been little food with the Mahdists, Farrag now "nearly starved" as the army's rations shrank. The situation reached emergency proportions in January 1885, when there began to be talk of capitulation if a rumored British relief expedition did not arrive soon. Farrag's thoughts turned dark as he contemplated the fate awaiting him if he fell back into the Mahdists' hands. But "kismet" intervened when he joined a contingent of Sudanese soldiers detailed to provide security for three steamers sent up the Nile to expedite the relief effort by bringing back soldiers and provisions.[101] He thus was not in Khartoum when the fatal Ansar attack on the fort occurred.[102] After Gordon's defeat, Farrag traveled with the British back to Dongola, and then to Cairo. His regiment disbanded as part of the British military withdrawal from Sudan, and Farrag again found himself unemployed.

Farrag's narrative effectively ends here, with Leue providing a moving conclusion:

> "Indeed, Abdulcher," [Leue] said, as the soldier came to an end, "you have experienced much evil, but you have also had much luck."
>
> The ombascha nodded and turned silently back to the column.

In the last paragraph of this chapter, entitled "Kismet," Leue explained how Farrag, who had so miraculously survived so many dangerous campaigns in Egypt, Sudan, and German East Africa, had died in battle after all, thus becoming "a victim of his soldierly duty." The last sentence in the chapter—"So that was his kismet"—invokes a common trope, which held that Sudanese soldiers (and Muslim soldiers more generally) espoused a particularly fatalistic view of the world and the events that affected their lives.[103] Yet this line also acknowledges Farrag's way of remembering his life and the many brushes with death he experienced as a soldier. In noting Farrag's silence as he returned to the column, Leue evokes the traumas of war and the pain of losing comrades in a way that rarely surfaces in representations of the askari. Farrag's silence thus amplifies reflections on the sacrificial "deaths for the Fatherland" suffered by both Africans and Germans that Leue uses to conclude the chapter.[104] Farrag presented his life story to Leue in a way that emphasized key experiences and realizations that led inexorably to his life in the Schutztruppe, to the moment he was sharing with Leue as they marched through German East Africa in the early 1890s.

On the other hand, Farrag omits aspects of his life that one might expect to see in an askari narrative. For example, Farrag's narrative offers no information on the four years between his separation from the Egyptian army and his enlistment with the Wissmanntruppe. It was a period of abjection for the unemployed, poverty-stricken ex-Egyptian soldiers, who were living in "wretched conditions" when Wissmann arrived on his 1889 recruiting trip to Cairo.[105] The British saw them as "journeymen unusable for anything but the warrior-trade" and were happy to be rid of them.[106] The Wissmanntruppe eagerly took them on as the foundation of their hastily assembled army for East Africa. Taking into account Farrag's role in shaping the narrative, his failure to mention the years between the dissolution of his Egyptian army unit and his employment with the Wissmanntruppe becomes clearer. Discussing a life without soldierly work would have diminished the image he wanted to project to Leue.

The incompleteness of Farrag's narrative leaves much to the imagination. For example, Farrag's failure to mention a family is another significant silence, since many of the Sudanese soldiers recruited to the Schutztruppe from Egypt brought their families with them to German East Africa. One British commentator pointed out the central importance of family to the Sudanese soldiers of the Anglo-Egyptian army: "Devoted to their wives, it is essential to provide for the welfare of their women as the best means of keeping these wild but lovable men in order, and in some cases where this item of battalion economics was neglected serious trouble ensued."[107] German officers of the imperial era also believed that fatherhood, based on "fundamental" virtues of "domesticity" and "sensitivity," contributed directly to manliness. Indeed, they viewed these qualities as "prerequisites for patriotism and valour."[108] In leaving out any discussion of his family, Farrag avoided having to account for this possible chink in his masculine armor. Askari respectability was based in part on being householders, so if for some reason Farrag had not yet married and become a head of household, he had reason not to draw attention to this point in a narrative meant to highlight his askari qualities. We can only speculate on why Farrag might not have married, or why he remained silent on this issue in the narrative.

Despite the narrative's lacunae, given the upheaval and social mobility of the period and place, Farrag's story testifies to the circuitous routes Sudanese men took to becoming Schutztruppe askari. Joining the Schutztruppe offered men like Farrag a way out of a life of poverty in the Cairo slums, the possibility of building respectable lives in a new and distant context, and the potential for appreciation and respect from their German officers and patrons, as well as fellow askari. For men who had known only lives of warfare and soldiering, often under unfree or coerced conditions, the Schutztruppe offered a place to practice their only profession, and they knew the organization simultaneously promised them otherwise largely unattainable promotion, compensation, and prestige.

The narratives used here suggest how African men came to fight Germany's colonial wars. Farrag negotiated multiple, simultaneous subjectivities on his way to becoming an askari.[109] He constructed his past as a series of meaningful moments that ultimately led him to his "home" in the Schutztruppe in German East Africa. In representing himself to Leue, he highlighted numerous turning points and decisions that set him apart from others, particularly the Sudanese he characterized as "half-wild." In German East Africa, askari also set themselves apart from those they considered *washenzi*, or uncivilized people — the undifferentiated masses of East Africans the Schutztruppe sought to dominate. In becoming an askari, he engaged in a continual process of clarifying his personal allegiances, aptitudes, and affiliations, ultimately leading to a tight bond of comradeship with Leue, and through him, to the rest of the Schutztruppe.

Sudanese soldiers also viewed themselves as superior to their southeastern and eastern African Schutztruppe counterparts and seemingly maintained a kind of outsider status despite their absolute centrality to the Schutztruppe's ability to fight. Yet the historical processes that brought soldiers from southeastern and eastern Africa into the German colonial army, how they represented themselves to others, and how these soldiers might have understood their experiences in the Schutztruppe often mirror those expressed in Farrag's life history. This suggests that the Sudanese soldiers were not as exceptional as the Germans purported in their texts. Rather, their exceptional status emerged from their relative seniority and experience as practitioners of a particular European-influenced style of warfare. The rest of this chapter examines the meanings and processes behind recruitment within German East Africa, exploring the qualities that made these soldiers simultaneously different and similar to their Sudanese seniors.

FROM RUGA-RUGA TO ASKARI: RECRUITING WITHIN GERMAN EAST AFRICA

In 1889 the existence of a group of former Anglo-Egyptian soldiers espousing a Sudanese or Nubi martial identity facilitated Hermann von Wissmann's ability to rapidly assemble recruits for his conquest army. By 1895, however, the Schutztruppe faced a recruitment problem that substantially changed its makeup. After 1895, recruits from the central steppe and Great Lakes regions of Tanzania came to comprise the bulk of the Schutztruppe rank and file. Nyamwezi, Sukuma, and Manyema men from these regions became Schutztruppe askari for reasons that often converged with those of the Sudanese soldiers. For example, in nineteenth-century Sudan and East Africa, militarized polities and entrepreneurs relied on slave raids to fill the ranks of private armies and to acquire slaves for sale into local, regional, and overseas markets. Among Dinka and Shilluk men in southern Sudan, hunting skills were fostered and celebrated, and Sudanese Schutztruppe members' skills as hunters played a central role in expeditionary provisioning practices, for example. East African recruits also brought hunting skills with them to the colonial army. In addition, their distinct skills and sensibilities differentiated them somewhat from the Sudanese troops.[110] The everyday demands of the East African long-distance caravan trading network generated pools of young men from work cultures that celebrated practical skills as trackers, scouts, guards, and soldiers. As we have seen, Schutztruppe narratives about Sudanese soldiers celebrated intangible qualities like stoic resolve, calmness under stressful conditions, and unmitigated dedication to superior officers. In contrast, descriptions of East African recruits to the Schutztruppe noted that they were responsible, industrious, ambitious, and lively. How might we explain these descriptive and narrative differences? How did the soldiers themselves and their German commanders contribute to shaping an askari identity that lasted well beyond the German colonial era?

Before embarking on the East African recruits' story, a small detour through southeastern Africa is warranted. The case of the Shangaan ("Zulu") recruits offers a contrasting vantage point from which to consider what was at stake in the construction of Schutztruppe askari identities. In other words, because these recruits did not stay on as soldiers past about 1895, their story shows that the making of the Schutztruppe was not a foregone conclusion.

During the Schutztruppe's "experimental" phase of building a conquest army (1889–91), German officers recruited some four hundred Shangaan men, referred to as Zulus, from Inhambane in southern Portuguese East Africa, today's Mozambique.[111] They were likely descendants of the followers of Soshangane, one of the Nguni leaders who migrated from what is now South Africa into the Inhambane region in the 1830s following wars with Shaka. Shoshangane founded what became known as the Gaza Empire.[112] With few exceptions, these soldiers remained in the Schutztruppe for only about three years before returning to Portuguese East Africa.[113] A combination of administrative, economic, and psychological factors likely contributed to their brief presence in the German colonial army. For example, the Portuguese placed limits on the soldiers' enlistment terms before allowing the Wissmanntruppe to enlist them in 1889. Like the British in Egypt, the Portuguese balked at allowing the Germans unrestricted access to new recruits within Portuguese East Africa.[114] In addition, Shangaan soldiers knew that the Sudanese soldiers received higher pay than they did and, understandably, found this unfair. And the massive casualties suffered by the Schutztruppe in the 1891 Zelewski expedition fell disproportionately on Shangaan men, demoralizing those left behind.[115]

But there was more going on between Schutztruppe officers and Shangaan recruits than these practical explanations reveal. Schutztruppe officers represented the Shangaan soldiers somewhat schizophrenically, sometimes finding them dependable and "first-rate recruit-material"—if decidedly less impressive than the Sudanese troops—and sometimes finding them uncontrollable and cowardly.[116] To some officers, the Shangaan recruits appeared as "pure nature children," in need of strong guidance and careful handling to compensate for their "great pettishness" and "strong sense of honor."[117] Another described them as displaying a "larger than life cowardice" during a raid on an enemy compound in Ukaguru in 1891.[118] Remarkably, however, a Shangaan recruit named Plantan rose through the ranks to become effendi, the highest possible rank for Africans in the Schutztruppe. His ward, Kleist Sykes, followed in his footsteps, serving as a signaler and scout during World War I.[119] According to Sykes's descendants, he also served as an orderly to General von Lettow-Vorbeck during World War I, until a severe illness disabled him. His career as an askari ended with his capture by Belgian troops in late 1917.[120] Although not many Shangaan men remained with the Schutztruppe past 1892, the few who did distinguished themselves as dedicated soldiers whose esteem among officers rivaled that of the Sudanese soldiers.

So how do we explain these discordant reviews of the Shangaan soldiers' performance? For one thing, in contrast to the Sudanese, they had received only minimal, if any, Western-style military training before their recruitment in Portuguese East Africa and subsequent transport to German East Africa, in 1889. While they showed great enthusiasm for going to war, they found German training methods and military praxis less than compelling.[121] Whereas the Sudanese troops struck German officers as "serious," "ill-tempered," and "quiet," the Shangaan soldiers were represented as prone to loud singing, whistling, and joking, as well as "extraordinarily interesting" and spontaneous dance sessions.[122] The Shangaan recruitment experiment may in fact have been destined to fail, given Portuguese security considerations and Shangaan perceptions that they were being treated unfairly vis-à-vis other soldiers, especially the Sudanese. Still, stopping with these explanations forecloses an opportunity to point out how the Schutztruppe, and other colonial armies, worked. In other words, unlike the identifications that developed between Sudanese soldiers and German officers, the relationships between Shangaan soldiers and German officers revealed unequal expectations for soldierly conduct, compensation, and treatment. Ultimately, the Shangaan soldiers did not fit into Schutztruppe culture, and they returned home, leaving few traces of their presence in the Schutztruppe's organizational development through the rest of the 1890s.

This diversion through the Shangaan piece of early Schutztruppe history helps illuminate the qualities that positioned certain groups of East African men to become the German colonial army's choice for rank-and-file recruitment. The moral economy of the nineteenth-century East African regional caravan trading system, and the emergence of centralized polities that aimed to control these networks, produced young men whose masculine identities rested on certain positive valuations of martial skills and ideals. Whereas the Sudanese troops manifested qualities congruent with German ideals of military leadership, the East African askari brought regional expertise and practical soldiering skills to the organization. Dramatic socioeconomic changes in nineteenth-century Tanzania changed the conditions under which East African men could achieve manhood and respectability. For some, soldiering for the Schutztruppe represented a prime socioeconomic and political opportunity amid a turbulent period of narrowing opportunities and increasing dangers.

MAKING BIG MEN:
THE MARTIAL WORLD OF UNYAMWEZI

The German conquest of central Tanzania around 1893 brought profound changes for those who lived there, particularly around the small town of Tabora. As the Germans increasingly ensconced themselves in local affairs, they reshaped power relations around Tabora and beyond, backing up their claims to authority with military strength.[123] A Nyamwezi Schutztruppe veteran named Ali, who before the German arrival claimed to have been a wealthy slave raider, expressed memories of dismay and humiliation at German demands for labor and their unwillingness to differentiate between different status groups:

> We were all rounded up and told that we now belonged to the new government, the German government, and that we would all have to work for the invaders. No one in the community was spared this information—not the families of high standing, not the nobility, not the slaves, no one. We were all treated as one. This was frightening news, as we did not understand what it might entail. To those of us who had enjoyed the freedom and masterdom of the entire country of Unyamwezi this came as a shock. We were horrified that we now owed our allegiance to a so-called superior people.[124]

Having been forced to do hard labor clearing land to build a new German fort, he felt "ready for a change," wanting the "greater freedoms" that would come with a salaried position in the German colonial apparatus.[125] Realizing that his past as a successful slave raider might make him a suitable candidate for the German army, he decided to join. His explanation of this transitional moment in his life course exemplifies John Lonsdale's notion of "agency in tight corners": recognizing that regional politics were undergoing rapid transformation, Ali threw in his lot with the new power brokers. He explained his decision to join the Schutztruppe as one of the only ways to restore any semblance of his previous status as a "wealthy nobleman."[126]

The economic and social changes that occurred in Unyamwezi in the wake of the Schutztruppe's arrival substantially altered existing paths to becoming a big man. With colonial officials single-mindedly working to curb the slave trade in East Africa, slave raiding had become an untenable occupation for men like Ali.[127] The Schutztruppe also wrested control of the central caravan route from those who had previously controlled it, initiating a de-professionalization of the old porterage system.[128] Although a few other paths to respectability—such as migration to sisal plantations for wage labor—opened up with the colonial presence, others diminished in importance.[129] Ali hoped that becoming an askari would put him on a path toward the "greater freedoms" that might come of being a salaried employee of the German regime. He also imagined, incorrectly, that as an askari he would free himself from arduous forced or wage labor demands in the colonial economy—an economy that in its extractive and ad hoc character departed significantly from older understandings of reciprocal obligation that underpinned local political legitimacy.

Nyamwezi men came from cultural and socioeconomic contexts where serving in a strong patron's retinue enabled passage to manhood and accumulation of wealth that might then lead to respectability. They grew up observing specific military traditions structured by the patronage of wealthy and influential leaders who dominated the central caravan trade routes in the second half of the nineteenth century. Following the German conquest of these polities in the 1890s, young men transferred their loyalties to the Schutztruppe because it was one of the only suitable martial options left to them under the colonial security regime. Their historical and cultural linkages to the professional caravan trading network, where young men served as porters and guards, appealed to Schutztruppe officers in search of resourceful types accustomed to rough, expeditionary living. They recognized that these soldiers brought a vital and inimitable set of new skills to the army—mobility, stamina, and familiarity with interior lands, caravan routes, and social conventions.

Unlike their Sudanese soldiers, however, Nyamwezi soldiers came from within German East Africa, and in the minds of some Schutztruppe officers, that posed a potential risk. Their ties to local communities, old trading networks, and other kinds of cultural and religious networks set them apart from Sudanese and Shangaan soldiers. The

Nyamwezi soldiers thus posed a particular challenge to Schutztruppe officers, who doubted their trustworthiness in the event of anticolonial rebellion.[130] On this question, however, askari surprised their superiors—the Schutztruppe experienced few major acts of indiscipline until the latter stages of World War I. Official Schutztruppe historian Ernst Nigmann, reflecting on the organization's history in 1911, took this as "proof of the health of the whole organization."[131] One year later, as if to prove this sentiment, the governor's office wrote to the Colonial Office in Berlin to report that one of the last of "rebel leaders" of the Maji Maji war had been arrested by his own nephew, an askari named Marambira. Echoing Nigmann's description, the letter noted, "This should be seen as a pleasing sign of how the askari understand their belonging to the government."[132] The letter also made special note of the captured rebel leader's involvement in the "ambush and massacre" of a Sudanese effendi's column during the war, thereby suggesting that the soldier Marambira had come to prioritize his askari identity over the kinship tie with his uncle. By most accounts, East African askari fought wherever and whenever their officers ordered them to. Why was this so?

The answer lies in a surprising correspondence between the military cultures and practices that socialized many East African boys and young men, and the evolving Schutztruppe way of war. Askari willingness and aptitude to fight for the Germans stemmed from a sense that what was being asked of them was a continuation of regional military practices. The small-unit combat methods used in the Schutztruppe bore resemblances to precolonial practices of raiding warfare.

However, this continuity between military cultures only partially explains why the recruitment of Nyamwezi and other East African soldiers worked so well for the Schutztruppe.[133] As Ali's narrative suggests, one reason Nyamwezi men became askari was that the nascent colonial state created an environment in which options for achieving respectability through accumulation of prestige items narrowed significantly. German consolidation of power in the interior of East Africa intensified the population's involvement in the already existing, but more narrowly focused, cash economy.[134] As John Iliffe argues, "the Germans gave monetization high priority, paying their employees in cash and gradually demanding that tax should be paid in specie and not in kind."[135] German tax demands, designed to raise revenue as well as to have an "educational" effect on East Africans, forced profound changes in their everyday lives. It forced people to "use money, sell surplus corps, work for Europeans, and obey a distant government."[136] In order to accumulate enough cash to pay taxes and to procure socially vital prestige items such as livestock or cloth, East Africans increasingly had to take on wage labor. German taxation and labor demands thus undermined existing relationships between labor, prestige, and exchange that had characterized previous economies. Under these conditions, the cash poor could only with great difficulty accumulate enough prestige goods to exchange in important sociocultural transactions, such as bridewealth. On the other hand, those who earned cash through migrant wage labor might accumulate enough cash to purchase livestock and prestige goods to exchange with prospective fathers-in-law as bridewealth in order to build their own households through marriage.[137] Colonial taxes forced African householders to recast household-level production around both subsistence-level farming or herding, *and* earning wages to pay taxes. German labor demands, both paid and unpaid, also took a toll on householders' abilities to manage domestic production. Migrant labor became one of the few remaining options for accumulation of the cash and goods essential to social mobility. Another possibility, albeit available only to very few, was to occupy one of the rare salaried positions in the colonial government. These included East African administrators who came from "a bewildering variety of frameworks of local rule," clerks, teachers, and of course, the askari.[138] In this context, becoming askari made sense to East African men with military backgrounds or proclivities who also hoped to improve their status.

Well before the *Schutztruppe*'s arrival in Unyamwezi, the political upheavals and "military revolution" that occurred between 1860 and 1890 in Unyamwezi had exerted some influence on young men who grew up there. The upstart leaders Mirambo and Nyungu-ya-Mawe consolidated power in Unyanyembe through political acumen, backed up by the creation and deployment of well-organized standing armies with widespread reputations for ruthlessness. The men who fought in these armies, known as *ruga-ruga*, came from a range of social backgrounds. Their common experiences as soldiers in the armies of Mirambo, Nyungu-ya-Mawe, and their successors, gave them skills that Schutztruppe officers found useful in the 1890s.

The Schutztruppe recruited men from other groups within German East Africa, including the Hehe and Ngoni.[139] The numbers recruited from these groups, however, did not approach those of the Nyamwezi recruits until World War I, when manpower needs obviated adherence to previous martial race paradigms of recruitment. Tracing a prehistory of the Schutztruppe askari thus requires accounting for particular Nyamwezi contributions to being askari. Tracing the historical processes by which men from Unyamwezi became ruga-ruga in the precolonial context lays the basis for understanding how they became askari in the 1890s and how men from this second, non-Sudanese Schutztruppe recruiting wave contributed to being askari and the askari way of war.

RUGA-RUGA

The Schutztruppe began recruiting Nyamwezi and other men from the central steppe in large numbers around 1895. In 1911, Ernst Nigmann, the official historian of the Schutztruppe, described them in glowing terms:

> The good Nyamwezi, who from the beginning approached our rule with open trust, provided an even larger number [than the Manyema] of capable, responsible soldiers. It was also obvious that many Nyamwezi porters, who through their employment in government service had in any case found access to the [Schutztruppe], easily exchanged the admittedly more freelance work of the porters for the more contractually bound, but also more respected and profitable, work of the soldier.[140]

The ethnographer Karl Weule noted, "For purposes of the colonial economy, the Nyamwezi, because of their physical and mental disposition, are decidedly the most promising element in German East Africa."[141] These assessments of how the Nyamwezi received German rule tell us something of their perceived suitability as Schutztruppe soldiers. But they reveal little of the social dynamics behind the complex and violent regional history that preceded the Schutztruppe's arrival on the scene.[142]

Nyamwezi refers to the peoples who live in the western part of the region that now makes up Tanzania.[143] The name was of foreign origin, and not one that those who lived in the region used themselves. Instead, they referred to themselves using more specific monikers, such as Kimbu, Nyanyembe, and Sukuma. Nyamwezi thus became a shorthand descriptor for diverse peoples who lived in the region and who shared certain cultural and social practices and labor cultures. These peoples, Andrew Roberts argues, "achieved a kind of unity by being involved together in certain major historical trends and events," including the caravan trade, Arab, Swahili, and Ngoni encroachments, and the rise of leaders like Mirambo. In addition, "the memory of such shared experiences" helped solidify a Nyamwezi identity that floated above other local specific identities.[144]

Until around 1860 the peoples of Unyamwezi tended to live in small polities oriented around local rulers known as *batemi* (sing., *mtemi*).[145] With small populations, no standing armies, and fragmentary political organization, these polities did not attempt to dominate each other.[146] Hostilities between them were usually limited to raiding and counter-raiding for livestock or goods, or to exact revenge, but not to assert authority over other polities.[147] And because the small Nyamwezi polities seldom built up herds large enough to tempt concentrated attack from outside, they rarely fell victim to cattle-raiding peoples like the Maasai, who sought bigger prizes when they conducted raids.

Around 1860, Nyamwezi peoples began playing "leading roles" in regional trading systems because of their geographic position within Unyamwezi, and because the region had been relatively peaceful until that time.[148] They traded cultivated crops and the goods gathered from nearby forestlands for iron tools and weapons, salt, and livestock available from neighboring peoples. When not cultivating, they worked as intermediaries in regional exchanges.[149] Stephen J. Rockel argues that around this time arose "a Nyamwezi merchant class, the *vbandevba*, who were of mixed aristocratic and commoner origin, and who took accumulation and profit making seriously."[150] The vbandevba were "great cattleowners and farmers" who imported slaves from Manyema, west of Unyamwezi, to work for them.[151] Also around this time, and in association with the intensification of the caravan trade, emerged the socioeconomic category of the *waungwana* (sing., *mwungwana*), to which anyone, slave or free, could aspire. The word connoted the "general qualities of urbane gentility" typically associated with coastal Swahili culture.[152] Waungwana tended to think of themselves as "autonomous agents, as gentlemen and as entrepreneurs."[153] These descriptors—vbandevba and waungwana— are pertinent to understanding the socioeconomic aspirations of many East Africans after about 1860.

Between 1840 and 1860, Nyamwezi men and women began staking claims as central actors in the emerging East African trading system, developing reputations as long-distance travelers who routinely journeyed to such distant destinations as the copper fields of Congo and the Swahili coast. Unyamwezi increasingly became the engine behind the growth of the caravan trading network connecting the interior regions of central and eastern Africa with the Swahili coast. Before 1800 the central routes linking Unyamwezi to the coast had been "pioneered by [Nyamwezi] trade specialists" carrying small amounts of trade goods, including "a few tusks."[154] In the 1820s, Arab coastal merchants established trading centers in Unyamwezi, and began reaping handsome profits from these interests. Through a process of "interaction and competition" between coastal and Nyamwezi caravan traders, a major center developed at Kazeh (later Tabora), where regional political stability, and an advantageous position at a major trading crossroads, led to its expansion.[155] As Tabora's reputation as a large market grew, Arab traders brought in commodities such as beads, cloth, firearms and gunpowder. They then exchanged these items for ivory, as well as for captives brought to the market to be sold to coastal "patricians," Zanzibaris, or anyone who could afford them.[156] From Tabora, young and middle-aged men employed as porters transported the ivory, other goods, and captives to the coast for sale into the Indian Ocean system. "By doing so," Unomah argues, "some of them earned enough wealth to begin their own small-scale trading." Their presence as small traders, porters, and soldiers throughout east and central Africa widened. Increasingly they became involved in slave-raiding operations in eastern Congo and elsewhere.[157] Rockel reinforces this portrait of an emerging economy when he writes, "The development of a labor market for caravan porters was an early and significant stage in the transition to capitalism, which began in a period of violence and political upheaval."[158] By 1860, Nyamwezi men and women were at the epicenter of a rapidly intensifying trading network with a scope that reached across eastern Africa, into the Indian Ocean, and beyond.

CARAVAN CULTURE

Divisions of labor and skill specializations within Nyamwezi labor culture of the 1870s and 1880s allowed individuals with particular skills to flourish. Participants exercised some personal autonomy in selecting

what kinds of porterage activities to undertake. Some porters only con-
tracted for work during the dry season, returning to Unyamwezi during
the wet season to tend to their agricultural lands.[159] Individuals might
also choose whether or not to carry heavy loads to the coast and back,
or to travel individually to the coast with just a few trade goods in order
to find more lucrative work with a large caravan for the way back. Each
season, porters evaluated the wage-earning and status-building potential of different combinations of caravans, journeys, and goods, and
chose the best opportunities. Caravan culture had its own hierarchies
and divisions of labor, with qualified individuals performing distinct
tasks such as load allocation, labor recruitment, supervising caravans,
ritual protection, and physical security.[160] Women participated actively
in a wide range of caravan work as well—a precursor to their presence
in the Schutztruppe campaign communities later on.

Nyamwezi porters had reputations among European explorers
and company representatives as hardnosed professionals who negotiated their own terms, holding their employers to standards of proper
compensation and work conditions.[161] Specialized porters made long-
term commitments to the occupation, "[learning] the skills necessary
for success and survival, and [proving] their endurance and strength."
They worked according to a "code of honor that regulated customary
practices." Strikingly, Rockel's research on Nyamwezi caravan porters
shows that this code "provided the 'grammar' for the labor culture of
the caravans, which over time, and drawing on other resources, shaped
communal interactions across Tanzania."[162]

Not all Nyamwezi became professional porters, and cultivation
remained a central feature of life in Unyamwezi regardless of social
position. Yet involvement in the long-distance caravan system, either
as porters or guards, became a rite of passage to manhood. Nearly all
men, and a significant number of women, undertook the journey to
the coast and back at some point in their youth. Nyamwezi boys began
preparing for caravan life very early. In the 1880s a German explorer-
scientist reported that Nyamwezi boys amused themselves by making
little bows and arrows that they sometimes used to shoot birds. They
also played "war games" among themselves and role-played scenes
in which they protected precious cattle from lion attacks.[163] Boys also
sometimes used sticks and grass to construct small versions of typical
porters' loads, which they then used to "imitate a caravan."[164] Boys aged

thirteen to fifteen reportedly exhibited great bravery, making them ideal candidates for bodyguard and soldiering duties, in which they could be entrusted with special missions.[165] By their young adulthood, most had been socialized in the everydayness of the caravans, and they imagined futures in which they too would participate in the long-distance marches that criss-crossed Tanzania. A Nyamwezi man who had not completed a journey to the coast and back was considered *mutini*, an "unripe fig," someone "who did not know the ways of the world," and who was therefore less than a man.[166] Young men of all social ranks, including the royal lineages, participated in this rite of passage, often as porters although, according to Norman Bennett, "a more usual role among the Nyamwezi was for the sons of chiefs to lead caravans and act as commercial agents for their [vbandevba] fathers."[167] In this way, caravan hierarchies began to map onto hierarchies of political authority throughout Unyamwezi.

Ali, the Nyamwezi ex-askari whose reflections appeared earlier in this chapter, grew up the son of a "wealthy nobleman" (perhaps a vbandevba) in Kazeh just outside Tabora. Ali's memoir provides no dates, but he probably came of age sometime in the mid-to-late 1880s. He recalled with pride the "metamorphosis" he experienced when, at age fourteen, his father taught him how to shoot a muzzleloader: "I felt a head and shoulders taller than [the boy I was]. I was becoming a man, partaking in the business of men."[168] Shortly thereafter, Ali's father helped him organize his first safari, "[a] hefty charge for a young man," he recalled many years later. Ali received a supply of guns and ammunition, as well as "bales of cloth, rolls of wire and boxes of beads—all for the purpose of bartering and buying slaves."[169]

Ali's trial safari took him only as far as Lake Tanganyika, offering preparation for the next challenge of transporting the captives to the coast, a journey of about three months.[170] Having previously accompanied his father on other safaris, he was familiar with the logistical, communicative, and strategic intricacies of managing such an operation. He also already understood the ruthlessness required of one aspiring to become a big man like his father: "There was no question of entertaining emotion in the business of slave-trading."[171] Upon successfully completing the test safari and returning to Tabora, Ali's father organized a feast marking both Ali's safe return and his coming of age. The accompanying ngoma, with its singing, dancing, and storytelling, lasted "well into the following day."[172] Ali took great pride in having completed his first safari. With his father's approval, he passed unequivocally into manhood.

Like many other Nyamwezi men, Ali associated the beginning of his metamorphosis from boy to man with the moment of learning how to fire a muzzleloading rifle. After 1860 warfare and political upheaval intensified, exacerbated by a massive influx of firearms into central Tanzania. Armed conflict became inexorably linked to the extension of trade in the region, and possession of firearms took on new meanings. As Michael Pesek argues,

> Firearms served not only as [trade] goods and tools of killing, but were also symbols of power. . . . And it was not only that ownership or use of them in the many wars of the nineteenth century made them into one of the most important catalysts of social change. It was more their specific tie-in to the political and symbolic economies of African societies that made them so important for the history of East Africa.[173]

For these reasons, many men became porters in order to acquire a weapon. By 1870 or so porters received their wages in firearms and cloth, with cloth taking the secondary position in terms of value.[174] Owning one's own firearm enhanced one's chances for upward mobility in the caravan hierarchy, because it marked a man as having enough experience to acquire a firearm, and also showed that he could access the same symbols of power that previously had been associated more narrowly with the batemi. Nyamwezi oral traditions show that new batemi used firearms in their installation rites. Firearms also announced an mtemi's arrival at his destination, and they marked the arrival of caravans at their destinations after long journeys.[175] Weapons were also traded for ivory, which alongside slaves remained the most valuable trade good throughout the 1870s and 1880s.[176] The proliferation of weapons in association with the caravan system contributed to the birth of a formidable new way of war between 1860 and 1890.

Nyamwezi caravan culture encouraged independent and adventurous spirits and militated against young men remaining *mutini* for very long. Young men's "wanderlust" infused their economic goals of acquiring the prestige goods (mainly firearms, cloth, and livestock) that would lay the foundation for respectability back in Unyamwezi.[177] As

Iliffe observes, "Respectability demanded, first, sufficient economic independence to allow the individual to reshape his lifestyle."[178] In Unyamwezi, respectability could mean having accumulated enough wealth to establish oneself as an independent trader, to marry, to acquire livestock, or to purchase slaves to work in one's household.[179] Between 1860 and 1890 many Nyamwezi men had set themselves on the path to achieving respectability through the caravan system.

MIRAMBO, NYUNGU-YA-MAWE, AND THE ARMIES OF UNYAMWEZI

The centralization of regional trade at Tabora and its domination by Omani and coastal Arabs marked a turning point in Unyamwezi's history. By 1860 Unyanyembe, the land surrounding Tabora, had become wealthy and powerful vis-à-vis its neighbors. Population growth led to prosperity, and the reigning mtemi, Mnywa Sele, defended his interests using firearms and private slave armies provided by his wealthy Arab allies. Around 1860, however, disagreements between Mnywa Sele and Unyanyembe's Arab merchants and vbandevba over control of trade and taxation resulted in his overthrow and exile from Tabora.[180] His distant relative Mkasiwa, in alliance with an Arab named Muhammad bin Juma, became the new mtemi.[181] Between 1860 and 1865, Mnywa Sele built a new army, which attacked Mkasiwa, other Unyamwezi polities, and Arab trading caravans. Despite some military successes, he failed to reclaim his position as mtemi and was killed in 1865. The struggle for power in Unyanyembe and the expansive tendencies begun under Mnywa Sele unleashed a series of defensive realignments among the smaller polities of Unyamwezi, as well as the fragmentation and dispersal of Unyanyembe's political elite.[182] Before this period, batemi typically had little personal wealth, and accession was matrilineal. But with the intensification of trade in Unyanyembe, many batemi accumulated personal wealth, which they passed to their sons. Local "princes" began to find the role of mtemi more appealing, and they began to vie amongst themselves for increased authority within their small polities.[183] This marked a significant transformation in regional politics.

Out of this competitive and fluid political environment emerged two pivotal figures of nineteenth-century Tanzanian history—Mirambo and Nyungu-ya-Mawe. The two had much in common, and they even became allies for a time. They were "exact contemporaries"—both were born around 1840, and both died in 1884.[184] Both were also born to batemi families who administered minor polities around Tabora. Mirambo was raised in Uyowa, a small state northeast of Tabora, and Nyungu came from Itetemia, a royal village also just outside Tabora. Their careers began when local "kingmakers" recognized them as potentially "dynamic" leaders capable of steering their respective polities, or *butemi*, through the increasingly complex and violent regional politics of the age.[185] Nyungu began making a name for himself as a commander, or "war captain," of one of Mnywa Sele's armies.[186] These war captains had grander ambitions than presiding over small butemi, however, and they used their local political footholds to dominate smaller polities, ultimately becoming major regional power brokers. They backed their claims to dominance with military forces of unprecedented size and organization. By 1880, Mirambo's army of ruga-ruga numbered about ten thousand men.[187] The fact that both men became known to the wider world not by their birth names but by nicknames that announced their ruthlessness and battlefield skill attests to the centrality of war making to their identities.[188] The standing armies they created, and the campaigns those armies undertook, ratcheted the violence that had begun under Mnywa Sele to new levels.

Under Mirambo and Nyungu, the term *ruga-ruga*, previously associated mainly with caravan protection duties, took on an expanded and altogether more terrifying meaning.[189] Before the 1860s ruga-ruga referred to soldiers who protected the caravans from brigandage and who prevented porters from absconding with goods on long-distance marches.[190] Simultaneously, European explorers and military officers used the term ruga-ruga to refer to the armed irregulars who accompanied their columns as guards. Columns were advised to march "pressed together as tightly as possible, [with] patrols [ruga-ruga] in the lead and on the sides."[191] The ruga-ruga also raided villages for supplies and manpower on their officers' orders.[192] Thus a member of the Emin Pasha relief expedition (1887–92) noted in his journal, "The ruga ruga came in this morning bringing me four live fowls and three kids. . . . They got a good supply of goat meat for themselves and their comrades which I let them keep."[193] Between 1860 and 1890 the term *ruga-ruga* accommodated some flexibility, and its usage related directly to whether one benefited from, or was victimized by, their raiding practices.[194]

Mnywa Sele was one of the first batemi to assemble around him a regular group of soldiers called ruga-ruga. Following him into exile, they fought a five-year guerrilla war in southern Unyamwezi, harassing caravans on the central route as they passed through an expansive area of dry and barren terrain known as the *mgunda mkali*, or "burning plain."[195] Mnywa Sele's capture and death in 1865 turned him into a "legendary hero among . . . loyalist Nyamwezi." One who was impressed by Mnywa Sele's example was Nyungu-ya-Mawe, who as mentioned above, likely served as one of his war captains, and "believed [that] the mantle of Mnywa Sele had descended on his shoulders."[196] By 1871 he had become the "leader of a warrior band" in his own right, building a force of ruga-ruga at his home in Itetemia.[197] He organized his ruga-ruga into companies led by lieutenants with fearsome war names. He creatively combined the companies to respond to different military challenges, using both small (twenty to sixty men) and large (four to five hundred) formations.[198]

Meanwhile in Uyowa, Mirambo also began asserting authority over several smaller kingdoms to create a unified polity called Urambo. He moved his royal residence, or *kwikuru*, to Iselemagazi, building a large enclosed and fortified compound that reportedly enclosed some two square miles of land. According to the missionaries who described the *kwikuru* in 1879, "In this enclosed space about 200 huts, well built and some fifty feet in diameter, give habitation to about 10,000 inhabitants, at least another 5,000 live in the houses built against the wall."[199] Ensconced in a fortified compound, and with a large population to draw on, Mirambo became a threat to Unyanyembe's commercial power and political dominance in the region.[200]

While engaged in the conquest of smaller butemi around Urambo, however, Mirambo determined that to seriously challenge Unyanyembe a better-organized military force was needed. Having "absorbed . . . the new tactics of warfare introduced into the Nyamwezi regions by the Ngoni," he began to model his army after them, paying particular attention to an Ngoni subgroup known as the Watuta.[201] Mirambo began building "what was very close to a permanent standing army," which combined men of Urambo with men from groups Mirambo's army had defeated. Many of these men were quite young, some of them just boys who were easily molded to fit Mirambo's expectations for a disciplined force.[202] One historian of the Nyamwezi described them as a mixture of "runaway slaves, war-captives, deserting porters, social outcasts and rest-less young men eager for adventure."[203] They were organized into age sets, with a regiment for young, unmarried men between twenty and thirty years of age, who fought offensive campaigns, and another for more experienced men, who could marry and build homes, and whose military duties were primarily defensive.[204] In Urambo a version of Kin-yamwezi called Kirugaruga developed to accommodate this mixture of soldiers from all over Unyamwezi.[205] Young soldiers in Mirambo's army were allowed to marry and build homes only after their "fighting ca-reer" was over, at which time they received "slaves and land according to the extent of their faithful service."[206] This was a departure from pre-vious marriage practices, which typically occurred between the ages of fourteen and sixteen.[207] By 1880, Mirambo's ten thousand ruga-ruga made his army the most formidable in the region, alongside Nyungu's. Military leaders rewarded soldiers for their battlefield performances by distributing captured women, cattle, and cloth based on each soldier's ability to prove his battlefield accomplishments. They reportedly did this by displaying to their leaders dead combatants' body parts and captured weapons.[208] The young soldiers thus absolutely depended on their leaders for their livelihoods. Although they could eventually as-cend to the senior age set and be allowed to set up a household, until that time they had little to do but fight. Ruga-ruga were expected to subordinate any personal goals and desires to those of their leader until they passed into the next age set. They delayed fulfillment of these goals until they had proven a sustained contribution to their leader's battlefield success and the furtherance of his territorial, economic, and political aims. These leaders' most significant accomplishment in military terms was that they convinced young soldiers to "submerge the self" to a collective military identity. Before the 1860s, Nyamwezi ways of war involved "small-scale raiding," which was "essentially an *indi-vidualized* activity."[209] The new ruga-ruga armies, armed with a range of weaponry including swords, bows and arrows, spears, shields, and guns, followed the Ngoni model in building esprit de corps by emphasizing drill, formal training, and specific bodily adornment and clothing that expressed their group membership.[210]

The outward appearance and battlefield behaviors of the ruga-ruga became a staple of European representations of Tanzania in the nineteenth century, which consistently depicted them in ways that buttressed their reputation as fearsome soldiers. Caution is warranted, however, in how we read, interpret, and use the sources that represented the ruga-ruga in these ways. As explained earlier, most available sources for this period were European mediated, and they were written to appeal to audiences in Europe who expected to read lurid stories about Africa. These sources show deep investment in presenting soldiers like the ruga-ruga as "other" than European soldiers. For example, observers described the ruga-ruga as wearing feathers, beads, and bright pieces of cloth on their heads.[211] Their hair was "plaited in long hanks," with "wooden amulets, strings of beads, and little horns from duikers [antelopes]" worked in as charms that were meant to aid the soldiers in their abilities to seize spoils and slaves in war.[212] The hairstyles were supposedly modeled after those of ritual practitioners, whose braids presented "a frightening exterior" that encouraged people to keep their distance.[213] The headdresses they wore also indicated how many enemies they had killed in battle. All ruga-ruga wore headdresses with black feathers into battle, and once a young soldier had killed an enemy, his comrades gave him a guinea fowl feather to indicate his battlefield prowess. More experienced soldiers received heron feathers.[214] The embeddedness of these displays in Nyamwezi social and cultural practices was largely irrelevant in these European renditions of the ruga-ruga. Thus, it mattered little that such headdresses belonged to an elaborate hierarchy of regalia in Nyamwezi court and military culture that used different kinds of feathers to indicate rank and status. Instead, the readers' focus is drawn to reports of gruesome behaviors and displays, including trophy taking and cannibalistic acts. Reports of atrocities such as these must be placed within the wider historical contexts of genres of writing, circulation of pernicious images of Africans and others deemed uncivilized, and comparative histories of battlefield behaviors.[215]

In addition, most of these accounts were produced by explorers and missionaries whose interventionist agendas prompted them to describe Mirambo's and Nyungu's soldiers as bloodthirsty savages.[216] As Norman Etherington explains regarding missionaries who wrote exaggerated accounts of the impact of Shaka's violence in South Africa, "they spun tales that accorded perfectly with [their] self-image as emissaries of peace and love to a land convulsed by heathen barbarism and chaos."[217] Some authors' accounts were not published until years, and even decades, later than the events being described. Colonial administrators and commanders used such stories to justify or stand in for the extreme violence they ordered and oversaw during colonial conquest.[218] The point here is not to deny that significant violence occurred in this time and place but rather to prompt circumspection about how sources were produced and what discursive outcomes they may have had on future historians.

With these cautions in mind, it nevertheless seems reasonable to argue that ruga-ruga organizational efficiency and purposeful use of terror evoked "constant dread" among East African villagers, reshaping regional patterns of violence and increasing its frequency and magnitude.[219] Additionally, the accelerated building of enclosed fortified villages indicated the emergence of new defensive sensibilities among the peoples of the central steppe in response to this new and unpredictable military entity. A British traveler's report from 1877 conveys this sense of pervasive fear throughout the area between Lake Victoria and Tabora:

> The neighboring country is in rather a disturbed and unsettled state, the people living in constant dread of being attacked by Mirambo and his Ruga-Ruga. On my return I and my party were taken for these dreaded robbers, the whole district turning out to resist us, and it would have fared badly with us but for the timely appearance, like a "deus ex machina," of an old nyampara or chief, who had once travelled with me, and who took my part against the excited villagers. Everything here shows that the people are in constant dread of invasion; the villages are surrounded by strong thorn fences, with narrow openings, which can be easily defended by a few men, the cattle are sent out to graze under strong armed escorts, and even the farmer when at work in his mtama [sorghum] fields, has his spear stuck in the ground beside him, ready for a fight.[220]

The armies of Mirambo and Nyungu set in motion many far-reaching changes to the practices of everyday life in the central steppe of Tanzania.

Among the many gaps in our understanding of the ruga-ruga, we know very little about the ways that they made meaning of their violent activities. Still, a few intriguing details can be teased from the sources. Rituals performed by specialist practitioners (*waganga*) provided ruga-ruga with spiritual armor before battle, motivated them during battle, and also prepared them to return to community life after war. Waganga prepared war medicines for ruga-ruga to consume before and after battle.[221] Any ruga-ruga who had shown cowardice received a separate and differently composed medicine prepared by the chief's senior wife—a clear effort to publicly gender-shame the cowardly soldiers by diminishing their masculinity.[222] One chief also reportedly threatened, "If you are afraid again, you will not come back to the village; I will have you murdered outside [the village]."[223] Waganga performed cleansing rituals on soldiers before allowing them to return to their homes, to "emphasize that what was hostile is now united again in harmony, including the spirits of slain enemies."[224] Beyond the threat of being executed for cowardice then, dying outside the village before going through cleansing rituals risked soldiers' ability to transition properly to the afterlife. In these ways, the ruga-ruga solidified bonds with their leaders, found outlets for the range of emotions attached to the violence they committed, and ensured that their communities would accept them again.

Soldiers' coping methods are another intriguing area of inquiry that unfortunately raise more questions than answers. A widely reported factor in ruga-ruga wartime behavior was their use of *banghi*, a type of hemp, which supposedly rendered them hallucinatory, "wild and excitable," and unpredictable.[225] Smoking banghi may have contributed to their performances of invulnerability, and perhaps also produced hallucinatory or numbing effects that buffered them from the effects of participation in terrible violence. Later on, similar dynamics seemed to be at work within the ranks of the Schutztruppe, with the widely reported use of banghi and other intoxicants such as locally brewed beer (*pombe*) and palm wine (*tembo*) among askari. A phrase book published in 1911 for the purpose of familiarizing Schutztruppe officers with useful Kiswahili phrases included the phrase "it is forbidden to smoke hemp," perhaps indicating some level of usage among askari, and certainly the Schutztruppe's negative view of its consumption. A similar entry exists for opium, but not for beer or wine.[226] Here again, it makes sense to take these observations with a grain of salt. Phrase books can only indicate what notions circulated among Schutztruppe officers regarding their troops' behaviors. Moreover, as Johannes Fabian has so convincingly argued, European explorers and missionaries whose writings described central and eastern African practices of consumption of banghi and other substances were themselves often "'out of their minds' with extreme fatigue, fear, delusions of grandeur, and feelings ranging from anger to contempt."[227] They suffered psychoses brought on by tropical diseases and were frequently under the influence of alcohol, opiates, and other substances used as medications, such as quinine and arsenic.[228] Their abilities to comment sensibly on the behaviors of Africans should thus be viewed with some skepticism. Still, especially in light of what is known about soldiers, fear, and trauma in other historical contexts, evidence suggests that substances may have influenced ruga-ruga combat behaviors.[229]

In the ruga-ruga way of war, the terror-inducing elements described above complemented the tactics they employed to overcome Unyam-wezi's fortified-village defenses. They favored ambushes conducted at dawn so that they would surprise the villages under attack, forestalling "any well-organized resistance" from the villagers."[230] Ruga-ruga armies avoided long sieges because they did not have artillery pieces, and because neighboring areas could not support their needs for provisions for long periods. Nor could they carry large stores of provisions on campaign. At the outset of a surprise attack, the ruga-ruga fired a few shots to bring out the village's defenders. Concealed ruga-ruga would then "jump out . . . and surprise the people from the village, overcome them, and plunder the village."[231] They carried with them ladders to scale the outer walls, as well as bundles of grass to be used for burning the village once they had overrun it.[232] In taking large villages, they employed familiar siege tactics, digging holes to use as cover as they progressed closer to the palisade's wall. Once at the wall, they stormed the fort:

> A few [ruga-ruga] shot through the wall's loopholes, others climb up the backs of their comrades and climb on the roofs of the *tembe* and shoot [down] into the village. One lets himself down into the village and opens the door, whereupon all [of them] storm in and plunder the village. [They] yell continuously during the shooting: Forward! You men, forward![233]

The ruga-ruga killed the majority of adult males, seizing women and children, who their chiefs later distributed as rewards for battlefield prowess.[234]

In this way, leaders like Mirambo and Nyungu-ya-Mawe constantly revitalized soldiers' ties to the *ruga-ruga* armies, encouraging them to remain soldiers. Under Nyungu-ya-Mawe, *ruga-ruga* who achieved distinction on the battlefield became trusted lieutenants, or *vatwaale* (sing., *mutwaale*). These men then became "keystones" of the chief's political apparatus as military governors of his provinces.[235] This arrangement allowed him to maintain oversight and control over his consolidated territory without necessarily removing sitting chiefs from their positions, as long as they cooperated. According to Aylward Shorter, "where chiefs remained, all the rights and duties of effective government lay with the vatwaale. It was their task to police the area, settle disputes, and most important of all, collect all ivory and forward it to [Nyungu's capital] Kiwele."[236] The vatwaale also regularly raided for slaves within their provinces, sending the captives on to Nyungu's court. In his effort to reward ruga-ruga with war spoils, accolades, and to single out some for increased authority, status, and power, Nyungu's "empire of the *ruga-ruga*" foreshadowed German methods of consolidating power after 1890.[237] In contrast, Mirambo killed the "legitimate chiefs" of the areas he conquered and installed members of the royal family to replace them. Mirambo was therefore dependent on his appointees' "gratitude to keep them loyal," and had to keep up a "succession of lightning punitive raids" in order to maintain authority.[238]

Both Mirambo and Nyungu-ya-Mawe died in 1884. The polities they built survived past their deaths but lost cohesion as the years passed. Both leaders had challenged Unyanyembe's power during the 1860s and 1870s, but they had never been able to dislodge Mkasiwa's son and successor, Isike, from power. Isike's alliance with Tabora's Arab trading elites and their private armies helped him defeat Mirambo and Nyungu. When they both died, in 1884, Isike became the most powerful leader in Unyamwezi, notwithstanding his still heavy reliance on Arab military support. The proliferation of traders and other smaller rulers who "maintained heavily armed followings of their own" also weakened his position.[239] This was the political situation in Unyanyembe when the Schutztruppe, after securing the coast in 1890, began its advance inland with the goal of establishing hegemony over the trade routes from the coast to the Great Lakes and the areas around Lake Victoria into Uganda.[240]

In August 1890 a German column led by Emin Pasha brazenly, and against orders, asserted German control of Tabora. "It is really a piece of impertinence on my part," he wrote, "to dash, so to speak, into people's houses and without further ado to annex country and people; but it cannot be helped, and we cannot deal so gently here as is the custom in Europe."[241] He established an alliance with the Tabora Arab elite and immediately set about trying to undermine Isike's authority, sending him an ultimatum demanding that he not only hand over ivory and guns (including a machine gun), but that he also "surrender his country" to Germany. "Isike," however, "maintained a cool reserve," and thus also kept his autonomy for the time being.[242] Meanwhile, Emin departed Tabora toward Usukuma, leaving behind a contingent of twenty-five askari. In February 1891, Wissmann ordered the establishment of a small military post at Tabora with a German lieutenant in charge of the twenty-five askari left behind by Emin. From this outpost, the Germans began making "treaties" with local rulers in the surrounding areas, including in Urambo, Mirambo's former stronghold.[243] The Schutztruppe found allies in different pockets of Unyamwezi, as those who had grievances against Isike or his allies began to throw their support to the Germans as the emergent dominant power in the region. These allies hoped that the Germans would aid them in their bids for local authority following Isike's future demise. Among them were "ruga-ruga who, since the disintegration of Mirambo's state, had reverted to small bands of raiders on the periphery of Nyanyembe."[244] Isike, recognizing the growing threat to his authority in Unyanyembe, decided to preemptively strike the Schutztruppe outpost at Tabora in April 1892. His assault failed and provoked the Germans to pursue war against him in earnest. Over the next year the Schutztruppe attempted several times to breach Isike's boma. Finally, in January 1893, the Schutztruppe overran it after three days of digging siege trenches, which ultimately "reached the base of the boma, undermined its outer walls, and provided protection for the bulk of the attack force moving through the breach to engage in hand-to-hand combat."[245] Isike's defeat and suicide cleared the way for the Schutztruppe's effective occupation of Unyamwezi, giving it a military and political foothold that endured through the rest of the German colonial era.

First envisioned as a reserve force for the Wissmanntruppe during the coastal war, by 1895 the Nyamwezi became one of the staple groups from which askari were recruited throughout German rule. Graf von Götzen, an officer who traveled extensively in central Africa in 1893 and 1894, and who later became governor of German East Africa, described the ruga-ruga as a "type of Freikorps [voluntary army]," comparing them to locally based militias in German history.[246] A contingent of Nyamwezi ruga-ruga took part in the assault on Bushiri's boma in Bagamoyo in May 1889, supplementing the Schutztruppe force of one thousand Sudanese, Shangaan, and assorted other soldiers from Africa and the Middle East and, of course, Germans. Thus Nyamwezi ruga-ruga served as auxiliaries from the founding moments of the Schutztruppe. Their battlefield performance at Bagamoyo made an impression, if not an entirely favorable one: "The Nyamwezi, who because of the thick firing line [formed by other soldiers in front of them] were hindered from pushing to the front, could not enmesh themselves in the battle, fired off their weapons randomly, and struck up a terrible war cry, which drowned out the deafening noise of the rifle and artillery fire."[247] The Shangaan soldiers joined them in their war cry, in contrast to the Sudanese troops, who reportedly fired with the "calm of veteran soldiers."[248] This description, with the Nyamwezi shouting and randomly firing their weapons in the heat of battle, suggests some continuity of Nyamwezi ways of war that came with them into the Schutztruppe from the ruga-ruga military complex. It also points up a contrast between Nyamwezi ways of war and those of the Sudanese recruits with whom Schutztruppe officers so readily identified. Nearly all recruits, regardless of origin, lacked firing discipline until they went through the Schutztruppe's training regimen, and even then results varied. Familiarity with firearms did not necessarily connote any ability to fire accurately or with discipline. Sudanese soldiers fighting in the Anglo-Egyptian army had been trained to use their weapons primarily for bayonet charges. And as we have seen, firearms carried significance to Nyamwezi men that only partly had to do with their killing potential.[249] Firearms had symbolic value as prestige goods that marked a man's passage to manhood, his experience as a long-distance traveler, and his ability to wield a terrifying weapon that was laden with symbolism in Nyamwezi understandings of power. The contrast drawn between the raucous Nyamwezi, who fired their weapons indiscriminately, and the stoic Sudanese, who fired calmly, can also be read as a German valuation of particular cultural qualities that mirrored their self-image as soldiers.

Nyamwezi men had much to learn before they rated as askari in the eyes of Schutztruppe officers. Still, by 1895 they had managed, as a social category, to position themselves as suitable candidates to make the transition to the askari ranks. In 1897, Richard Kandt, the colonial administrator at Tabora, reported that "a large number of people, some of them not inspiring much trust, reported for service as askari." He discovered that most of them "understood as little about shooting as [he] did of walking a tightrope."[250] He ended up choosing only three to join the Schutztruppe, and two of them, he noticed with amusement, had taken German names.[251] Kandt's selectivity in recruiting speaks to the continuation of Nyamwezi ways of war at the same time that it highlights the growing appeal of the Schutztruppe as a suitable place for Nyamwezi men to remake themselves inside of a new, yet partly familiar, martial complex. Equally important, the Schutztruppe created the possibility of earning a living as a soldier and salaried employee. Such earning power opened new paths to respectability in a socioeconomic environment where opportunities to do so had narrowed substantially for men so inclined, or without other viable options.

THE SCHUTZTRUPPE'S NEW RANK AND FILE

Young Nyamwezi and other men from the central steppe and lakes regions of Tanzania began joining the Schutztruppe in the 1890s because it was a new martial community with which to identify, a place to legitimately exercise military skills, and an alignment with a powerful new patron. In fact, the Schutztruppe option was one of the only viable paths to military respectability for men who came of age in Unyamwezi in the 1890s. During this time, the Schutztruppe established itself as a major new regional power broker. It offered new East African recruits visible trappings of prestige in the khaki uniform, salaries that outstripped any others in the colonial labor force, and virtually unchecked authority over others. The Schutztruppe steadily eroded or diluted the authority of East African leaders as German colonial rule progressed toward the interior. Parallel to these developments, Nyamwezi material culture showed signs that being askari had become integral to Nyamwezi subjectivities. For example, Moravian missionaries operating near Tabora between 1897 and 1921 collected a variety of pieces, including carved wooden toys and musical instruments made from gourds, depicting askari, both as individuals and as parts of caravan collectivities.[252]

Schutztruppe officers rarely made explicit the qualities they valued in their Nyamwezi askari. Nigmann's comment in the official Schutztruppe history that they were "capable" and "responsible" is qualitatively different from the kinds of praises given to soldiers with origins in Sudan. Schutztruppe officers initially distrusted Nyamwezi recruits, often describing them in the same terms they had used to describe the Shangaan soldiers who fought in the first few years of the Schutztruppe. They emphasized Nyamwezi sociability, their love of spontaneous song and dance, and their independent "freelance" spirit. They expressed ambivalence about these behaviors, finding them at once charming and annoying, unifying and disruptive, calming and threatening. Whereas the soldiers from Sudan were described as steadfast and calm, the Nyamwezi were described as uncontrollable and unpredictable. Yet these qualities had their place in the Schutztruppe, dependent as the Germans were on the ability of their askari to move independently and confidently in small units, with or without white officers or NCOs. The sociability cultivated by the Nyamwezi in camp, on the march, and in the maboma disrupted German officers' beloved sense of order at times. But it also guaranteed a social life and sense of community that reduced the temptation to desert under harsh conditions. The boma communities were places where askari retreated to deal with the psychic and physical traumas of warfare, among others who had experienced the same. For the most part, the askari's moral community excluded German officers, a condition that undoubtedly gave the soldiers much-needed space within which to restore themselves mentally, to share with others the pain of losing comrades, or to grouse about their officers.[253] German officers were intimate outsiders who knew much about their troops' lives, but Nyamwezi soldierly expression was antithetical to the stoic Prussian model of soldierly masculinity that Schutztruppe officers performed. Recognizing that the East African recruits made up the army's backbone, however, German officers accepted that they were good askari, even if they were not Sudanese.

German ambivalence about the Nyamwezi also had to do with their position as the first group to be recruited en masse from within German East Africa's territorial boundaries. Although Schutztruppe officers claimed that their goal was to station askari outside their homelands, thereby isolating them from any communal ties, with the Nyamwezi this was wishful thinking. The Nyamwezi were expert travelers, with extensive knowledge of travel routes, impressive physical stamina, and involvement in intricate social networks based in regional competitive dance associations (*ngoma*), joking relationships (*utani*), and Islamic beliefs and practices.[254] Had they wanted to foment or support rebellion against the Germans, they certainly could have. During the Maji Maji war (1905–7), the Schutztruppe thought it prudent to deploy a seven-hundred-man composite unit to Tabora to guard against such a possibility.[255] But Nyamwezi askari identified with their Schutztruppe officer-patrons who—despite their obvious differences from nineteenth-century East African military leaders—embodied an appropriate mixture of emotional toughness, calm under pressure, dedication to procedure and training, paternal generosity, and resolve. Through experience, and through the Nyamwezi askari's proven abilities as demonstrated in the coastal war of 1889–90, they gained their officers' trust. With the colonial cash economy placing respectability further out of reach, and with the German military conquest severely limiting expression of other martial identities, Nyamwezi men who volunteered to be askari put their trust in their latest patrons, the Schutztruppe officers, to nurture them as new elites in a changing order. Under the combined tutelage of Sudanese senior askari and Schutztruppe officers and NCOs, this second wave of recruits from eastern Africa became the new German rank and file.

2 ～ Making Askari Ways of War
Military Training and Socialization

AROUND 1895 the Swahili poet Mbaraka bin Shomari wrote a poem honoring the sitting governor of German East Africa, Friedrich von Schele. In keeping with the conventions of Kiswahili epic poetry, after some thirty stanzas of praising Schele's nobility, generosity, and wealth, bin Shomari called attention to the military might that underwrote the governor's authority:

> Bullets and gunpowder fill up the houses.
> Even in the ammunition belts they are placed in a special way.
> All the soldiers assemble if the trumpet sounds.[1]

The poet's description of Schele's military strength identifies obvious markers such as munitions stores. In addition, however, these lines communicate the poet's impression of another highly visible component of the governor's authority — his ability to efficiently and quickly mobilize his troops and equipment in the face of perceived threats. Stockpiled bullets, gunpowder, and ammunition belts visibly conveyed colonial military strength, but being able to assemble soldiers at the sound of a trumpet conveyed a different kind of mastery. Backed by such performances of soldierly discipline, colonial authorities communicated their vision of mastery to audiences across German East Africa. But how did the Schutztruppe organization create disciplined soldiers out of men who came from such disparate geographic locations, linguistic backgrounds, and cultural contexts? What was the "glue" that tied these soldiers to each other, to their officers, and to the Schutztruppe for the three decades of its existence?[2] To answer these questions, this chapter undertakes a close reading of the set of practices that socialized and trained recruits to become soldiers. Military training in German East Africa should be understood as a multidirectional educative process.[3] German officers and NCOs (German and African) laid the contours of a training regime for their African recruits. Within that regime, diverse groups of recruits contributed distinct military cultural practices to the ongoing development of an effective Schutztruppe way of war. Through these intersecting and fluid processes, askari developed the professional sensibilities and skills necessary for advancement in the Schutztruppe, laying the basis for their claims to respectability within colonial society. The askari's dedication to the Schutztruppe sprang not from some organic loyalty to the German Empire, but instead from their sense that Schutztruppe officers and NCOs were capable patrons and leaders who could help the askari become big men as they climbed the military ranks.

MAKING ASKARI:
TRAINING AS SOCIALIZATION PROCESS

After the initial conquest of the coastal region (1889–91), the Schutztruppe began establishing military outposts (maboma) throughout German East Africa. Conquest of the territory took the next fifteen years.[4] German colonial officers and administrators used these outposts and the military forces assigned to them to cultivate an illusion of military control over the colony by practicing rituals that proclaimed military dominance. Through the German-designed training regimen, askari acted out the German vision of a powerful colonial state. Given the colonial government's inherent legitimacy problems, that vision took the shape of a "martial paradigm" that "displayed an idealized model of organization . . . [that] tended to aid in the imposition of social control on civilian society—whether enforced or voluntary—in a wide variety of contexts."[5] Prussia's central role in the development of European martial paradigms in the 1800s shaped colonial officers' visions of the colonial state as a machine, even if local realities hardly measured up to such ideals.[6] Colonial rule in German East Africa was in fact a hodgepodge of ad hoc local arrangements with friendly leaders and itinerant administrative practices, reinforced with the threat of military force.

Military training was central to the socialization processes that ultimately bonded askari to the Schutztruppe organization, their fellow soldiers, and their officers, contributing to the making of a colonial military culture. This military culture included constant reinforcement of discipline and combat readiness, construction of a professional ethos, performance of rituals (drill, ceremony, customs, and courtesies), and maintenance of soldiers' morale.[7] A mixture of practical military considerations and more nebulous concerns about cultivating esprit de corps underwrote German officers' obsession with training their troops in drill, proper uniform wear, and following the Schutztruppe's organizational and operational rules. To create well-trained and disciplined units, they had to convince their recruits to conform to German specifications for good order and conformity.

But creating the conditions for outstanding battlefield performance through training was only part of what Schutztruppe officers had in mind when they exercised their soldiers each day. In addition, German officers wanted each askari to feel confident that he would be successful against any enemy, regardless of numerical superiority, as long as he followed his officers' orders and trusted in the Schutztruppe training regimen[8] In other words, Schutztruppe officers wanted their African soldiers to feel militarily competent, and preferably superior, in combat situations in which they seemed to be at a disadvantage because of numerical weakness, lack of familiarity with local surroundings, and a range of other concerns.[9] They believed that by cultivating an abiding confidence in German leadership alongside faith in rigorous training and technological superiority, the askari would be prepared to confront any military challenge they faced. Punishment, including in some cases extreme physical violence, reminded the wayward or faint of heart to refocus their attention on these fundamental organizing principles.

Schutztruppe officers' diaries and memoirs routinely emphasized the importance of military training and just as routinely expressed disappointment in askari military skills during these sessions. Philipp Correck, a Schutztruppe lieutenant stationed in the southern highlands during the 1905–7 Maji Maji war, peppered his diary with descriptions of simply "dismal" early-morning training sessions with his askari, comparing them to "[new] recruits in their first days."[10] Such negative portrayals of the askari, even in the midst of an ongoing war, fit uncomfortably with other descriptions of the askari—often by the same authors—that instead described the askari as soldiers who showed remarkable skill and resolve under fire.

This disconnect might be explained in different ways. First, soldiers' willingness to conform to training demands could be motivated by the kind of reinforcement they got from their officers. Lieutenant Correck's askari gave him the Kiswahili nickname Bwana Moto, "Mr. Fiery Temper," based on his outward behavior, and especially his predilection for beating askari and porters with a hide whip (*kiboko*) and sometimes with his fists.[11] Correck complained in his diary that his "paw [*Pfote*]" still hurt four days after punching one of his askari during a morning training session.[12] Such behavior among Schutztruppe officers and NCOs was not uncommon, and any number of explanations might account for it, including the accepted use of such methods in German military culture more generally, the stress of being deployed in an unfamiliar environment during wartime, sadistic tendencies, and frustration with being unable to properly communicate with their troops, given significant language differences.[13] Under such conditions, soldiers likely performed their duties more out of fear than dedication to Schutztruppe ideals or training principles.

By contrast, soldiers who perceived the worth of their training through officers' encouraging comments and gestures, or through combat experiences that proved the benefits of training, might be more inclined to treat *Exerzierplatz* activities as preparation for combat.[14] General Lettow-Vorbeck, for example, apparently garnered the respect of many askari who marched with him during World War I. His leadership style included positively reinforcing his troops with verbal encouragement, rest time, and when possible, new supplies, food, and drink.[15] That most of these rewards came from plundering villagers' supplies and requisitioning their livestock made little difference to weary and malnourished soldiers with superiority complexes whose way of war had long relied on expropriating goods from civilians both in peace and war.[16] In fact, as we have seen, these practices had been the norm during East African warfare even before the Germans' arrival. From most askari's perspectives, a commander's willingness to take such action showed a requisite toughness that equated to effective leadership.[17] Soldiers were far more likely to cooperate with inspections, drill, and parades if their officers took care of them, whether in terms of survival needs or preserving their status vis-à-vis colonized East Africans.

The Schutztruppe's numerous violent military expeditions in the first fifteen years of the German occupation of Tanzania may also have contributed to lackluster drilling sessions.[18] Often enough, the askari's everyday experiences brought them face to face with the real thing, so playing at war while in garrison paled in comparison to their combat experiences. Not surprisingly, the value of their repetitive training came through most clearly in combat situations that taxed them to the limits of their mental and physical endurance.[19]

The training process generated emotional bonds between soldiers and the Schutztruppe organization, increasing the likelihood that men could depend on each other, and on their officers, during crisis moments.[20] Askari were expected to wear their uniforms properly, march in good order, and comport themselves appropriately while standing in formation partly because their officers also believed such activities would reinforce the troops' discipline and obedience as they prepared for war.[21] They believed that drill and ceremony would lead their soldiers to bond emotionally with the Schutztruppe organization—the stuff of esprit.[22] Askari abilities to apply what they learned from drill, target practice, and field exercises undergirded their abilities to fight under physically and mentally stressful conditions.

In addition, the skills they practiced on the Exerzierplätze helped them perform the "military show" that reinforced German claims to authority across the colony by enacting a vision of military discipline and concentration of force that was distinct from anything that had existed in Tanzania before the German conquest.[23] While tedious and physically exhausting, hours of Exerzierplatz training nonetheless shaped askari experiences off the training field, where they had opportunities to execute the skills they had learned in training. In these situations, askari experienced meaningful—maybe even ecstatic—feelings of purpose, belonging, and organizational identification that infused their hardships with value. In their marching songs, and in conversations with their superiors, they often expressed affection for the distant kaiser. They did so not because of loyalty to the German Empire per se, but because for them, the kaiser was the ultimate patron, the one who made their aspirations to becoming big men possible.[24] "Anyone who could do so much for his soldiers," they thought, "must really be a good emperor."[25] Training thus contributed to the development of vertical and horizontal ties to the Schutztruppe organization through their officer-patrons, who backed their claims to status as respectable men, and through their fellow askari, their comrades-in-arms.

TRAINING PRACTICES: INTERACTIONS AND COLLISIONS

The military sensibilities that German and African men brought with them to the training grounds interacted, but sometimes collided, to produce new social and cultural relations within the Schutztruppe, and new modes of communicating with those inside and outside the Schutztruppe. Thinking about military training as a distinct form of socialization and identity formation within colonial culture helps us better understand how colonial soldiers related to each other, to their officers, and to diverse populations of colonial subjects. It helps explain what held colonial armies together.

German assumptions about what made a good soldier sometimes differed from the soldierly values askari brought with them from the disparate African military cultures they had previously known. German officers and NCOs had much to learn about fighting in East Africa, as well as how to best manage their African troops in ways that would encourage them to remain with the Schutztruppe. Before World War I, mutinies among askari happened very rarely. When they did, it was generally because of an inability or unwillingness of officers to treat the askari in accordance with their understanding of social and military hierarchies and prestige.[26] Much more was at stake in the colonial military training regime than the ability to execute maneuvers or fire accurately on command. In significant ways, military training also communicated expectations back and forth between German officers and askari so that both sides had working assumptions, and perhaps sometimes "working misunderstandings," about their roles in the Schutztruppe.[27]

Most of the training methods used in the Schutztruppe originated in nineteenth-century German military training philosophies and practices. Most German Schutztruppe members came from the Prussian army, with a significant minority also coming from Bavaria, Saxony, and Baden-Württemburg.[28] Notoriously harsh in terms of discipline, the nineteenth-century Prussian military relied on constant repetitive training to foster combat effectiveness. According to one military historian, "it took a year to teach an infantryman the basics of using his weapon and marching with his platoon."[29] The recruits received "very elementary and very repetitious" training that involved "learning to march in step, to load and fire a [firearm], and to perform platoon or company maneuvers."[30] Officers believed that such training, though tedious, would help prepare infantrymen to quickly assess situations, to respond to battlefield circumstances appropriately under stress, and to "elevate" in them a "soldierly spirit."[31] After 1815 the Prussian general staff developed war games as a way of testing "operational features and possibilities."[32] Such war games later featured prominently in Schutztruppe training methods in East Africa.

Germany's nineteenth-century military history had a significant impact on how junior officers, some of whom became Schutztruppe officers, developed their abilities to lead troops in combat. Particularly after the Franco-Prussian War, the concept of *Auftragstaktik* (mission tactics) fostered expectations that junior officers should be able to confidently lead troops without specific direction from superiors. According to Isabel Hull, mission tactics "encouraged risk taking and excess, and it promised to forgive mistakes ('wrong expedients') taken in that spirit."[33] Officers who later served in colonial armies benefited from the German military's encouragement of mission tactics, since it gave them great latitude to act in the interest of securing colonial objectives. With usually no more than two or three German officers at each Schutztruppe station—and stations sited at great distances from Schutztruppe headquarters, in Dar es Salaam—officers in East Africa had to be able to decide how and when to use military force in their districts without supervision or oversight. For similar reasons, they also entrusted small unit operations and expeditions to their senior askari, especially their Sudanese soldiers. *Auftragstaktik* thus encouraged independent action in the field. The excessive violence of the conquest and consolidation of authority in German East Africa must partly be attributed to the premium placed on officers' and NCOs' abilities to decisively plan and execute operations without supervision or prior approval.

German officers assigned to the Schutztruppe underwent some preparation before they traveled to their posts in East Africa, but it was hardly systematic, especially in the early years. They read the recollections of fellow officers with previous postings in Africa to gain perspective on how to fight "small wars" against African armies, as well as how to prepare for life in East Africa more generally.[34] They may also have studied what they could of other colonial armies in Africa.[35] In fact, in

1909, with international political tensions steadily building, the *Reichs-kolonialamt* went so far as to encourage Schutztruppe officers traveling home on leave to route their travel through "the neighboring colonies of foreign powers for the purpose of studying the local military relationships and dispositions."[36] Although officers had to pay for such travels out of their own pockets, the *Kommando der Schutztruppen* agreed to grant them leave extensions so they could work up any materials gathered on such a trip.[37] Literary treatments of colonial wars fought in very different contexts also influenced Schutztruppe officers' assessments of local conditions once they arrived in East Africa. Some officers appear to have used parts James Fenimore Cooper's *Leatherstocking Tales*, a series of novels set in eighteenth-century North America, as makeshift field manuals for life on the march.[38] Some studied Kiswahili at the Seminar for Oriental Languages in Berlin before they departed for East Africa, with some gaining fluency in the regional lingua franca over time.[39] Others merely muddled through, learning to communicate with their troops and other employees in a mixture of German and Kiswahili. Lieutenant Philipp Correck, for example, began learning Kiswahili on the voyage to East Africa but complained throughout his deployment of his inability to master it despite expending "all his energies" on it.[40] Officers who made the effort to learn Kiswahili were rewarded with better insight into their troops' lives, as well as the ability to recognize some of the subtleties of Kiswahili wordplay and East African nicknaming practices, which frequently mocked Europeans.

Between 1889 and 1892 the Schutztruppe included soldiers from Egypt/Sudan, Somalia, Portuguese East Africa, and the coastal hinterland of Dar es Salaam.[41] In the early years of the Schutztruppe (Wissmanntruppe), officers managed the polyglot army's substantial language difficulties by segregating soldiers from the different geographic regions into separate units and by using interpreters, including "Turks" from the Egyptian army and German officers who spoke Arabic, French, Portuguese, and Kiswahili.[42] The layers of translation that characterized these early years proved quite challenging to the goal of assembling an army, as one officer noted in his memoir:

> For the Arabic-speaking Sudanese we had plenty of translators, who spoke very good French, a few of whom even spoke German, for the Zulus, however, only one translator was to be found, whose only other language was Portuguese, which only

[Wissmanntruppe founder] Wissmann [and two other lieuten-
ants] understood. In addition the translator, José, a half-caste, soon
showed himself to be a dark gentleman [i.e., untrustworthy], and
the Zulus disproportionately preferred to communicate with us
directly through sign language than through that person.[43]

As German officers tried to find ways to surmount linguistic obstacles
to training and command, the Shangaan ("Zulu") recruits refused to
cooperate with this particular solution to communication problems by
refusing to simply allow a translator to speak for them.[44] In this way, they
interpreted their new social situation in German East Africa through
the colonial politics of their homeland. Eventually the Schutztruppe
settled on giving commands in German, with most other communications taking place in Kiswahili. Schutztruppe officers who attended the
Berlin-based Seminar for Oriental Languages learned to translate common commands into Kiswahili so that they could begin using some of
them upon arrival in Dar es Salaam.[45] In 1911 the Schutztruppe published a phrasebook offering translations of words and phrases from
German to Kiswahili.[46] The degree to which the phrasebook was disseminated among German personnel is unclear, but at the very least
its printing in 1911 showed that a corpus of translations from German to
Kiswahili had been collected over time.

Askari communicated among themselves first in their mother
tongues and later in Kiswahili. Egyptian-Arabic phrases were used in
certain contexts, as during sentry duty when soldiers placed at specific
intervals called out to each other to prove they were awake, alive, and at
their posts.[47] Songs were sung in different languages, including Arabic,
Kinyamwezi, and Kiswahili, and mixtures of all three.[48] Senior askari
responsible for leading training sessions also developed a vocabulary of
German commands and insults. The German word *Schwein*, overheard
from German officers and NCOs, appeared to be a favorite way for senior askari to denigrate junior askari (as well as enemy captives).[49] In
using German military commands as well as German insults toward junior troops, senior askari expressed their identification with the German
officers and NCOs whom they heard using these words each day. Yet
African soldiers' vocalizations of these words and phrases also formed the
basis for their later usage in everyday life around the military stations.[50]
Some askari even learned to speak enough German to receive monetary
awards from the *Kommando der Schutztruppen*.[51] Thus although the

Schutztruppe's first few years presented formidable language challenges, by the mid-1890s officers and troops had found common ground for day-to-day communication through a mixture of German and primarily Kiswahili, with sprinklings of other languages interspersed as well.

After the Schutztruppe's rapid assembly, in 1889, and the final defeat of the coastal rebellion, in 1891, the army opened up recruitment to a wider pool of volunteers. Normally, askari volunteers reported to the *Rekrutendepot* in Dar es Salaam for training, which lasted three months (see fig. 2). Stations in the interior also sometimes accepted recruits to fill manpower needs when senior askari retired, although authority to do so varied with the colonial government's fiscal status.[52] As colonial rule progressed, soldiers were also sometimes recruited on short notice from areas where concentrations of ex-askari lived. In 1896, for instance, a Prussian army lieutenant and geographer raised a unit of ex-soldiers from the coastal town of Bagamoyo to accompany him on a research expedition to Irangi.[53] Recruits underwent a medical exam, and if they passed, they were accepted into training and outfitted with a uniform. After the askari received their uniform components, they were expected to maintain and keep track of every item, and their NCOs were supposed to ensure that all askari in fact possessed the items they had been issued.[54] Periodic inspections helped reinforce the soldiers' responsibility for looking after their gear. After this initial training, officers sent them out to individual units stationed around the colony to fill each post's personnel needs. At their new stations, the recruits continued to train regularly under command of a German officer or NCO. Senior askari also worked separately with brand new recruits. Schutztruppe military training in German East Africa closely resembled Prussian rank-and-file training in Germany and was based on Prussian infantry drill regulations issued in 1888 and 1906.[55] Training sessions, where askari practiced military bearing, shooting, and individual and group marching, began first thing in the morning.[56] Soldiers awoke to a bugle playing reveille at five-thirty. Two-hour training sessions then took place on the station's Exerzierplatz. The Kiswahili phrase used by askari for these "exercises" was *kucheza tabur*.[57] Although it is glossed as "to drill," the phrase is actually an interesting combination of the Kiswahili word "to play" and a Turkish word for "battalion." A literal translation would be "to play battalion," again evoking the multilayered history of the Schutztruppe.

FIGURE 2. This photo shows an askari standing at the gate of the boma for the Schutz-truppe's Fifth Company in Dar es Salaam, which also served as the colony's recruit-ment reception station, or *Rekrutendepot*. The askari looks into the boma courtyard. Although the askari is in uniform, he is not wearing boots, highlighting a common way in which askari undermined Schutztruppe ideas of military order. On either side of the boma gate are two placards listing the names of German officers and NCOs who died in action, and two carved wooden "Swahili" doors. The right side of the photo also shows an askari's guard box, painted in bold stripes in the German imperial col-ors black, white, and red. The photo captures the mixture of influences visible at the Schutztruppe maboma, as well as their role as nodes of security for the colonial state. *Used with permission of the Photo Archive of the German Colonial Society, University Library, Frankfurt am Main.*

Morning training sessions were followed by a midday break that co-incided with the hottest hours of the day. During this time, askari rested, ate, and took care of mandatory tasks like cleaning their weapons (see fig. 3).[58] Afterward, askari worked around the station, making repairs, build-ing new structures, and keeping things tidy.[59] They also assisted with colonial administrative and disciplinary duties, delivering messages and summonses, escorting officials between stations and on expeditions, act-ing as witnesses or ceremonial representatives in judicial proceedings, and guarding prisoners and chain-gang laborers. During military expedi-tions, commanders kept up training regimens, with overnight campsites serving as temporary Exerzierplätze until they received orders to con-struct a new permanent post, or until the company marched on to its next site.[60] In these ways, askari received constant reminders of Schutz-truppe order and discipline, whether in garrison or on the march.

FIGURE 3. Taken at Ujiji station in 1912, this photograph shows three junior askari cleaning their rifles. When in garrison, such duties consumed part of each soldier's day. Note the variations in how the three soldiers wear their uniforms. For example, none are wearing their leg wraps, or puttees, and the one in the center is not wearing boots. All three wear fezzes, but these show no uniformity, suggesting a degree of choice in uniform wear, or perhaps the unavailability of uniform parts at different times. Rank chevrons are visible on the sleeves of the askari on the left and in the center. Insignia designating achievement in marksmanship decorate the sleeves of the askari on the left and the right. Uniforms thus communicated considerable information about those who wore them. *Used with permission of the Photo Archive of the German Colonial Society, University Library, Frankfurt am Main.*

In addition to the repetitive training modes used to instill obedience and familiarity with battlefield skills in its African soldiers, Schutztruppe officers used war games to prepare their askari for a range of armed combat contingencies with East African armies. The Schutztruppe handbook for field exercises (*Felddienstübungen*), published in 1910, documents twenty-seven different kinds of war games that officers might use in training their African troops. Using these scenarios, officers trained askari in a variety of potential military confrontations, including attacking units while on the march, attacking fortified field positions, and conducting battles of retreat.[61] Most of the exercise scenario texts began with a variation on the phrase "The colony is in rebellion."[62] To add realism to the elaborate war game scenarios, officers sometimes had small contingents of "dependable, long-serving" askari costume themselves and perform the roles of East African military enemies against the khaki-clad active askari.[63] In 1906 the settler newspaper *Usambara Post* reported on plans to employ African sailors and senior students of the government school at Tanga to "fight" the local askari unit, using firearms loaded with blanks.[64] Askari sometimes also played the roles of ruga-ruga auxiliaries to help units practice incorporating them into regular tactics.[65] These exercises were supposed to sharpen askari's abilities to fight against enemies who practiced styles of warfare Schutztruppe officers considered dangerous, even if judged primitive by their standards.[66]

Most exercises incorporated "the numerically stronger, but poorly armed native as the enemy," and the different scenarios focused on "divergent" tactics from those used in Germany, suggesting that the Felddienstübungen had at least as much to do with helping officers imagine East African warfare as it did with finding ways to train askari for combat.[67] Indigenous practices of warfare specifically identified in the Felddienstübungen included "surprise engagement at close range and the cautious employment of open order."[68] To counter these styles of warfare, field exercise training objectives sought to anticipate and undermine indigenous armies' few possible advantages, which usually stemmed from the relative simplicity of their weapons and tactics. Soldiers in East African armies typically used old muzzleloading guns, spears, or bows and arrows. They used camouflage and concealment to hinder detection and to mask movement, fleeing into hiding when necessary. They also used numerical advantage to overwhelm their better-armed opponents and force them to engage in close combat. The Schutztruppe tried to train their askari to anticipate all these possibilities in combat against East African armies. They also practiced reacting to sudden alarms signaling surprise attacks or fires, and they were judged on their abilities to respond with "extreme speed" to unpredictable deadly threats.[69] Askari companies periodically received regular inspections of their proficiency in reacting properly during such exercises.[70]

As in most militaries, physical training also featured prominently in daily training regimens. Askari companies undertook "practice marches" for several days to test their endurance, as well as marches for "exploratory purposes" to help familiarize soldiers with "terrain, routes, water, and provisioning" conditions in the areas they traversed.[71] This

kind of practical knowledge, it was thought, would contribute to successful expeditions and column maneuvers in the future. In one such
instance, in July 1904 a company commander planned to have part of
his company complete a "battle-like" firing exercise with live ammunition and targets on their return from a five-day, 160-kilometer practice
march from Dar es Salaam to Kisiju and back.[72] Coincidentally, the
firing exercise soon became a real demonstration of colonial firepower
when the company passed through the Rufiji delta district. Some time
earlier, uncooperative local inhabitants murdered a police-askari who
had recently been dispatched from Dar es Salaam to Rufiji District.
Although the unit appears not to have been directly involved in ar-
resting the alleged guilty parties, its nearby simultaneous display of
firepower and sharpshooting attracted many "curious and interested"
African observers. Germans in Dar es Salaam, clearly worried about
the proximity of this minor rebellion to the colonial capital, hoped this
military show would "cure them of their childish insubordination."[73]
The unit returned to Dar es Salaam twelve days after its initial departure to great celebration.[74] This example certainly illustrates how training prepared askari for the physical and emotional demands of military
confrontation. Schutztruppe exercises also served wider communicative purposes for the colonial state by reminding local populations of
its intent and ability to use force on short notice.[75]

German officers used other methods for physical training as well.
They erected gymnastic and other training equipment on some stations.
Three-dimensional military training structures helped soldiers simulate
combat activities such as scaling walls or buildings and crossing rivers
or other narrow spaces in single file, helping soldiers build physical endurance too.[76] Askari trained on these apparatuses with varying degrees
of enthusiasm.[77] German officers' gymnastic exercises reminded some
askari of monkeys, dampening their eagerness to participate.[78] Although
they seemed to enjoy exercises involving jumping, their efforts on the
high bar appeared to one officer "awkward."[79] While it is difficult to
know much about the askari's thoughts on these forms of training, it
is tempting to imagine that they perceived such activities as trivialities
having little to do with what they would face in war. In this respect,
practice marches probably made much more sense to the troops.

Askari also received training in a range of military skills fundamental to effective military operations. All askari learned to shoot the

Mauser M/71, a single-shot .450-caliber rifle that used black-powder cartridges famous for giving off clouds of black smoke and betraying soldiers' locations. Askari regularly undertook strictly monitored target practice, with sharpshooters receiving special recognition and insignia.[80] Specialists also learned how to maintain and fire the Schutztruppe's machine guns, and a still smaller group of specialists, some of whom were children, learned how to operate the heliograph for field communications. At any given time some twenty askari also served in the *Musikkapelle* (band) based in Dar es Salaam, which performed on special occasions such as the kaiser's birthday.[81] Individual askari also served as company buglers and drummers. In addition, askari also carried out many of the day-to-day tasks that enabled colonial governance, including tax collection, vaccination campaigns, and providing escorts for European travelers.[82] Askari were indispensable to the colonial state as colonial intermediaries as well as soldiers (see chapter 5).

Askari did not, however, accept their orders wholesale, despite potentially harsh consequences for noncompliance. Rather, they identified with some aspects of German military culture but simply tolerated others in order to avoid punishment. Ali Kalikilima's narrative of his time as a young recruit reveals something of the experience of Schutztruppe military training. His narrative intertwines remembered feelings of admiration for the Germans and feelings that their disciplinary harshness was excessive:

> Training lasted many months. We were taught how to march properly, how to handle a variety of weapons and most importantly, how to be fearless. The training was so intense that at times when I fell down to sleep I often wondered whether I'd made a wise choice [in joining the Schutztruppe]. Our instructors were ruthless and cruel. It seemed they did not know how to speak. It intrigued me that it was necessary for all orders to be shouted. The smallest mistake was punished with hard labour, not only for the culprit, but for all of us.[83]

For Ali, training imparted more than valuable combat skills. It also instilled a strong sense that his instructors had in fact made him "fearless" by putting him and his fellow-recruits through a strange, exhausting, and life-altering experience. He respected his leaders even if he did not like them.[84] Fear of disciplinary action for moral or technical failure during combat also should not be discounted as a key factor in keeping askari on task. Such was the basis of the working relationship at the heart of the Schutztruppe's ability to operate effectively as an expeditionary force.

Throughout the Schutztruppe's existence, officers frequently commented on what they perceived to be substandard shooting skills among their troops.[85] As we have seen, Schutztruppe officers and askari also had different ideas of what it meant to possess and use a firearm. In late-nineteenth-century East Africa among Nyamwezi men, for example, owning a firearm visibly illustrated that its owner either had the means to purchase the weapon or that the weapon had been bestowed on him by a wealthy and powerful patron.[86] Either way, ownership of the weapon meant at least as much, and perhaps more, than actual shooting ability. Ali's specific fear that he would not be able to handle his weapon properly in combat mirrors similar feelings experienced by soldiers in other wartime contexts and should in part be attributed to generalized nervousness about the great unknown of impending battle.[87] Yet Ali recalled with great pride the moment in his pre-askari youth when his wealthy slave-raiding father initiated him in "the art of shooting with a muzzle-loader gun."[88] Some askari gave themselves nicknames related to "weapons-craft," such as Powder, Flint, or Bullet, which they kept throughout their Schutztruppe enlistment period.[89] Schutztruppe officers' recurring observations that individual askari lacked shooting skills should perhaps be interpreted in this light. Interestingly, officers complained far less about askari units' abilities to fire salvos, where individual accuracy mattered less, suggesting that small-unit firing discipline in combat situations actually met their standards much of the time, even when results during target practice disappointed.[90]

Recruits expressed their willingness to adhere to the rules and norms of their new organization, and thus also at least their nominal acceptance of colonial civilizationist ideals, in different ways. For example, their experiences of receiving pay changed over the course of the Schutztruppe's existence, reflecting an increasing engagement with the German colonial state's vision of modernity. In the Schutztruppe's early days askari received their wages in goods. Schutztruppe officers meticulously recorded these payments in individual soldier paybooks—a complicated and time-consuming affair. Later, the askari became salaried employees who received their regular pay in cash, simplifying the process. The paybooks also recorded information about individual recruitment history, campaign participation, decorations, punishments, achievements in target practice, and family status.[91] In effect, the paybooks provided European Schutztruppe personnel with a summary of each askari's professional life history, enabling them to quickly fit soldiers into units after transfers, to measure progress toward specific training and behavioral goals, to monitor health, and to manage inheritances for soldiers who died while on duty. Officers also corresponded with each other about askari when they transferred them between posts, noting their health statuses, shooting histories, special skills or qualities, and the equipment they had been issued.[92]

Another means by which Schutztruppe military training transformed askari into colonial agents was to inculcate in them new understandings of time and order. In coastal East Africa, time is reckoned on a twelve-hour cycle, beginning with six o'clock in the morning. Seven o'clock in the morning is thus "hour one [*saa moja*]," eight o'clock is "hour two [*saa mbili*]," and so on until six o'clock in the evening, when the cycle begins again. This practice of reckoning time spread to other parts of Tanzania via the caravan trade routes. In rural areas, where "life and production" were tied to daylight hours and seasonal changes, this way of measuring time prevailed.[93] With the establishment and expansion of colonial rule, askari were expected to structure their days using European concepts of "industrial time," eschewing the old ways of telling time.[94] Sudanese soldiers likely had longer experience with European time concepts, but for other recruits, this sort of change probably required some adjustment. Such new ordering practices influenced how askari interacted with their superiors as well as colonial subjects. As they conducted their duties, their ability to operate in both modes helped transmit knowledge between the colonial state and its subjects.

The Schutztruppe also attempted to instill German ideals of order in their African soldiers by insisting on specific measures for managing health and hygiene. Staff doctors and officers monitored the health of askari companies and offered treatment for illnesses in boma infirmaries (*Lazarette*) or, if the troops were on campaign or expedition, in field hospitals. Askari at some locations took quinine to "cure" malaria, and they also served as test subjects for different quinine dosages.[95] Doctors studied sick soldiers to assess transmission, progression, and treatment of specific diseases, including malaria, relapsing fever, sleeping sickness, and dysentery.[96] Soldiers were given specific guidelines for constructing and maintaining latrines in the maboma as well as in field encampments.[97] Askari also assisted Schutztruppe medical personnel with large-scale vaccination efforts, which further associated them with colonial projects.[98]

Treatment protocols for infirmary personnel were interwoven with Schutztruppe disciplinary practices as well, making askari responsible for certain aspects of their own health. Soldiers admitted to infirmaries for treatment of "self-inflicted" illnesses were subject to deductions from their pay. According to a 1904 Schutztruppe directive, illnesses falling into this category included "sexually transmitted diseases, diseases related to the use of alcohol, opium, hemp, or other intoxicating stimulants, injuries received in brawls, and self-inflicted wounds."[99] In 1910 a revision to the 1904 document allowed that "sexually transmitted diseases should only be characterized as self-inflicted if the man does not report [himself] sick directly after infection. If the sick notice happens promptly, there will be no punishment or reduction in pay."[100] Officials likely realized that efforts to arrest the spread of diseases around the colonial centers, which included physical examinations of women identified as prostitutes, had largely failed.[101] For one thing, women who underwent successful treatment for sexually transmitted diseases often returned to sex work following their recovery, risking reexposure.[102] In addition, colonial authorities apparently released from "control" any woman who could prove she intended to marry—an interesting elevation of European gendered marriage ideals over public health concerns.[103] And in light of the relatively recent Schutztruppe experience of being militarily unprepared in the face of the Maji Maji war in 1905, it made little practical sense to continue punishing askari for contracting these diseases. In shifting to punishing soldiers who failed to seek treatment, colonial officials gave them the opportunity to demonstrate personal responsibility for their own health and safety, and to place faith in the efficacy of colonial medicine—another marker of their engagement with colonial values.

Another signature way that askari performed their roles as Schutztruppe members and colonial agents was by adhering to rules of proper uniform wear. Uniforms serve vital purposes within military organizations. Up close, the insignia and rank placed on a uniform archives the wearer's rank, accomplishments, and skills, and thereby transmits information about experience, status, and authority to fellow soldiers.[104] Uniforms also produced new postures and bodily practices in young men unaccustomed to wearing the elaborate layers of clothing, insignia, headgear, puttees (leg wraps), and boots issued to each Schutztruppe askari.[105] By accepting these sartorial practices, askari recruits made their first steps toward full Schutztruppe membership.

In Kiswahili, the German word *Uniform* translated to "askari clothes" (*nguo za askari*), so that this linguistic signifier denoted the fusion between the men's identities as soldiers and outward expressions of those identities, as well as the distinctiveness of the clothing ensemble.[106] One scholar contends that "wearing a uniform properly—understanding and obeying rules about the uniform-in-practice and turning the garments into communicative statements—is more important than the items of clothing and decoration themselves."[107] Particular items of clothing could in fact be quite important, since cloth and specialized clothing items had intrinsic value as currency, prestige goods, and practical pieces in East African cultures. A number of colonial employees and local leaders wore uniforms or uniform-like clothing in their day-to-day lives. But only the askari could legitimately demonstrate membership in the Schutztruppe, the most potent arm of German colonial administration, by wearing uniforms according to the organization's specialized rules and regulations. Photographic evidence shows that askari also sometimes altered or combined their uniforms with elements drawn from East African clothing practices.[108] But on the whole, uniforms set the askari apart from most other East Africans, whom they and their superiors referred to as *washenzi*, or barbarians. These distancing practices provided a psychological buffer for the askari as they waged war against Schutztruppe enemies. They also confirmed and reinforced individual askari's sense of belonging to the dominant military and political actor in the territory and thus their claims to status as big men.

For the thousands of East Africans who were not part of the Schutztruppe, uniforms reinforced the idea that the askari were part of a larger whole, or cogs in a machine. That is, uniforms created the impression of there being many more askari than there actually were, that they were interchangeable with each other, and thus that any one of them might be as dangerous as the next. By massing together large numbers of uniformed soldiers, armies appeared large and formidable, producing lack of confidence and fear in their military opponents. A government's ability to assemble a uniformed army sent unspoken but quite clear messages about its strength, because such an undertaking required substantial economic and human resources. These messages would not have been lost on East Africans, whose notions of "wealth in people" informed their decision-making processes at every socioeconomic level, from households to larger polities. In addition, as literary scholar Paul Fussell astutely observes, "The uniform . . . assures its audience that the wearer *has* a job, one likely not to be merely temporary and one extorting a degree of respect for being associated with a successful enterprise. The uniform attaches one to success."[109] In German East Africa, the wearing of uniforms by those most directly associated with the colonial state conveyed permanence, authority, and status in ways that stood out from the vast majority of East Africans living with colonialism. Askari and other colonial employees found "success" through their attachments to the colonial state, and in wearing uniforms that represented those attachments, they helped disseminate a message about the potential benefits of cooperation with the colonial state.

Like soldiers everywhere though, the askari did not always meet their officers' expectations of fastidiousness in uniform wear. The official German-Swahili military language guide for East Africa provides insights into the everyday struggles that characterized relationships between German officers and African soldiers. A number of entries suggest officers' everyday recurring frustrations with askari deficiencies in properly wearing their uniforms, and how to maintain complete uniform sets. For example, an entry for "leg wraps [*Beinwickel*]" is followed by a series of German phrases with their Kiswahili translations, including "wrap your leg wraps around," "wrap your leg wraps tighter," and "where are your leg wraps?" For "trousers [*Hosen*]," we find "your trousers [*siruali*] are torn," and for "tunic [*Rock*]," "your coat [*koti*] is torn," "pull your coat down," "hang your coat up there."[110] Phrase books, of course, cannot be taken as definitive examples of how officers addressed their askari. Still, they give some indication of German obsessions with proper uniform wear on the one hand and askari noncompliance, apathy, or misunderstanding on the other.

Uniforms also sometimes undermined askari abilities to accomplish their goals, because their distinctiveness marked them as potential targets of violence against colonial figures and their local allies. Uniforms announced a soldier's arrival from afar, giving people opportunity to flee, or to plan acts of resistance and self-defense. In one of many examples, East Africans living around Kilimanjaro in 1904 saw askari tax collectors approaching from a distance and fled into hiding, refusing to return until they were sure the askari had departed.[111] Not only did the askari wear distinct uniforms, they also carried weapons and printed documents with striking visual markings recognizable to literate and non-literate alike. The black, white, and red of the German imperial flag, as well as the eagle insignia, appeared on summons documents (*Schaurizettel*) issued by colonial authorities to order people to attend the judicial hearings known as *mashauri*. The flags also flew over every boma and accompanied officials on expeditions and tours. The intended political symbolism would not have been missed by anyone with even a minimal history of interaction with the colonial government. Indeed, it appears that nonaskari sometimes stole uniform parts if opportunities to do so arose, raising the possibility that outsiders might have tried to impersonate askari.[112] One uniform item that may have been especially compelling was the identification tag (*Erkennungsmarke*), a metal plate that the askari were supposed to always wear on a lanyard under their tunics. A 1908 missive from Dar es Salaam to all police-askari units reminded commanders of this rule and also warned them that "the usual keeping of these by women and boys [was] not allowed and punishable." Askari who lost their identification tags "through their own fault" had to pay a fine of half a rupee.[113] Uniforms and other visible trappings of the state helped cement the soldiers' place in colonial practices of power, differentiating them from nearly everyone else in the colony. At the same time, nguo ya askari served as a common symbol around which the soldiers began to identify with each other across their differences in origins, languages, and military traditions.

Belonging to the Schutztruppe meant conforming to a set of rules and expectations disseminated by the headquarters in Dar es Salaam and enforced by officers and NCOs at their stations. Disobedience or failure to comply with regulations could result in harsh punishments. These punishments included extra duty, confinement with or without chain-gang labor, flogging, fines, dismissal from the Schutztruppe, or some combination thereof.[114] The highest-ranking officer at each station or outpost was authorized to give out these punishments as he saw fit. Floggings—usually twenty-five lashes with a kiboko—were administered by the senior African askari on site in front of the entire unit, and indeed, the whole boma or campaign community.[115] Askari received the hamsa ishirini, as it was known in Kiswahili, for many types of offenses. Officers' diaries provide examples of askari being flogged for such infractions as sleeping or inattention while on watch duty, stealing goods from local populations, and negligence or abuse against a child.[116] In keeping with their reputations for stoicism, Sudanese soldiers reportedly received their lashes "without batting an eyelash."[117] They set the example for other soldiers, "who [made] an effort to do as the Sudanese and not express any pain."[118] Particularly egregious offenses could result in the death penalty, but such judgments had to receive the colonial governor's approval. Officially, death penalty cases were divided into "not purely military crimes," punishable by hanging, and "military crimes," punishable by close-range gunshot to the head or heart, although little evidence has survived to show how often executions of askari occurred.[119] In one 1894 case, a "crazed" senior askari was hung after shooting an NCO, but it appears that such cases were quite rare.[120] As with floggings, executions were carried out by senior African soldiers. "Naturally whites are absolutely excluded from this duty," wrote Wissmann in a book meant to prepare Schutztruppe personnel for African postings.[121] In theory, by making senior African troops responsible for disciplinary violence, German personnel created the appearance of being above the fray, or as neutral adjudicators in cases against their askari.

In fact, German officers also rendered unsanctioned violent punishments against their soldiers, often the manifestation of an intense rage that seemingly came out of nowhere. This is not to discount the presence of violent disciplinary practices as part of normal military practices at the time, especially within the Prussian army. Still, we might also interpret this behavior as part of a syndrome referred to in German East Africa as *Tropenkoller* (tropical madness) and elsewhere as tropical neurasthenia. The syndrome was a set of psychological afflictions experienced and reported by white Europeans living and working in tropical Africa for extended periods. Medical experts of the age explained the maladies as features of the supposed degenerative processes that occurred in white Europeans' mental and physical health during long-term exposure to tropical environments, with its combined stresses of hot and humid weather, long marches, consumption of intoxicants, and pervasive fear of being surrounded or ambushed by hostile peoples.[122] Recent scholars have also argued that the notion of tropical neurasthenia reflected contemporary "social anxieties" about "white masculinity and racial robustness [that] made it ripe for export to the colonial setting" from its North American and European ideological origins.[123] Furthermore, as Anna Crozier argues for British East Africa, ideas about tropical neurasthenia served as a "rational means of filtering, regulating, and managing the behavior of . . . colonial personnel."[124] The combination of official and unofficial disciplinary actions officers and NCOs took against underperforming askari was constitutive of the everyday violence of the soldiers' work lives. Perhaps we can also read these actions as reflective of the complex mechanisms by which colonial officials' perceptions that their masculinity and racial superiority were under siege influenced their behaviors against even their most trusted African agents.

Physical forms of punishment made wayward soldiers' infractions visible to fellow soldiers and to the boma communities. The Schutztruppe also reserved the right to punish their troops by taking deductions from their pay—a less visible, but nonetheless consequential means by which to remind them of their positions as military subordinates and clients to their superiors. For example, soldiers serving "middle or strict" detention lost their monthly pay for the duration of their sentence. Instead, they received a much reduced, but rank-appropriate, "detainee payment," out of which they had to cover their own subsistence.[125] Soldiers sentenced to dismissal from the Schutztruppe and awaiting confirmation of the judgment from superiors were detained in prison and assigned to chain gangs. They received no pay but instead only the same provisions as other chain-gang members.[126] In some cases, "legal" wives or children received small allowances while the askari served out their sentences, helping them weather the decrease in household income. Still, the combination of detainment with diminished pay added additional humiliation to the experience for askari, since it temporarily placed them in the same socioeconomic category as average chain-gang prisoners. Many of these prisoners ended up on chain gangs for failing to pay taxes, suggesting that they were cash poor and living at subsistence level. Thus embedded in the Schutztruppe punishment process was an effort to remind askari of the value of remaining in good standing with their officer-patrons if they wanted to retain their socioeconomic status as local big men.

On the other hand, Schutztruppe headquarters staff members continued to tweak disciplinary regulations throughout the organization's existence.[127] This suggests that the askari, metropolitan critics of German militarism abroad, or other concerned colonizers such as staff doctors, influenced Schutztruppe leadership to remind subordinates and civilian authorities that any punishments rendered needed to be proportional to the infractions committed and that they needed to be administered by appropriate personnel.[128] In fact, in 1913 Schutztruppe headquarters sternly admonished traveling civilian officials that they had no authority to administer punishment to askari and that failure to heed this warning would result in them losing the privilege of askari guards for protection during travel. A clear disdain for civil servants' failure to understand askari motivations emerges from the 1913 Schutztruppe circular: "Worst of all, in one case a European let his head of porters perform the flogging of a police-askari. Europeans, who so clearly lack any feeling for the position of the askari, should never again have askari as escorts. The askari has a very fine sense of the belittling of his status that such treatment inflicts on him."[129] In short, punishment existed to keep askari in line, but the privilege of disciplining askari belonged almost exclusively to members of the Schutztruppe. In this way, officers sought to maintain askari status vis-à-vis others, including African and European colonial employees.[130]

MARTIAL RACES, LEADERSHIP, AND SOLDIERING

As previous chapters have illustrated, African Schutztruppe recruits contributed skill sets and military traditions to the making of an askari way of war. In recruiting the initial contingent of askari from Egypt ("Sudanese"), Portuguese East Africa ("Zulus") and assorted East African ("Abyssinians" and "Swahili") and Red Sea ("Somali") locations, Wissmann and his officers drew on the DOAG's practical knowledge, experiences from previous African travels, as well as prevailing martial race stereotypes regarding potentially cooperative and portable military populations. Sudanese soldiers dominated the senior askari ranks because of their proven experience in the Anglo-Egyptian army, their military seniority, and their age. Very quickly, they gained reputations as dedicated and unflappable leaders. Yet quite early in the Schutztruppe's history, officers judged the Sudanese troops as best suited to garrison duty, sentry duty, and drill instruction. These tasks did not require great physical exertion, sensory skills, or tracking acumen, but they did require attentiveness, knowledge of procedures and rules, patience, and gravitas.[131] Although most Sudanese soldiers received firearms training during their Egyptian service, they reportedly did not measure up to German standards for firing discipline and accuracy.[132] Schutztruppe officers came to overlook these flaws, however, because in their estimation the Sudanese soldiers embodied the exemplary qualities of loyalty, bravery, and stoicism they held in such high esteem. British prohibitions against German recruitment in Egypt after 1895 meant that Sudanese recruits who died, retired, or returned to Egypt could not be replaced.[133] This political fact reinforced German officers' enshrinement of these soldiers' status at the top of the Schutztruppe's martial races hierarchy. They thus became the soldierly models for later cohorts of new recruits drawn from within German East Africa.

In Schutztruppe eyes then, by 1900 essentially two categories of askari—Sudanese and non-Sudanese—existed. Calls from budget-conscious administrators back in Germany to get rid of the "expensive" Sudanese soldiers in favor of men recruited locally in German East Africa met strong opposition from colonial administrators on the ground, who insisted that the Sudanese soldier was "on average consistently a better soldier than the local native."[134] Despite Schutztruppe officers' early representations of Sudanese soldiers as best suited to garrison duties, they routinely led flying columns, organized and carried out small patrols, and established and managed outposts without direct supervision. Most descriptions of the roles Sudanese soldiers played emphasized their leadership qualities, which are best explained by their relative age and experience in European-style armies vis-à-vis younger askari recruited from other regions and contexts.

In contrast, most other recruits to the Wissmanntruppe were younger and had little or no experience of fighting in European-led armies. Shangaan soldiers, who had more in common with East Africans than the Sudanese linguistically, developed skills as patrol leaders and spies.[135] Only a few of these soldiers remained with the Schutztruppe after 1895, with one (Effendi Plantan) eventually achieving the African officer's rank of effendi.[136] In 1906 only two soldiers with that rank were still in service.[137] Later, Nyamwezi, Sukuma, and Manyema soldiers brought sensibilities garnered from the caravan trade and the standing armies of Mirambo and Nyungu to the Schutztruppe. Over time, these soldiers received promotions and began occupying the askari-NCO ranks (ombasha, shaush, beshaush, sol) alongside the remaining Sudanese soldiers.[138] The polyglot heterogeneity of the Wissmanntruppe eventually became submerged in a Schutztruppe ethos that celebrated the achievement of creating the kind of homogeneity that made it a formidable army. At the same time, Schutztruppe members of all ranks continued to acknowledge difference in significant ways that ultimately reinforced certain qualities as desirable for askari. Pay and privilege differentials between soldiers spoke volumes about which askari the Germans valued most. A combination of factors, including overall seniority and existing payment agreements with the Egyptian colonial army, ensured that the Sudanese soldiers received the highest pay of all askari. Still, their higher rates of pay also communicated to other soldiers that their Sudanese superiors were soldierly models worthy of emulation. On the other hand, rank-and-file soldiers commanded a range of indispensable practical skills the Schutztruppe needed for success in its way of war. As these soldiers moved up the ranks, they reshaped and expanded the image of the model soldier to include not just the calm resolve and discipline of the Sudanese, but also the creativity, energy, and resourcefulness of the Nyamwezi troops.

Here again, considering groups of East African men who ultimately did not become part of the Schutztruppe suggests the qualities Schutztruppe officers valued in new recruits. In the 1911 official history of the Schutztruppe, Major Ernst Nigmann noted that neither the Maasai nor the Hehe, whose young men purportedly held the martial life in high esteem, had proven suitable for long-term service in the Schutztruppe. The Maasai, according to Nigmann, were "mushy," "flaccid," and usually "had to be let go [from the Schutztruppe] before their time [ended]." The Hehe, for their part, supposedly suffered terribly from homesickness when sent outside their "lovely, cool" southern highland home, Nigmann asserted.[139] The gendered and sexualized overtones in Nigmann's descriptions of the Maasai and the Hehe tell us far more about Schutztruppe officers' visions of who made good askari than they do about any objective realities regarding Maasai and Hehe abilities as soldiers. Indeed, Nigmann's description of these groups smacks of defensiveness in the face of these men's reluctance to join the Schutztruppe for reasons that emanated from their own martial histories and gendered understandings of soldiering. Moreover, significant parts of

Maasai and Hehe populations experienced terrible socioeconomic disruption caused in part by Schutztruppe-driven violence in the 1890s, followed by colonial political interventions that forced major changes in their societies.[140] Nigmann's attribution of feminine, unmanly, or childish traits, such as softness and emotional fragility, to these groups should be seen in this light.

His descriptions reveal hallmark Schutztruppe ideals, including physical tautness, emotional toughness, and stoic resolve. "Zulu" soldiers, on the other hand, had exemplified some of these hallmarks, but they lacked the calm effectiveness of the Sudanese, to whom they were incessantly compared. As Tom von Prince put it in his memoir, "Zulus were more warlike, [the] Sudanese more soldierly."[141] Through these discursive processes, Schutztruppe officers reified the martial race hierarchy and delineated the masculine qualities they desired in their troops. For the most part, these processes reflected German conceits and insecurities about their own history of soldierly masculinity, coupled with defensive rationales for why certain men seemed not to measure up.[142]

But the discursive making of Schutztruppe masculinities could not have existed without askari participation.[143] They brought a range of sensibilities, aptitudes, and qualities with them that German officials attempted to alter through training and socialization processes, but which could work only if the soldiers cooperated (see chapter 1). Available evidence suggests that the askari conformed much of the time, but they also had their own ways of living within and testing the strictures of military life. In addition, the Schutztruppe's practical manpower needs throughout the 1890s changed its recruitment patterns, necessitating continual adjustments to the discursive hierarchy to reflect the fluid mixture of African soldiers who actually comprised the Schutztruppe. Perhaps even more important, the Schutztruppe's combat experiences between 1890 and 1918 both reinforced and challenged how officers and askari saw themselves vis-à-vis their battlefield opponents and forced the Schutztruppe to reconsider and adjust its methods in the face of failure. The next chapter explores how askari experiences during three periods of warfare between 1890 and 1918 reflected their training, socialization, and aspirations, as well as the conditions under which some askari opted out of continuing to fight for the Germans.

3 ⇌ The Askari Way of War

SCHUTZTRUPPE MILITARY socialization undoubtedly played a crucial role in turning African recruits into askari. Yet the soldiers' practical experiences of combat—of learning by doing—featured at least as centrally in their ability to fight as the formal training they undertook while in garrison. The conquest decade of the 1890s and its numerous "pacification campaigns" and "punitive expeditions" provided askari of all ranks and backgrounds with ample opportunities to hone the military skills and develop the mental practices that later sealed the Schutztruppe's reputation as a ruthlessly effective colonial army.[1] The military culture that coalesced in the 1890s laid the basis for how askari would fight after 1900, especially in the two major wars that caused Tanzanians the most widespread suffering of the entire German colonial period—the Maji Maji war (1905–7) and World War I (1914–18). Between 1890 and 1918, the askari way of war blended East African and European practices of warfare to deadly effect. The Schutztruppe's methods, including scorched-earth tactics, highly mobile operations, concentrated firepower, and the use of family members, porters, and military auxiliaries for logistical and tactical support, proved devastatingly effective against diverse East African opponents. Later, during World War I, similar methods also proved successful against European-led Allied colonial armies.

Thinking about an askari way of war as a "soldiers' culture" that existed as a subset of Schutztruppe military culture helps us see their violent wartime practices as the "logical products" of the training, socialization, and combat experiences that molded them into soldiers.[2] Military historians have increasingly concerned themselves with exploring "culture"—understood as "habitual practices, default programs, hidden assumptions and unreflected cognitive frames"—as a way of better grasping the range of contextual factors that influenced militaries to act in particular ways.[3] As one military historian explains military historiography's cultural turn, the concept "'way of war' serves as the water in which the human actors swim, filled with unstated assumptions and default settings of which they may be only dimly aware; it is the envelope of possibilities and expectations in which they live."[4] The askari way of war made possible the Schutztruppe conquest of German East Africa. The soldiers' military actions also expressed their vision of themselves vis-à-vis those against whom they fought. As one witness to the askari's wartime violence during Maji Maji put it, "All people were barbarians to the askari."[5]

Adopting an askari vantage point for interpreting military actions from the conquest era through to 1918 helps explain the askari way of war as a central feature of their subjectivities. The style of war that began during the conquest decade of the 1890s continued into the next two decades, with the grander scale of the Maji Maji war and World War I taking their way of war to new levels of destructiveness and bringing terrible consequences for significant portions of the African population. Much has been written about these two wars, their prosecution, and their effects. The askari occupy a prominent place in descriptions and analyses of both wars, where they emerge as the primary agents of colonial violence, as brutes, and as loyal soldiers to the German colonial cause.[6] Tracing some askari combat experiences from the 1890s through Maji Maji and World War I shows how these violent contexts shaped their abilities to perform the roles of big men and colonial state makers. Their actions in these colonial wars also cemented their reputations as dedicated and resourceful soldiers who could effectively operate without supervision from German officers or NCOs.[7] Any doubts Schutztruppe officers may have had about the African soldiers' abilities or loyalty were obviated by askari performances in the two wars. And East Africans who opposed the Schutztruppe learned that while the askari way of war was by no means infallible, it was relentless, callous, ruthless in its execution, and deadly.

It would seem natural to draw contrasts between the wars of the 1890s, Maji Maji, and World War I. The conquest wars of the 1890s ranged from "punitive expeditions" of short duration to more protracted conflicts such as the war with the Hehe, which lasted most of the decade. Maji Maji began as an intense anticolonial war that provoked a pitiless response from the Schutztruppe. And the East African campaign of World War I, frequently described as a sideshow to the European war of 1914–18, was fought against Allied African troops under the leadership of European officers and NCOS, and accustomed to fighting in the mode of European colonial armies. Certainly these distinctions are accurate and worth noting, since the Schutztruppe had different objectives in these wars. The wars of the 1890s were fought to establish German control over this portion of their new empire. In Maji Maji, the Schutztruppe wanted to decisively defeat the rebels, to force into submission areas believed to be supportive of them, and to discourage further rebellion. In World War I, Lettow-Vorbeck wanted to force the Allies to divert essential resources away from Europe to East Africa, and secondarily, to retain German East Africa as a colonial possession.[8]

But if we adopt a soldiers' perspective on the wars, looking beneath the geopolitical and military demographic differences between the two, we see that these kinds of distinctions mattered little to how soldiers fought. In fact, the askari way of war that began with the conquests of the 1890s exhibited significant continuities with Maji Maji and World War I. Of course, there were also differences between how and why the askari fought in the 1890s, in Maji Maji, and in World War I. By emphasizing what the askari did, what they thought they were doing, and what they hoped to gain (or feared losing) when they went to war, this chapter illustrates some of the continuities and changes in askari ways of war between 1890 and 1918. In so doing, it offers a further glimpse into the askari's identities as soldiers and sheds light on the extent to which their soldierly objectives meshed with those of their officers and other colonial officials.

THE ASKARI WAY OF WAR AND "SMALL WARS"

In 1896, British field artillery officer and war theorist Colonel Charles E. Callwell published *Small Wars: Their Principles and Practice*, a compendium of imperial war experiences that offered its readers practical advice regarding the "broad rules which govern the conduct of operations in hostilities against adversaries of whom modern works on the military art seldom take account."[9] Conceding that the term *small war* evaded simple definition, Callwell nonetheless defined it as an expedition "against savages and semi-civilised races by disciplined soldiers," especially in cases where "organized armies" engaged opponents who "shirked engagements in the open."[10] He noted that the term signified nothing about the scale of any given campaign. Instead, it referred to any military confrontation that occurred between a *regular* and an *irregular* army.[11] In twenty-seven thematically organized chapters, Callwell used examples of imperial warfare drawn from around the world to enumerate the challenges every colonial army would face in such wars, as well as what he called "principles" for overcoming such challenges and defeating the enemy. Most notably, Callwell argued that "civilized" armies must always be prepared to "overaw[e] the enemy by bold initiative and by resolute action whether on the battlefield or as part of the general plan of the campaign."[12] Callwell thus fused evidence of Western armies' organizational and technological superiority with assumptions about European (and North American) racial superiority to generate an influential essentialist argument about the nature of warfare between "civilized" and "savage."

Callwell had little interest in the specific processes by which British, French, and other colonial armies recruited, trained, and deployed their soldiers in Africa and elsewhere. And with the exception of short discussions of German failings in the war against the Herero and Nama in Southwest Africa (1904–7), he largely ignored German examples of colonial warfare in making his case. For Callwell, colonial soldiers were simply "regulars," whose combat modes against "irregulars" fit neatly into his paradigm of small wars. For example, in combat against "guerrillas," regular troops had little choice but to "resort to punitive measures directed against the possessions of their antagonists."[13] In other words, colonial soldiers' routine practices of seizing enemy livestock and other property, or destroying their food stores, communicated their intent to punish guerrilla fighters for waging war against the colonial army in the first place, as well as for refusing to "meet them in the open field" to fight.[14] Callwell's treatise on small wars thus unsurprisingly presented colonial soldiers as interchangeable, faceless regulars whose motives, desires, and objectives in the wars they fought mapped directly onto those of the colonial authorities for whom they fought. Callwell's audience of military practitioners probably also did not look to *Small Wars* for perspective on what made colonial soldiers tick during military operations.

Still, Callwell's prescriptions for how small wars should be prosecuted provide helpful markers for understanding the framework within which askari went to war. That framework in turn helps connect the askari way of war with the range of tangible and intangible gains they hoped to achieve in war and provides the basis for comprehending continuities and changes in their way of war between 1890 and 1918.

The foundation of the askari way of war was each company's ability to conduct small-unit operations in formations reminiscent of Callwell's "flying columns," or "self-contained bodies of troops roaming through the theatre of war."[15] Led by German officers, NCOs, or senior askari, these columns acted as escorts, patrols, or strike forces to suit local conditions and military imperatives. Askari moved between these different modes of operations as needed. Any given Schutztruppe officer or NCO also routinely participated in or organized such small-unit operations, because such operations constituted the baseline of Schutztruppe actions throughout the colonial period. The Schutztruppe relied on mobility, surprise, deception, and superior firepower to compensate for their manpower disadvantages.

The unpublished diary of Schutztruppe NCO Josef Weinberger, who served in the Fourth Company from 1891 to 1896, affords an early, unvarnished view of the day-to-day activities of the Schutztruppe's columns. His diary documents a life of constant marches, rapid decision making with scant or faulty military intelligence, inconsistent access to food and water, and the ever-present threat of ambush. Weinberger arrived in German East Africa in October 1891, and in February 1892 the Fourth Company received orders to march to Kisaki to found a station, contain the Schutztruppe's enemies (collectively referred to as *mafiti*) in the area, and defend a nearby mission station at Tununguo.[16] Shortly thereafter, part of his company (forty-five askari and fifteen porters) undertook a "punitive expedition" against local leaders in response to their refusal to attend a colonial *shauri*. Eight days into the expedition, as they climbed onto high ground, they began receiving heavy fire from enemy soldiers who, in Weinberger's words, "skulked around [them] like hyenas." This guerrilla style of attack continued "day and night" over the next few days, with the enemy refusing to directly engage the company in battle. Local informants also told the company that all wells in the area had been poisoned, so the soldiers were suffering from terrible thirst. In the midst of all this, Weinberger's commander fell ill with malaria and transferred leadership authority to him. Leaving behind a few askari to "cover" the commander, Weinberger decided to pursue the enemy at night. His column surprised and defeated several "densely occupied mountain villages" that had presumably been serving as havens for the enemy soldiers. His notation of the single word *peace* after his description of these events stood in for a description of standard Schutztruppe practice in these kinds of situations. To deny enemy soldiers the possibility of using such villages for provisioning or as hiding places, askari burnt them to the ground, an element of the askari way of war that recurred throughout the German era.[17]

Askari bore much of the responsibility for the effectiveness of these small-unit operations. They conducted patrols in areas considered insecure, gathered intelligence about local politics and geographies, and provided security details for European civilians, sick or injured German Schutztruppe personnel, and sometimes for allied African notables. They guarded the porter trains that often accompanied them on the march, both to protect them from raids, and to deter them from absconding with the column's supplies. They scouted for sources of food and water, commandeering supplies from villagers they encountered on such missions. They also hunted game to supplement column provisions as opportunities arose to do so.

Askari NCOs were at the heart of the Schutztruppe's ability to execute this style of warfare. Indeed, senior askari routinely influenced Schutztruppe officers' and NCOs' decision-making processes in the field. Weinberger's diary again offers useful examples of the face-to-face interactions between German Schutztruppe members and askari that often helped determine the outcomes of violent encounters with their enemies. For instance, on 26 August 1892, the Fourth Company's senior askari NCO, the Sudanese *sol* Mabruk, advised company commander Lieutenant Kurt Johannes to send a ten-man unit to patrol the area around the company's new station in Kisaki. A *beshaush* named Ramadan led the patrol. Half an hour after the patrol's early-morning departure, enemy soldiers attacked the camp, and an intense battle between the besieged askari and the attackers ensued.

In the midst of the battle, Beshaush Ramadan's patrol returned bearing news that three additional bands of enemy soldiers were approaching on three sides of the encampment. Shortly thereafter, and just as Be-shaush Ramadan had described, an attack of even greater intensity occurred. Rallied by a Sudanese askari's rousing "war dance," the askari returned "furious fire," eventually forcing the enemy soldiers to flee. Rather than "energetically undertaking pursuit" of the enemy, how-ever, the company commander ordered them to remain encamped, assuming a defensive mode, a stance that was anathema to the Schutz-truppe ethos. Much to Weinberger's frustration, Johannes denied his request to undertake a follow-up attack with Sol Mabruk.[18] Two hours later, encumbered by a nervous and unwieldy group of allied civilians, the company commander ordered the column to march toward Kisaki. The column again came under attack.

Sol Mabruk proved indispensable in restoring order among the soldiers, directing their uncontrolled fire toward a goal. He also calmed and organized the column's civilians and porters, allowing for a more effective defense. Attending to unit morale, he pointedly informed Weinberger that Lieutenant Johannes's poor leadership skills—includ-ing his failure to take the offensive and his inability to communicate with his troops in Swahili—had undermined the askari's trust.[19] Thus, like other senior askari, Sol Mabruk's soldierly experience helped glue the unit's leadership and rank-and-file together under stressful and dangerous conditions.[20] Beshaush Ramadan's patrol provided impor-tant intelligence to the company, even if timing and circumstances prevented its troops from acting on it. Things likely would have gone much worse had askari NCOs not been present. The Schutztruppe's ability to recruit experienced senior soldiers from northeastern Africa and elsewhere had compensated somewhat for the haste with which Wissmann and his fellow officers assembled the army. The presence of soldiers like Mabruk and Ramadan amplified the organizational and technological advantages the Schutztruppe columns brought to bear in East African warfare in the 1890s and later.

The columns formed the organizational basis of the Schutztruppe and underpinned the most identifiable elements of the askari way of war. Small subunits broke off from the larger columns in order to con-duct reconnaissance, patrols, and searches for provisions, as Beshaush Ramadan's early-morning patrol near Kisaki illustrates.[21] These smaller units could operate less conspicuously than the columns, and they did not have to concern themselves with managing the logistics train that usually made up a major section of any given column. They could maneuver with speed and flexibility. In attacking encampments or villages, they used predawn ambushes and sieges to maximize the advantage of surprise. Indeed, during World War I the Allies found that the askari's skills as patrollers made them frustratingly elusive and dangerous opponents, seemingly able to strike at will, only to then disappear into their surroundings.[22]

The ways the Schutztruppe askari fought had much in common with styles of warfare used in other European colonial armies. Still, within both Anglophone military historiography and Tanzanian history and memory, the askari came to be known for certain practices of warfare that differentiated them, even if only by degrees, from the colonial soldiers of other armies. One such difference was that only rarely did they descend into the kind of complete unit indiscipline that could undermine or derail field operations. This is not to argue that they were always the brave, loyal, and dependable askari of German myth. Nor do I want to argue that they were invincible in battle, for they were not. The 1891 Zelewski expedition, in which Hehe soldiers destroyed an entire Schutztruppe column, is a case in point, and one to which I shall return later in this chapter. Rather, despite their predictable flaws and failings as soldiers, their training and discipline saw them through the chaos of the numerous battles the Schutztruppe fought between 1890 and 1918.

Their consistently high levels of discipline and cohesion laid the foundation for some of the most destructive aspects of the askari way of war. Commonly, the Schutztruppe responded to real or perceived military threats by attacking and destroying local villages and communities believed to be working with or supporting enemy combatants.[23] Often enough, such attacks took the form of burning villages and cultivated fields to the ground, forcing surviving residents to flee into hiding to avoid capture.[24] The Schutztruppe's use of scorched-earth methods of warfare continued throughout the colonial period, with the askari their primary practitioners. Frequent notations, both terse and detailed, in Schutztruppe officers' diaries, memoirs, and official military records sampled from across the German period underline the point that the askari practiced this mode of warfare as a matter of course.[25]

As the askari companies campaigned, the challenges of provisioning the columns set the stage for another highly destructive aspect of their way of war. As already noted, the columns marched with contingents of porters who transported most of the unit's supplies, munitions, and equipment. Invariably, however, the columns ran short of food, and officers dispatched them to locate communities where supplies were available. More often than not, the askari seized any goods they could find without compensating those unfortunate enough to lie in the Schutztruppe's path. Even when officers attempted to make restitution for goods seized by askari, it could hardly make up for the loss of subsistence food items during times of war.[26] The soldiers' practice of living off the land reinforced their scorched-earth tactics. Taking advantage of the wartime conditions that made populations especially vulnerable, askari exploited these opportunities to seize food stores, livestock, and any other useful goods in conjunction with their general pattern of destroying local communities believed to be resisting German authority and encroachment.[27] And of course increasing their wealth in livestock and goods also contributed to their abilities to perform the big-man roles to which they aspired.

This pattern of expropriating goods from civilians, destroying their homes and livelihoods, and placing survivors in a state of dependency, contributed directly to individual askari's goals of increasing their wealth in people and further building their domestic labor pools out of women and children captured on campaigns.[28] One case deserves mention here. In January 1898 a column operating in the southern highlands during the hunt for Hehe leader Mkwawa captured three women, one of whom the askari recognized as "an old acquaintance from Iringa." According to the officer who recounted the episode in his diary, she had been captured during the Schutztruppe's taking of Iringa three years earlier, thereafter becoming an "askari wife." In a later confrontation between the Hehe and the Schutztruppe, she "preferred" to be recaptured by the Hehe. Thus, at least this one case makes visible not just a line of continuity between East African and Schutztruppe practices of warfare but also the extent to which the askari way of war was entangled with regional practices and gendered notions of proper conduct.[29]

The askari, of course, made up only a small subset of each column's personnel. The presence of large numbers of noncombatant column members also influenced the askari way of war. The Schutztruppe depended on additional manpower, including porters, "campaign community" members, such as askari wives, askariboys, and for the Germans, African servants and cooks, and military auxiliaries (referred to as "ruga-ruga" or "irregulars").[30] All column members had parts to play in the labor demands generated by keeping an army in the field for extended periods of time.[31] Askari were responsible for setting up camps for officers and NCOs at the end of each day's march. They also bore responsibility for finding sufficient provisions for themselves and other column members, and for providing security for the columns and encampments. When permanent boma sites were selected, askari typically comprised a significant portion of the labor force needed for construction of the forts, housing, and other facilities in and around the maboma. Porters, family members, and the askari's dependents transported most of the column's supplies and matériel, including very heavy and cumbersome equipment like machine guns and artillery pieces. Askariboys—dependent boys or sons who acted as servants to their "fathers" (babas)—carried their gear and firearms, and handled myriad other duties for the askari, including cooking and assembling their camps at the end of each day.[32] The women of askari households carried out a range of essential domestic duties on the march, including cooking, laundering, and gathering food and water.[33]

The campaign communities formed mobile microeconomies that performed most of the Schutztruppe's logistical functions, but which also generated recurrent challenges for the Schutztruppe's officers, NCOs, and senior askari. Most notably, feeding large numbers of noncombatants who could not as easily live off the land like independent askari platoons proved to be almost a daily stressor for column leadership while on campaign. In the later stages of World War I, when Schutztruppe units began experiencing extreme hardship as they desperately maneuvered to escape Allied pursuit, General von Lettow-Vorbeck attempted at one point to force the "askari wives" to separate from the main column and head south, "where they would have it better and would no longer burden" the column.[34] The women rebelled, refusing to follow Lettow-Vorbeck's orders and forcing his column to continue provisioning for them by hunting additional big game.[35] In an earlier instance, a German officer allowed the women to accompany the askari on a march to a new station so that the soldiers would not have to wait for their arrival. He soon regretted his decision, however, because like many askari themselves, he noted, the women "had especially long fingers," and took every opportunity to steal foodstuffs from the small subsistence farms they passed along the way. The officer resolved to punish the askari for any further such acts.[36] Such cases demonstrate that the presence of women and other dependents was integral to the askari way of war.[37] As aspiring big men, it was incumbent on the askari to provide for the welfare of their household members in order to prove their status credible. The easiest way to do so was to bring family members on campaign with them, which brought the additional benefit of providing some comforts of home while on campaign.[38]

This element of the askari way of war also complicated military operations beyond the seemingly omnipresent provisioning problems that characterized Schutztruppe operations. In addition to being micro-economies, the campaign communities encompassed quite a differentiated set of social relations. Everyday household dramas, jealousies, and love stories that characterized garrison life continued to unfold during campaigns, with added complications brought on by the hardships of war.[39] Social hierarchies and gendered identities interacted to shape relations between the different categories of column members, ensuring that Schutztruppe leadership spent considerable amounts of time settling disputes, negotiating compromises, and keeping the peace between them. Moreover, these hierarchies modeled the Schutztruppe vision of the colonial social order, in which German officers occupied the top position, followed by other Germans and Europeans. The askari, especially the Sudanese, came next. Porters, auxiliaries, dependents, and all other column members occupied lower positions in this social order. Particular tensions existed between the askari and the porters, since the soldiers viewed the porters and their labor as beneath them.[40] Officers and NCOs encouraged this labor hierarchy by allowing the porters to perform household labor tasks for the soldiers, like pounding grain for flour.[41] Typically, women or askariboys did this work in askari households. In addition, askari roles in protecting porters from attacks and in preventing them from pilfering goods reinforced the porters' subordinate, feminized position in the column's gendered hierarchy.

Here it is worth pausing to make a starker analytical point about women, in particular, as the askari's "constitutive others"—those who provided the feminine basis for the construction of the askari's masculinity. In addition to the gendered divisions of labor described above, which reflected the gendered and racialized hierarchy of Schutztruppe culture as a whole, the presence of women in the columns in fact created askari manhood. In other words, the askari's gendered understanding of the world "presume[d] the existence of women."[42] To put it even more starkly, it presumed that women were integral to their way of war, whether at the level of practice, or in more symbolic terms. In practical terms, women's labor as cooks, farmers, provisioners, and porters underwrote the askari's household economies, even while on expeditions. Women were also the askari's emotional and sexual companions, and alongside the askari, they shared in expressing campaign community cultural values, for example through song and dance performed at the end of each day's march. As mothers, they socialized the next generation of askari and campaign community members. Symbolically, their presence in the columns marked the askari as men of status, in effect displaying the askari's ability to reproduce themselves both socially and biologically. In addition, women were targeted for capture in warfare precisely because of their future value in both practical and symbolic terms—as productive and reproductive laborers in the household, as status markers, and as the basis of askari masculinity itself.

Askari women's lived experiences within the askari way of war varied depending on their relationships to the Schutztruppe through the askari. Their experiences also depended on many of the same factors that affected the askari and other members of the columns during wartime, such as scarcity, illness, injury, and the risk of death. Captive women lived the most precarious existences within the campaign communities, since they suffered the trauma of being violently uprooted from their previous lives, as well as the degradation of being treated as prisoners, outsiders, and subordinates to those who were already column members. Moreover, askari and others, including German Schutztruppe officers and NCOs, abused and violated them in "ghastly" ways.[43] The Schutztruppe also forced captured women to report information about provisions, routes, and locations of enemy soldiers or leaders.[44] Failure to provide good information, or refusal to cooperate with Schutztruppe demands, sometimes resulted in summary execution.[45] In August 1894, during operations in Ungoni, a captured woman's "foolish" behavior created a disturbance in the camp. She was shot the next morning.[46] Women captured in war clearly suffered terrible consequences that might lead to incorporation into soldiers' households under conditions that at best would provide security and kinship ties over time. At worst, their captivity might lead to death.[47]

By contrast, *mabibi* with established attachments to the askari often behaved with striking boldness in asserting their belonging to the campaign community and claiming the resultant associated privileges. Recorded incidents between askari women and Schutztruppe officers while on campaign appear most frequently in sources for World War I, but earlier examples also exist to demonstrate how women helped define the askari way of war through the demands they directed at Schutztruppe officers. Most often, these confrontations seemed to revolve around the assumption that askari wives would accompany askari on military expeditions. Thus in May 1906, in the midst of Maji Maji, a captain held a "shauri with the bibis" because they "absolutely" wanted to go with their men on campaign. He refused to allow them, anticipating that their presence would cause disorder among his troops. Early the next morning, when a few tried to follow the askari out of camp, the lieutenant threatened them with a kiboko, which "convinced them otherwise."[48] They stayed behind, "to the horror of the askari." The officers drew a line between military campaigns, which they believed should exclude women, and long marches between campaigns, where women were an expected, if not always entirely welcome, presence. The women's responses to the officers' decisions, however, which in the example provided above necessitated a shauri between an officer and a group of askari wives, indicate that their expectations were often vastly different.

Several reasons explain these differences in expectations between German officers and the mabibi. First, women's involvement in military expeditions and caravan culture had long-standing precedents in many eastern and northeastern African contexts. Askari wives viewed their participation in the columns as essential and as a part of their everyday lives, in much the same way that many Nyamwezi women had viewed their roles in long-distance trading caravans in the mid- to late nineteenth century.[49] Second, and related to the first explanation, many mabibi believed that their rightful place was alongside their men, whether in garrison or on the march. Source limitations make it difficult to ascertain the extent to which these women, who came from backgrounds at least as wide-ranging as the askari, entered into formal marriage arrangements with the soldiers.[50] A range of marriage, cohabitation, and companionship practices characterized relationships in the askari communities. In addition, these relationships reflected diverse and tangled emotional and sexual attachments, dependency, and desires for the belonging and security that came from community and kinship. They also may have had concrete security concerns with being left behind, since the presence of armed men in the columns offered better defenses and provisions than the camps. Status claims likely also heightened the need for askari women to be near their husbands, since a bibi's status vis-à-vis other women derived from her relationship to an askari. None of this is to discount the coercive and violent practices that without question kept some women in the campaign communities against their will. Instead, it is to make the point that women had good reasons to engage in open confrontation with German officers over the question of whether or not they might accompany their men on campaign.

A third explanation for askari women pushing to join their husbands on the march had to do with competing conceptions of gender between the women and the Schutztruppe officers. While the women saw no reason to limit their presence in the columns, German officers had very different ideas of what constituted appropriate feminine behavior. They were prone to viewing askari women as prostitutes or camp followers who would harm military order and discipline. Yet quotidian realities, and the women's own assertiveness, thwarted officers' abilities to stabilize this gendered reading of column life. As we have seen, askari women made up a significant portion of the column's labor force. German assumptions about what constituted women's work sometimes clashed with the women's ideas of what was appropriate. Another example from Correck's journal illustrates this point. He noted that his ruga-ruga and porters had "cleaned up" some farm plots, seizing "six [head] loads of beans" in the process. Correck told the women at his camp to sort the beans, to which they responded that "they were no askaris," implying that he had no authority to order them to do anything. In keeping with his usual practice, he threatened them with a kiboko, and "right away [there was] quiet."[51] Moreover, the women's presence clearly improved troop morale. In weighing the costs and benefits of including askari women, officers often concluded that they could not afford to disappoint the women or the troops. Nor could they afford to go without the camp and column services these women provided each day. In the end, the women's position at the center of the campaign community's ability to socially and culturally reproduce itself, as well as their role in the "reproduction of labor power" through their children, made them indispensable to the askari way of war, and thus also to the Schutztruppe.[52]

The military auxiliaries known as ruga-ruga also had parts to play in the askari way of war, as well as in column social relations. Evidence to underpin this point, however, like evidence on the ruga-ruga more generally, makes generalizing difficult.[53] Ruga-ruga who fought alongside the regulars of the Schutztruppe generally came from the private armed retinues of local leaders seeking to maintain friendly relations with the Germans.[54] At least until World War I, they rarely wore uniforms, although they sometimes wore simple insignia such as red scarves so that askari would not mistake them for the enemy.[55] They typically did not receive pay, but the Schutztruppe allowed them to take war spoils as compensation. During World War I, the Schutztruppe's need for trained and experienced manpower led them to regularize some ruga-ruga contingents, providing them with uniforms, similar firearms to the askari, and in some cases, a salary.[56] Some ruga-ruga were recruited, as needed, from among "young fellows" who had received training as scouts and messengers at the colonial stations.[57] For most of the colonial era, ruga-ruga operated as irregulars, often deployed in similar numbers as the askari within the columns.[58] In effect, the ruga-ruga at least doubled the Schutztruppe's manpower resources.

Great variety characterized the different ruga-ruga contingents, with some receiving high praise from officers for their resourcefulness, and others being described as brigands and brutes.[59] For example, during Maji Maji the ruga-ruga "distinguished themselves" in the destruction and plunder of fields, livestock, and provisions that the Schutztruppe harnessed as central aspects of scorched-earth warfare. They also proved "indispensable" in their abilities to conduct ambushes against Schutztruppe enemies, and in carrying out the "unrelenting pursuit of the fleeing rebels into their most secret, most isolated hiding places."[60] They also acted as advance scouts, spies, and skirmishers.[61] In short, Schutztruppe officers tended to view the ruga-ruga as the decisive element in countering their opponents' guerrilla tactics, even if they sometimes decried their lack of discipline or courage, inability to execute field movements properly, and inefficient use of firearms.[62] On the whole, sources represent the ruga-ruga as more resourceful, less controllable, and lower-maintenance versions of the askari. Their presence complemented and amplified the askari's ability to fight effectively in unfamiliar local contexts. The complementarity of their different aptitudes tied their fortunes in and after wartime together. Perhaps because of this, regular and irregular soldiers worked well together despite what would appear to have been a laboratory for competing masculinities and status claims. Askari also felt secure in their longevity with the Schutztruppe and likely viewed the ruga-ruga merely as temporary reinforcements during violent crises and thus not a threat to their status.

Diverse column members necessarily found community with each other in the Schutztruppe field formations. They depended on each other for survival and differentiated themselves from those they viewed as *washenzi*—those East Africans they perceived as uncivilized, and those who were at war with the Germans. Weinberger's diary again offers an instructive example to highlight this dynamic. Passing through Ugogo in November 1892, Fourth Company commander Tom von Prince ordered local inhabitants to attend a shauri. When nobody showed up, the company set up camp "about six hundred [meters] from the Sultan's *tembe*," making a show of force to reinforce the point. Shortly thereafter, a "magician" appeared at the camp. With what Weinberger considered exceptional "cheekiness," the ritual specialist sprinkled the entrance to the camp with *dawa* (medicine). Weinberger, finding this behavior "too much," grabbed the man by his hair and beat him "mercilessly" with a kiboko "under the scornful laughter of our soldiers and porters."[63] Soon after this violent and humiliating episode, the "Sultan" appeared, offering goats, chickens, flour, and rice as gifts. As part of the Schutztruppe community, the soldiers and porters viewed the ritual specialist as an *mshenzi* outsider, deserving of the punishment he received from their NCO, as well as their ridicule, for daring to use local spiritual practices to engage the column. In such moments, whatever tensions existed within the columns waned in favor of a temporary expression of common interest and identification with Schutztruppe ideals regarding the defining characteristics of civilization and barbarism.[64]

One marker that starkly differentiated the askari from those they considered washenzi was their use of specific military technologies that gave them advantages over their opponents. A number of scholars have argued against simplistic explanations of colonial conquest as the natural result of European technological superiority alone.[65] Indeed, even Callwell cautioned against assuming that weapons superiority by itself would guarantee victory against adversaries in colonial wars.[66] After all, newer military technologies were being imported into Africa throughout the latter half of the nineteenth century, and colonial adversaries used them in defending themselves against colonial invasions.[67] Thus a colonial army's true advantages came from being able to deploy advanced technologies such as breechloading rifles, machine guns, artillery pieces, and communications devices in conjunction with tightly organized and highly mobile military units composed of trained, experienced African soldiers (see fig. 4).[68] Although their slow-moving logistics trains made them vulnerable, their organizational and financial capacity to assemble large contingents of porters allowed them to conduct field operations for significant stretches of time without needing to be tied to depots, harbors, or railways. The fusion of all these elements usually resulted in colonial armies' victories over their enemies, as well as widespread destruction in the areas at war.

FIGURE 4. Positioned just off a beach, with four machine guns pointing toward the sea, a unit of askari appears in full kit, prepared for war. The photo's original caption ("Askari Exercises") reveals that this was an askari machine-gun training exercise, perhaps in the last few years before World War I began, or shortly after its outbreak. Visible on the sleeves of a number of the soldiers in the image are insignia indicating achievement in marksmanship and skills as gunners. This photograph illustrates the level of trust Schutztruppe placed in the askari, and also reminds us of the independence with which askari units often operated. BArch, Bild 105-DOA5042/Walther Dobbertin. *Used with permission of the Bundesarchiv-Bildarchiv.*

That said, the Schutztruppe's use of breechloading rifles and Maxim guns often determined the outcomes of their violent encounters. Most notably, the use of these weapons reduced askari casualties while exponentially increasing enemy casualties, resulting in terribly lopsided Schutztruppe victories.[69] Single-shot breechloaders like the Mausers (M/71s) used by the askari gave the soldiers' longer firing ranges and better accuracy than most armies they encountered in East Africa, whose arsenals were generally limited to muskets, muzzleloaders, spears, and arrows.[70] The Maxim gun, usually operated by a German Schutztruppe member, added a new dimension of lethality to East African warfare, for it was "light enough for infantry to carry, it could be set up inconspicuously, and it spat out eleven bullets per second."[71] Armed with these weapons, the Schutztruppe killed thousands of people indiscriminately and with astonishing speed. In addition, their firepower communicated unequivocal messages about their intentions to conquer and subjugate the region, the futility of continued resistance, and the perceived inferiority of their victims.[72] In the Schutztruppe's racial logic, nearly everyone outside the campaign community were washenzi, and the askari's weapons afforded them enough distance from the targets of their violence that an imagined line between civilization and barbarism remained intact.[73] Recalling an askari attack on Maji Maji fighters near Kilosa in 1905, one witness vividly reported, "It was tragic, I tell you, because people fell down like flies. . . . People were massacred like ants."[74]

The machine gun's lethality set the stage for the askari's scorched-earth tactics, producing terror, devastation of land and livelihood, and massive loss of life for many Tanzanian peoples. Summarizing his feelings about the efficacy of the machine gun, Weinberger made a chilling note in his diary on 4 July 1895: "From directly nearby we receive fire from the bush. The Maxim gun does *everything*. 2 villages set on fire; jumbes [local leaders] of the surrounding areas hurry [to us] with gifts to show us their subjection."[75] The askari way of war made such scenes all too familiar across Tanzania. For those who survived such attacks, the image of the askari as perpetrators of mass violence was indelibly imprinted. This worked to the askari's advantage because it helped them perform the big-man roles to which they ultimately aspired.

The askari's use of such weapons and tactics also helped them overcome fortified or enclosed sites such as maboma or matembe.[76] While on campaign, askari frequently encountered fortified villages and structures, a particular defensive outgrowth of the nineteenth-century East African wars.[77] These diverse kinds of fortifications varied in defensibility and complexity according to regional construction styles, available materials, and the status and wealth of those who built and occupied them. Generally, assaults on fortified villages took place before sunrise, usually following a night march, so that defenders would be caught unawares and thus unable to properly mobilize a coordinated response. Artillery, Maxim guns, and sharpshooters targeted the corners of outer defensive walls to weaken them and prepare the way for designated askari to storm the site.[78] Once a fort's walls had been breached, soldiers began their assault accompanied by "hurrahs, trumpeting, and drumming and all possible means of intimidation."[79] Officers were advised to assemble their soldiers before allowing them to begin house-to-house searches in order to prevent them from being surprised by hidden defenders or setting up friendly fire incidents. In addition, soldiers were not to set the site on fire until they received orders to do so. This allowed adequate time for the askari to search out valuable provisions, including weapons, powder, and food, without overzealously or inadvertently destroying them. Ruga-ruga were to pursue and capture refugees and, in theory, to place them in the commanding officer's custody. Many, however, ended up being incorporated against their wills into soldiers' households. Once provisions had been seized, and the village cleared, officers gave the word to allow plundering to commence, during which soldiers and auxiliaries took "anything that could serve the soldiers' needs and anything else not riveted and nailed down."[80] Designated askari were then given orders to burn the village to the ground.[81] Wissmann viewed this pattern as absolutely essential to the Schutztruppe's ability to defeat its enemies and secure its own ability to continue fighting: "In Africa, the destruction of a fortified village is often the only possible means of punishment, because the natives will often leave the villages as soon as the assault begins, taking everything of any worth at all with them."[82] Schutztruppe officers thus authorized and condoned these practices as legitimate, and askari (and ruga-ruga) used them as opportunities for increasing their socioeconomic standing.

Although the Schutztruppe and other colonial armies enshrined these practices as the most effective means of conquering African lands, they had also shaped aspects of warfare in eastern Africa well before the German arrival. Fortified settlements and structures of all kinds had featured in eastern African defensive practices since at least the 1850s.[83] They spread across Tanzania in response to the creative and destructive tactics of men like Mirambo, who nurtured a "culture of fear" by using surprise and "attack by guile" to keep enemy forces off balance.[84] Mirambo also pioneered the "systematic destruction of villages by fire." By the 1880s he had become the "the region's foremost practitioner of siege warfare," with his troops highly skilled at overcoming fortifications.[85] His armies were also known for their high degree of mobility, their use of extreme physical violence, and their single-mindedness in striking population centers as opposed to rural areas. Like the askari later on, Mirambo's ruga-ruga used his quest for authority and control over Unyanyembe to secure for themselves the spoils of war and higher socioeconomic standing. This is not to argue for direct lines of continuity between the precolonial and colonial eras in Tanzania. Instead, I want to suggest that the patterns of warfare characteristic of the Schutztruppe askari manifested some of the same qualities as armies like Mirambo's. There is a good reason for this. As Richard Reid observes, both Mirambo and the Schutztruppe needed to control population centers in order to make credible claims to regional authority. Their ability to convincingly pull this off relied on creating the perception that they were "phantoms" with the ability to strike in multiple places at once, to ambush unsuspecting opponents, and to overcome enemy defenses through coordinated tactics.[86] In this sense, the askari way of war shared much with that of Mirambo's armies.

It is not that the soldier's methods changed substantially from one conflict to the next. Rather, the spectrum of violent conflicts askari fought between 1890 and 1918 produced a range of contexts within which askari acted on their aspirations to increase the markers of status they already had. In important ways, the differential scale, scope, and intensity of the wars the Schutztruppe fought determined the extent to which the askari viewed their relationships with the Germans as beneficial. In addition, each particular war's character, as manifested in Schutztruppe opponents' abilities to cause harm, how the Schutztruppe fared against their opponents, and the duration of any given conflict shaped how the askari viewed the desirability of belonging to the Schutztruppe. Fortunately for the Germans, over the long haul most askari generally found it better to belong to the Schutztruppe than not. Still, many of them also chose other options. The remainder of this chapter explores how the askari way of war connected with their willingness to fight under the different circumstances they encountered between 1890 and 1918.

THE HEHE WARS: CONTINGENT LOYALTIES

Recent scholarship allows us to connect the dots between Schutztruppe experiences in the conquest wars of the 1890s, through Maji Maji (1905–7), and into World War I (1914–18).[87] Considering these experiences from an askari perspective opens up possibilities for making the connections even clearer. In particular, by closely examining a moment when things went badly for the askari during war, or when they opted not to stay with the Schutztruppe, we gain further insight into what factors they valued as soldiers and aspiring big men.

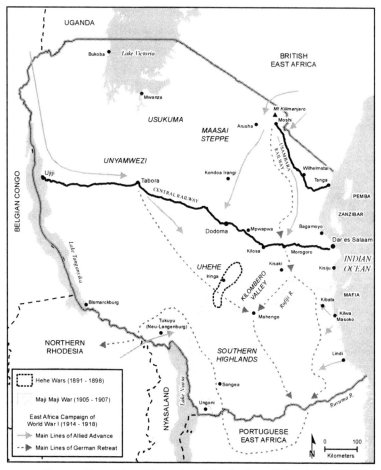

MAP 2. German East African Campaigns. *Map by Brian Edward Balsley, GISP*

The disastrous Zelewski expedition of 1891, in which Hehe soldiers loyal to Mkwawa nearly destroyed an entire Schutztruppe column, provides a good starting point for discerning the contingent nature of askari service in the Schutztruppe, for at least two reasons. First, this event occurred very early in the Schutztruppe's history and firmly established that some of their eastern African opponents had the capacity to cause them great harm. Second, it helps balance military historiography, which has often insisted on a heroic narrative about the askari's dependability and loyalty.

The demise of the Zelewski expedition has been extensively analyzed elsewhere, so a short summary suffices here.[88] Soon after defeating the coastal rebellion that had served as the Wissmanntruppe's founding moment, Wissmann ordered a captain named Emil von Zelewski to lead a column into the southern highlands to militarily engage the Hehe, judged the next major polity in need of subjugation. Mkwawa, the Hehe leader, received warning from his intelligence agents of Zelewski's advance from Kilwa.[89] This advance warning enabled Mkwawa's brother, Mpangile, to assemble an army of three to five thousand men. Mpangile's army ambushed the Zelewski column on 17 August 1891, killing some five hundred soldiers, porters, and Europeans (including Zelewski), and capturing numerous weapons, including two machine guns and three hundred rifles.[90] One-fifth of the Schutztruppe's manpower had been wiped out in one morning.[91] Nearly the entire company of Shangaan troops under Zelewski's command died in the attack. Zelewski had wholly underestimated Hehe capabilities, famously remarking, "The fellows haven't even got guns, just shields and spears."[92] Zelewski had such confidence in the Hehe's inability to truly threaten his column that he ordered his lieutenant, Tom von Prince, to take his company of "Zulus" back to the coast, thereby foreclosing any possibility of reinforcement.[93] Having also become accustomed to conducting warfare against fortified positions, Zelewski neglected to deploy patrols or to protect the column's flanks. The column's destruction undid the Schutztruppe's sense of invulnerability, and ignited a strong desire for vengeance among young officers like Tom von Prince. In addition, it emboldened some Tanzanian leaders to consider military confrontation instead of political negotiation or accommodation as a viable option against the encroaching Germans.[94] The result was a decade-long escalation and expansion of violence between the Schutztruppe, the Hehe, and their respective allies.

The Zelewski catastrophe had an immediate impact on some rank-and-file soldiers' willingness to fight, even as it inspired a burning desire for revenge in German officers and NCOs.[95] After marching back to the coast and learning the news of the expedition's near annihilation, Tom von Prince received orders to make ready for a "reconnaissance" expedition to Mpwapwa, which seemed to be the next likely Hehe target.[96] Prince noted that "Sudanese and native" troops stationed in Bagamoyo had heard about the destruction of Zelewski's column and could not be "inspired" to participate in this mission. Prince's clear affection for his company of Shangaan soldiers almost certainly influenced his negative depiction of the Bagamoyo contingent. Still, the constant punitive expeditions and the hardships involved began to take a toll on the Shangaan soldiers as well. Much to Prince's dismay, in late June 1892 a contingent of nine Shangaan askari deserted his column. Prince noted that they, along with many other askari, had developed a healthy fear of the Hehe's fighting abilities. The deaths of their fellow Shangaan soldiers in the Zelewski expedition had shaken them. Moreover, their contracts were close to expiring, and most had no intention of staying in German East Africa after their contract periods ended.[97] Disciplinary problems also manifested when a new commander, Brüning, attempted to get his soldiers underway one morning.[98] Instead of obeying Brüning's repeated orders to stand at attention, the Shangaan soldiers chanted in increasingly loud and "worrisome" tones, "We want to go home."[99] Prince intervened and restored order, and the soldiers undertook the expedition without further incident. Still, their behavior illustrates their attachment to a particular commander—Prince—and their unwillingness to perform for an officer whom they did not trust, particularly in light of privations and dangers they had experienced in over a year's worth of campaigning against the Hehe. Prince's memoir suggests that he gained the trust of his Shangaan soldiers through small but meaningful gestures, such as appreciating their forms of musical expression or assisting them in sorting out administrative and financial issues.[100] This does not rule out the strong possibility that some askari also feared what their commanders would do to them if they disobeyed orders or otherwise acted out. But it does suggest that askari discerned between strong or weak leadership qualities and responded to their officers based on these assessments.

While it is true that the Schutztruppe rarely experienced ruinous acts of indiscipline among its soldiers, askari nonetheless had limits to what they would tolerate from their commanders and campaign conditions. Askari viewed their officers not as interchangeable parts in a military machine but as their personal patrons. In other words, askari tended to see their officers as men who bore responsibility for their well-being, broadly construed. Wissmann believed that he had worked out a formula for keeping the askari in good spirits and combat ready, but not all officers followed his advice.[101] In another instance of early indiscipline in the Schutztruppe, in January 1895 a company of Sudanese soldiers on their way back to their garrison on Lake Malawi went on strike against their officers, threatening to shoot them.[102] They cited "cruel treatment" as grounds for the strike. For example, they complained against their commander's decision to sentence one of their comrades to work on a chain gang alongside "base criminals," an affront to his status as a Sudanese askari.[103] The soldiers demanded to present their complaints against company leader Paul Fromm to Schutztruppe commander and military governor Friedrich Freiherr von Schele in Dar es Salaam—the man they viewed as their true commander. Manyema soldiers joined the Sudanese askari in their protest the next day. Recognizing that failure to address their concerns promptly might stir anger among other Sudanese companies operating nearby, Fromm ordered Sergeant Weinberger to escort the soldiers to the coast to air their grievances to Schele. In contrast to their expressed disdain for Fromm and his abusive methods, they supposedly declared their loyalty to Weinberger, saying, "We will only go with you, or if you do not want us, then we will leave."[104] After Weinberger's company arrived at the coast, Schele admonished the troops for not following official procedures in making complaints against their superiors but acknowledged their right to register their complaints to him as the highest Schutztruppe authority. He warned them that further disobedience would not be tolerated. The "ringleaders" were sent back to Egypt, and the rest of the company was placed under a new commander.[105] These early instances of askari disobedience stemmed from a combination of frustrations with leaders perceived as unfit for command, the often harsh conditions of campaign life, and the unsurprising growing pains of the young Schutztruppe organization. By the time of the start of the Maji Maji war, in 1905, many of the problems that characterized the early years of the Schutztruppe had been overcome by longevity and experience among the askari and their officers, more practical recruitment patterns, and the defeat of most polities that might have posed a serious challenge to Schutztruppe authority.

MAJI MAJI: WAR AS OPPORTUNITY

Mkwawa's final defeat, in July 1898, spelled the end of resistance in Uhehe, but numerous patrols, expeditions, and battles waged to assert control of different parts of German East Africa continued through 1903. The official Schutztruppe history lists no engagements for 1904 and the first half of 1905.[106] Then, in July 1905, the war that later came to be known as Maji Maji began in a southeastern region of German East Africa, between Kilwa and the Rufiji River. It eventually encompassed some hundred and fifty thousand square kilometers of German East Africa. In late July 1905, aggrieved residents of the region, motivated in part by prophetic pronouncements by a local ritual practitioner named Kinjikitile, organized themselves in opposition to colonial interests.[107] When the worst of the fighting ended in 1906, some three hundred thousand Africans had died through the combined effects of combat, massive famine, and rampant disease.[108] An unknowable number of others experienced loss of livelihood, capture and imprisonment, and long-term disruption of community and family life caused by famine and low birthrates in the war's aftermath.

Maji Maji had multiple and complex local origins.[109] Excessive colonial demands for labor and taxes; interference in local practices of trade, cultivation, and exploitation of forest resources; and intervention in local political practices contributed to frustration and anger across diverse East African populations and regions. Many who lived in the southeastern and southern highlands regions of Tanzania realized the extent to which illegitimate and exploitative colonial economic and political practices, if allowed to continue unchecked, would irrevocably alter their livelihoods, political autonomy, and ability to provide for households. Some also began to actively contemplate and plan the overthrow of colonial rule. Representatives of the colonial state, including European missionaries, soldiers, and African employees and allies of the colonial state became the targets of this new resolve to use violence to change the colonial order.

This heightened and widespread anger over colonial injustices converged with a sharp rise in the numbers of diverse peoples who participated in protective and restorative rituals involving the use of consecrated water (*maji*). Such rituals had been features of everyday life in southeastern Tanzania and elsewhere, where they were used to preserve the health of the land and to ward off danger. As historian Thaddeus Sunseri puts it, maji was one among several "medicines disbursed by spirit mediums in the greater Rufiji basin on the eve of the uprising [that] were intended primarily to protect crops, bring rain or otherwise ensure a good harvest."[110] The maji rituals that accompanied the move to war in 1905 emerged out of these regional traditions. The prophet Kinjikitile, and others who heard his message and helped spread it, preached that the maji would protect believers from European soldiers' bullets. As messengers (*hongo*) spread the word of the maji's professed efficacy across Matumbi and beyond, some who heard the message (also called *hongo*) took up arms against colonial agents and symbols.[111] Although the first reported act of war was the uprooting of cotton plants at a Matumbi plantation, rebels soon followed this symbolic act in August and September 1905 with armed attacks against Europeans, their African employees, and their forts. During this period, Maji Maji rebels killed a Catholic bishop and laid siege to the German boma at Mahenge. These initial successes against colonial targets caught German officials and their soldiers by surprise, calling to mind the destruction of the Zelewski expedition in 1891. Schutztruppe columns were vulnerable to the rebels' early use of guerrilla-style tactics, using concealment, deception, and harassment to unsettle Schutztruppe efforts to engage in set-piece battles.[112] The Germans also were psychologically disadvantaged by their complete inability to comprehend the scope or purposes behind the insurgency. Additional troops, auxiliaries, and equipment arrived from Germany, Eritrea, and elsewhere to reinforce the Schutztruppe in October 1905.

From this point on, the Schutztruppe sought to regain the initiative by launching a deadly new phase of the war. They organized the assembled troops into three columns, which began marching inland from their coastal bases along separate routes to the southern region. As in the conquest wars of the 1890s, the columns conducted numerous expeditions against the rebels. By the end of October, Schutztruppe officers had concluded that only scorched-earth tactics—an "alliance with hunger"—would give them the necessary edge to defeat the rebels quickly.[113] Maji Maji fighters continued to attack the columns, sometimes quite brazenly, but the Schutztruppe's machine guns caused horrible casualties that forced them to retreat. In late November 1905, German machine guns forced some two thousand Maji Maji soldiers to retreat during "the greatest pitched battle of the war" near Kibata in the Kilombero valley. Three hundred Maji Maji fighters were killed.[114] Thereafter, askari terror tactics shifted the war's momentum decisively to the Schutztruppe.

The askari returned to their way of war with zest, reducing much of the southern half of German East Africa to wasteland and causing horrendous casualty rates and mass destruction of property and livelihoods for the region's populations. Schutztruppe officers initially worried that if the rebellion spread to the central steppe or the Great Lakes region, the presence of so many Nyamwezi, Sukuma, and other locally recruited askari in their ranks would result in divided loyalties and compromised military effectiveness. Their worries proved unfounded. First, the shock of the rebels' initial successes against the Schutztruppe provided motivation for the soldiers to track down, arrest, and execute their attackers and anyone else perceived to be involved in the insurgency. The askari became deeply frustrated with the rebels' abilities to escape and hide, as well as what one Schutztruppe officer labeled the "age-old scheme of African people" to abandon their villages and go into hiding in the wilderness, taking their goods and livestock with them. When askari arrived in these empty villages, they found "huts without supplies, stalls without domesticated animals," which "made it difficult for a large company to provision itself."[115] By denying the askari the ability to seize useful supplies, to capture laborers, or to benefit from war spoils, the villagers thus denied them the usual rewards of attacking villages. Askari almost certainly viewed these denials not just as blows to their ability to prosecute their way of war but also as affronts to their prestige.

Enraged by this cycle of chasing rebels only for them to disappear into the bush, and the recurring frustration of finding villages devoid of people and provisions, askari conducted a deliberate terror campaign as they marched into the southern highlands.[116] In a familiar pattern taken to greater dimensions, they burned villages, fields, and food storage huts to the ground. The deaths of individual askari at the hands of Maji Maji fighters stoked the soldiers' rage. Their counterinsurgency tactics thus encompassed a desire for revenge against their *"shenzi"* enemies, and simultaneously communicated the Schutztruppe's message that restoring the colonial order justified their use of exterminatory violence. The askari's infamous brutality during Maji Maji was at least partly an expression of anger and frustration at being challenged and sometimes outdone by soldiers they considered militarily inferior, as well as by the East African civilians, whom they viewed as generally subordinate in their social station and inferior in their humanity.[117]

Still, in this war as in others, the askari way of war created opportunities for them to bolster their status claims and to position themselves for the postwar period. As the Schutztruppe gained momentum against Maji Maji insurgents at the end of 1905, askari and Schutztruppe auxiliaries took advantage of the devastation caused by war to increase their wealth in people, goods, and livestock. Thousands of women from the southern highlands were taken prisoner by askari or auxiliaries, and many were forcibly incorporated into Schutztruppe households, exchanged into local slaving networks, or forced to labor for the colonial government raising crops.[118] Some women surrendered to the Germans in order to escape conditions they considered worse than life with the askari.[119] As in the Schutztruppe's past wars, livestock seizures also continued to be a standard method of increasing the size of government herds, while simultaneously diminishing Schutztruppe enemies' wealth, sources of nourishment, and morale.[120]

In a few cases, the colonial government made some restitution for the damage its army caused, especially for those who demonstrated "loyal service" to the Germans.[121] But the vast majority of Tanzanians who lost property, crops, or livestock during the war never received compensation. Interestingly, some askari and ex-askari successfully filed claims against the colonial government for losses incurred during the war.[122] In this way, Schutztruppe soldiers and allies who lost material goods during the war were at least partly restored to their former prosperity at a time when most people around them, especially in the southern highlands, were destitute. The Schutztruppe also made arrangements for askari wives to receive a portion of their husbands' pay while the troops were on campaign, allowing for askari households to continue functioning despite their absences.[123] Askari continued to receive their pay on time, and in some cases they received additional monetary rewards for exemplary performances during wartime.[124] Schutztruppe leadership prioritized troop provisioning, so that askari did not go without food for very long despite the desperate conditions they created for others as they marched through the southern highlands. Thus, askari households collectively emerged from the war better positioned in socioeconomic terms than many of their former competitors, and certainly better than most Tanzanians from the southern regions, whose lives changed for the worse during and after Maji Maji.

WORLD WAR I: UNMAKING THE ASKARI

When World War I began in East Africa, in 1914, the peoples of the southern highlands were just beginning to recover from the staggering effects of famine and disease that resulted from Schutztruppe actions during Maji Maji.[125] The Schutztruppe's scorched-earth policy disrupted crop cycles—a problem exacerbated by the masses of people fleeing the askari and auxiliaries. Areas became underpopulated, causing labor shortages. Land previously under cultivation fell to wild vegetation and animals. A drought in 1913 exacerbated these existing difficulties of raising subsistence crops. During World War I, this region again became an epicenter of military destruction with dire consequences for southeastern African populations.

World War I in East Africa lasted far longer than anyone anticipated at its outset and consequently caused terrible hardships. Lettow-Vorbeck's purpose at the beginning of the war was to force the Allies to commit resources to the East African theater so that they could not be used in Europe. In this objective he was largely successful. Early Schutztruppe victories against British forces in battles at Tanga and around Kilimanjaro in the initial phase of the war kept troop morale high. The colonial government continued to function until 1916, most notably allowing for the minting of money so that troops could be paid. But as the war dragged on, and Allied strength became more concentrated in German East Africa, the Schutztruppe's military capacity worsened significantly. The colonial capital, Dar es Salaam, fell to the British in 1916, and the temporary capital at Tabora also fell to the Belgians later that year. A coastal blockade closed off most possibilities for the Schutztruppe to receive supplies from outside, so that they increasingly depended on supplies and equipment captured from their enemies following battles. Between late 1916 and November 1918, Lettow-Vorbeck whittled down his last remaining column to enhance its mobility as it assembled south of the Rovuma River in preparation for crossing into Portuguese East Africa (Mozambique) to escape Allied pursuit and capture. For the remainder of the war, the Schutztruppe continued living off the land, also raiding Portuguese colonial maboma for goods when possible. The Allies pursued them through southeastern Africa until Lettow-Vorbeck's surrender, in November 1918, in Northern Rhodesia (present-day Zambia). As in 1905 and 1906, the undersupplied Schutztruppe committed many abuses, although Allied armies, struggling to provision their own columns, similarly contributed to stripping the region of provisions and manpower.

Lettow-Vorbeck's single-mindedness in pursuing this strategy caused grave suffering for many East Africans. As previously noted, civilians in the southern half of German East Africa endured the worst consequences of multiple armies attempting to live off the land as they marched through an already damaged region. The result was long-lasting famine and pandemic that affected southeastern Africa long after the war's end, in November 1918. Inside the armies, losses were also significant. For example, both the Schutztruppe and the Allied forces used thousands of under- or uncompensated porters to transport their supplies and equipment, but continual shortages of provisions for such massive columns made them especially vulnerable to malnutrition, disease, and exhaustion. Soldiers also experienced these crises. Unlike most porters and other column members, however, the askari had firearms at their disposal, giving them the ability to take supplies by force, or to efficiently hunt for game, helping them avoid hunger.

The stresses and privations of the second half of the East Africa campaign placed the askari in a qualitatively different collective position from that of the post–Maji Maji era. Unlike the circumstances of Maji Maji, in which many askari benefited from the devastation they caused in the southern highlands, there were only limited opportunities during World War I to accrue additional wealth, or even to protect their prewar status. A number of factors contributed to the Schutztruppe's waning credibility in backing their soldiers' status claims. After 1916 soldiers stopped receiving pay because the government could no longer mint money. Widespread scarcity made it difficult to find even basic provisions, let alone to commandeer herds of livestock or large stores of other goods. After all, anything they took also had to be transported, and finding able-bodied porters became increasingly difficult in the second half of the campaign. The Allied armies' pursuit of the Schutztruppe also detracted from the askari's previous distinction as the only uniformed military operating in the region. In fact, as the Schutztruppe's situation worsened, in 1917 and 1918, a number of askari deserted the Germans and went over to the King's African Rifles because they perceived the British army as a place that might better position them for a postwar sociopolitical landscape. Finally, the constant forced marches the Schutztruppe undertook in the last half of the war took a toll on askari abilities to maintain family units and further undermined their abilities to demonstrate their status as householders and big men.

Still, some of them maintained and even increased their wealth in people after 1916. For example, to compensate for their manpower losses, the Schutztruppe began forcibly conscripting young men living in the regions through which they marched. Some of these conscripts became askariboys, and thus also part of askari households and the larger campaign communities. Similarly, it seems clear that the askari continued to incorporate women and children into the columns even under the campaign's most dire circumstances, and sometimes even against their officers' orders.[126] This element of the askari way of war, which had been so central to their self-identities from the founding moments of the Schutztruppe, remained so for those who surrendered with Lettow-Vorbeck in November 1918. Schutztruppe officers' efforts to reduce numbers of noncombatants in the columns met with resistance from the askari and their dependents because separation from the column also meant socioeconomic insecurity. Moreover, officers understood that removal of dependents from the columns would cause logistical difficulties by reducing the amount of labor available for camp duties and porterage. They also knew that failure to accommodate the askari on this issue might result in serious morale problems and indiscipline, which they did not want to risk, given their precarious military position (see fig. 5).

Militarily, too, the askari were in a different position from earlier combat experiences. Their opponents in the British, Belgian, and South African colonial armies typically had levels of training and experience in colonial warfare that differed from the styles used by their previous East African opponents, as in the Hehe wars or Maji Maji. For one thing, soldiers in the Allied colonial armies received similar training as the Schutztruppe askari. They wore similar uniforms and

FIGURE 5. This famous photograph, entitled *Kriegssafari 1914*, vividly captures a foundational element of the askari way of war. It shows a long column of askari on the march through a steppe landscape, with European officers in front riding mules. Porters and dependents of column members walk behind the askari, carrying the column's supplies and equipment. The photo's title combines German and Kiswahili, rendering a word that means something like "war journey." Askari and other column members referred to such marches as *safari ya Bwana Lettow* (Mr. Lettow's journeys). This photo has become the iconic representation of the East African campaign of World War I, but it also helps us imagine how the *Schutztruppe* went to war throughout the German colonial era in East Africa. BArch, Bild 105-DOA0966/ Walther Dobbertin. *Used with permission of the Bundesarchiv-Bildarchiv.*

operated within similar disciplinary regimes. Allied armies were better prepared to resupply their troops' equipment, and the equipment they used was often technologically superior to that of the Schutztruppe. Technological superiority did not guarantee superior performance in battle, and in fact the simplicity of the Schutztruppe's weapons helped the askari remain mobile and self-sufficient. But it enhanced the Allies' advantages in manpower and logistical flexibility in 1917 and 1918.

Perhaps the most important difference between the askari experience of World War I and those of previous wars was that the East African campaign laid bare their dependence on the survival of German colonial rule. At no other time in the Schutztruppe's short history had the askari experienced such long-term hardships or sustained challenges to their positions as big men in German East Africa. The askari who surrendered with Lettow-Vorbeck in November 1918 probably remained with him because they believed that path to be the most viable option for protecting their interests in a rapidly changing geopolitical environment. After 1916 they surely understood that their previous status roles as Schutztruppe askari were in jeopardy, but their only real alternative was desertion, either to try to try and make it on their own or to throw in their lot with the British. Either way, such acts severed the relationship between the Schutztruppe and the deserting askari. The sharp rise in askari desertions after 1916 bespeaks their recognition that the Germans were no longer credible as long-term patrons. Their collective postwar socioeconomic decline resulted from their inability, under British rule, to reclaim the status they had enjoyed and exploited under German rule.

POSTWAR PHANTOMS: THE DEMISE OF THE SCHUTZTRUPPE ASKARI

The askari way of war proved militarily effective in tying up Allied resources in East Africa for over four years. But whereas in previous conflicts the askari way of war had often yielded economic or status benefits for its practitioners, the East African campaign was different. Askari who survived World War I did not emerge from the experience as big men. In fact, it appears that most ex-Schutztruppe askari lived out marginalized, even destitute, existences. Surviving askari who could prove their identities as ex-Schutztruppe members received back pay, pensions, and charitable gifts from the German government and private citizens between 1918 and the early 1960s.[127] These efforts helped the askari and their families survive in political environments—the British mandate, then independent Tanganyika/Tanzania—where they had lost any basis for claims to authority or status. After the war, they lived together in enclaves in Tanga, Dar es Salaam, Iringa, and the Kilimanjaro area. They seem not to have remained an identifiable pan-regional interest group in the mode of francophone and anglophone colonial veterans' organizations that emerged following World War II. As a collective of ex-soldiers, their trail in the historical record largely fades after 1919, although disparate individual histories have somewhat illuminated a range of postwar askari experiences.[128]

One reason their visibility as a collective decreased so substantially after World War I was that they no longer had roles to play in successor states' performances of authority and dominance. The prestige and autonomy they had enjoyed as Schutztruppe members dissipated as soon as the British became the new colonial power. The next chapter examines the askari beyond their soldiering roles, as everyday practitioners of colonialism in German East Africa, in order to sketch the full extent of what they lost after 1918.

4 ꙮ Station Life

JUHANI KOPONEN has noted that "colonialism . . . created spatial structures of its own; once created, these began to influence and condition people's action, while at the same time being reproduced by means of the same action."[1] Koponen's observation encapsulates how the military stations, or maboma, enabled a range of processes that resulted in the making of local colonial communities. For the askari, their kin and dependents, and others, the maboma were the militarized spaces that defined their professional lives, as well as the domestic labor and leisure spaces that completed their personal lives. Contrary to past portrayals of the askari as isolated from surrounding communities in German East Africa, I argue that they were connected in various ways to communities outside the maboma where they lived and worked. In fact, their local connectedness stands out as a specific feature of early colonial state formation processes, which have not been analyzed to the same extent as later processes. In addition to the intermediary roles of their work lives, which included military and policing duties, askari's off-duty lives incorporated meaningful economic and socio-religious interests and activities that tied more and more people to the colonial state and the local cultures being produced around the maboma. Many of these ties were certainly fleeting, tenuous, or even involuntary, but they exposed people to colonial sensibilities and practices in lasting ways.

Askari communities developed in conjunction with, and in proximity to, the maboma. Askari homes and neighborhoods, referred to as askari villages, were usually situated close to the maboma, if not actually within the maboma walls. Proximity between the maboma and the askari villages served colonial interests by ensuring that soldiers could respond quickly to military emergencies. And living in or near the colonial centers afforded the soldiers' household members new kinds of socioeconomic opportunities. At the same time, outsiders came to the maboma for many reasons, some in search of ways to improve their life circumstances through work or trade, some because colonial agents compelled them to appear at the maboma for judicial business, some out of curiosity or for entertainment. Whatever importance the maboma had as colonial centers came from this mix of inhabitants and interlopers who brought them to life each day.

A close look at the fixed sites where the askari and their community members lived and worked illustrates how boma life continually enacted and reenacted everyday colonialism in German East Africa.[2] Askari communities, like other kinds of communities, were constantly "coming into being," fluctuating in their details, but also retaining identifiers that expressed belonging and set them apart from others.[3] The boma communities thus expressed both colonial authority and colonial ambivalences about that authority.

Like other Kiswahili words German colonial authorities appropriated to express everyday concepts, the word *boma* accommodated a variety of usages in the East African context. East African peoples used the term to refer to many different kinds of enclosures, including those meant to protect livestock, to indicate the boundaries of large domestic compounds, or to fortify villages against military attacks. German colonizers initially used the term to refer to the fortresses they built or occupied to instantiate their military presence. Later, as this military presence became the basis for practices of governance and state making, *boma* began to connote not just the actual fortress structure at most military stations but also the complex of structures that grew up around the fortress, which eventually came to resemble what we might think of today as a military base.

The German colonial maboma served mainly as military strongholds and administrative centers, and they came to include many other functions as they became more entrenched and widespread throughout the colony. In the early years of establishing their authority, colonial officials often occupied and inhabited existing structures that then doubled as administrative spaces for the fledgling government. For example, in May 1890, during the coastal war, Wissmann began building a permanent station at Kilwa, on the southern coast. He designated four existing Arab stone houses on the beach to be "renovat[ed] and exten[ded]" to create the basis for a permanent station, and construction of the "provisional fortress" proceeded quickly.[4] The Kilwa fortifications allowed the Schutztruppe to defend the site with limited manpower and freed the bulk of the unit stationed there to march inland to fight the Hehe, who took up arms against the Germans beginning in 1891.[5] The Schutztruppe also purposely destroyed old maboma and built new forts on top of the old sites, which reinforced both the idea of a permanent Schutztruppe presence and the imprudence of challenging German military strength.[6] These processes of building maboma and stations as bases for further military expeditions continued throughout the 1890s as the Schutztruppe presence expanded throughout German East Africa.

After the coastal war of 1889–90, officers began choosing the locations of the military stations more deliberately, with an eye to guarding against the unnerving possibility of a colonywide rebellion. The network of garrisons that took shape throughout the 1890s was designed to protect the areas they considered critical to controlling the colony's most valuable economic and geopolitical sites—caravan routes, lakes, mountain regions, and later, railways. Throughout the colonial period, the military garrisons doubled as administrative centers and over time came to coincide with the civil districts set up to administer the huge territory. A major shift—at least on paper—from military to civilian administration of the colony's districts occurred after the Maji Maji war of 1905–7, when Colonial Secretary Bernhard Dernburg determined that the Schutztruppe had much to answer for in provoking the devastating conflict. But despite real efforts to expunge military influence from senior leadership positions in the districts, "the acute lack of civilian personnel . . . led to military officers continuing to perform administrative and political functions."[7] More often than not, top colonial officials in the districts were either current or former Schutztruppe members. Moreover, veteran askari residences dotted the lands around the stations, extending the government's reach into communities that otherwise would have had only tenuous connections to the maboma.

Schutztruppe founder Hermann von Wissmann had learned from experience the importance of officers exercising great care in siting

MAP 3. German East African Administration. *Map by Brian Edward Balsley, GISP*

military stations and camps.[8] This meant not only placing the stations in strategically useful positions but also successfully navigating local political and social relations to accommodate Schutztruppe military needs. In addition, the sites had to be able to accommodate the living-space needs of European and African employees using "what the wilderness offered" in the way of available building materials and on a limited budget.[9] To that end, askari helped construct the maboma and surrounding buildings when they were not on campaign, carrying out colonial duties, or otherwise engaged.[10] African laborers recruited from surrounding areas, usually through local leaders allied with the Schutztruppe, comprised the bulk of the labor forces that built the maboma, however. In design and execution, the maboma blended German ideals of order and security with African uses of space and materials.

Each of the stations (of which there were thirty in 1903) differed in layout and composition, but they also shared many common features.[11] A colonial judge described them as haphazardly and "artlessly" built according to "purpose and need," a "motley" collection of old and new.[12] Before the Germans arrived, East Africans had used *boma* to refer to many different kinds of enclosure, from "the most simple hedge [built] to protect a piece of land to the impregnable walling-in of a village."[13] European explorers and company agents began using the term in the 1870s and 1880s, calling their camps and stations *maboma* even before the formation of the Wissmanntruppe. During the military conquest of the interior, Schutztruppe units regularly faced such barricades and defensive structures.[14] Officers often described African fortifications and military practices with some derision, since they rarely reflected German security sensibilities or fortress architecture. Still, their experiences of fighting against fortified villages in the 1890s revealed to them the value of integrating local building styles and materials into their defensive plans.

The maboma were built to defend against what Schutztruppe personnel perceived to be the primary features of East African styles of warfare. Assuming that "the natives of our tropical colonies are not acquainted with a proper siege" and that "their preferred fighting style is, since time immemorial, the raid," the Schutztruppe built maboma to withstand these anticipated styles of warfare.[15] As the first layer of defense, they constructed barriers made of thorny euphorbia branches.[16] Given time and resources to construct more elaborate rings of defenses, laborers built palisades constructed from long, narrow tree trunks bound tightly together, sometimes two to three layers deep, then entrenched in ditches and reinforced with additional trees and branches. These techniques placed formidable obstacles in the way of soldiers' storming the boma and also helped defend against incoming arrows, bullets, and other projectiles. "Accidental" holes left in the palisades during construction functioned as loopholes for firing against attackers.[17]

The idealized Schutztruppe vision of how a boma should be built grew out of German military aesthetics and self-understanding, as well as practical assessments of how to defend colonial space and interests.

Made of whitewashed stone, clay, or brick, one observer described a typical boma, located at Moshi, as resembling a "small knight's castle."[18] The need for defensibility against potentially overwhelming numbers of soldiers with only minimal manpower dictated each fortress's size. In fact, this imperative sometimes trumped others, such as the racist "hygienic" considerations that called for the spatial separation of European and African housing within the maboma.[19] Ideally, each fortress was square, with bastions set up at two diagonal points to create a zone of enfilading fire. A two-hundred-meter field of fire was supposed to be left open around the fortress, and laborers cleared the land around the maboma for that purpose. The maboma sometimes also incorporated special redoubts to improve defensibility and to protect weapons, munitions, and provisions.[20]

In graphic representations and official documents, German colonial officials depicted the maboma as strictly demarcated and orderly sites that reflected their desires for military and administrative control over German East Africa. Of course, these idealized renditions of the stations could not capture the life that made them into dynamic centers of colonial rule, as well as places where the day-to-day dramas of familial relationships often took center stage. A Sunday afternoon in a boma is described in a colonial memoir as peaceful and routine:

> Deep quiet reigns over the boma courtyard. In front of the gate stands the bored guard, in the guards' room[,] cigarette-smoking askari. Storehouse and office rooms are closed today. [One] side of the fortress forms the European living quarters, [another side] the prisoners' room. We all lived together that way in harmony. Nothing disturbed the pleasantness. And that is how one lived on all stations in German East Africa.[21]

Suddenly, a woman's shouting disturbed the quiet scene. The senior askari's (shaush's) wife, having apparently learned of a recently issued government order prohibiting the flogging of women, decided to test the system. She began behaving "wildly," flailing about and resisting all attempts to restrain her. Her husband, a shaush named Ramassan, had her arrested and confined in the boma. He viewed the government order with contempt, seeing it as an affront to household gender hierarchies and even as a threat to the colonial order itself.[22] She continued shouting throughout the day, and all efforts to calm her failed.

To escape the racket, the German officer in charge of the boma, Hermann von Bengerstorf, left to take a walk, and when he returned, the fort had returned to its peaceful state. But as soon as the bibi detected his return she resumed shouting.[23] Tired of her yelling, he ordered an ombasha to release her. The officer then described her actions: "The African suffragette strode proudly across the courtyard, looked over at [his] veranda, and smiled. Goodbye, mister! [she said]."[24] Realizing that he had been "tricked" by the shaush's wife into participating in a performance meant to ridicule her husband and all other men at the station for their newly imposed punitive impotence, Bengerstorf wryly remarked, "A new era had dawned. I comforted myself with the thought: 'The cleverest one gives in.'"[25]

In this anecdote, the boma's "immense strength" contrasts sharply with the inability of its male agents to regulate the askari wife's behavior. She disrupted their routines simply by refusing to cooperate. To restore order to the boma, they had to accommodate her, however briefly. The anecdote thus discourages facile acceptance of German portrayals of control over life in the maboma and, by extension, life in the colony. It helps us understand the maboma beyond their idealized official purposes. In the boma, official concerns easily spilled over into domestic ones, and vice versa.[26] German and African colonial personnel lived in the maboma, but these spaces also included prisons, storage spaces, offices, and open courtyards where diverse social interactions occurred. Reconstructing the texture of everyday life in, around, and between the military stations shows the fluidity between official "colonized" spaces like the maboma and external spaces that the colonial state wanted to claim. Movement back and forth across the maboma's boundaries by colonial agents, family members, and others exposed a growing dependence between the colonial centers and surrounding local economies, especially as German colonialism became entrenched across more territory through the 1890s. In effect, the maboma became nodes that aided in the consolidation of colonial rule. The maboma and the askari embodied colonial military might, reminding everyone of the stations' essential purpose—protection and expansion of colonial interests. Yet at the same time, they generated a range of economic, social, and political opportunities for many people, including the askari and their dependents, which activated everyday colonialism.[27]

The above anecdote also again illustrates women's constitutive place in the making of askari, and indeed, Schutztruppe masculinities. The woman's behavior in the anecdote is depicted alternately as hysterical, then clever, and even subversive, on that Sunday afternoon in the boma. Most striking though, is that her acts challenged the shaush's domestic authority, at the same time undermining military order and making it all appear fragile, at least for a moment.

She was not alone in acting in small ways to protect her interests. In turn, she exposed the outward appearance of Schutztruppe order as being a bit flimsier than one might guess. As in the campaign communities (see chapter 3), askari women in garrison performed myriad practical and symbolic roles that bring the Schutztruppe's gender order into sharp analytical relief. Their everyday activities and concerns emerge in surprising ways from the sources, in large measure because Schutztruppe officers seemed to spend considerable administrative time sorting out askari family affairs. Questions around the soldiers' pay, for example, appeared to absorb the officers' attention. While soldiers were on expeditions, "lawful" wives were allowed to draw portions of their husbands' pay. In order to make such claims, the wives had to present an identification document (*Frauenteilzahlungsausweis*) to bursary officials.[28] Still, officials seemed wary of fraudulent requests for allotments of askari pay.[29] Askari women also sometimes lodged complaints against soldiers for failing to provide money to them while away on expeditions. In at least one case, a colonial official in Urundi gave some of his own money to two askari women who came to him with complaints about their husbands' irresponsibility. He wrote to the soldiers' commander asking him to compel them to reimburse his money and to "take care of their wives."[30] At Iringa, an askari wife named Faida complained to Major Ernst Nigmann that her askari husband, Abdu, "an inveterate drunkard" but a fine soldier, was not bringing home his "full pay" as a result of military disciplinary action being taken against him for bad behavior.[31] In all these instances, we may assume that askari women acted to provide for their families while the askari were away. Perhaps some of them saw the absence of the soldiers as an opportunity to access money without their husbands' oversight. Whatever the reasons behind their actions, they indicate that Schutztruppe officers took them and their claims seriously. On the one hand, this earnestness in hearing out women's complaints can be interpreted as evidence that they viewed the women's presence as vital to the army's ability to function. On the other hand, though, the women's grievances focused attention on the askari's failings as heads of household and as men. While this kind of negative framing meshed with German racial thinking that positioned askari (and all African men) as children in need of strong guidance from their white leaders, it also threatened the military masculinity that the Schutztruppe so jealously cultivated.

Askari household stability also mattered greatly to colonial officials. Their interventions in domestic disputes allow us to see askari wives in a variety of encounters that again give the lie to the Schutztruppe's carefully cultivated picture of order in the maboma. A singular archival find affords us a rare glimpse of just how messy askari domestic arrangements could be. In January 1915, Juma bin Abdallah, an askari of the Eighteenth Feldkompanie in Dar es Salaam, appeared in the district court (*Bezirksgericht*) of Dar es Salaam to accuse a thirty-three-year-old businessman named Max Miersen, also of Dar es Salaam, of attempting to rape his wife, Habiba binti Mkondo.[32] According to Abdallah's testimony, around eight o'clock on the evening of 14 January 1915, he heard his wife screaming. Entering the hut, he saw her standing on a bed, crying, with Miersen standing nearby. When Miersen noticed Abdallah, he ran away without saying a word, jumped into a rickshaw, and was driven to a hotel. Abdallah followed and confronted him, but Miersen admitted nothing. Abdallah then went directly to an executive officer named Seidel to make a report. Seidel sent him to the Bezirksgericht. Abdallah reported that, according to his wife, Miersen "had wanted to force her to have sexual intercourse," and when she refused, he slapped her. Abdallah further claimed that Miersen had been there on two other days for the same purpose but that Habiba had escaped each time.

Habiba also provided a statement, which noted her age as fifteen. Habiba reported that on the evening in question, "a big fat man" had come to her house. He closed the door, stripped the cloth wrap from her body so that she was naked, and demanded that she sleep with him. She refused and screamed for her mother. He grabbed her roughly and forced her to the floor, but she managed to get up again. Finally, her husband arrived and the "fat man" ran away. She stated for the record, "I have never had sexual intercourse with a man. I mean of course a European." She also submitted a complaint against "the fat man" for insult (*Beleidigung*) and causing bodily harm. Her statement ends with a remark that the accused had never before demanded sex from *her* but that he had tried to "grab" a woman in the neighboring house.

In addition, "the Catholic Christian [African] woman" Luise, aged twenty-three, gave her witness statement. According to Luise, Habiba lived in her house. Luise, too, had heard screams, and when she entered, she saw Miersen, "whom [she knew] well," hitting Habiba. Luise claimed that she scolded Miersen, saying, "That is no [proper] custom, this is not a European, but a native house, I will report this to the sol." Luise then saw Askari Abdallah looking through the window, and when Miersen saw him, he ran away. Luise concluded by stating that the accused had often come to their area to "grab" women. Further testimony by Luise a few days later revealed that Habiba owed her money and had therefore taken employment with Luise to repay the debt. Another Christian witness named Susanna, aged twelve, confirmed Luise's story, and added that Miersen had tried to "grab" her as well two days earlier.[33]

The next day, Miersen disputed the accusations made against him. He claimed that on the evening in question he had gone to Luise's hut to give her money he owed her for darning his socks. He said he saw a woman in the hut whom he had never seen before and asked her if Luise was there. According to him, the woman replied no and then offered herself to him sexually. Miersen said that he refused the offer, and she responded, "What do you want here? Get out of here!" He thought to himself that maybe she was drunk or otherwise disturbed and asked her if she was crazy. She then grabbed him by the jacket and hit him in the face. In order to make her release him, he slapped her, and she screamed. He then left, got into a rickshaw, and went to the hotel. Suddenly an askari appeared and accused him of hitting his wife. Miersen ordered him to go away. He ended this statement by noting that "at present I have no regular bibi."[34]

Miersen asked the *Bezirksamt* (district office) to find out more information about Habiba's past, and to confirm whether she actually was "the wife of the askari in the legal sense," or whether she was instead, as he suspected, Abdallah's *mchumba*, or girlfriend.[35] He also requested that the native judge (*Eingeborenenrichter*) be called to attest to Habiba's reliability as a witness.[36] After observing her at the district office, the Eingeborenenrichter Karl Treuge confirmed Miersen's suspicion that Habiba was not Abdallah's lawful wife, but his mchumba. She spent her days working in Luise's home, and her nights with the askari at the boma. In his expert opinion, Treuge found it "improbable" that she had propositioned Miersen, that he would have turned her alleged sexual advance down, or that she had struck him during the incident.[37] Treuge expressed his doubts about this aspect of Miersen's version of the story:

> Even if she wasn't the askari's [legal] wife, she still must have feared that the askari might surprise her at any time in the hut, and that actually, the askari would come when Miersen hit her. She also must have feared that one of the women would betray her. Even conceding that she might have been drunk, I do not believe that she would have acted so irrationally as to proposition the accused. I cannot, however, guarantee [that this is the case].

Saying that he had known Miersen for a long time, and that he could not say anything detrimental about his character otherwise, Treuge nonetheless remarked, "I know that he especially likes Negro women [Negerweiber]." He said that in a previous incident, he had learned of Miersen's proclivities and become "convinced that the accused is a dangerous hunter of girls [Mädchenjäger]."[38] Owing to lack of sufficient evidence, he had not followed up on the case. He expressed doubt over Miersen's testimony that he had come to Luise's hut solely to pay for the mending work she had done: "Miersen would hardly conduct himself this way and go to uncivilized huts, as long as he has a boy to take care of it for him."

On the basis of all this information, Miersen was charged with forcing a woman to participate in an adulterous sexual liaison, and a trial took place on 25 January 1915. Although the court members agreed that Miersen was known to be a Mädchenjäger, and noted that much of the evidence against him was indeed incriminating, they felt that the reliability of several of the African witnesses was questionable.[39] For example, the court's final report mentions that Miersen had, at some previous time, been involved in a breach-of-contract case in which Abdallah was sentenced to a "long time" on a chain gang. The court thus viewed Abdallah's motive for accusing Miersen with suspicion.[40] They also doubted Habiba's representation of herself, since it came to light through other African testimonies that she had, a few years previously, resided in a quarter of the city known for prostitution. Treuge, the native judge, also pointed out that in his observations of Habiba, "she did not make a good impression" and had problems dealing with "the truth." Although in her statement she said she had just that year reached sexual maturity and had never before had sexual intercourse with a European, Treuge countered that he had "determined that two years ago she lived in Dangeroni [sic], where there are only sexually mature women," and that she had indeed had sex with Europeans.[41] Her claims that she had never had sex with a European man were thus, to his mind, not credible. The court exonerated Miersen.

This case provides tantalizing evidence for understanding the kinds of projects askari women like Habiba undertook in their domestic lives. Women living under colonialism experienced new kinds of mobility and opportunity that allowed them to pursue a kind of independence, especially in urban centers like Dar es Salaam.[42] Indeed, Habiba's experience exemplifies those of young women trying to make their ways in the colonial economy through a combination of different occupations and social relationships. Even if she did not live in the boma proper, she was connected to it through her *mchumba* (boyfriend), the askari Abdallah. She also generated her own income by working for Luise, who lived outside the boma. Habiba's debtor status, too, speaks to a longer relationship with Luise and hints at the kinds of intricate community relationships and small-scale economies that existed around the maboma.[43] Previously, Habiba may also have worked danguroni, and perhaps this is where she met Abdallah.[44] As Luise White has shown for colonial Nairobi, different categories of "prostitution" accommodated a variety of arrangements between women seeking to earn money and men who came to them as clients. Women who worked danguroni sometimes established relationships with men that "mimicked marriage" in that they "demanded the greatest investment of women's time in cooking, cleaning, skilled entertainment (if any was offered), and simply being home and being available there."[45] Habiba's efforts to hide her danguroni past (including the possibility that she had sexual relations with European men) from the court might be read as an attempt to defend her honor in the European courtroom context. In the "nonnative" court, a past as a prostitute perhaps played differently than in the local East African urban context, where her sense of personal dignity (*heshima*) was not necessarily linked negatively to her previous occupation as a prostitute. On the surface then, Habiba understood herself as Abdallah's mchumba, as a woman who had to earn a living and a woman who deserved her own measure of respect because of her efforts. Of course, this case can only be taken as one intriguing example of the social complexities of being a member of a boma community. Yet it also underlines the need for thinking of the boma geographies as places where African masculinities and femininities were made and remade within local frameworks that encompassed African and European moralities, social practices, and understandings of justice, however defined.[46]

A number of examples throughout this chapter advance the more general argument about the roles of askari women in station life. For all the sources' limitations and silences on the askari women, they sometimes make the mabibi come alive, particularly when their subject matter involves the maboma and askari villages. This is hardly surprising given German colonial gender categorizations, which located women's natural positions within the home. But in reading the sources with an eye to the women's perspectives, we also come away with a stronger sense of how they positioned themselves in the boma communities.

Perspectives on the multiple and sometimes contradictory purposes and uses of the maboma emerge clearly from colonial descriptions, in which the schematic depictions of these structures found in colonial blueprints, handbooks, and manuals contrast productively with lively anecdotes and descriptions found in colonial memoirs. Let us take the example of the Mwanza boma, carefully described by a Schutztruppe doctor in his 1905 memoir. The boma was sixty meters square. To the right of the entrance gate a long *tembe* housed the mailrooms and storage area.[47] On the other side of the gate stood a desolate-looking bastion that served as a storage space for random items, including a folding boat, animal pelts, and old shoes, all under a corrugated tin roof.[48] The ground floor of the bastion included a confinement space for prisoners [*Arrest*]. Nearby stood a large open hall for the guards, as well as the comptroller's room, where boxes of rupees and ivory that served as regional currency were stored. The officers' residence, housing the station chief, doctor, and comptroller were also nearby and included a mess where the officers ate their meals and socialized. Housing for NCOs similar to the officers' was under construction. In the middle of the space enclosed by these buildings stood the Schutztruppe company office, a round structure with a pointed straw roof set among grassy areas and mango trees, "making for a pretty patch of garden." The back exit opened onto a scenic avenue lined by eucalyptus and other trees leading to the edge of Lake Victoria.[49] Local African allies of the Germans lived in proximity to the maboma, facilitating communication between them and colonial administrators.[50] The typical boma's appearance emphasized the aesthetic, practical, and political needs of the colonizers.

Unsurprisingly, however, boma spaces also clearly showed the extent to which ostensibly German colonial spaces were products of their East African geographical positions. The open courtyard at the Mwanza station resembled the open areas of many East African villages, with a large shady "village tree" at the center surrounded by an open area. "Public life," including formal colonial proceedings such as the town hall–style meetings known as *mashauri*, and informal gatherings such as dances, occurred in these spaces.[51] Because European officials, askari, their families, and other temporary residents such as prisoners often lived so close together in the maboma (especially on the coast), incidents like the one involving the screaming wife of a senior askari occurred with some regularity. In 1907, for example, the Bagamoyo district office asked the governor's office in Dar es Salaam to fund the building of new barracks to accommodate the local askari contingent. The boma housed over fifty prisoners and thirteen askari who had nowhere else to live, and this arrangement caused some serious problems. The Bagamoyo district officer reported repeated incidents of "stabbing and other disruptions of order," especially in the communal cooking area of the courtyard, because prisoners, askari, and askari dependents all shared the same tight space within the boma. "To eliminate this unwholesomeness, which is irreconcilable with safety and order in the prison," the officer wrote, "I recommend that the askari currently billeted in the ground floor cells be removed."[52] Such a move, he noted, would free cells for use as separate housing for women or sick prisoners. The letter concluded by observing that constructing new barracks was "thoroughly desirable from a disciplinary perspective, and [it serves] the interest of immediate troop readiness."[53]

German disciplinary sensibilities often did not jibe with how askari and their dependents used space in the boma and did not easily accommodate the potential for conflict when "outsiders" like prisoners' families entered the mix. As the above example shows, cramped conditions inside the Bagamoyo boma created tense conditions as askari, prisoners, and their respective family members engaged in their everyday activities. Prisoners' family members, who came to the maboma to bring food, reacted angrily to the askari and their associates. Askari dependents used the boma courtyard as they would have used courtyards in other kinds of East African compounds—as a space for food preparation and socializing.

Descriptions of everyday life in the maboma reveal the extent to which Africans may have treated them as both exceptional and typical East African spaces. They were exceptional in their relationship to colonial authority and in the ways they forced people who otherwise might not have had reason to interact into close contact with reach other. But they were typical inasmuch as Africans who lived in or entered the maboma used the spaces for purposes other than what the colonizers envisioned.

Day-to-day interactions between colonizers and colonized in the maboma also challenged German ideals of security. The example above shows that what German officials judged as rigid boundaries between groups, such as "guards" and "prisoners," were often not so rigid for Africans. For example, colonial judge Hans Poeschel witnessed a confounding scene on a street in Dar es Salaam. A chain gang assigned to improving the dockside street seemed overly friendly with their askari guards. Poeschel wrote, "A chain of women shook sand from baskets onto the hardpacked ground. Across from them stood a chain of men, each with a piling hammer, pounding the sand. A couple of askaris watched over them. And the whole group [*Gesellschaft*], men, women and askaris, . . . laughed and flirted incessantly, so that it sounded down the length of the dock."[54] The prisoners' seeming lack of concern with their status as members of a chain gang flew in the face of German ideas about shame and honor.[55] Yet chain gangs were a ubiquitous feature of daily life in German East Africa, and because prisoners stayed on chain gangs for months at a time, they became accustomed to daily interactions with their askari guards. Cultural, linguistic, or religious networks that were largely invisible to the colonizers might also have shaped communications between prisoners and askari. For example, Germans had little understanding of East African joking relationships (*utani*), a set of mutually recognized protocols that organized intergroup social relations between East African ethnolinguistic groups. These understandings often grew out of regional histories of conquest and subjugation that preceded the German invasion. In short, what the Germans viewed as a clear-cut relationship of obedience between prisoner and guard conceivably encompassed much more.[56] The proximity of askari to East African colonial subjects, both inside and outside the boma walls, underpinned their roles as colonial functionaries but also caused anxiety for Europeans, whose fantasies of total control generated unrealistic expectations for fixed, impermeable boundaries between prisoners and askari. As agents of colonial authority, askari routinely abused prisoners, both verbally and physically. But these examples illustrate that everyday relations between askari and East African colonized peoples took many forms and grew out of East African social processes that European commentators often could not readily grasp.

MABOMA AS NODES OF AUTHORITY

The Schutztruppe's ability to project authority rested on performances of the colonial state's message of mastery over German East Africa, and the maboma, as nodes of authority, were central to these performances.[57] These performances, which we might think of as "acts of transfer," encompassed both "theatricality" and "spectacle." Performance scholar Diana Taylor encourages us to distinguish between theatricality and spectacle within performance as a way of discerning how performances communicate in different modes or registers:

> theatricality, like theater, flaunts its artifice, its constructedness; it strives for efficaciousness, not authenticity. It connotes a conscious, controlled, and thus always political dimension that *performance* need not imply. It differs from spectacle in that theatricality highlights the mechanics of the spectacle. A spectacle . . . is not an image but a series of social relations mediated by images.[58]

The maboma's bombastic architecture and displays of technology provided the theatrical backdrop to the spectacles the colonial state staged for the communities surrounding them. Thus the askari's training, drill, and ceremony combined with the theatricality of the boma spaces to create spectacles that drew East Africans into a set of communications about German ideals of civilization and dominance in East Africa.[59] These were largely one-way messages that were not intended to produce conversation but rather to induce silence, fear, and awe among the subject populations. Still, the maboma were also sometimes spaces where colonial officials attempted to convince local populations of the benefits of colonial civilizationist endeavors. For example, Schutztruppe staff doctors used station market halls as sites for conducting mass vaccination efforts in which African hospital workers and askari worked to immunize "all market visitors [including] town residents, Indians and colored alike, caravan porters from the hinterland, market visitors from the surrounding villages, [and] adults and children of both genders" against smallpox.[60]

But the maboma were also centers of everyday colonial life where quotidian relationships and activities involving Germans and Africans, colonizers and colonized, men and women, old and young, helped communicate far more ambivalent and complicated messages about the nature of colonial authority (see fig. 6).[61] As much as the stations were "islands of rule" that housed and secured the apparatus necessary to maintaining a visible and convincing military presence, each boma depended for its survival on local economies that provided station members with vital goods and services such as food, laundry, and transportation.[62] The German fantasy of achieving self-sufficiency for its stations required a sizable and diverse African labor force. African laborers, traders, and others came to the stations to look for employment or business opportunities. The stations also housed market halls (some of which were compulsory), drawing sellers and buyers from the surrounding countryside, and intensifying the process of monetization that began in the early 1890s.[63] Traders also set up their small businesses on the fringes of the stations to target the askari and other colonial employees, especially on paydays. Literate Africans worked as clerks in the station's post and telegraph offices, teachers in government schools, and scribe-translators for judicial proceedings. These kinds of jobs were exceptional and went to a very small African elite who had the requisite skills for such work. Most people who came to the maboma looking for work ended up building, cleaning, tending livestock, gardening, or performing other manual labor for very little pay. For some of these workers, employment at a boma led to voluntary or involuntary incorporation into askari or German households.[64] Young men who became members of askari households sometimes later became askari themselves after working as askariboys.[65]

Deutsches Kolonial-Lexikon.   Zu Artikel: Tabora.

Neue photogr. Gesellschaft, Berlin.

Die Boma (Feste) von Tabora.   Vorn Leute, die zum Schauri (Rechtsprechung) gekommen sind und warten
(Deutsch-Ostafrika.)

FIGURE 6. The caption of this photo explains that it shows crowds gathered outside the Tabora boma, waiting for a shauri to begin. Appearing in *Deutsches Kolonial-Lexikon* in 1920, the photo accompanies an encyclopedic entry on Tabora, which emphasizes the town's strategic and commercial value to the colonizers. The boma creates an imposing backdrop to the scene in front, where people casually wait to be let through its gates. On the right side of the photo, an askari, also looking relaxed, walks toward the boma. The image captures the boma's function as a strongpoint as well as a multipurpose and well-trafficked site. *Schnee, ed., Deutsches Kolonial-Lexikon, vol. 3, plate 187.*

Everyday life in the maboma included nearly constant construction, maintenance, and beautification projects that employed askari, their dependents, and both compensated and uncompensated African laborers. At Mwanza, for example, the local commander noted, "There is always building going on, here a bastion, there a storage space, a work shed, a European's house; the huts for askari, boatsmen, court messengers, etc., all have to be renovated about every three years."[66] This work relied solely on African labor. Colonial officials learned to adjust their construction expectations to local practices and materials. Hildebrandt complained that left unsupervised, the askari and other "Negroes" living at the station would build their homes "crookedly," which offended the German military sensibility of ensuring "order" through "straight building lines."[67] Station construction also required accommodation to local labor practices.

While overseeing the building of the Kilosa station, Lieutenant Tom von Prince learned through trial and error that efficiency in procuring laborers was best achieved by asking local leaders, known as *majumbe* (sing., *jumbe*) to provide them. To secure the German levies, majumbe could mobilize, with or without compensation, their clients or slaves. By having the majumbe fill station labor requirements, Schutztruppe officers avoided having to negotiate individual contracts with people over whom they had little legitimate authority or leverage and who had different ideas about work schedules and pace.[68] Local workers reported to the maboma early in the morning with their tools and were then divided into work groups under askari supervision and set to work on station projects.[69]

As part of the askari's garrison duties when not on the march, they also participated in station construction projects, including building their own homes. Many askari received training as "craftsmen" as well, so that following their early morning training routine, they could be industrious around the station: "A number of askari patch shoes and clothes, others lay bricks, one supervises the garden work, one is trained as a military hospital assistant, two are police, the ordnance-askari cleans the Maxim gun, others watch the tribute-workers."[70] By using the askari to perform such a wide range of station work, often alongside "tax laborers" or chain-gang prisoners, government officials kept construction and operating costs low.[71] This work scheme kept idle askari busy, while also allowing them to supervise the station's laborers.[72] The communities surrounding the maboma thus developed, or were forced into, social and economic ties to the stations reflective of the fluidity between civil ("colonized") and military ("colonizer") milieux. Some of these work relationships turned into other kinds of relationships, including marriages, domestic servitude, or becoming askariboys. The askari translated their roles as supervisors of workers into *babas*, or "fathers," to vulnerable men and women in search of kinship, protection, and community membership.

ASKARI VILLAGES

The ways that the askari lived in and around the stations helped the colonial state project its message of authority. The soldiers' presence around the maboma and their relative cash wealth as salaried employees encouraged small-scale local economies that supplied them with the goods and services they desired. The askari villages were also work and leisure spaces for the soldiers and their families, and they also sometimes attracted people from outside the community to participate in the "askari subculture."[73] The askari villages spilled into larger station villages, often arranged on both sides of the wide, well-traveled roads that connected interior towns. The station villages, with their mixture of shops, small businesses, hotels, and mosques, underpinned the development of future interior towns such as Tabora, Iringa, Songea, and Bukoba.[74] The proximity of the askari villages to main roads, market halls, the maboma themselves, and the growing frontier towns, ensured frequent interactions between askari, their household members, other East Africans who lived and worked nearby, and Europeans.

Askari housing arrangements and styles varied tremendously between stations.[75] On the coast, Europeans and askari lived crowded together in the old stone fortresses they had taken over during the conquest phase. By 1901 officials at the old coastal fort at Bagamoyo had reached their breaking point with the crowded conditions and began clamoring for funding from the Gouvernement to build new housing for askari, or at least to subsidize their salaries to cover rental costs for living in private homes in Bagamoyo town.[76] In the interior, soldiers generally lived in separate askari villages sited close to the stations. Typically, single askari lived in barracks, while askari with dependents lived in individual apartments or houses, but this was not absolute. For example, at the lakeside stations Mwanza and Bukoba all askari lived in separate "round huts built in the local style."[77] A 1912 orientation handbook for German officers and NCOs inexperienced with field duty in East Africa advocated that the askari should live in separate askari villages instead of coastal-style barracks. Despite the flammability and relative impermanence of East African huts, which tended to be wattle and daub with grass roofs, the handbook insisted that these provided better living arrangements for the African soldiers: "Our Askari, who are now almost exclusively composed of soldiers drawn from within the protectorate or from tribes directly neighboring them, feel most comfortable in the familiar, simple but well-built native-style huts."[78] The handbook even recommended that each askari should have his own separate dwelling in order to accommodate their "more or less numerous family [members] and other dependents" at the stations.[79] Officers were urged to accommodate the "needs and customs" of the askari in their construction planning. Schutztruppe captain Heinrich

Fonck praised the detached houses, which had "the advantage of hindering arguments between families" and offering more space and privacy than other arrangements.[80] Ideally every eight families shared a common veranda, or *baraza*, which opened onto a courtyard where food preparation and social activities took place. For example, Iringa station built two identical compounds in 1902, one for a sol and one for a beshaush. Their residences each had two rooms, separated from each other by a corridor. Nearby annexes housed the kitchens, supply rooms, accommodations for servants, animal stalls, and latrines.[81] The annexes encircled large courtyards.[82] These spacious compounds reflected the senior askari's positions in the Schutztruppe hierarchy, as well as their social rank in local hierarchies. The spaces could accommodate many dependents, a variety of domestic subsistence practices, and even small businesses run by household members—all of which enhanced individual askari's status and visibility within local orbits.[83]

The size of an askari's home, and the materials with which it was built, depended on the soldier's rank. House sizes and quality of building materials improved incrementally as the askari progressed through the ranks.[84] In 1903 at Kilimatinde senior soldiers moved into recently completed "stone structures." Stone and brick structures with corrugated tin roofs (as opposed to wood-framed adobe structures with straw roofs) were markers of rank and status, since they were more expensive and harder to acquire than other locally derived materials. Meanwhile, the rank and file moved into new "barracks" built to replace "damaged askari houses" that had formerly stood on the site.[85] Most rank-and-file askari lived in block or row houses, with each askari family (of which there were about 160 per station) having small, separate, enclosed rooms in the building. Using mats and pieces of cloth, they subdivided the rooms into smaller areas to accommodate different household members (wives, children, "boys," etc.). An unmarried askari at Tabora lived in a one-room hut that served simultaneously as "living room, sleeping chamber, and kitchen," with just enough space for a bed with a mosquito net and a stone hearth.[86] Even with dependents, junior askari lived in smaller spaces than their superiors.[87] For East Africans seeking to change their personal circumstances by attaching themselves to askari communities, the sizes of the dwellings likely mattered less than the possibility of achieving personal economic security (if not always personal safety) through inclusion in an askari household.[88]

The soldiers' neighborhoods were not physically isolated from surrounding populations in any meaningful ways. The askari village at Mwanza lined both sides of the main road to Tabora, a major stop on the old East African caravan trading route that connected the coast to the Great Lakes region.[89] A similar circumstance obtained at the station in Moshi, in the Kilimanjaro region, where "the black soldiers had their houses along the road from the Bezirksamt to the steppe."[90] Official Schutztruppe guidelines recommended that the askari villages not be any closer than two hundred meters from the fortress so that they would not be in the boma's line of fire if it came under attack.[91] There seemed to be little to stand in the way of askari and non-Schutztruppe populations living in proximity to each other.

In fact, the askari villages were far enough away from the maboma that they sometimes became targets of destructive acts undertaken by local residents who elected not to risk attacking the maboma themselves. Fires occurred frequently in the askari villages because the askari homes were built with flammable materials, and open fires burned throughout the day and night for cooking and other purposes. Sometimes, though, askari villages were purposely set on fire as an expression of discontent over the Schutztruppe's presence. The Schutztruppe commander at Mwanza related a story in his memoir that underscores this point. He recalled a series of incidents that occurred while the askari and station personnel were away from the boma on an expedition. During their absence, someone began setting fires in the askari village "every other night." A local "magician," concerned with his "sinking prestige" in the area, circulated rumors that a ghost was burning askari homes to express its rage against "whites" having planted a flag on a mountain near the askari village. Confusion reigned in Mwanza: "Women became unruly, men did not obey, and everything became unhinged."[92] The magician was caught and subsequently hanged to death from a tree on the exercise field. The fires stopped after the man's execution.[93] The askari's proximity to surrounding communities thus potentially made them and their households vulnerable to small acts of resistance, revenge, or subterfuge. Despite these dangers, however, askari villages provided separate space within which they could live their lives with some measure of autonomy from their officer-patrons, while still remaining connected to the maboma.

The askari villages were lively scenes of work, recreation, and sociability, night and day.[94] The askari's dependents contributed greatly to the oft-reported bustle of the askari villages. The everyday lives of the wives, daughters, companions, and servants and of the askari themselves played out on the verandas and courtyards in front of their homes, where they caught up with each other's news, pounded grain for porridge, or braided each other's hair. The askari's sons, who sometimes also later became askari, imitated their fathers' military training, practicing the salutes and commands they had seen performed on the parade grounds.[95] Dancing, drumming, and singing also took place regularly, to judge by colonial commentators' frequent references to the askari villages' musical activities.

The askari and their community members also actively participated in local economic consumption and production. Askari spent their salaries on many commodities for their personal use and recreation, and high on the list were locally produced alcoholic beverages. Askari partook regularly of the local brews known collectively as *pombe*, versions of which were found throughout the colony. Women who lived on the edges of the stations brewed pombe to sell to the soldiers, despite governmental efforts to regulate its production and sale.[96] As a military historian describing another context observes, "It was much easier for commanders to deal with the frequent incidents of inebriated soldiers getting themselves into trouble than it was to take the unpopular step of trying to restrict or remove their men's alcohol ration."[97] The pombe women were only a fraction of the various agents who waited each month for the askari to receive their pay in order to extend them credit, and to "palm off their junk" on the cash-rich but "reckless" troops.[98] In addition, some askari ran small businesses or drew on the productive capacity of their households to earn extra income through the sale of surplus produce or household crafts. Soldiers' wives also sometimes brewed beer in their homes, which they then sold.[99] Local economies developed around these households because of their relative wealth and willingness to readily spend their cash. This dynamic again highlights the askari villages as sites of opportunity for some East Africans.

ASKARI, ISLAM, AND CHRISTIAN MISSIONS

Religious communities also provided spaces where the askari and their family members interacted with people who did not officially belong to the boma communities. Most askari were Muslim, but significant numbers of them also converted to Christianity and participated in Christian-mission community life. Christian missionaries fixated on the askari in two ways. First, they viewed them as responsible for the spread of Islam throughout German East Africa.[100] Second, they considered it part of their missionary duties to prod the colonial government into counteracting what they perceived as an outsized Muslim influence on colonial affairs by recruiting more Christian men to the Schutztruppe. Government officials were largely indifferent to these efforts, but the missionary focus on the colony's religious makeup helps illuminate some aspects of askari involvement in spiritual communities.

The askari did in fact play a significant role in creating new communities of Islam in some parts of German East Africa that may not have had them before the German conquest. The station villages that grew up around the maboma included mosques, which marked the coalescence of new Muslim communities as part of the Schutztruppe's gradual spread across the interior of the colony.[101] These sites became sources of tension between Christian missionaries and colonial administrators. For example, the askari village at Moshi had a small mosque made of corrugated tin—a status material—which a local missionary cited as evidence "that Islam [was] standing on watch here."[102] In nearby Arusha in 1912, a new mosque also appeared, which "was meant [primarily] for the soldiers and traders in the area of the district substation."[103] Ever sensitive to what they perceived as the unchecked spread of Islam through the German colony, missionaries complained that "every German military station in the interior acts as propaganda for Islam, because the askari are mostly Muslim."[104] Missionaries also viewed communities of ex-askari as transmitters of Muslim influence, especially within their own households, where askariboys might easily emulate their *babas*.[105] Government officials gave lip service to the idea that Christianity was important to the German colonial endeavor, but they also accepted that most of their African employees, and especially the askari, were Muslims. Colonial officials had little stake in supporting the missionaries in their anti-Muslim agenda, although they encouraged missionaries to send "suitable and capable mission pupils to the individual [Schutztruppe] companies for employment as recruits."[106] But, as Governor von Götzen himself cautioned in 1903, "the Gouvernement cannot today, nor still for a long time to come, go without the service of mohammedan askaris." In support of this contention, he cited Muslim soldiers' "proven bravery," and the dearth of suitable Christian recruits within German East Africa.[107] On another occasion, the Gouvernement denied a missionary society's application to build a new station in Masoko, where a Schutztruppe company was stationed. Arguing that some twenty-five Christian askari families and forty-five other Christians living in Masoko needed a ministry, the missionaries pointed out how unfair it was that Muslims in Masoko could "do as they liked," while Christians were forced to travel a long distance to attend schools and services.[108] In March 1914 the Gouvernement issued an order that Christian askari should be given the opportunity to practice their beliefs at their stations, although it is unclear to what extent that directive was heeded by local officials.[109] The issue of the treatment of Christian askari flared from time to time in correspondence between colonial-government officials and missionaries for the whole period of German rule, but it had little effect on actual recruiting practices. In 1913 the Gouvernement estimated that only 4.4 percent of the askari were Christians, while 67.3 percent were Muslims, and 28.3 percent practiced other religions ("heathens").[110] Some missionaries may also have been ambivalent about sending converts to become askari. Lutherans around Moshi sent some of their pupils to the Schutztruppe, but only after "alerting them to all the dangers, to the bodily or the spiritual realm, that would await them in this service."[111] The percentage of Christian askari remained low until World War I, at least in part because officers judged them to be less effective and less dedicated to the Schutztruppe than Muslim troops.[112]

Islam featured prominently in askari self-understandings as respectable men, and there is good reason to believe that part of the process of becoming askari involved becoming Muslim. Young askari reportedly "followed the example" of senior Muslim troops, and askariboys followed the example of their "fathers," in adopting Islam.[113] The askari's connections to other Muslims in the colony through brotherhoods and dance associations may have networked them in ways that further bolstered their claims to respectability. These connections also made colonial officials nervous and worried Christian missionaries, who viewed the askari as obvious proselytizers. These insecurities appeared to have some basis in July 1908, when a batch of incendiary letters, known as the Mecca Letters, suddenly appeared in coastal German

East Africa. These letters, which mirrored texts that had circulated in other millenarian contexts such as Sudan and Somalia, admonished Muslims that "the Day of Judgment was approaching, and that they must therefore return to piety and discipline, holding themselves aloof from unbelievers."[114] Rumors began circulating that the askari would be inspired by these letters, and that they would turn against the Germans, creating a dangerous security environment.[115] In light of the relatively recent events of Maji Maji, colonial authorities were shaken by the rumors and undertook thorough investigations of what was behind them. In the end, these inquiries yielded little evidence that the letters had influenced the askari to rebel against German rule, although askari certainly knew about the rumors.[116] Some askari in Tabora had in fact attended sermons at a local mosque, where a *mwalimu* had "preached against German rule." Askari had also collected money to support him following his exile from Tabora.[117] Effendi Plantan, the highest-ranking askari in the Schutztruppe's organizational history, had also been approached by a Zanzibari proponent of the Mecca Letters who tried, unsuccessfully, to convince the effendi to incite a rebellion against the Germans.[118] But in general, the Mecca Letters failed to compel the askari to act against colonialism. This is hardly surprising given the level of dependence that had developed by this time between askari and the Schutztruppe organization. Still, the question of Islam's place in German East Africa, and especially the prominent place of Muslim intermediaries—including the askari—in the day-to-day governance of the colony, remained a tense point for the rest of the period of German rule in East Africa.[119]

Despite missionaries' frustrations with the colonial government's tepid interest in trying to limit Islamic influence by changing the makeup of the Schutztruppe, mission stations worked out practical relationships with the military stations that yielded small dividends for them in terms of their ability to access askari families as potential converts. In fact, mission stations took on some of the government stations' workloads. For example, during development of the Langenburg station in 1898, the district officer Arnold von Eltz handed over the "dispensation of justice for native criminal and bagatelle cases" to the Moravian station because he had "no time for other things and also had no askaris available."[120] The friendly tone infusing interactions between missionary and government stations enabled additional interactions between the askari communities and others. At some locations, askari and their children attended classes and sermons given by missionaries. In 1902 at the Moshi station, for example, Captain Kurt Johannes gave the missionaries a small stone house with a corrugated tin roof to hold classes for "the servants of the Europeans and the children of the askari." Local Chagga children also attended the school. The use of this house came to a "sudden end," however, when Johannes decided to use it for another purpose.[121] Five months later, with the new station chief's blessing, the Lutherans set up a new school in the allied Chagga leader Meli's boma. The missionaries took pride in the number and variety of students they now reached: "Right away the number of students grew in a pleasing way, so that a few times we had one hundred students. . . . The majority of the visitors are Wachagga, mostly boys, but also quite a few men, ten to thirty girls, as well as a number of women. Besides these, a number of Swahili boys and Nubian children came."[122] These Swahili boys and Nubian children were probably the children of askari and other colonial employees. The missionary singled out the Nubian children for their appearance, intelligence, and air of entitlement vis-à-vis the Chagga children.[123] By 1912 missionaries near the Moshi boma had again changed venues, teaching askari and their children in an open hall where colonial officials usually held judicial proceedings.[124]

Askari community members around Moshi thus participated in mission education for at least the better part of a decade. The effects of such education on askari and their dependents cannot be ascertained, but their presence in mission classrooms challenges the notion that they were isolated from other East Africans. In fact, askari community members appear to have interacted quite frequently with others in a range of ways that were not directly tied to the exercise of colonial authority. Allowing the askari and their families to receive mission educations benefited the colonial government by contributing to a larger pool of literate or multilingual intermediaries from which to replenish their ranks.[125] Their involvement in the mission communities, as in the mosques, was part of the fabric of everyday colonialism. Askari and their kin could pursue paths to respectability through the mosques and the missions, since both provided the connections and practical skills necessary to perform respectability within the colonial grammar of power.

VETERANS: ASKARI BECOME PATRONS

Ex-askari often settled near the maboma to keep their connections to the colonial establishment alive. Their continuing ties to the maboma enabled additional channels of colonial power beyond those of the active askari. They made themselves available as Schutztruppe reserves in times of emergency. But veterans also oriented themselves to life outside the boma in order to promote themselves as local patrons. After askari left the Schutztruppe, they used their relative status and wealth to position themselves as men of influence in various ways. They established their own businesses, managed large herds of livestock, and cultivated cash crops. Some of them took positions as local colonial functionaries. Others found employment with local rulers. For example, the Lutheran missionary Wärthl, traveling through Turu in 1912, encountered an ex-askari working as a bodyguard for a local leader named Sangeda. He described his hosts:

> [Sangeda] is of slight, almost frail build, with slyly flickering eyes. All the larger, however, are the bodyguards whom he had chosen. One of them claimed to have served as an askari in the Schutztruppe; he asserted [that he had served] for seven years, and it amused me not a little to hear German commands colorfully mixed up and pronounced such that only with effort could a German recognize them in their original meanings.[126]

The ex-askari, whose stature contrasted so markedly with that of Sangeda, took pride in his connection to the German colonial regime and seized the opportunity to reaffirm it through the German missionary. The veteran's performance of German commands for the missionary signaled a continuing attachment to the organization that had trained and socialized him, even as he served a new patron.[127]

Not surprisingly, communities of ex-askari congregated in areas that afforded them access to colonial power centers and arteries, as well as economic hubs such as caravan routes. Colonial officials also had a hand in choosing the sites where ex-askari would set up new villages. The Morogoro district officer Lambrecht wrote in a 1901 report that the station had settled some former askari along an "abandoned" stretch of the caravan road lying in a valley between Kilosa and Kidete. According to him, the soldiers' presence promoted an air of safety along the route, convincing local residents to rebuild settlements there. The report indicates that

the former askari made themselves into local patrons, building the settlers "clean houses and straight roads," which created a "friendly view."
The askari borrowed a supply of seeds and livestock from the district office. Lambrecht was favorably impressed with their industry: "The effort
they dedicate to cultivating the fields and [performing] other work on the
land is admirable."[128] One year later, in 1902, Lambrecht again reported
enthusiastically on the "progress" the ex-askari settlements had made in
cultivating rubber trees, potatoes, and coffee, all from seed stores the district office had provided in the previous year.[129] In the summer of 1903 a
Schutztruppe officer conducting an inspection of interior stations noted
that the "four Sudanese settlements on the caravan route are proving
themselves and flourishing generally well." Equal success marked the
"four Wanyamwezi settlements near Kilossa [sic], [which have] a total
of over one thousand heads."[130] In 1911 a military handbook reported that
some thirty-five former askari, mainly "Sudanese," lived in different locations in Morogoro District and could be counted on as reservists.[131] In
May 1900 the Tabora district officer, Rudolf Gansser, reported a similar
plan to build "rest houses" with markets at two days' distance from the
Tabora boma. He planned to settle "old Sudanese" at the marketplaces.
The veterans were allowed to buy sixty-pound sacks of sorghum from
the station for 1 rupee, which they could then sell at a profit, earning 25
rupees on every 100 rupees they spent.[132] The district officer eagerly anticipated the completion of the network of "rest houses": "Through [the
building of the rest houses and markets] I will achieve simultaneously a
kind of road police, and the eternal robberies on the caravan road will
cease. Additionally [with this plan] it will also be possible to resettle the
areas around the caravan road, which will also be a great advantage."[133]

The colonial officers' keen interest in these developments related
directly to their interest in protecting the central caravan route and facilitating European travel across the colony. At the time of these reports,
the area was slowly recovering from at least two decades of war-related
devastation. Before the arrival of the Schutztruppe, in the 1880s, the
Hehe raided the area to target the caravan route as part of their quest
to consolidate regional power. Then in the 1890s the Hehe fought an
extended war against the Schutztruppe. The final defeat of the Hehe,
in 1898, marked the Schutztruppe's ascension to military dominance
in the area, which in turn fostered a new regime of security around
Kilosa and Morogoro. In the aftermath of this consolidation of power,

the government decided to settle ex-askari at strategic points along the caravan route and to provide them the resources to found new communities. This served multiple purposes. First, it encouraged settlers to return to the area, and thus set in motion new economic, social, and political possibilities of benefit to the colonial regime and some Africans. Second, the veterans' presence reinforced the settlements' ties to the colonial center at Kilosa, extending the colonizers' reach into communities and households that otherwise might have been beyond their influence. Third, the Schutztruppe could keep track of veterans in case they needed to call them up as reserves. Finally, as more settlements reestablished themselves along the caravan route, Schutztruppe officers and other colonial officials could rely on them as safe and well-provisioned places to rest while traveling between the coast and the interior, or between neighboring districts.[134] The veterans gained influence and wealth, proving themselves indispensable intermediaries for the colonizers. And the government benefited from having its emissaries dispersed along the major trading routes.

The constitutive role of violence in askari self-understandings, which bolstered their sense of entitlement vis-à-vis others in the colony, also influenced their conduct in their post-askari careers. For example, former askari who had settled along the caravan route between the coast and the interior town Tabora reportedly forced porters to work for them for free. Instead of allowing the porters to take their necessary rest at the end of their journeys, ex-askari forced them to build houses or to "cheaply manage their agricultural plots [shamba]."[135] The anonymous author of an article on the porter shortage expressed dismay over what he considered one veteran askari's egregious behavior:

> Yes, it happened that a former sol who lived on the *barabara* [road] showed the [passing] caravans a certificate, noting that this was permission from the *bwana mkubwa* [local European official] obliging the porters to work! This same sol had the audacity [to] forcibly hold up a small animal transport of four goats being sent to the coast by a European because they ate a bit of his cultivated grain or sorghum, which was planted all the way to the edge of the road.[136]

Although the caravan leader tried to pay the sol "damages," and he informed the former askari that the goats belonged to a European, the veteran kept the animals.[137] In this brazen act, the ex-askari demonstrated not only a lack of regard for the caravan leader's effort to make amends for the errant livestock but also a lack of concern that the goats belonged to a European. As a veteran with land adjacent to the road, he could easily repeat such expropriations as often as he liked, at least until colonial authorities stopped him from doing so. In fact, he and others like him thought of such behavior as appropriate, given their standing as local power brokers and men of means.

These behaviors were nothing new. Askari had of course also participated in the practice of forcing porters to work while serving in the Schutztruppe. An 1893 governor's order had decreed that during "periods of uprisings," the government could requisition any and all "available" porters "without regard to any previously existing agreements between [the porters] and private persons."[138] Punishments for anyone caught "hindering" government efforts to secure porters included a three-month prison term or a hefty fine, and the threat of being exiled from the colony.[139] Over the next two decades, the Schutztruppe routinely demanded that local "chiefs" provide it and its European associates (missionaries, explorers, scientists) with porters to haul their equipment and personal items on expeditions.[140] Schutztruppe officers fostered these behaviors in the interest of perceived military necessity. In turn, the askari used this authority as a basis for improving their personal circumstances. Ex-askari continued such practices once they left the Schutztruppe. Having borne colonial authority for so long, veterans saw no reason to change, and their age enhanced their social standing even beyond the status they had enjoyed as askari. Such practices brought veterans into conflict with resentful European settlers, but since the ex-soldiers had the backing of colonial officials, only rarely did they experience official consequences for their actions.[141]

Ex-askari also remained tied to the Gouvernement through awards of land parcels to those who finished their terms of service in good standing. At a time when many East Africans were losing land to settlers establishing plantations, these land grants to ex-askari helped them subsist and perhaps accumulate some additional wealth, further buttressing their social status.[142] The askari did not own the land but could use the plots to support themselves and their households. In Bagamoyo District, the Gouvernement awarded different-size plots ("classes") based on how many young coconut palms the colonial government had planted on the land.[143] Officials assessed the ex-soldiers' service records and disabilities and then awarded them land grants according to their merit and need. After receiving these grants, the askari were responsible for nurturing, at their own expense, any young trees planted on the plots. They were forbidden to tap the trees for *tembo* (palm wine), and they were liable for any damage done to the trees.[144] They could keep the fruits from the trees, but both the trees and the property remained in government hands. They also received 30 rupees to build a hut on the land within the first three months of settlement. To generate additional income, veterans could rent out individual trees to others, as long as they cared for the government trees within their purview.

Disabled or elderly veterans used the plots to help them live through their retirement. For example, in 1911 a colonial official requested that an askari named Asmani, who had served fourteen and a half years, receive a plot of land. According to the request, Asmani had "always conducted himself very well" and "had given the police unit many years of good service," but he also suffered from epilepsy and "because of that [could] hardly earn the necessary [subsistence] income anymore."[145] Another request was made for the "Sudanese" askari Belal Chatad, who had served since 1892 and who had gone blind. As recipients of the land grant, the request also included Belal Chatad's wife and "his very intelligent son," who was serving at that time as a teaching assistant in the Bagamoyo government school.[146] Veterans' dependents had to be taken care of as well if they were to remain reliable agents of colonial rule.

Not all veterans were impressed with this program, however. Shaush Almas Hussen, who had served in Lindi since 1902, rejected a settlement of seventy-five trees because he would not own the land himself.[147] In addition, he complained that 30 rupees was a paltry sum for building a hut on the land and argued instead that the Gouvernement should pay him 150 rupees to construct a home. The Bagamoyo district officer sympathized with the shaush, who had been wounded during Maji Maji: "People cannot build huts here for 30 rupees." He pointed out that in one recent case, in order to "prevent people from spending money needlessly" on building houses they could not complete for lack of money, he used district money to purchase the necessary materials to build the house. He then ordered sailors and chain-gang prisoners to build the hut, thereby ensuring minimal, if any, labor costs.[148]

Almas Hussen's "stubborn" rejection of the settlement offer led to him being sent back to the *Rekrutendepot* in Dar es Salaam, where he had been before his arrival in Bagamoyo.[149] His unwillingness to accept the Gouvernement's offer shows that at least some askari felt slighted by what they perceived as the Gouvernement's inadequate recognition of their sacrifices during their Schutztruppe enlistment. Hussen's stance on the issue of land ownership and housing suggests that his standard of mutual obligation had not been met by the Gouvernement's gesture. The colonial officer at Bagamoyo registered Hussen's complaints as potentially threatening to local order, since his "continual appeals to government authority [*amri ya serkal*] and tradition [*desturi*]" might incite other veteran "settlers" to question their awards' adequacy.[150] Too much of this kind of sentiment among ex-askari, colonial officials imagined, would be disruptive to the colonial order, since the veterans also had a significant part to play in its maintenance.

Veteran askari proved useful as intermediaries for the colonial state. They circulated among local populations, continuing to represent colonial authority as men of influence, local administrators, and police-reservists. The colonial government did not offer official approval of their marauding behaviors along the trade routes, but neither did its representatives act with any resolve to curtail their activities. Even veterans in poor health still exerted influence through their privileged access to land, and they likely helped maintain and sometimes improve their dependents' socioeconomic circumstances and social mobility. Their presence and activities, alongside the colonial government's practices of everyday colonialism, helped disguise the colonial state's inherent weaknesses by increasing its visibility and reach in areas outside the immediate station environs.

☙

The maboma, askari villages, and veterans' settlements described here were sites that bolstered the colonial state's ability to project its claims to authority, however "vague and unfinished," across German East Africa.[151] The local cultures and economies that developed around these sites laid the basis for colonial centers that encompassed new social geographies and hierarchies reflective of both colonial ideals and African aspirations within a changing political and economic environment. From these sites, the askari and other colonial agents launched military expeditions and patrols, undertook a variety of administrative and punitive duties, and communicated the colonial state's messages across long distances. Chapter 5 explores some of the concrete and symbolic ways that the askari performed these intermediary roles both within and outside the maboma.

5 ⸺ Askari as Agents of Everyday Colonialism

ASKARI ROLES in expanding colonial state interests tied directly into their everyday lives in and around the maboma. The policing roles they undertook while in garrison also enabled the state to accomplish the practical goals essential to its continued existence, such as taxation and labor levies. The impact of this part of askari duties went beyond these mechanics of rule, however. Their routine movements as patrollers, escorts, and messengers in the vicinity of the maboma expressed colonial officials' desire to project authority beyond the maboma. Similarly, the drill, ceremony, and training they conducted every day as soldiers served the obvious purpose of keeping the askari ready for their military duties. In addition, however, these military scenes were performances designed to display the state's mastery, or potential for mastery, over the subject population. In certain ways then, the soldiers' (and former soldiers') everyday lives in and around the maboma completed the image that colonial officials wanted colonial subjects to see — of African men and women participating in, benefiting from, taking advantage of — what German colonialism brought to East Africa. In other ways, their quotidian activities also exposed the ways that East Africans rejected German colonialism, whether in whole or in part. This chapter reconstructs the everyday lives of askari in and around the maboma, illuminating the processes that on the one hand enabled the state to carry out its priority functions of taxation, labor recruitment, and keeping order, and on the other hand, exposed some its dependence on webs of relationships and networks over which they had minimal, if any, purview. I then focus on how askari performed authority in military parades that drew on and influenced East African cultural practices, both reinforcing and challenging German colonial state-making ideals.

EVERYDAY COLONIALISM: TAX COLLECTION

In their everyday lives, askari traveled from place to place conducting a number of duties in the name of the colonial state. One such everyday duty was to collect taxes from communities living around the maboma. Despite some halfhearted government efforts to rein in the askari's abusive tendencies, tax collection gave them abundant opportunities to abuse those who resisted. A Lutheran missionary working in the Kilimanjaro region in 1904 witnessed the fear an askari tax collection visit provoked among his congregation. As he began his sermon one day,

> the people saw a few soldiers appear in the distance. Immediately, everyone fled, the elderly in front, the women with the children and infants behind. I asked them if they had not paid their taxes; when they said yes [they had], I said to them, that they then had no reason to flee. "But the soldiers harass and beat us," they replied, running away.
>
> When the soldiers came, I said, "You should go elsewhere, the people paid their taxes." "Would someone flee, if he had paid?" said one of the soldiers. "You know that the Wakamba are fools, who run away without reason when they see soldiers," I said. With that, the soldiers left. In vain I tried to call the people back. Even after four days I found a woman with her two children from [Mbaa Masi] staying with [an elder], but she came back that day when I told her that the soldiers had long since moved on.[1]

This report echoes many others from the period that indicate widespread fear of the askari, even in places that were in good standing with the Schutztruppe, as was generally the case around Kilimanjaro by 1905.[2]

Tax collection occurred in two ways, both through colonial intermediaries. First, local rulers collected taxes from the people in their purview and delivered them to the stations. Second, tax collectors, including askari and other trusted agents such as clerks, traveled through the tax districts "to urge delinquents to make their payments, thereby preventing too many from escaping taxation." Taxes were paid in cash, livestock, and other goods (such as cereals and wax).[3] In Songea the tax collectors included "two scribes from Kilwa, three mission students, two locally living [i.e., in Songea] Swahili, one half-Arab living in the Luwegu area[;] in total eight civilians, [and additionally] the literate effendi[,] a beshaush and an ombasha serve as temporary personnel."[4] Colonial authorities mobilized this mixture of civilian and military colonial intermediaries to collect taxes because they brought to bear different skills, such as literacy or language facility, which made tax collection possible. The high-ranking askari, described as "temporary personnel," provided the coercive and security element that backed up the other intermediaries in their efforts to make people pay taxes to an alien government.

Even if colonial officers described tax collection as a fair and well-organized process, and even if they claimed a desire to limit abuses by askari and other intermediaries, they could not be everywhere. Numerous interactions escaped their supervision, and that lack of oversight left open many possibilities for askari to expropriate local residents. In July 1914 a Catholic bishop complained to the Bagamoyo district officer that some askari detailed to work for a local African administrator (*akida*) had "harshly" punished an African Christian man for not paying his taxes in a timely manner.[5] Other Christians had been detained (and later set free) for the same reason. The Bagamoyo *Bezirksamtmann* Michels wrote to the governor that the bishop's charges were overblown:

> The one positive case mentioned by the bishop in his . . . letter of 19 July concerns a policeman [askari] . . . who twice struck a man . . . with a small stick [made of] tamarind [wood]. The man who was hit—and this cannot be called abuse—immediately came to the district office, the case was investigated, the askari was punished, and the injured man was awarded half a rupee in damages. . . . This is the only violation during tax collection that has come to my attention, and it was redressed right away, before the bishop even had any knowledge of it.[6]

He called the bishop's accusation that the askari had "locked up" others "untrue and petty, not to say frivolous," and further noted that the bishop had provided "not even a shadow of proof" for the events described.[7] Michels's defense of the soldiers' behavior and dismissal of the missionary's complaint against their violent actions was quite typical of colonial administrators. Colonial government officials elevated the prestige of the state and enforcement of colonial order over the interests of other Europeans in the colony, such as missionaries, businessmen, or settlers. The askari thus continued their abuses unchecked, believing that they were entitled to their "illegal exactions."[8]

EVERYDAY COLONIALISM II:
ASKARI, MASHAURI, AND SCHAURIZETTEL

Local residents also came to the maboma to participate in recurring events referred to as *shauri*. These were forums for "public deliberation of issues concerning the administration of a district and its population, including legal matters and problems brought to the meeting by the audience."[9] Or, as colonial judge Hans Poeschel put it, "The shauri can mean anything. Shauri is the court session, shauri is every deliberation and every gossip session. . . . Having a shauri is the greatest enjoyment the black knows. For him, it replaces the newspaper, theater, and cinema. [It] is to him what playing skat [a popular card game] and drinking beer [is] for the Germans, [what] boxing and football [are] for the English."[10] Poeschel's emphasis on the shauri as a form of entertainment for African attendees captures the element of spectacle the shauri embodied. But it ignores the graver aspects of peoples' attendance at mashauri. Colonial officials handed down serious sentences at the end of deliberations, usually either the hamsa ishirini or a period of confinement and labor on a chain gang. Most stations had a special hall or other space designated for conducting the mashauri, which occurred regularly (but contingent on the presence of a German colonial official) and dealt with all manner of local government affairs, judicial matters, private disputes, and public complaints. For example, the courtyard of the Moshi boma was especially "lively" on Wednesdays and Fridays because of "mashauri, court cases, and tax appointments."[11] Mashauri took place in Tabora District "almost daily" with the primary purpose of "enlightening and educating the natives," and they "always brought together a significant mass of people."[12] At Kilosa in the mid-1890s, mashauri also occurred daily.[13] An officer stationed at Iringa in 1898 complained that although the daily mashauri were "thoroughly necessary," they were an "unpleasant intrusion on [his] map work."[14] Streams of people showed up on shauri days to present their complaints, to make requests, and to respond to summonses.

Mashauri featured prominently in the everyday affairs of colonial officers and other colonial functionaries, including the askari. They were simultaneously sites where colonial power and authority was enacted and spaces of appearance where colonial sociality played out. Colonial officers presided over mashauri at the maboma, but also conducted them ad hoc during their periodic district tours. They devoted excessive time to presiding over mashauri, complaining frequently about being overworked. But they also recognized that mashauri instantiated state authority through the face-to-face paternalistic exercises that made manifest the German colonial civilizing ideal.[15]

Askari were directly involved in the mashauri in several ways. For example, they sometimes served as "native" observers (*Beisitzer*) of the proceedings.[16] Askari also spread the word about *mashauri* and court days to surrounding areas so that local residents would know when to show up for them.[17] When complaints were made against specific individuals, the district office issued a form known as a *Schaurizettel* authorizing plaintiffs to summon the defendant to the station for a shauri. If those summoned did not report to the boma, askari were sent to arrest them. The Schaurizettel served as their authorization to arrest the accused and escort them back to the boma for the shauri. This preprinted official form featured bold black, white, and red diagonal stripes, with a picture of the imperial eagle in its center. Colonial officials filled in spaces on the form to indicate who was being summoned, when and where they should report, and other details as required. These "well-known and feared" documents had a Kiswahili nickname — "*bendera*-notes" (flagnotes) — because of their resemblance to the flags that flew over all the stations in German East Africa. According to one colonial memoirist, "Even if [the recipient] did not command the art of reading, he still knew what the black-white-red piece of paper [with the] strange bird with tattered feathers in the middle meant; it was the unmistakable official order to follow the askari."[18] Failure to do so could have dire consequences.[19] After escorting accused offenders back to the station, askari were also responsible for carrying out punishments for noncompliance with the Schaurizettel, often a mere prelude to a further punishment for the complaint that had generated the document in the first place.[20]

For example, a Schaurizettel issued at Marangu in 1905 stipulated that an askari named Kasi Moto was to pick up Msaba, a Chagga man who was living at a Lutheran mission station in Mamba.[21] Upon arrival he located Msaba's wife, Salime, but not Msaba. The askari struck Salime and accused her of hiding Msaba. The incident generated a short correspondence between the government station at Marangu and the missionary station at Mamba. Lieutenant Willmann at Marangu promised that Kasi Moto would be punished, noting that "the askaris should not hit" people.[22] Incidents like these reveal the processes through which askari independently carried out the will of the colonial state. Their presence incited fear among civilians, but askari also abused people because they were operating alone or in small patrols and needed to demonstrate their strength through violence or the threat of potential violence.

Documents like the Schaurizettel proved to other colonial officials that the askari had reason to be escorting specific people, or carrying valuable items or dangerous materials. In conducting the affairs of the colonial state, individual askari routinely traveled great distances as escorts, messengers, and guards. They were entrusted to move people and goods expeditiously and more or less safely, notwithstanding the challenging security and environmental conditions they often faced when traveling. Another official document, the *cheti cha rukhsa* (*Erlaubnisschein*, or permission slip) was preprinted in German and Kiswahili and included spaces for officials to enter information such as the number of women and children accompanying the traveler; number of weapons; pounds of gunpowder or lead (or both); and number of fuses the traveler carried. An example of a cheti cha rukhsa from 27 November 1902 shows that a junior officer at the Kilimatinde station sent an askari named Husseni to escort a prisoner to Mpwapwa, a minimum of five days' walk. The cheti directed that upon completing the trip, the askari was to return "immediately" to Kilimatinde, along with the pair of handcuffs he had used to secure his prisoner. Askari transited back and forth between the maboma, visibly transmitting the state's authority through their uniforms, their weapons, the bits of paper they carried, and the people and goods they guarded.

In carrying the Schaurizettel and other similar documents such as the cheti cha rukhsa, which authorized them to move unimpeded through the colony on colonial business, askari embodied state authority.[23] The documents also conferred legitimacy on their actions as they performed their duties, which reflected the itinerant nature of colonial administration. The authority and legitimacy manifested in these bits of paper expressed the power of the boma, emboldening askari to carry out violent acts against those they encountered in their everyday duties and whom they considered *washenzi*. Askari sometimes received punishment from their superiors for their violent behaviors, but they got away with most of their abuses. Generally, askari acted with impunity because their superiors did not witness their actions, and their victims may have feared making reports to skeptical colonial officials, or calling additional attention to themselves. Askari benefited tremendously from the colonial state's reliance on itinerant practices of power. These practices allowed them much freedom to act out their superiority complex, and to wrap their abusive actions in the state authority they carried with them.

EVERYDAY COLONIALISM III: EXPEDITIONS AND THE MABOMA AS SITES OF AUTHORITY

The fixity of the stations and their symbolism as colonial strongholds operated in relation to a fundamentally itinerant style of governance. Expeditions, whether "punitive" or otherwise, characterized day-to-day management of the districts. A colonial newspaper contrasted the boma with the relative weakness of Europeans outside the boma:

> The Negro has fear and respect for the boma. The *bwana mkubwa* is there, he has Askaris available, one can be locked up by him and receive his 25 kiboko strokes from him. All Negroes know that. The other Europeans, mainly those who don't belong to the Gouvernement, are not so powerful and dangerous, they don't need to have so much respect for them, all the less if the European concerned somehow, somewhere ever gets called *bwana ndogo*. It has indeed become clear to the Negro that Europeans who are not officials are not worth much.[24]

This author specifically referenced an ongoing debate within colonial society regarding settlers' perceived lack of stature vis-à-vis colonial administrators and a corresponding lack of respect from Africans. But in singling out the boma as the source of the European officials' strength, he also drew attention to a weakness in the colonial state—its reliance on mobility and "theatrical" performances of power, in which the askari played starring roles.[25]

Askari acted on the boma's authority with or without the presence of a German official on the scene. Their presence invariably made Europeans feel more secure, and equally invariably struck fear in the hearts of African civilians. The soldiers' reputation for violence preceded them, and news of the imminent arrival of an askari unit could cause villagers to flee their homes and go into hiding.[26] For this reason, askari were also frequently assigned to protect Europeans on their travels or on sites that the government considered strategically or economically valuable. Clement Gillman, an engineer involved in construction of the central railway line between Dar es Salaam and Morogoro in 1906, asked the government to send some askari to help him "manage" the railway workers: "I got one askari today with the right to punish my workmen with the usual '25.' This was done owing to the fact that some fresh workmen sent to me a few days ago, did not like to stay here and are running away by the score and don't do decent work. Now, however, having seen the askari and being afraid of the whip, they are alright."[27] Two weeks later, Gillman also sent for an askari to "research" a theft that occurred in his hut while he was asleep. The askari arrived three days later. The "research" into the theft yielded no useful information, but the askari nevertheless impressed Gillman by patrolling his camp overnight and reporting to him first thing in the morning while standing at attention and saluting.[28]

For Gillman, who supervised a large, diverse African labor force working on a difficult, protracted, and backbreaking project, the soldiers' presence shored up his authority.[29] The askari also gave him a sense of security in a dangerous environment, for the Schutztruppe and Maji Maji fighters were at war with each other in the regions directly south of the railway line at this time. An askari presence, even if only consisting of one or two men, signified that the Schutztruppe were not far away and that they would almost certainly respond to attacks on German interests with disproportionate retributive violence.

One further example of an itinerant practice of colonial rule illustrates how German authority moved from the maboma to areas surrounding them. In June 1902 the Tabora district chief, Oberleutnant Ledebur, set off with twelve askari on a five-week district tour. Along the way he visited various local rulers, as well as Moravian and Catholic missionary stations. According to his report, "Everywhere along the way there were shauris."[30] In the eastern part of the district, he heard mashauri in which complaints were made against an Ngoni leader accused of committing "a series of violations." The Schutztruppe considered the Ngoni a "warlike" people, and according to Ledebur, "Every man who is able to carry weapons indeed has them, and loves to carry them." "Several hundred" fully outfitted Ngoni soldiers, led by their "sultan," met Ledebur's column as it approached.[31] Ledebur's report provides specific evidence of how the soldiers' presence enabled Schutztruppe officers to enact colonial authority under such circumstances:

> The mashauri ended with me deciding to send the sultan, accompanied by an askari, to Tabora to bring an elephant tusk as tax. A report was sent there, [informing them] that the sultan should stay under the station's custody for four weeks so that he would get a lasting impression of the power of the government. I avoided telling him my decision on the spot because I only had a few askari with me and I wanted to avoid [causing] agitation among [his] people.[32]

The tusk "tax" was actually a significant fine, since by this time elephants were increasingly rare in the territory. And although the Ngoni leader's confinement was perhaps a more lenient punishment than being confined in chains or being publicly flogged, Ledebur assumed that the shame of being made to submit to the Germans in their boma would have the desired effect. The askari accompanying him provided a reassuring presence, but Ledebur clearly recognized his vulnerable position vis-à-vis the Ngoni. Ledebur thus decided to avoid outright confrontation with the Ngoni leader's soldiers.

Ledebur's strategy of secretly sending the "sultan" to Tabora under askari escort let him use the element of surprise to reinforce the colonial government's resolve.[33] It also allowed him to slip away to his next rendezvous before the Ngoni learned what had happened. But after Ledebur got under way to his next destination, he encountered a Tutsi informant who shared a rumor that the Ngoni had been harassing the Tutsi, a regional rival to the Ngoni. The informant told him that the "sultan" had not followed Ledebur's orders to leave for Tabora and that in fact he had even detained the askari assigned to escort him.[34] That news caused Ledebur to hurriedly march nine hours back to the Ngoni settlement. Upon arrival, Ledebur learned that his Tutsi informant had lied. The "sultan" had left "without resistance" for Tabora, as Ledebur had ordered him to do. The Tutsi's apparently fabricated story of the askari's detainment succeeded in pushing Ledebur to the urgent response he then undertook, which also suggests the extent to which Schutztruppe alliances could be manipulated by local intermediaries or agents.

Upon arrival in the sultan's land, Ledebur singled out a few people for "special punishment" to once again make manifest the colonial government's authority:

> For the collectivity, I ordered that 150 spears and 150 shields, as well as clubs, be delivered [to me]. This was carried out without delay. I could have just as easily gotten double the number. The weapons were burned outside the location. The Wangoni showed themselves to the end [to be] calm and obedient, so that I could soon march off without misgivings.[35]

The reference to exemplary punishments meted out to "a few people," probably hangings or floggings, hints at the violence that surely accompanied this disciplinary action against the Wangoni. Askari performing escort duties and other constabulary functions were always on the verge of such violent confrontations. It was this constant threat of askari violence that underwrote colonial claims to vast numbers of people and amounts of space. This example illustrates the degree to which the colonial government relied on the askari, as agents of everyday colonialism, to convince East Africans of the state's strength, represented most vividly by the maboma. Although these formidable structures helped the state perform military strength, it was colonial intermediaries like the askari who in their everyday activities made the state a tangible presence in the lives of many East Africans.

PERFORMING AUTHORITY

While in garrison, askari participated in training, labor, and administrative activities. As their omnipresence in German colonial visual evidence suggests, they also regularly performed in a variety of ceremonial roles that directly linked them with colonial authority. The military training askari underwent as recruits not only turned them into soldiers, but also transformed them into the quintessential ceremonial representatives of the German colonial state. Marked as the embodiment of colonial ideals of order and discipline, their uniformed presence at mashauri, floggings, executions, and parades helped colonial officials produce the "practical yet ghostlike effect" that indicated the presence of the colonial state.[36]

Military bases are obvious sites for analyzing the ways that states communicate their claims to authority and their ideals of governance to surrounding communities. Soldiers and militaries project ideas about order, hierarchies, and dominance through their routine practices and displays, as well as in their extraordinary performances of military might, many of which take place on or around military bases. Military officers cannot guarantee that their troops' sentiments will match with the ideals their bodies express in parades and other kinds of ceremonial performances. But for the purposes of producing the mystique of the state, ultimately their troops' sentiments are not all that important. From the officers' perspectives, what matters most is the performance itself and its ability to persuade audiences that they are witnessing a spectacle of mastery or dominance. Askari involvement in such performances placed them at the heart of local colonial politics, even if their presence was largely silent. The many ceremonial displays put on by colonial authorities played to different audiences. For Schutztruppe officers and NCOs, they reinforced what it meant to be good Schutztruppe soldiers. To East African observers of these colonial rituals, the askari performed the roles of obedient representatives of colonialism. And as they played these two roles, they conducted themselves in ways consistent with their self-understandings as big men.[37] In performing these ceremonial roles that required absolute stillness and silence, they likely experienced a blend of professional pride and boredom. Yet in performing these roles, they instantiated colonial dominance and expressed the very attributes that cued others to see them as men of standing.[38]

In their ceremonial capacities, askari helped shape perceptions of a world "fundamentally divided into state and society" (or colonizer and colonized, or perhaps even soldier and civilian).[39] Colonial officials set the process in motion by arranging—choreographing—these ceremonial settings for audiences made up of colonial subjects. The askari then performed their prescribed roles as soldiers and state agents, contributing to processes of state spatialization, whereby the presence of the askari also indicated the presence of colonial state authority.[40]

Yet askari performed the ritualized roles that created the structural effects of state making only as a subset of their more general roles as soldiers and state agents. After all, standing at attention in parade formations, executions, or judicial proceedings occupied only part of their time. Upon completion of these and other duties each day, they returned to their homes, families, and villages, where they assumed roles as friends, fathers, husbands, householders, and local authority figures. Moreover, the settings where they usually performed rituals of state dominance became spaces of social interaction and opportunity that drew increasing numbers of people to the maboma. Through their participation in the repetitive processes of constructing an image of a spatialized state through rituals of authority and dominance—practices that James Ferguson and Akhil Gupta call "vertical encompassment"—they became emblems of the opportunities and excesses of colonial politics and economies.[41]

Their back-and-forth movement between the contrived ceremonial settings in and around the maboma and the less formal spaces where they spent their leisure time point up the tensions that inhered in colonial governance practices, which relied so heavily on African agents. The rest of this chapter explores this tension by examining how askari involvement in many colonial practices of "enframing"—of presenting "the state" as something fixed, enduring, and outside of ordinary peoples' everyday worlds—worked in tandem with their positions as men of influence in local communities.[42] Their community involvement in dance associations known as ngoma, in turn, provided outlets for using some of the same elements of these enframing practices to different purposes. Moreover, the audiences who observed askari in these state-making performances used them as the starting points for improvising their own performance innovations, which bespoke local hierarchical concerns as well as concerns over the relationship between the maboma and Africans who lived in their orbits. Following the askari from their state-making activities to the less formal settings of their everyday work and leisure, reveals that the channels of colonial authority flowed through everyday social interactions and cultural expressions, tying increasing numbers of people to the colonial centers, some quite tightly, others less so. These patterns had at least as much to do with East African evaluations of the myriad changes colonialism brought as with colonizers' vision of a state that would accommodate its ideological, economic, and political goals.

In a diary entry for 22 October 1907, Schutztruppe lieutenant Philip Correck tersely described events held that day at the southern highlands military outpost of Gumbiro in honor of the German empress's birthday:

> Kaiserin birthday. The square is nicely adorned with garlands. 11 o'clock parade formation, speeches, pass-in-review. — [In the afternoon] big public entertainment. . . . Askari and natives produced almost an unearthly fervor.[43]

Though brief, his recollections of the day's events captured a transition from an official standard military celebration of a quintessentially German holiday to an informal, wider one that showcased East African festive practices and expressive cultures.

Correck's description of the "unearthly fervor" produced by the askari and other Africans that afternoon almost certainly referred to the East African phenomena of *ngoma*. In Kiswahili the word *ngoma* can mean drum, dance, or party, and indeed often encompasses all three at the same time. This chapter discusses ngoma as festive occasions during which dancing and drumming occur. In addition, ngoma are often sites where competitive dance associations (also called ngoma) perform in front of large, diverse audiences.[44] Ngoma were forms of entertainment and social interaction that drew audiences from far and wide, entangling soldiers, colonial employees, peasants, laborers, and household members in what one noted historian of East Africa has described as "total social phenomena." The attractiveness of the ngoma and the excitement that infused them came in part from the unpredictable combination of a regionally recognizable grammar of dance practices on the one hand, and the dancers' creativity in performing new movements and themes on the other.[45] In addition, ngoma were overwhelming aural and visual spectacles, in which liberal and widespread consumption of palm wine (*tembo*), locally brewed beer (*pombe*), and marijuana, or hemp (*banghi*), reportedly heightened the participants' mood.[46] German colonials differed greatly in their tolerance of ngoma, with some considering them little more than an annoying racket and others revering them as authentic folk customs. Still, the sheer volume of German descriptions of ngoma, and the consistent features that observers noted about them across time and space, speak to their centrality in East African sociocultural history.

FIGURE 7. In addition to their soldiering and policing duties, askari routinely practiced for the military parades that often accompanied special occasions and holidays in German East Africa. The formation pictured here marked the kaiser's birthday celebration in Dar es Salaam sometime between 1906 and 1917. On the left side of the photo is an askari band playing military music. The soldiers' khaki uniforms contrast starkly with the Europeans' white ceremonial uniforms. The parade ground is decorated with flags and garlands. A close look at the tree in the middle of the photo reveals that a number of African observers are watching the spectacle from above, providing an interesting contrast with the straight lines and rigid postures of the soldiers' formation. BArch, Bild 105-DOA6492/Walther Dobbertin. *Used with permission of the Bundesarchiv-Bildarchiv.*

Beyond their obvious festive purposes, ngoma embodied local articulations and struggles over meanings and practices of authority. German enthusiasm for honoring their holidays abroad as they would at home provided the occasions for colonial military parades to transition into ngoma. Parade pageantry and spectacle set the stage for ngoma by visually expressing colonial ideas about authority and the civilizing mission (see fig. 7). But in the ngoma themselves, African men and women had opportunities to interpret and challenge these ideas in settings that blurred ostensible boundaries between colonizers and colonized. This aspect of ngoma—as a kind of performance where East Africans interacted socially, expressed their understandings of how they related to authority figures, and entertained each other—lends itself to analysis of the everyday, local underpinnings of colonial cultures.

African soldiers, as agents of the colonial state, transmitted information about political authority and dominance through their physical movements and sartorial practices. They participated in and expressed colonial authority through uniform wear, drill, training, and parades. These practices also underwrote their personal authority and claims to status as men of influence in German East Africa. Thus elements of physical expression and bodily adornment contributed to African soldiers' abilities to project both personal and state authority, especially around the maboma.[47] Audiences who witnessed the askari in their various military performances rightly interpreted these activities as displays of authority and dominance, but they almost certainly interpreted them in other ways as well. Askari military performances, and local peoples' participation in the activities that followed, created zones within which people witnessed a colonial military culture that performed its violent tendencies while it also advertised itself as a site of economic opportunity and cultural advancement.[48] As East Africans gathered in and around the maboma on occasions like the German kaiserin's birthday, they participated in a range of social, cultural, and economic interactions that defy easy categorization. These multifaceted interactions took place within the orbit of German colonial authority but were not necessarily beholden to German authority claims. Instead, celebrations and festivals, with their associated parades and ngoma, provided spaces and opportunities for local colonial cultures to develop, reproduce themselves, and spread to other areas both near to and far from the maboma. It is thus useful to focus on the connections between parades and ngoma as interrelated instances that perhaps most vividly show the askari in their performative capacities as colonial intermediaries and men of influence in the communities around the maboma.[49]

Alongside practical military training, modern armies trained their soldiers for a variety of ceremonial roles, and the Schutztruppe was no different. Combining their training in proper uniform wear with their abilities to execute certain bodily movements "together in time"[50] and on command, askari performed in a number of ceremonial roles, such as standing for review when dignitaries visited their stations, or representing the state at mashauri, punishments, and executions. And of course, they marched in parades. On special occasions like the kaiser's (or kaiserin's) birthday, openings of railway lines, and visits from dignitaries, the Schutztruppe organized parades, concerts, and shooting contests. During these festivities, the askari paraded for European

colonial residents and employees, visiting European and African dignitaries, and East African crowds. These spectacular and "mesmerizing"
ceremonial displays performed colonial authority and ideals of order
and discipline for mixed audiences, including European soldiers, settlers, administrators, businessmen, and missionaries, and sometimes
their wives.[51] A local Tanga newspaper described one such celebration
of the kaiserin's birthday in 1902:

> The celebration of Her Majesty the kaiserin proceeded according
> to plan. In the morning, our police troops formed up behind the
> new boma. While the askari presented [arms], [Gouvernement
> Secretary] Sperling gave a short, pithy address, which ended
> in a toast to Her Majesty. Local leaders from the whole district
> gathered in great numbers for the celebration.[52]

These events always included parades, and German observers took
pride in the precise, controlled movements askari performed as they
executed the parade patterns. When the kaiser's son, Prince Adalbert,
visited Tanga in February 1905, a reporter for a local settler newspaper
described the scene:

> A command resounds, the weapons fly, rattling, from the shoul-
> der and click into the fist, and the honor guard of black askari
> motionlessly present for the high visit, while the black musi-
> cians, students of the government school in becoming sailors'
> uniforms, belted out the presentation march as if it were [hap-
> pening] on the Tempelhof field.[53]

In another example, the Usambara railway opened in Moshi on 7 February 1912 to great fanfare. A Lutheran missionary working in the Kilimanjaro region described the festivities as "colorful," with "festively
dressed Europeans" and local "chiefs" from the Kilimanjaro region in
attendance. The chiefs wore "European garb" as they arrived with their
entourages. He contrasted the chiefs with other African participants
who appeared to him more exotic, noting that "amongst the colorful
masses of many hundreds of natives . . . a band of wild [Maasai] in
warlike adornments [attracted one's eye]." The Gouverneur arrived
from Dar es Salaam to officially open the railway, taking the opportunity to decorate the senior railway engineer for his achievement. Finally, local police-askari paraded for the assembled crowd, marking the

beginning of the real festivities, including a feast and dancing.[54] On the parade ground, the askari reportedly lived up to the highest standards of Prussian military tradition while they performed one of the colonial government's favorite rituals of authority. Askari parades marked the beginning of festivities that lasted through the rest of the day and into the night. In honor of these occasions, askari also received small gifts of cash or goods such as tobacco. Once they were released from parade duties, they joined the crowds gathered around the maboma and in the streets to continue the festivities.[55]

Men and women who visited the maboma on such occasions per-haps considered the German parades and drilling sessions to be the Schutztruppe's specific style of ngoma.[56] This was unsurprising since the *beni*, the prevalent form of ngoma in East Africa, incorporated el-ements of European-style brass-band and military drill. Additionally, the Kiswahili word *kucheza*, which means to play or to dance, was also used to describe askari drilling sessions. Beni, from the English word *band*, developed out of a well-established complex of competitive dance associations that originated in Swahili coastal cultures of Kenya and Tanzania. The dance form, according to Terence Ranger, took its name "from its essential musical feature—the attempt to reproduce the effect of a military brass-band."[57] Although the dances performed to *beni* music varied widely across regions, all of them somehow in-corporated military drill as a theme. Each *beni* association also had "a hierarchy of male and female officers, with elaborate ranks (such as kaiser, *Gefreite*, *Soldat*), uniforms, and titles of honour." The ngoma leaders not only danced, but administered the group's competitions, memberships, and mutual-aid functions as well.[58]

By 1914 two branches of *beni*—the *marini* and the *arinoti*—had spread throughout German East Africa from their coastal origins in Tanga.[59] Marini and arinoti corporate identities had roots in regional status hierarchies that opposed "elite/coastal" and "vulgar/interior" social groups. The marini became associated with "the elite, the educated, the smart" peoples of the coast, and the arinoti became "essentially the society of the unskilled labour migrant" of the interior of Tanzania.[60] Schutztruppe askari and their dependents participated in these ngoma, with their membership in one or the other determined by when and where they were recruited into the organization.[61] The most senior soldiers dominated the marini, while more recent recruits became arinoti, thereby reinforcing existing rank and status hierarchies within the Schutztruppe itself.[62] To more fully grasp what was occurring in the kinds of performances held on the festive occasions described above, we must imagine the askari in two interrelated circumstances. On the one hand, askari drilled to German specifications on the parade field. Afterward, on the other hand, askari performed ngoma versions of these same specifications alongside other members of their ngoma and against members of rival associations.

It is no wonder then that such large African audiences came to the maboma to witness or participate in these and many other kinds of special events. In May 1898 a Schutztruppe major recorded his observations of a celebration associated with Ramadan at the Iringa station in the central highlands. His remarks offer a lush description of the ngoma as "total social phenomenon":

> Because it is a Mohammedan holiday, one sees festively dressed people walking around all over the place. The natives celebrate these festivals as soon as they have any contact at all with eastern African Mohammedans, enthused with it less because they have suddenly become convinced Mohammedans, but more because they enjoy the day off associated with the holiday. Everywhere on the streets the people performed their native dances, the so-called [n]Goma, and indeed in separate groups that correspond to their tribal affiliation. In the middle of the group a few men squat and with their fists pound [on] a variety of musical and other instruments: drums, empty tin boxes, upside-down water bowls, wooden boxes, and so on. People who understand music say that melodies are even recognizable in the spectacle. I clearly am not one of these people. Dancers move around the musicians, making a big circle and gradually moving themselves sideways, meaning in the direction of the periphery. Depending on the kind of [ngoma], the steps they make to move forward are different [from each other]. Everyone, musicians and dancers, sing simultaneously a text of constantly repeating text, [which is] mostly composed of only a few words. In the end, the monotone noise of the so-called music and the hours-long moving around in a circle has a quasihypnotic effect on the dancers, [so that] they often forget their surroundings. They fall into a kind of delirium, which for them seems to form the climax of the revelry. A large circle of

onlookers is formed around the dancers, who frequently give loud expression to their admiration for the featured spectacle.[63]

This rich description and the officer's admitted incomprehension of the "spectacle" he witnessed help us envision the social possibilities generated by the boma contexts that perhaps would not naturally come to mind when thinking about militarized geographies. The maboma exemplified colonial authority through their appearance and their everyday purpose as administrative and military headquarters. When ngoma occurred in such settings, they partly reinforced Schutztruppe efforts to stage their message of authority and paternalist generosity.[64] But as the passage above so wonderfully illustrates, ngoma were primarily occasions where African peoples expressed themselves through dance, or through their appreciation of others' dance abilities and creativity. Europeans' inability to comprehend or appreciate what they observed underlines their place on the fringes of the ngoma, although their numerous written descriptions of them show that they found these events endlessly fascinating.[65] The maboma, askari, and parades communicated colonial ideals of military, political, and ideological control, but East African revelers made and shared their own interpretations of the messages in tangible, if temporary, colonial communities. The ngoma form expressed itself against German notions of order and the values system that informed the German civilizing mission. In a fascinating way, however, the ngoma also incorporated military order, turning it into one of many dance forms and reinterpreting the concept of order within an East African framework.

As the askari transitioned from Prussian-style parade to post-parade revelry, they mingled with the gathered crowds, feasting, drinking, and dancing. Their celebratory mood and the competitive nature of ngoma created an air of potential mischief, confrontation, and violence.[66] On at least one such occasion, a celebration of the kaiserin's birthday in 1891, ended in a fight between "Sudanese" and "Swahili" askari, resulting in two serious injuries. The officer who reported the incident was very thankful that the "Zulu" contingent had "marched off" earlier in the day, insinuating that had they been present, the situation would have escalated into something much worse.[67] Fighting between different askari contingents was part of the dynamic of internal rivalries within the Schutztruppe, especially in its early years. Perceived insult or mockery between different groups of askari played out in ngoma displays that then turned violent. Indeed, mock fighting (*manova*, from *maneuver*) was part of ngoma choreography. The chance to observe dance styles, to experience the competitive atmosphere, and to verify rumors about the soldiers' novel performances drew sizable audiences to these events. Although clearly related in their fundamental characteristics, East African styles of competitive dance varied across different regions and social groups, and they changed according to economic conditions and tastes.[68] The musical and dance performances of the "Sudanese" soldiers' and their wives impressed observers, probably because they came from outside a more familiar East African complex of dance styles.[69] Commenting on an ngoma that occurred in Tabora in the mid-1890s, August Leue compared variations in East African dance styles to European dance cultures:

> As we Europeans have our waltzes and ländler, our françaises and quadrilles, so were the people of Tabora not limited to one single way of dancing. *Kibangi, Kimrima, Kiunguya* and [all the others], changed [from one to the next] in regular succession. On the whole it was always essentially the same thing; and the different attributes revealed themselves only to the eyes of the knowing.[70]

Leue emphasizes similarities between East African styles while also noting the variations that formed the basis for competition between groups. The built-in competitive features of ngoma added to the drama of the celebrations. His description also evokes the fluid creativity of the ngoma performers and the ways that these events blurred distinctions between community insiders and outsiders. Whether they occurred in the immediate vicinity of the maboma or in smaller settings elsewhere, the ngoma provided opportunities for all kinds of people to intermingle. The competitive aspect of ngoma reinforced, but also redefined, "communities of commitment" among participants.[71]

The public celebrations served several purposes for their German sponsors. For one thing, these festivities reasserted and reinvigorated an internal sense of *Heimat* and community for all Germans in the colony.[72] Europeans also used these occasions to socialize with other white people, celebrating the rarity of having so many together in one place at one time. The celebrations were also clearly designed to communicate to their colonial subjects messages about German political and military power, as well as the values of order and discipline they promulgated not just for their troops and employees but as part of their general civilizing-mission ideal of "education to work."[73] Festive occasions created opportunities to demonstrate their largess by relaxing the rules, providing food and drink, and distributing gifts to their employees and subjects. These actions also helped them enact the civilizing mission by conveying paternalistic notions of themselves as generous patrons.

German observers interpreted major ngoma associated with events like Prince Adalbert's visit as expressions of adoration for the European dignitaries involved, and "an approval of colonial rule."[74] But ngoma were also occasions where participants expressed their evaluations of German patronage and their abilities to carry out their "duties of reciprocity."[75] Danish planter Christian Lautherborn, who operated a plantation in northeastern Tanganyika in the 1890s, recorded a much smaller ngoma scene that shows the dynamic of reciprocal obligation in microcosm. Upon returning to his plantation from a visit to Europe in 1892, he was greeted by his workers:

> At the plantation I was received with jubilation by my Negroes, and I, naturally, had to go out with something good for them to eat—rice and a couple of goats. . . . The entire village of Bweni paid me a visit the other day with both of the chiefs with all of their wives and slaves, about three hundred men in all I believe. They had brought music and performed a dance with singing in the middle of the garden. "Bwana Malete is here again from Europe. He cleans his cotton with steam now. He himself is as strong as a steam engine, because he has eaten his mother's good food. She had not seen him for many years, and therefore, gave him the best she had. But it is good that he is strong, because he uses his strength to work and not to beat the Black people. We hope that he may be long among us." When the dance was finished, I passed out a couple of cases of mineral water among them, which they gladly drank. To the chiefs I gave the clothes I had brought, which pleased them greatly.[76]

The villagers praised Lautherborn, but not out of any simple joy over his return. Nor did they celebrate solely out of admiration for his skill as a cotton planter or his kindness as bwana. Their praise served to remind him of his obligations to his workers. It also perhaps expressed admiration for Lautherborn's immersion in modernity, as evidenced by the reference to the use of steam to clean cotton. The ngoma gave him an opportunity to demonstrate his generosity, and therefore his suitability as patron. Ngoma also had the potential to be tense affairs, because the "loosening" of social restraints on such occasions made "uninhibited mockery of authority" a common feature.[77] Such mockery included giving Europeans nicknames that poked fun at particular physical or behavioral traits or commented on their particular professions (for example, Bwana Fedha, or Mr. Money, was a bursar).[78] Dancers sometimes integrated these characters into their performances.

African audiences interpreted such occasions within local frameworks of mutual obligation or reciprocity. Along with other public spectacles such as executions or mashauri, German-sponsored festivities shaped new colonial sociabilities. These in turn produced new conversations, relationships, and ways of thinking about everyday colonial life. We can surmise that they expressed local identities, values, and hierarchies operating under the surface of the German fantasy of political and military control. Of course, the maboma also had darker purposes as spaces of oppression, where those who fell afoul of colonial authority received their punishments and, often enough, met their deaths. Yet as much as these occasions contributed to the colonial state's ability to express its claims to authority and dominance, they also helped generate local colonial cultures that gave people means and opportunity to discuss, perform, and imagine possibilities for living with, or perhaps even undermining, colonialism.

The most visible sites of these local colonial cultures were the "askari villages," where soldiers lived with their family members and dependents. As we have seen, these villages were usually sited right outside the maboma. Day and night they were lively scenes of work, recreation, and sociability.[79] Photography from this period shows askari in their home environments in relaxed poses, wearing interesting mixes of Schutztruppe uniform parts and coastal Swahili-style *kanzu* (long white robes worn by men) and *kofia* (close-fitting circular caps worn by men). Askari community members sometimes also appear in such photography, reminding us that life around the maboma was not strictly about soldiering. While out on an evening walk, the wife of a Schutztruppe officer stationed in the interior during the 1890s recorded her observations of "the life hidden beneath the apparent order of the askari village":

I saw a variety of [ngoma] . . . [Upon seeing me] the dancers attempted to show me their finest steps and movements performed, naturally, at the highest tempo. To walk through the wide streets, which are kept extremely clean, is a fascinating experience. All life is played out on the street. Everything moves through the night air, dancing or sitting on the verandahs — the houses are used only for sleeping or to protect against the cold. The doors are always open and as the streets are always dark, the figures around the fire can be seen as magnificent silhouettes in the distance.[80]

As with the Iringa Ramadan ngoma scene described earlier, it is easy to imagine that many different kinds of people were present at these evening dances in the askari villages, just as they were for ngoma that happened inside the boma proper or on the streets of the towns.[81] Partly for this reason, Schutztruppe officers preferred that their soldiers live in the slightly detached settings of the askari villages, instead of housing them inside the actual maboma. They helped "control the nightly tumult so relished by the Africans" — a reference to the frequent ngoma that continued until taps on many evenings.[82] German officers included information on ngoma in the handbooks and memoirs they produced for their peers and successors — a testament to their ubiquitous presence wherever askari were found, whether in garrison or on the march.[83]

In the end, however, officials could do little to control askari village life in any lasting way. Efforts to curtail evening drumming and dancing through curfews, fines, and taxes had minimal impact. In the end, Schutztruppe officers concluded that the ngoma helped maintain their troops' "healthy minds," and the regularity of the ngoma, which occurred whether they were in garrison or on campaign, perhaps served as a barometer of troop morale.[84] Another anecdote from Leue's memoir illustrates how much these spaces mattered in the everyday making of colonial cultures. An askari named Juma invited an enslaved Manyema woman named Schausiku, with whom he had fallen in love, to return with him to the *Askaridorf* to see the "Sudanese-ngoma" that followed festivities for the kaiser's birthday.[85] She agreed, giving Juma the opportunity to show off his house to her. He bragged of his aspirations to achieve higher rank, which would lead to a bigger house.[86] Later, after being promoted to the higher rank of ombasha, he bought her freedom and married her, creating the occasion for another ngoma: "On the same day [that Juma received permission from his officer to marry] in the askari village, the marriage was celebrated, in which nearly the whole company . . . participated. A phenomenal ngoma was held, and the honey pombe flowed in streams."[87] This anecdote indicates that life in the askari villages created possibilities for new social connections that furthered the growth of askari households, and by extension, the colonial stations. In these everyday moments, askari and other colonial intermediaries interfaced with colonizers and colonized, spurring the spread of colonial cultures, at least until 1918, when the age of German rule formally ended with Lettow-Vorbeck's surrender to the British.

HOUSEHOLDS AND STATE MAKING

In order to make everyday colonialism work, German colonial authorities tried to communicate a vision of modernity, civilization, and order to an East African public that they constructed as a mass of undifferentiated washenzi, even as they tried to categorize them using scientific methods developed in Europe. At the same time, they needed practical means of extracting from African populations monetary, material, and labor resources if they were to keep German East Africa viable as a colonial state. For this work, they relied on colonial functionaries who brought to bear a flexible combination of linguistic facility, literacy, local knowledge, and of course, the ability to threaten and use violence. Askari, as soldiers and agents of everyday colonialism, were integral to the state's ability to convey its messages about modernity, and to handle the face-to-face business of convincing or forcing people to comply with its objectives. At the same time, through their work, household relationships, and leisure activities, askari undertook the making of local colonial communities around the maboma. Colonizers also relied on their employees to draw others into the colonial orbit through family ties, business interactions, and communities of belonging such as ngoma. These colonial communities were spatially linked to the maboma, but were also mobile and porous, allowing people to become new or temporary community members with some ease. Thus in using colonial intermediaries, the state should have reckoned with some unpredictability in the conveyance of their message and how it was received.

Similarly, being part of the boma communities promised certain benefits, but it also involved acceptance of certain risks. Inclusion in an askari household meant that the askari, as *baba* (father), would provide food, shelter, clothing, and the security of kinship ties to his household members. In the best cases, dependents found comfort, companionship, and love in their homes. They became part of a recognizable community that, for all its flaws, also benefited from its enmeshment in the colonial state. In exchange, however, askari expected their dependents to work and to be obedient. Failure to do so could, and did, result in abuse. Dependents might choose to escape abusive households on occasion, but giving up socioeconomic security in these difficult times was not necessarily an obvious choice. In any case, these households and the communities that encompassed them were at the very heart of the colonial state's ability to function. It is for this reason that it is so important to consider how phenomena such as ngoma engaged different social groups across economic, social, and spiritual categories. Without understanding these spaces where new relationships were formed, and colonial relationships were reinterpreted, we also fail to understand all the ways that ordinary people are consciously and unconsciously enmeshed in apparatuses of authority and dominance. And this is why it is also important to study agents of state authority like the askari within their everyday contexts, as people with aspirations and projects that, in all their complexities, shaped everyday decisions and actions.

CONCLUSION
Making Askari Myths

THE SMALL Schutztruppe column that surrendered to the British in Northern Rhodesia in November 1918 had survived a long and exhausting campaign. Its members had stayed with General Paul von Lettow-Vorbeck through the hardships because they imagined his column to be the one place that would protect their position in the postwar colonial setting. Although many askari had deserted the Schutztruppe during the war because they felt the Germans had lost their *nguvu*, the twelve hundred askari who remained to surrender in November 1918 had stayed because they believed that Lettow-Vorbeck still possessed his ability to protect and restore them to their former status.

The problem was that the colonial society they had known before 1914 was undergoing rapid revision by the Allied victors, and there was no meaningful place for the askari in the new colonial order. The British War Office declined a request from General Jacob van Deventer, the Allied commander on the spot, to advance money to General Lettow-Vorbeck so that he could pay his former askari and porters. Instead, the War Office directed van Deventer to treat the German askari as prisoners of war and to hold them at internment camps in Tabora "or other centres in proximity to their homes, receiving subsistence only." The War Office further directed van Deventer to release them "by successive batches" and to have them "escorted by armed parties to their destinations[,] receiving subsistence."[1] And with that, the Schutztruppe in East Africa came to an unceremonious end. General Lettow-Vorbeck, their ultimate patron, eventually secured some of their back pay from the German government, but not until 1927.[2] In the meantime, the soldiers were left to find their ways in a devastated postwar political and economic environment. German askari did not join the KAR or any other regional colonial militaries in large numbers. Ali Kalikilima became a scout for the British mandate government's Locust Control Department. Others later became part of the tiny Western-educated class in Tanganyika who were active in missions, schools, trade enterprises, governmental administration, and ultimately the nationalist movement.[3] A few even traveled to Germany and made lives there. Like other people of African descent living in Germany at the time, however, they experienced significant hardship and tragedy, especially after Hitler's seizure of power, in 1933. Mahjub bin Adam Mohamed, the son of a veteran Sudanese askari who likely worked as a machine gun porter or askariboy during the war, moved to Germany in the 1920s, married a German woman and made a living as a language instructor and entertainer.[4] He was arrested in 1941 for violating Nazi racial laws, and although formal charges against him were never filed, he was interned in the concentration camp Sachsenhausen in September 1941, where he died of unknown causes just over three years later.[5]

On the whole, though, the askari became largely invisible as a social group after 1918, although some of them continued to live in the larger towns of Tanganyika or in enclaves around former Schutztruppe stations. The British district officer in Lindi in 1919 reported that "an unknown number of [former] German askaris [were] living a freelance existence in a series of miniature native republics" across the border in Portuguese East Africa, alongside "over a hundred . . . K.A.R. deserters."[6] Another "small discordant element" of ex-German askari lived in Songea in 1920.[7] And in 1924 Lutheran missionaries at a station near Kilimanjaro expressed dismay that some former German askari, described as Sudanese, were "propagat[ing] their [Muslim] faith" among local Chagga residents.[8] The soldiers' dispersal over a great geographic expanse, coupled with British inattention to the long-term fate of the Schutztruppe askari, has made them difficult to trace in the existing historical record.[9]

It is hardly surprising that men who had dedicated their lives to soldiering for the Germans were devastated not only by the demise of the

Schutztruppe but also by the lack of opportunity to continue soldiering in British-administered Tanganyika.[10] Ali Kalikilima recalled a visceral reaction to learning of the German defeat:

> For the first time in my life the harsh African sun chilled my flesh and I shuddered in its heat. My throat was tight and my saliva had dried up. I tried to swallow but the muscles in the back of my throat constricted. The hand of defeat, of shame, gripped me so tightly that I thought I would vomit and collapse, but I did not. I stood straight and tall, my head held high. The shocking news had drained my face, drained my spirit but Allah was at my side that day. I could only imagine how the general [Lettow-Vorbeck] must have been feeling, but he too stood straight and tall, his God at his side.[11]

Ali struggled to uphold his military bearing, even as his physical reaction to the "shame" of defeat threatened to betray him. By identifying with Lettow-Vorbeck, he acknowledged his comradeship with the rest of the Schutztruppe who surrendered at Abercorn. Ali's physical response to the news of defeat was a manifestation of the shame of defeat, but also his fears of an uncertain future. Mzee Ali was one of the "loyal askari" who surrendered alongside General Lettow-Vorbeck, but as we have seen, his reasons for staying to the end had more to do with his image of himself as a professional soldier and a man worthy of respect than with any abstract loyalty to the German Empire.

Ali's narrative in fact gives voice to a story that has been obscured by the German myth of the loyal askari, which celebrated the askari as heroes of the German colonial cause without taking into account their lived experiences and histories. The myth emerged in its most fully articulated form after World War I and continued circulating well beyond World War II. It presented the askari as brave and loyal soldiers who held out against all odds to the end of the arduous campaign in East Africa. It ignores or explains away askari desertions, which occurred in surprisingly high numbers, as the unfortunate choice of a few bad elements who did not measure up to Schutztruppe standards of professionalism and honor.[12] The loyal askari myth served its authors and audiences as an expression of German colonial nostalgia and longing for a return to the military virtues of the Wilhelmine era. As Roland Barthes so beautifully explains, "Myth deprives the object of which it speaks of all History. In it, history evaporates. It is a kind of ideal servant: it prepares all things, brings them, lays them out, the master arrives, it silently disappears: all that is left for one to do is to enjoy this beautiful object without wondering where it comes from."[13] The "beautiful object"—the askari—floats above history, disconnected from the realities of colonialism and war in East Africa in which every askari participated. Moreover, in using the askari to construct a myth about Germany's past as a model colonizer, colonial apologists elided the devastating toll that nearly three decades of German colonialism had exacted on East African peoples. The askari were thus more than just innocuous constituents of German colonial fantasies, and the myth of the loyal askari was hardly innocent.[14]

Colonial revisionists deployed images of the askari pictorially and in written form as a symbol containing different meanings. The loyal-askari symbol was used to stand in for certain dark realities in the German colonial experience. In addition, colonial apologists used the askari's image as a discursive symbol that helped them construct and maintain their own identities in postwar Germany, a period of pervasive uncertainty and turmoil. The colonial fantasies harbored by this particular group of Germans were based on experiences from their colonial past and postcolonial present—a present distinguished by military defeat, occupation of the Rheinland by francophone African soldiers, and the sudden absence of actual colonies following the Versailles settlement.[15] Colonial apologists who wrote during this period, mainly men who had lived and worked in the colonies as soldiers or administrators or both, used the askari to point up what they perceived as the gross injustice done to Germany in the postwar international settlement.[16] For this small group of colonial activists, the askari became a potent symbol of Germany's former military glories at home and abroad. In an interesting way, however, the figure of the stoic, uniformed, loyal askari acted as a substitute for any real engagement with Germany's history of violence in its overseas colonies.

In East African historiography, on the other hand, the askari emerged indisputably as the physical embodiment of colonial violence in all its forms. Mythmaking around this version of the askari had much firmer roots in the history of askari experiences and behaviors than the German colonial version described above. After all, their abusive and murderous acts were widely reported by Europeans and Africans alike.

Still, the depiction of askari as outsiders to Tanzanian history, as discon- nected or isolated mercenaries, requires some modification. This book takes a step in the direction of including the askari as makers of Tanza- nian history by foregrounding their involvement in colonial violence, while also linking their histories of violence to their socioeconomic aspirations and their immersion in everyday colonial life.

The askari's rapid demise as a visible social group following Ger- many's defeat in World War I resulted from their sudden lack of local patronage and their inability or unwillingness to transfer their soldierly skills to the new government. German efforts to help them were im- peded by geographic distance, lack of resolve on the part of successive German governments, and dwindling interest in Germany's colonial past as it grew more temporally distant to postwar Germans.[17] The ex- askari's marginality in the states that succeeded German East Africa (mandate Tanganyika and independent Tanzania) can be traced to de- pendence on the Schutztruppe organization. Their story is distinctive inasmuch as the colonial state for which they fought ended without adequate time or political will to prepare them to transition to a post- Schutztruppe life.[18]

Yet their story is also part of a larger pattern of veterans' experi- ences in global military history. In short, veterans are almost always disappointed in how their former employers treat them after they leave the military. Soldiers commit to military service with expectations that a patron or state will help them achieve their aspirations and a com- fortable lifestyle in their postmilitary lives. As long as the state contin- ues to uphold its part of the contract, the relationship between soldier and state remains intact. Wrapped in heroic platitudes and rhetoric intended to mask the realities of what the state asks its soldiers to do, that relationship flourishes in good times. However, when patrons be- come insolvent, or states cut their budgets, veterans come face to face with the limits of the rhetoric and the flimsiness of promises made. The incentives that convince soldiers to fight—citizenship, steady pay, health care, professional training, social capital, education, land, hous- ing, and so on—and that once appeared permanent and unassailable, begin to erode. Veterans become living, breathing everyday reminders of the incalculable and untold costs of militarization, militarism, and war, and societies tend to look away, not wanting to think too deeply about the work that soldiers do, how states authorize them to do it, and how it all relates to our lives. For the Schutztruppe askari, who had been responsible for so many abuses against Tanzanians, their postwar economic and social impoverishment does not seem at all surprising in retrospect. Studying soldiers in the multiple contexts in which they live and work—and thinking of them as intermediaries—makes it difficult to ignore how the potential for different modes of violence in their everyday lives affects those around them in a range of ways. This book uses a specific African colonial case to highlight the pattern, but its applicability is not limited to German East African temporal or spatial boundaries. This pattern should give us pause. If we better understand how diverse incentives and coercions are conceived and used by states and others to assemble armies to fight for them, we might also develop more sophisticated ways of thinking about soldiers and veterans beyond the heroic platitudes that tend to disavow their everyday realities, past and present, as well as the effects of their realities on the communities and societies who must find ways to live with them long after the wars soldiers fight come to an end.

Chronology

1821	Mehmed Ali Pasha begins Egyptian army modernization program
1820	"Arab" trading posts established in west-central Tanzania and Great Lakes region
184?	Nyungu-ya-Mawe and Mirambo born
1860	Mnywa Sele exiled from Tabora
1865	Mnywa Sele captured and killed
1881	'Urabi Revolt; Mahdiyya begins
1883	Hicks Pasha defeated at el-Obeid
1884	Carl Peters travels to German East Africa (GEA); Berlin Conference; Mirambo and Nyungu-ya-Mawe die; Mahdist siege of Khartoum begins
1885	Gordon defeated at Khartoum; Kaiser Wilhelm signs imperial charter; DOAG begins operating in GEA
1887	Emin Pasha relief expedition
1888	Abushiri Revolt begins; coastal blockade
1889	Wissmanntruppe assembled; Bushiri's fort at Bagamoyo stormed
1889	Second Emin Pasha expedition
1890	Emin Pasha claims Tabora; Wissmanntruppe sets up small post at Tabora
1891	Bushiri and allies defeated; GEA becomes crown colony; Wissmanntruppe becomes Schutztruppe; war against Hehe begins; Zelewski expedition
1892	Isike attacks Schutztruppe at Tabora
1893	Schutztruppe defeats Isike
1895	Nyamwezi recruitment to *Schutztruppe* begins

1898	Hut tax imposed; Hehe defeated (Mkwawa dies); Mahdiyya defeated
1902	Forced cotton cultivation in southern half of GEA
1904	Herero-Nama war (Southwest Africa) begins
1905	Maji Maji war begins; construction of central railway begins
1907	Maji Maji war ends
1908	"Hottentot" election; Dernburg reforms initiated
1912	Heinrich Schnee becomes governor of GEA
1914	Lettow-Vorbeck arrives in GEA as commander of Schutztruppe; World War I begins
1916	Dar es Salaam falls; Tabora falls; Lettow-Vorbeck stages troops south of Rufiji River
1917	Germans retreat into Portuguese East Africa
1918	Lettow-Vorbeck surrenders to Allies
1919	Lettow-Vorbeck returns to Berlin
1927	Ex-askari receive back pay
Late 1940s	Mzee Ali tells story to MacDonell

Notes

INTRODUCTION: RECONSTRUCTING ASKARI REALITIES

1. German East Africa comprised today's mainland Tanzania, Rwanda, and Burundi.

2. Marine-Oberingenieur Bockmann, "Berichte über Deutsch-Ostafrika," RM 8/368, p. 159, Bundesarchiv (hereafter cited as BArch), Germany. See also "Addendum to Mr. Feetham's memorandum on German East Africa," CO 691/20, p. 474, National Archives, Kew (hereafter NAK). See also Michelle Moyd, "'We don't want to die for nothing': *Askari* at War in German East Africa, 1914–1918," in *Race, Empire, and First World War Writing* (Cambridge: Cambridge University Press, 2011), 90–107, for more on this episode. All translations from German and Kiswahili are mine unless otherwise noted. *Askari* is an Arabic and Kiswahili word for soldier, police, or guard. European colonial armies operating in eastern and northeastern Africa used the word to refer to their African troops.

3. Porter shortages plagued the Schutztruppe and their Allied opponents, especially in the last two years of the war. See Bockmann, "Berichte," RM 8/368, pp. 94–95, BArch; Geoffrey Hodges, *Kariakor: The Story of the Military Labour Forces in the Conquest of German East Africa, 1914–1918* (Nairobi: University of Nairobi Press, 1999).

4. The full name of the German East African colonial army was Die Kaiserliche Schutztruppe für Deutsch-Ostafrika (Imperial Protectorate Force for German East Africa).

5. Bockmann, "Berichte," RM 8/368, p. 160, BArch.

6. Ibid., 160–61.

7. Ibid., 163–64.

8. See Michael Pesek, *Das Ende eines Kolonialreiches: Ostafrika im Ersten Weltkrieg* (Frankfurt: Campus, 2010), 230–42.

9. Cf. Gregory Mann, *Native Sons: West African Veterans and France in the Twentieth Century* (Durham: Duke University Press, 2006), 66–68.

10. See, for example, R. W. Beachey, "Macdonald's Expedition and the Uganda Mutiny, 1897–98," *Historical Journal* 10, no. 2 (1967): 237–54; David Killingray, "The Mutiny of the West African Regiment in the Gold Coast, 1901," *International Journal of African Historical Studies* 16, no. 3 (1983): 523–34; Bertrand Taithe, *The Killer Trail: A Colonial Scandal in the Heart of Africa* (Oxford: Oxford University Press, 2009). Perhaps the most famous mutiny in the history of African colonial armies took place at Camp de Thiaroye in Senegal during World War II. See Myron Echenberg, *Colonial Conscripts: The Tirailleurs Sénégalais in French West Africa, 1857–1960* (Portsmouth, NH: Heinemann, 1991), 100–104.

11. Thomas Morlang, *Askari und Fitafita: Farbige Söldner in den deutschen Kolonien* (Berlin: Links, 2008), 93–94.

12. Beachey, "Macdonald's Expedition"; Killingray, "Mutiny."

13. Bror Urme MacDonell, *Mzee Ali: The Biography of an African Slave-Raider Turned Askari and Scout* (Johannesburg: 30° South Publishers, 2006), 213; Moyd, "'We don't want to die.'"

14. On Lettow-Vorbeck's efforts to secure the askaris' back pay, see Marianne Bechhaus-Gerst, *Treu bis in den Tod: Von Deutsch-Ostafrika nach Sachsenhausen—Eine Lebensgeschichte* (Berlin: Links, 2007), 54–57; Stefanie Michels, *Schwarze deutsche Kolonialsoldaten: Mehrdeutige Repräsentationsräume und früher Kosmopolitismus in Afrika* (Bielefeld: Transcript, 2009), 135; Nachlass (hereafter, NL) von Lettow-Vorbeck, N103/94, BArch.

15. Benjamin Lawrance, Emily Osborn, and Richard Roberts, eds., *Intermediaries, Interpreters, and Clerks: African Employees in the Making of Colonial Africa* (Madison: University of Wisconsin Press, 2006), 6. See also Ralph Austen, "Colonialism from the Middle: African Clerks as Historical Actors and Discursive Subjects," *History in Africa* 38 (2011): 21–33; Emily Lynn Osborn, "'Circle of Iron': African Colonial Employees and the Interpretation of Colonial Rule in FrenchWest Africa," *Journal of African History* 44, no.

1 (2003): 29–50. For a helpful historical overview of colonial states in Africa, see Heather J. Sharkey, "African Colonial States," in *The Oxford Handbook of Modern African History*, ed. John Parker and Richard Reid (Oxford: Oxford University Press, 2013), 151–70. For the German colonies specifically, see Sebastian Conrad, *German Colonialism: A Short History* (Cambridge: Cambridge University Press, 2012), 66–85.

16. Felicitas Becker, "Traders, 'Big Men' and Prophets: Political Continuity and Crisis in the Maji Maji Rebellion in Southeast Tanzania," *Journal of African History* 45, no. 1 (2004): 6, 16–19; Jan Vansina, *Paths in the Rainforest: Toward a History of Political Tradition in Equatorial Africa* (Madison: University of Wisconsin Press, 1990), 73–77.

17. John Iliffe, *Honour in African History* (Cambridge: Cambridge University Press, 2005), 246.

18. Marcia Wright, *Strategies of Slaves and Women: Life-Stories from East/Central Africa* (New York: Lilian Barber, 1993), 179–223; Edward A. Alpers, "The Story of Swema: Female Vulnerability in Nineteenth-Century East Africa," in *Women and Slavery in Africa*, ed. Claire C. Robertson and Martin A. Klein (Portsmouth, NH: Heinemann, 1997), 185–219. On the social history of slavery and emancipation in German East Africa, see Jan-Georg Deutsch, *Emancipation without Abolition in German East Africa, c. 1884–1914* (Oxford: James Currey, 2006), esp. 191–92. Abdulrazak Gurnah offers a fictional treatment of East African debt peonage and involuntary incorporation into a creditor's household. Gurnah, *Paradise* (London: Hamish Hamilton, 1994).

19. Jamie Monson, "Relocating Maji Maji: The Politics of Alliance and Authority in the Southern Highlands of Tanzania, 1870–1918," *Journal of African History* 39, no. 1 (1998): 113–16; Heike Schmidt, "(Re)Negotiating Marginality: The Maji Maji War and Its Aftermath in Southwestern Tanzania, ca. 1905–1916," *International Journal of African Historical Studies* 43, no. 1 (2010): 50–55.

20. I am by no means the first to reach this conclusion. See Frederick Cooper and Ann Laura Stoler, "Between Metropole and Colony: Rethinking a Research Agenda," in *Tensions of Empire: Colonial Cultures in a Bourgeois World*, ed. Cooper and Stoler (Berkeley: University of California Press, 1997), 24; Timothy Parsons, *The African Rank-and-File: Social Implications of Colonial Military Service in the King's African Rifles, 1902–1964* (Portsmouth, NH: Heinemann, 1999), 6. On the connections between households and statemaking, see also Emily Lynn Osborn, *Our New Husbands Are Here: Households, Gender, and Politics in a West African State from the Slave Trade to Colonial Rule* (Athens: Ohio University Press, 2011), 1–5.

21. Cooper and Stoler, "Metropole and Colony," 21. See also Clifton Crais, "Chiefs and Bureaucrats in the Making of Empire: A Drama from the Transkei, South Africa, October 1880," *American Historical Review* 108, no. 4 (2003): 1036.

22. On the coastal war of 1888–91, see Robert D. Jackson, "Resistance to the German Invasion of the Tanganyikan Coast, 1888–1891," *Protest and*

Power in Black Africa, ed. Robert I. Rotberg and Ali A. Mazrui (New York: Oxford University Press, 1970), 37–79; J. A. Kieran, "Abushiri and the Germans," in *Hadith* 2, ed. Bethwell A. Ogot (Nairobi: East African Publishing House, 1970), 157–201; Erick Mann, *Mikono ya damu: "Hands of Blood": African Mercenaries and the Politics of Conflict in German East Africa, 1888–1904* (Frankfurt: Peter Lang, 2002), 55–92. For a comprehensive history of the complexities that led to the conflict, see Jonathon Glassman, *Feasts and Riot: Revelry, Rebellion, and Popular Consciousness on the Swahili Coast, 1856–1888* (Portsmouth, NH: Heinemann, 1995).

23. On the history of the German East Africa Company (Deutsch-Ostafrika Gesellschaft, or DOAG) and Chancellor Bismarck's decision to allow a colonial army to invade the coast in 1889, see Juhani Koponen, *Development for Exploitation: German Colonial Policies in Mainland Tanzania, 1884–1914* (Frankfurt: LIT, 1994), 61–84; Arne Perras, "Colonial Agitation and the Bismarckian State," in *Wilhelminism and Its Legacies: German Modernities, Imperialism, and the Meanings of Reform, 1890–1930: Essays for Hartmut Pogge von Strandmann*, ed. Geoff Eley and James N. Retallack (New York: Berghahn Books, 2003), 154–70.

24. On the unusual constitutional position of the German colonial armies, see Tanja Bührer, "Ein 'Parlamentsheer' ohne 'preussische Erbstücke'? Die zivil-militärischen Konflikte um die Führungsorganisation der Kaiserlichen Schutztruppen," *Militärgeschichtliche Zeitschrift* 71, no. 1 (2012): 1–24.

25. Kirsten Zirkel, "Military Power in German Colonial Policy: The *Schutztruppen* and Their Leaders in East and South-West Africa, 1888–1918," in *Guardians of Empire: The Armed Forces of the Colonial Powers c. 1700–1964*, ed. David Killingray and David Omissi (Manchester: Manchester University Press, 1999), 97.

26. John Iliffe, *A Modern History of Tanganyika* (Cambridge: Cambridge University Press, 1979), 106.

27. Nancy Scheper-Hughes and Philippe Bourgois, "Making Sense of Violence," introduction to *Violence in War and Peace: An Anthology*, ed. Scheper-Hughes and Bourgois (Oxford: Blackwell, 2004), 1.

28. Older literature referred to this conflict as the Maji Maji Rebellion. While some authors continue to use this formulation, I prefer to use the word "war" to highlight the perspective of those who fought against the Schutztruppe, many of whom did not consider German rule legitimate. On the effects of the *Schutztruppe*'s actions during the Maji Maji war, see Ludger Wimmelbücker, "Verbrannte Erde: Zu den Bevölkerungsverlusten als Folge des Maji-Maji-Krieges," in *Der Maji-Maji-Krieg in Deutsch-Ostafrika, 1905–1907*, ed. Felicitas Becker and Jigal Beez (Berlin: Links, 2005), 87–99.

29. The others were Togo, German Southwest Africa, and Cameroon. See Hew Strachan, *The First World War in Africa* (Oxford: Oxford University Press, 2004).

30. Ludwig Boell, *Die Operationen in Ostafrika: Weltkrieg 1914–1918* (Hamburg: W. Dachert, 1951), 427, cited in Edward Paice, *Tip and Run: The Untold Tragedy of the Great War in Africa* (London: Weidenfeld and Nicolson, 2007), 387.

31. Some examples include Byron Farwell, *The Great War in Africa, 1914–1918* (New York: Norton, 1989); Brian Gardner, *German East: The Story of the First World War in East Africa* (London: Cassell, 1963); Charles Miller, *Battle for the Bundu: The First World War in East Africa* (New York: Macdonald and Jane's, 1974). In addition, the East African campaign served as the backdrop for the C. S. Forester novel (1935) and the John Huston film (1951) *The African Queen*. More recently, see William Boyd, *An Ice-Cream War* (1982; New York: Vintage International, 1999); Giles Foden, *Mimi and Toutou's Big Adventure: The Bizarre Battle of Lake Tanganyika* (New York: Vintage, 2006).

32. Paice, *Tip and Run*, 3–6. See also Strachan, *First World War*. For perspectives on the Carrier Corps of the King's African Rifles and other porters conscripted by the Allies during the war, see Hodges, *Kariokor*; Melvin Page, "The War of Thangata: Nyasaland and The East African Campaign, 1914–1918," *Journal of African History* 19, no. 1 (1978): 87–100.

33. Iliffe, *Modern History of Tanganyika*, 241.

34. Paice, *Tip and Run*, 398.

35. Boell, *Operationen*, 28; Strachan, *First World War*, 102. A nominally separate *Polizeitruppe* existed throughout the period of German colonial rule, but police-askari performed largely the same roles as Schutztruppe askari. Both served in constabulary roles, and both fought Germany's numerous colonial wars in East Africa. In this book, the word *askari* refers to men who served in either (or in the case of some veterans, both) of these organizations, unless the sources used permit specific identification of individual askari unit designations. See Stefanie Michels, *Schwarze deutsche Kolonialsoldaten*, 16.

36. Gardner, *German East*, 193; C. Miller, *Battle for the Bundu*, 326.

37. Susann Lewerenz, "'Loyal Askari' and 'Black Rapist': Two Images in the German Discourse on National Identity and Their Impact on the Lives of Black People in Germany, 1918–45," in *German Colonialism and National Identity*, ed. Michael Perraudin and Jürgen Zimmerer (New York: Routledge, 2011), 173–83.

38. Paul von Lettow-Vorbeck, *Meine Erinnerungen aus Ostafrika* (Leipzig: Koehler, 1920); Lettow-Vorbeck, *Heia Safari! Deutschlands Kampf in Ostafrika* (Leipzig: Koehler, 1920); Lettow-Vorbeck, *Mein Leben* (Biberach an der Riss: Koehler, 1957).

39. Heinrich Schnee, *Deutsch-Ostafrika im Weltkriege* (Leipzig: Quelle und Meyer, 1919); Schnee, *Die koloniale Schuldlüge* (Berlin: Sachers und Kuschel, 1924). See also various reports by German Schutztruppe officers in N 103/96, BArch.

40. On the the askari in post–World War I German political discourse, visual culture, and popular culture, see Susann Lewerenz, *Die deutsche*

Afrika-Schau (1935–1940): Rassismus, Kolonialrevisionismus und postkoloniale Auseinandersetzungen im nationalsozialistischen Deutschland (Frankfurt: Peter Lang, 2006); Sandra Mass, *Weisse Helden, schwarze Krieger: Zur geschichte kolonialer Männlichkeit in Deutschland, 1918–1964* (Cologne: Böhlau, 2006); S. Michels, *Schwarze deutsche Kolonialsoldaten.*

41. See Gisela Graichen and Horst Gründer, *Deutsche Kolonien: Traum und Trauma* (Berlin: Ullstein, 2005), 380; Katharine Kennedy, "African Heimat: German Colonies in Wilhelmine and Weimar Reading Books," *Internationale Schulbuchforschung/International Textbook Research* 24 (2002): 7–26; Lewerenz, *Deutsche Afrika-Schau*, 39–45; Wolfe W. Schmokel, *Dreams of Empire: German Colonialism, 1919–1945* (New Haven: Yale University Press, 1964), 16.

42. Ludwig Deppe, *Mit Lettow-Vorbeck durch Afrika* (Berlin: A Scherl, 1919), 280; Heinrich Schnee and William Harbutt Dawson, *German Colonization, Past and Future: The Truth about the German Colonies* (London: Allen and Unwin, 1926), 168–69.

43. Richard Meinertzhagen, *Army Diary, 1899–1926* (Edinburgh: Oliver and Boyd, 1960), 84, 178.

44. William Wynne Honeywood, sound recording, 1974, Imperial War Museum (hereafter, IWM), London, reel no. 3; Frank Lawson Musto, sound recording, 1985, IWM, reel no. 3. See also Leonard Mosley, *Duel for Kilimanjaro: An Account of the East African Campaign* (London: Weidenfeld and Nicolson, 1963), 12, 22. For a comprehensive historical biography of Lettow-Vorbeck, see Eckard Michels, *"Der Held von Deutsch-Ostafrika": Paul von Lettow-Vorbeck: Ein preussischer Kolonialoffizier* (Paderborn: Ferdinand Schöningh, 2008).

45. For more on this topic see Moyd, "'We don't want to die'"; Pesek, *Ende eines Kolonialreiches*, 127–53; Strachan, *First World War*, 103.

46. Stefanie Michels, "Macht der Bilder: Herrschaftspose, Hetzbild, Anklage—Streit um eine Kolonialfotografie," in *Macht und Anteil an der Weltherrschaft: Berlin und der deutsche Kolonialismus*, ed. Ulrich van der Heyden and Joachim Zeller (Münster: Unrast Verlag, 2005), 185–90.

47. "band of mercenaries": Helmuth Stoecker, "The Conquest of Colonies: the Establishment and Extension of German Colonial Rule," in *German Imperialism in Africa: From the Beginnings until the Second World War*, ed. Stoecker, trans. Bernd Zöller (London: C. Hurst, 1986); orig. pub. as *Drang nach Afrika* (Berlin: Akademie, 1986), 93. See also G. C. K. Gwassa, "The German Intervention and African Resistance in Tanzania," in *A History of Tanzania*, ed. I. N. Kimambo and A. J. Temu (Nairobi: East African Publishing House, 1969), 97.

48. Nationalist historiography also obscured many local histories of Maji Maji and other colonial-era conflicts. For criticism and contextualization of this historiography, see James Giblin and Jamie Monson, eds., *Maji Maji: Lifting the Fog of War* (Leiden: Brill, 2010), 10–16; Thaddeus Sunseri, "Statist

Narratives and Maji Maji Ellipses," *International Journal of African Historical Studies* 33, no. 3 (2000): 567–84.

49. For an earlier call for scholarship in this area, see Koponen, *Development for Exploitation*, 567, 568. In fact, a small group of Africanist scholars began studying "collaborators" in the 1970s, but their efforts were largely overwhelmed by the resistance trend in African historiography. See Anthony J. Dachs, "Politics of Collaboration—Imperialism in Practice," in *The Early History of Malawi*, ed. Bridglal Pachai (London: Longman, 1972), 283–89; Allen Isaacman and Barbara Isaacman, "Resistance and Collaboration in Southern Central Africa, c. 1850–1920," *International Journal of African Historical Studies* 10, no. 7 (1977); Ronald Robinson, "Non-European Foundations of European Imperialism: Sketch for a Theory of Collaboration," in *Studies in the Theory of Imperialism*, ed. Roger Owen and Bob Sutcliffe (London: Longman, 1972), 117–42; Charles Van Onselen, "The Role of Collaborators in the Rhodesian Mining Industry 1900–1935," *African Affairs* 72, no. 289 (1973): 401–18.

50. On the *Schutztruppe* in East Africa, see Tanja Bührer, *Die kaiserliche Schutztruppe für Deutsch-Ostafrika: Koloniale Sicherheitspolitik und transkulturelle Kriegführung 1885 bis 1918* (Munich: Oldenbourg, 2011); E. Mann, *Mikono ya damu*; Morlang, *Askari und Fitafita*; Michael Pesek, *Koloniale Herrschaft in Deutsch-Ostafrika: Expeditionen, Militär und Verwaltung seit 1880* (Frankfurt: Campus, 2005); Pesek, *Ende eines Kolonialreiches*. For French colonial armies in Africa, see Echenberg, *Colonial Conscripts*; Nancy Lawler, *Soldiers of Misfortune: Ivoirien Tirailleurs of World War II* (Athens: Ohio University Press, 1992); Joe Lunn, *Memoirs of the Maelstrom: A Senegalese Oral History of the First World War* (Portsmouth, NH: Heinemann, 1999); G. Mann, *Native Sons*. On British colonial armies in Africa, see David Killingray, *Fighting for Britain: African Soldiers in the Second World War* (Woodbridge, Suffolk: James Currey, 2010); Anthony Clayton and David Killingray, *Khaki and Blue: Military and Police in British Colonial Africa* (Athens: Ohio University, Center for International Studies, 1989); Melvin Page, *The Chiwaya War: Malawians and the First World War* (Boulder: Westview, 2000); Parsons, *African Rank-and-File*. For Portuguese East Africa, see Allen F. Isaacman and Barbara S. Isaacman, *Slavery and Beyond: The Making of Men and Chikunda Ethnic Identities in the Unstable World of South-Central Africa, 1750–1920* (Portsmouth, NH: Heinemann, 2004). For southern Africa, see Timothy Stapleton, *African Police and Soldiers in Colonial Zimbabwe, 1923–80* (Rochester, NY: University of Rochester Press, 2011); Stapleton, *No Insignificant Part: The Rhodesia Native Regiment and the East African Campaign of the First World War* (Waterloo, ON: Wilfrid Laurier University Press, 2006); P. S. Thompson, *Black Soldiers of the Queen: The Natal Native Contingent in the Anglo-Zulu War* (Tuscaloosa: University of Alabama Press, 2006). Unpublished studies include Kevin K. Brown, "The Military and Social Change in Colonial Tanganyika, 1919–1964" (PhD diss., Michigan State University, 2001); Michael Von Herff, "'They walk through the fire like the blondest German': African Soldiers Serving the Kaiser in German East Africa

(1888–1914)" (MA thesis, McGill University, 1991); Bryant Shaw, "Force Publique, Force Unique: The Military in the Belgian Congo, 1914–1939" (PhD diss., University of Wisconsin, 1984).

51. For a compelling East African example of this dynamic, see Timothy Parsons, "'Wakamba warriors are soldiers of the queen': The Evolution of the Kamba as a Martial Race, 1890–1970," *Ethnohistory* 46, no. 4 (1999): 671–701. On colonial martial-races theories in Africa, see Anthony H. M. Kirk-Greene, "'Damnosa hereditas': Ethnic Ranking and the Martial Races Imperative in Africa," *Ethnic and Racial Studies* 3, no. 4 (1980): 393–414; Joe Lunn, "'Les races guerrières': Racial Preconceptions in the French Military about West African Soldiers during the First World War," *Journal of Contemporary History* 34, no. 4 (1999): 517–36; Risto Marjomaa, "The Martial Spirit: Yao Soldiers in British Service in Nyasaland (Malawi), 1895–1939," *Journal of African History* 44, no. 3 (2003): 413–32; Parsons, *African Rank-and File,* 53–97. See also Heather Streets, *Martial Races: The Military, Race, and Masculinity in British Imperial Culture, 1857–1914* (Manchester: Manchester University Press, 2004), 1–17. On colonial military recruitment and socioeconomic status in West Africa, see Echenberg, *Colonial Conscripts,* 7–24.

52. Parsons, "Wakamba Warriors," 675.

53. Echenberg, *Colonial Conscripts,* 7–19. For a typology of recruitment styles based on research in Europe and the Middle East, see Jan Lucassen and Erik Jan Zürcher, "Conscription as Military Labour: The Historical Context," *International Review of Social History* 43, no. 3 (1998): 405–19.

54. On military slavery as a central factor in the building of the Anglo-Egyptian army in the late nineteenth century, see Ronald M. Lamothe, *Slaves of Fortune: Sudanese Soldiers and the River War, 1896–1898* (Woodbridge, Suffolk: James Currey, 2011), 12–19, 44–51.

55. See, for example, Echenberg, *Colonial Conscripts,* 22–24; Isaacman and Isaacman, *Slavery and Beyond,* 14–15, 61–68; David Killingray, "Gender Issues and African Colonial Armies," in Killingray and Omissi, *Guardians of Empire,* 221–48; E. Mann, *Mikono ya damu,* 237–41; Stefanie Michels, "Soldatische Frauenwelten," in *Frauen in den deutschen Kolonien,* ed. Marianne Bechhaus-Gerst and Mechthild Leutner (Berlin: Links, 2009), 122–30; Timothy Parsons, "'All Askaris are family men': Sex, Domesticity and Discipline in the King's African Rifles, 1902–1964," in Killingray and Omissi, *Guardians of Empire,* 157–78; Parsons, *African Rank-and-File,* 145–81; J. Malcolm Thompson, "Colonial Policy and the Family Life of Black Troops in French West Africa, 1817–1904," *International Journal of African Historical Studies* 23, no. 3 (1990): 423–53; Sarah Zimmerman, "*Mesdames Tirailleurs* and Indirect Clients: West African Women and the French Colonial Army, 1908–1918," *International Journal of African Historical Studies* 44, no. 2 (2011): 299–322.

56. Michelle Moyd, "Making the Household, Making the State: Colonial Military Communities and Labor in German East Africa," *International Labour and Working-Class History* 80, no. 1 (2011): 53–76.

57. I am grateful to Timothy Parsons for this astute observation.

58. Luise White, *The Comforts of Home: Prostitution in Colonial Nairobi* (Chicago: University of Chicago Press, 1990).

59. Lamothe, *Slaves of Fortune*, 72, 78–89.

60. J. Thompson, "Colonial Policy," 435; Zimmerman, "*Mesdames Tirailleurs*," 300.

61. Echenberg, *Colonial Conscripts*, 87–104.

62. G. Mann, *Native Sons*, 63–68.

63. But see Isaacman and Isaacman, *Slavery and Beyond*, esp. 1–18, which traces how the martial identity Chikunda was made and remade over the course of about two hundred years of Mozambican history.

64. Richard Reid, "Past and Presentism: The 'Precolonial' and the Foreshortening of African History," *Journal of African History* 52, no. 2 (2011): 136, 160.

65. Ibid., 150–51. But for early exceptions, see Joseph Miller, "The Imbangala and the Chronology of Early Central African History," *Journal of African History* 13, no. 4 (1972): 549–74; John Thornton, "The Art of War in Angola, 1575–1680," *Comparative Studies in Society and History* 30, no. 2 (1988): 360–78.

66. R. Reid, "Past and Presentism," 151.

67. T. O. Ranger, *Dance and Society in Eastern Africa, 1890–1970: The Beni Ngoma* (Berkeley: University of California Press, 1975); Michael Pesek, *Tänze der Hoffnung, Tänze der Macht: Koloniale Erfahrung und ästhetischer Ausdruck im östlichen Afrika*, Sozialanthropologische Arbeitspapiere, no. 72 (Berlin: Das Arabische Buch, 1997).

68. *Boma* [pl. *maboma*] is a Kiswahili word used to describe many different kinds of fortresses and enclosures in East Africa. The Schutztruppe built maboma as it established outposts throughout the territory. They were built in various styles, but all were multipurpose facilities meant to serve as fortress, community center, and administrative-military headquarters all in one.

69. For work that moves in this direction, see Parsons, *African Rank-and-File*, 110–24; Killingray, *Fighting for Britain*, 82–98, 101–8. See also Bruce Vandervort, *Wars of Imperial Conquest in Africa, 1830–1914* (Bloomington: Indiana University Press, 1998), which surveys colonial wars across the continent.

70. "more comparative work": Wayne Lee, "A Final Word," *Journal of American History* 93, no. 4 (2007): 1161–62; "cultural assumptions": Brian Holden Reid, "American Military History: The Need for Comparative Analysis," *Journal of American History* 93, no. 4 (2007): 1154–57. See also Brian P. Farrell, "Mind and Matter: The Practice of Military History with Reference to Britain and Southeast Asia," *Journal of American History* 93, no. 4 (2007): 1146–50. These essays were written in response to Wayne E. Lee, "Mind and Matter—Cultural Analysis in American Military History: A Look at the State of the Field," *Journal of American History* 93, no. 4 (2007): 1116–42. See also Robert M. Citino, Brian McAllister Linn, Peter Lorge, and James Jay Carafano, "Comparative Ways of War: A Roundtable," *Historically Speaking* 11, no. 5 (2010): 20–26; Aaron P. Jackson, "Expanding the Scope and Accessibility

of Non-Western Military History," *Journal of Military History* 75, no. 2 (2011): 603–13; Norman Etherington, "Barbarians Ancient and Modern," *American Historical Review* 116, no. 1 (2011): 31–57; Randolf G. S. Cooper, "Culture, Combat, and Colonialism in Eighteenth- and Nineteenth-Century India," *International History Review* 27, no. 3 (2005): 534–49. John Thornton offered an early pointed critique of the thin relationship between African military history and the wider field of military history. Thornton, *Warfare in Atlantic Africa, 1500–1800* (London: UCL Press, 1999), 1–18.

71. Lee, "Mind and Matter," 1119. See also Robert M. Citino, "Military Histories Old and New: A Reintroduction," *American Historical Review* 112, no. 4 (2007): 1084–90; John A. Lynn, *Battle: A History of Combat and Culture* (New York: Westview, 2003), xiv–xxii; Roger J. Spiller, "Military History and Its Fictions," *Journal of Military History* 70, no. 4 (2006): 1081–97.

72. Historians of Africa whose work analyzes the psychological, religious, and cultural meanings of violence in warfare include Inge Brinkmann, *A War for People: Civilians, Mobility, and Legitimacy in South-East Angola during the MPLA's War for Independence* (Cologne: Köppe, 2005); Stephen Ellis, *The Mask of Anarchy: The Destruction of Liberia and the Religious Dimension of an African Civil War*, 2nd ed. (New York: NYU Press, 2007); Ian Knight, *The Anatomy of the Zulu Army from Shaka to Cetshwayo, 1818–1879* (London: Greenhill Books, 1995). For insightful anthropological treatments, see Heike Behrend, *Alice Lakwena and the Holy Spirits: War in Northern Uganda* (Oxford: James Currey, 1999); Sverker Finnström, *Living with Bad Surroundings: War, History, and Everyday Moments in Northern Uganda* (Durham, NC: Duke University Press, 2008); Stephen Lubkemann, *Culture in Chaos: An Anthropology of the Social Condition in War* (Chicago: University of Chicago Press, 2008); Carolyn Nordstrom, *A Different Kind of War Story* (Philadelphia: University of Pennsylvania Press, 1997); Paul Richards, *Fighting for the Rainforest: War, Youth and Resources in Sierra Leone* (Oxford: James Currey, 1996).

73. Noteworthy exceptions include Bührer, *Kaiserliche Schutztruppe*; Lamothe, *Slaves of Fortune*; E. Mann, *Mikono ya damu*; Page, *Chiwaya War*; Pesek, *Ende eines Kolonialreichs*; Stapleton, *No Insignificant Part*; 'Ismat Hasan Zulfo, *Karari: The Sudanese Account of the Battle of Omdurman*, trans. Peter Clark (London: F. Warne, 1980). For a critical overview of the state of the field, see Richard Reid, "Warfare and the Military," in *The Oxford Handbook of Modern African History*, ed. John Parker and Richard Reid (Oxford: Oxford University Press, 2013), 114–31. See also John Lamphear, ed., *African Military History* (Aldershot, UK: Ashgate, 2007), for a useful collection of some of the most important journal articles dealing with Africa's history of warfare.

74. "warscapes": Nordstrom, *War Story*.

75. Lawrance, Osborn, and Roberts, *Intermediaries, Interpreters*, 3–7. In 1994, Koponen invited further study of these "intermediate" colonial employees but drew a distinction between "civil administration" and the "repressive wing of the colonial state, the armed forces." The askari's everyday lives show

this distinction to be less sharp than Koponen's description suggests. See Koponen, *Development for Exploitation*, 568–70. For examples of work that answers Koponen's call, see Pesek, *Koloniale Herrschaft*; John McCracken, "Coercion and Control in Nyasaland: Aspects of the History of a Colonial Police Force," *Journal of African History* 27, no. 1 (1986): 127–47. For a criticism of scholarship on "intermediaries" as being too focused on "African colonial actors as 'clients' of European colonial 'patrons' and as 'brokers' of imperial encounters," see Moses E. Ochonu, *Colonialism by Proxy: Hausa Imperial Agents and Middle Belt Consciousness in Nigeria* (Bloomington: Indiana University Press, 2014), 11–16. Ochonu's analysis of Hausa-Fulani "subcolonial rule" reveals similarities to the Schutztruppe askari, particularly in their shared belief in a civilizing mission that made them "colonials in their own limited rights," allowing them "to act in ways that went far beyond mediation" (13).

76. I am grateful to Timothy Parsons for this insight.

77. Christian Methfessel, "Spreading the European Model by Military Means? The Legitimization of Colonial Wars and Imperialist Interventions in Great Britain and German around 1900," *Comparativ* 22, no. 6 (2012): 42–60; George Steinmetz, "'The Devil's Handwriting': Precolonial Discourse, Ethnographic Acuity, and Cross-Identification in German Colonialism," *Comparative Studies in Society and History* 45, no. 1 (2003): 41–95.

78. The French and Portuguese cases are exceptional because of their longer colonial presence on the African continent.

79. See, for example, O. W. Furley, "The Sudanese Troops in Uganda," *African Affairs* 58, no. 233 (1959): 311–28, which maps Lugard's assembly of a small army of Sudanese soldiers for the British East Africa Company. This army formed the core of the Uganda Rifles, which was later incorporated into the KAR. For the German East Africa Company, see Pesek, *Koloniale Herrschaft*. In the case of France's West African empire, these processes happened much earlier, with the *tirailleurs sénégalais* becoming an official army in 1857. Still, the "conquest of the Sudan" embroiled French colonial forces in the "scramble" of the 1880s and 1890s in ways similar to the experiences of the British in northeastern and eastern Africa and the Germans in East Africa. See Echenberg, *Colonial Conscripts*, 8–19; Martin Klein, *Slavery and Colonial Rule in French West Africa* (Cambridge: Cambridge University Press, 1998), 77–93; C. W. Newbury and A. S. Kanya-Forstner, "French Policy and the Origins of the Scramble for West Africa," *Journal of African History* 10, no. 2 (1969): 253–76. For Portuguese East Africa, see Isaacman and Isaacman, *Slavery and Beyond*, 290–98.

80. David Killingray, "The Maintenance of Law and Order in British Colonial Africa," *African Affairs* 85, no. 340 (1986): 420. I am grateful to Timothy Parsons for this insight.

81. Thomas Morlang, "'Prestige der Rasse' contra 'Prestige des Staates': Die Diskussionen über die Befugnisse farbiger Polizeisoldaten gegenüber Europäern in den deutschen Kolonien," *Zeitschrift für Geschichtswissenschaft* 49, no. 6 (2001): 498–509. See also Marie Muschalek, "Policing Colonial

Africa: Rethinking a Research Agenda," unpublished seminar paper, History Department, Cornell University, 2009; Muschalek, "Everyday Violence and the Production of Colonial Order: The Police in German Southwest Africa, 1905–1915" (PhD diss., Cornell University, 2014).

82. Killingray, "Law and Order," 420–21; McCracken, "Coercion and Control," 128–38; Muschalek, "Policing Colonial Africa," 4–5. For French West Africa, see Gregory Mann, "What Was the *Indigénat*? The 'Empire of Law' in French West Africa," *Journal of African History* 50, no. 3 (2009); Henri Brunschwig, "French Expansion and Local Reactions in Black Africa in the Time of Imperialism," in *Expansion and Reaction: Essays on European Expansion and Reaction in Asia and Africa*, ed. H. L. Wesseling (Leiden: Leiden University Press, 1978), 116–40.

83. Jean-François Bayart, *The Illusion of Cultural Identity* (Chicago: University of Chicago Press, 2005), xii.

84. Koponen, *Development for Exploitation*, 129–42. See also Ben Jones, *Beyond the State in Rural Uganda* (Edinburgh: Edinburgh University Press, 2009), 9–10, 60–61, 163–65; James C. Scott, *The Art of Not Being Governed: An Anarchist History of Upland Southeast Asia* (New Haven: Yale University Press, 2009), 1–9.

85. A. H. M. Kirk-Greene, "The Thin White Line: The Size of the British Colonial Service in Africa," *African Affairs* 79, no. 314 (1980): 25–26, 38–44.

86. Michael Pesek, "Colonial Conquest and the Struggle for the Presence of the Colonial State in German East Africa, 1885–1903" in *Inventing Collateral Damage: Civilian Casualties, War, and Empire*, ed. Stephen J. Rockel and Rick Halpern (Toronto: Between the Lines, 2009), 163, 164–65. See also Johannes Fabian, *Out of Our Minds: Reason and Madness in the Exploration of Central Africa* (Berkeley: University of California Press, 2000), 102–27.

87. Pesek, "Colonial Conquest," 170.

88. Ibid., 164; Lawrance, Osborn, and Roberts, *Intermediaries, Interpreters*, 5–7.

89. "self-understanding" and "situated subjectivities": Frederick Cooper with Rogers Brubaker, "Identity," in *Colonialism in Question: Theory, Knowledge, History* (Berkeley: University of California Press, 2005), 73–75.

90. Lisa A. Lindsay and Stephan F. Miescher, "Introduction: Men and Masculinities in Modern African History," in *Men and Masculinities in Modern Africa*, ed. Lindsay and Miescher (Portsmouth, NH: Heinemann, 2003), 21.

91. Marcia Wright, *Strategies of Slaves and Women: Life Stories from East/Central Africa* (New York: Lilian Barber, 1993), 180.

92. Ibid.

93. See, for example, G21/592, Strafsache Miersen, Tanzania National Archives (hereafter, TNA), Dar es Salaam. I discuss this case further in chapter 4.

94. Bayart, *Illusion of Cultural Identity*, xii.

95. The term *wives* is problematic when referring to the women in the askari communities. Many women who lived and worked in askari households

may not have been recognized by the colonial state as formal wives. I therefore use the term askari *women* to refer to women who maintained some kind of domestic relationship to the askari, unless specific textual references provide better context or I am quoting directly from the sources. For comparison, see Zimmerman, "*Mesdames Tirailleurs*," 304.

96. Cf. Austen, "Colonialism from the Middle," 21–33.

97. Moyd, "Becoming *Askari*," 267–302.

98. The seminal work in this field is Susanne Zantop, *Colonial Fantasies: Conquest, Family, and Nation in Precolonial Germany, 1770–1870* (Durham, NC: Duke University Press, 1997). More recently, see the collected essays in Volker Langbehn and Mohammad Salama, eds., *German Colonialism: Race, the Holocaust, and Postwar Germany* (New York: Columbia University Press, 2011).

99. Richard Reid, *Warfare in African History* (Cambridge: Cambridge University Press, 2012), 150.

100. On "the strange career of African voices," see David William Cohen, Stephan F. Miescher, and Luise White, "Voices, Words, and African History," introduction to *African Words, African Voices: Critical Practices in Oral History*, ed. Cohen, Miescher, and White (Bloomington: Indiana University Press, 2001), 4–10.

101. An English-language exception is E. Mann, *Mikono ya damu*. For German-language treatments, see Bührer, *Kaiserliche Schutztruppe*; Susanne Kuss, *Deutsches Militär auf kolonialen Kriegsschauplätzen: Eskalation von Gewalt zu Beginn des 20. Jahrhunderts* (Berlin: Links, 2010).

102. Ann Stoler, "Colonial Archives and the Arts of Governance," *Archival Science* 2, nos. 1–2 (2002): 100. See also Steinmetz, "'Devil's handwriting,'" 46–51, 52–54.

103. Paul Steege, Andrew Bergerson, Maureen Healy, and Pamela E. Swett, "The History of Everyday Life: A Second Chapter," *Journal of Modern History* 80, no. 2 (2008), 374.

104. Wright, *Strategies of Slaves*, 180.

105. Sandra Greene, *West African Narratives of Slavery: Texts from Late Nineteenth- and Early Twentieth-Century Ghana* (Bloomington: Indiana University Press, 2011), 25.

106. See also James L. Giblin with Blandina Kaduma Giblin, *A History of the Excluded: Making Family a Refuge from State in Twentieth-Century Tanzania* (Oxford: James Currey, 2005), 3–4; Luise White, *The Assassination of Herbert Chitepo: Texts and Politics in Zimbabwe* (Bloomington: Indiana University Press, 2003), 12, 15; Stephan F. Miescher, "The Life Histories of Boakye Yiadom (Akasease Kofi of Abetifi, Kwawu): Exploring the Subjectivity and 'Voices' of a Teacher-Catechist in Colonial Ghana," in White, Miescher, and Cohen, *African Words*, 163, 187–88.

107. August Leue, *Dar es Salaam: Bilder aus dem Kolonialleben* (Berlin: Wilhelm Süsserott, 1903); Bror Urme MacDonell, *Mzee Ali: The Biography*

of an African Slave-Raider Turned Askari and Scout (Johannesburg: 30° South Publishers, 2006).

108. Greene, *West African Narratives*, 2.

109. Ibid., 10.

110. Ibid., 12. See also Dwight McBride, *Impossible Witnesses: Truth, Abolitionism, and Slave Testimony* (New York: New York University Press, 2001), 6–7.

111. "projects": Sherry Ortner, *Anthropology and Social Theory: Culture, Power, and the Acting Subject* (Durham, NC: Duke University Press, 2006), 143.

112. Clifford Geertz, "'From the Native's Point of View': On the Nature of Anthropological Understanding," *Bulletin of the American Academy of Arts and Sciences* 28, no. 1 (1974): 29–30.

113. Janet McIntosh, *The Edge of Islam: Power, Personhood, and Ethnoreligious Boundaries on the Kenya Coast* (Durham, NC: Duke University Press, 2009), 177–84, 189.

114. Abdulcher Farrag's narrative, as related by Schutztruppe officer August Leue, traces his life history from his youth in late-nineteenth-century Sudan to his death in German East Africa in the 1890s. I discuss his narrative at length in chapter 1.

115. The Zelewski column was attacked by Hehe soldiers, resulting in its almost total destruction. I discuss the Zelewski expedition more in chapter 3.

116. NL Prittwitz und Gaffron, Ergänzungstagebuch für die Zeit vom 16.4.1898 bis 30.3.1899 zu dem Haupttagebuch aus Deutsch-Ostafrika, 4.6.98, box 248, folder 6/248, p. 8, Leibniz Institut für Länderkunde, Leipzig (hereafter, LIL).

117. MacDonell, *Mzee Ali*, 20. Like Farrag's narrative, Mzee Ali's biography presents substantial analytical challenges because of the layers of mediation involved in its production. In the late 1940s, some three decades after the *Schutztruppe's* surrender in World War I, Ali narrated his life story to a British colonial employee, Bror MacDonell. Both Ali and MacDonell were employees of the British colonial government's Department of Locust Control, working mainly in southern Tanganyika and the northeastern corner of Northern Rhodesia (today's Zambia). No information on the languages involved is provided. MacDonell later dictated the account to a typist. In 2005, MacDonell's son gave the manuscript to the 30 Degrees South publishing house, which specializes in southern African nonfiction, military history, and memoirs. There, it was heavily edited. For more on the difficulties of using this text, see Moyd, "Becoming *Askari*," 117–20.

118. Leue, *Dar-es-Salaam*, foreword.

119. See also David M. Ciarlo, "Rasse konsumieren: Von der exotischen zur kolonialen Imagination in der Bildreklame des Wilhelminischen Kaiserreichs," in *Phantasiereiche: Zur Kulturgeschichte des deutschen Kolonialismus*, ed. Birthe Kundrus (Frankfurt: Campus, 2003). Comparative examples using similar tropes in later periods can be found in Bengerstorf, *Unter der Tropensonne*; Nigmann, *Schwarze Schwänke: Fröhliche Geschichten aus unserem*

schönen alten Deutsch Ostafrika (Berlin: Safari, 1922); Otto Stollowsky, *Jambo Sana! Lustige Geschichten, Plaudereien und Schnurren aus dem Leben in Deutsch-Ost-Afrika* (Leipzig-Anger: Walther Dachsel, 1935).

120. Cited in Glassman, *Feasts and Riot*, 253.

121. Wright, *Strategies of Slaves*, 180.

122. Thomas Kühne, "Comradeship: Gender Confusion and Gender Order in the German Military, 1918–1945," in *Home/Front: The Military, War, and Gender in Twentieth-Century Germany*, ed. K. Hagemann and S. Schüler-Springorum (Oxford: Berg, 2002), 233–54.

123. "human dimensions": David G. Thompson, "Villains, Victims, and Veterans: Buchheim's *Das Boot* and the Problem of the Hybrid Novel-Memoir as History," *Twentieth Century Literature* 39, no. 1 (1993): 59–78, 60. See also McBride, *Impossible Witnesses*, 6–7.

124. On the disputed presence of Africans, mainly as musicians, in German militaries from the seventeenth century to the end of the Kaiserreich, see Peter Martin, *Schwarze Teufel, edle Mohren: Afrikaner in Geschichte und Bewusstsein der Deutschen* (Hamburg: Hamburger Edition, 2001), 113–28.

125. Thanks to Paul Steege for reminding me of this point.

126. Jan-Georg Deutsch, "Celebrating Power in Everyday Life: The Administration of Law and the Public Sphere in Colonial Tanzania, 1890–1914," *Journal of African Cultural Studies* 15, no. 1 (2002): 93.

127. Alf Lüdtke, "What Is the History of Everyday Life and Who Are Its Practitioners?" introduction to *The History of Everyday Life*, ed. Lüdtke (Princeton: Princeton University Press, 1995), 6.

128. Ibid., 15.

129. E. Mann, *Mikono ya damu*, 11–12; David M. Anderson, "Massacre at Ribo Post: Expansion and Expediency on the Colonial Frontier in East Africa" *International Journal of African Historical Studies* 37, no. 1 (2004): 33–35, 53–54.

130. "problematic": Andreas Eckert and Adam Jones, "Historical Writing about Everyday Life," *Journal of African Cultural Studies* 15, no. 1 (2002): 5; "self-evident": Ben Highmore, *Everyday Life and Cultural Theory: An Introduction* (London: Routledge, 2002), 17–18. See also Lüdtke, "History of Everyday Life," 5–7.

131. Jakob Vogel, "Military, Folklore, *Eigensinn*: Folkloric Militarism in Germany and France, 1871–1914," *Central European History* 33, no. 4 (2000): 489. Alf Lüdtke defined *Eigensinn* as "stubborn self-reliance." See Lüdtke, "People Working: Everyday Life and German Fascism," *History Workshop Journal*, no. 50 (2000): 83, 85.

132. Eckert and Jones, "Historical Writing," 5.

133. Lawrance, Osborn, and Roberts, *Intermediaries, Interpreters*.

134. Ortner, *Anthropology*, 143; Steege et al., "Everyday Life," 371, 378. Modris Eksteins's formulation of politics as "all mediation between individual and group interests" is useful for interpreting askari community members'

behaviors and practices. Eksteins, *Rites of Spring: The Great War and the Birth of the Modern Age* (Boston: Houghton Mifflin, 2000), 43. See also Lüdtke, "History of Everyday Life," 19.

135. Ortner, *Anthropology*, 143. See also p. 139.

136. Steege et al., "Everyday Life," 363. See also Benjamin Lawrance, *Locality, Mobility and "Nation": Periurban Colonialism in Togo's Eweland, 1900–1960* (Rochester, NY: University of Rochester Press, 2007), 11–13; Gregory Mann, "Locating Colonial Histories: Between France and West Africa," *American Historical Review* 110, no. 2 (2005): 409–10.

137. Steege et al., "Everyday Life," 367.

138. Joan W. Scott, "The Evidence of Experience," *Critical Inquiry* 17, no. 4 (1991): 797.

139. Sherry Ortner, "Resistance and the Problem of Ethnographic Refusal," *Comparative Studies in Society and History* 37, no. 1 (1995): 191.

140. "Military culture" can be defined as "a kind of 'tool kit' [that] holds at least four distinct and commonly used tools: discipline, professional ethos, ceremonies and etiquette, and *esprit de corps* and cohesion. In general, however, one finds in each element an attempt to deal with (and if possible, to overcome) the uncertainty of war, impose some pattern on war, control war's outcome, and invest it with meaning or significance." See James Burk, "Military Culture," in *Encyclopedia of Violence, Peace and Conflict*, 2nd ed., Lester Kurtz (San Diego: Academic Press, 2008), 1243. See also Williamson Murray, "Does Military Culture Matter?" *Orbis* 43, no. 1 (Winter 1999); Don M. Snider, "An Uninformed Debate on Military Culture," *Orbis* 43, no. 1 (Winter 1999). The gendered dimensions of military culture have been explored in Cynthia Enloe, *Maneuvers: The International Politics of Militarizing Women's Lives* (Berkeley: University of California Press, 2000); John A. Lynn II, *Women, Armies, and Warfare in Early Modern Europe* (New York: Cambridge University Press, 2008); Regina Titunik, "The Myth of the Macho Military," *Polity* 40, no. 2 (2008): 137–63.

141. The term *Sudanese* presents thorny usage problems because of its use as colonial shorthand for complex ethnolinguistic, cultural, and regional groupings. For stylistic reasons, I use the term without scare quotes as a designator for soldiers recruited from this region. Where possible, I refer to specific identifications (such as Dinka, Shilluk, Nuba, Baggara, etc.). In referring to German or other perceptions of "Sudanese" behaviors, personal qualities, or group traits, I use quotation marks to differentiate these voices from my own.

142. Thomas Earl Rodgers, "Billy Yank and GI Joe: An Exploratory Essay on the Sociopolitical Dimensions of Soldier Motivation," *Journal of Military History* 69, no. 1 (2005): 97. See also Streets, *Martial Races*, 11–13.

143. Rodgers, "Billy Yank," 97.

144. Crais, "Chiefs and Bureaucrats," 1036–37, 1055.

145. Isaacman and Isaacman, *Slavery and Beyond*, 15.

146. Ibid.

147. Paul Steege, et al, "Everyday Life." 366.

148. Felicitas Becker, "Netzwerke vs. Gesamtgesellschaft: Ein Gegensatz? Anregungen für Verflechtungsgeschichte," *Geschichte und Gesellschaft* 30, no. 2 (2004): 315, 318–19; "in terms of ideas": Thomas Spear, "Neo-Traditionalism and the Limits of Invention in British Colonial Africa," *Journal of African History* 44, no. 1 (2003): 26.

149. Daniel Branch, *Defeating Mau Mau, Creating Kenya* (Cambridge: Cambridge University Press, 2009), 222.

150. John Lonsdale, "Agency in Tight Corners: Narrative and Initiative in African History," *Journal of African Cultural Studies* 13, no. 1 (2000): 5–16.

CHAPTER 1: BECOMING ASKARI

1. Ernst Nigmann, *Geschichte der kaiserlichen Schutztruppe für Deutsch-Ostafrika* (Berlin: Mittler und Sohn, 1911), 10.

2. Ibid., 8.

3. Ibid., 11.

4. Ibid.

5. Ibid.

6. For a study of one of these "Nubi" soldierly communities, see Timothy Parsons, "'Kibra is our blood': The Sudanese Military Legacy in Nairobi's Kibera Location, 1902–1968," *International Journal of African Historical Studies* 30, no. 1 (1997): 87–122. See also Johan de Smedt, "The Nubis of Kibera: A Social History of Nubians and Kibera Slums" (PhD diss., University of Leiden, 2011).

7. But for a comprehensive study of Sudanese soldiers in the Anglo-Egyptian army for the same time frame, see Ronald M. Lamothe, *Slaves of Fortune: Sudanese Soldiers and the River War 1896–1898* (Woodbridge, Suffolk: James Currey, 2011).

8. August Leue, *Dar-es-Salaam: Bilder aus dem Kolonialleben* (Berlin: Wilhelm Süsserott, 1903), 145.

9. Ibid., 143.

10. The Anglo-Egyptian army fought against the Mahdiyya through the 1880s and 1890s, finally defeating its forces in 1898. The bulk of the troops were former members of the Turco-Egyptian army who were then retrained by the British according to European standards. The Sudanese men Major Hermann von Wissmann recruited for the Wissmanntruppe, the predecessor to the Schutztruppe, were unemployed veterans of the Mahdi wars. Wissmann, an experienced explorer of central and eastern Africa, had noticed them while visiting Egypt in 1887. See Erick J. Mann, *Mikono ya damu: "Hands of Blood": African Mercenaries and the Politics of Conflict in German East Africa, 1888–1904* (Frankfurt: Peter Lang, 2002), 47.

11. C. E. Callwell, *Small Wars: Their Principles and Practice*, 3rd ed. (Lincoln: University of Nebraska Press, 1996). The term *small wars* encompassed most forms of conflict European armies undertook in their colonies, including "punitive expeditions" and "pacification" efforts.

12. Nigmann, *Geschichte der Kaiserlichen Schutztruppe*, 34. The Wahehe fought against the Germans for the better part of the 1890s and were finally defeated in 1899 when their long-standing leader, Mkwakwa, committed suicide after being cornered by Captain Tom von Prince's Schutztruppe unit. See Thomas Morlang, "'Die Wahehe haben ihre Vernichtung gewollt.' Der Krieg der 'Kaiserlichen Schutztruppe' gegen die Hehe in Deutsch-Ostafrika (1890–1898)," in *Kolonialkriege: Militärische Gewalt im Zeichen des Imperialismus*, ed. Thoralf Klein and Frank Schumacher (Hamburg: Hamburger Edition, 2006); David Pizzo, "'To devour the land of Mkwawa': Colonial Violence and the German-Hehe War in East Africa c. 1884–1914" (PhD diss., University of North Carolina, Chapel Hill, 2007).

13. Leue, *Dar-es-Salaam*, 158.

14. Nigmann, *Geschichte der Kaiserlichen Schutztruppe*, 170.

15. Heinrich Fonck, *Deutsch Ost-Afrika: Eine Schilderung deutscher Tropen nach 10 Wanderjahren* (Berlin: Vossische Buchhandlung, 1910), 10.

16. Nigmann, *Geschichte der Kaiserlichen Schutztruppe*, 69–71.

17. See Heinrich Schnee, ed., *Deutsches Kolonial-Lexikon*, 3 vols. (Leipzig: Quelle und Meyer, 1920), 3:434. On "Sudanese" and "Nubi" identities in Eastern African military history, see Mark Leopold, "Legacies of Slavery in North West Uganda: The Story of the 'One-Elevens,'" in *Slavery in the Great Lakes Region of East Africa*, ed. Henri Médard and Shane Doyle (Athens: Ohio University Press, 2007); Parsons, "'Kibra is our blood,'" 87–88.

18. Tore Nordenstram, "Descriptive Ethics in the Sudan: An Example," *Sudan Notes and Records* 48 (1967). See also Leue, *Dar-es-Salaam*, 118–20; D. Hay Thorburn, "Sudanese Soldiers' Songs," *Journal of the Royal African Society* 24, no. 96 (1925): 314–21; NL von Prittwitz und Gaffron, box 245, typescript (dated 19.9.97), p. 89, LIL.

19. David Brion Davis, introduction to *Arming Slaves: From Classical Times to the Modern Age*, ed. Christopher Leslie Brown and Philip D. Morgan (New Haven: Yale University Press, 2006), 9.

20. Stephen J. Rockel, *Carriers of Culture: Labor on the Road in Nineteenth-Century East Africa* (Portsmouth, NH: Heinemann, 2006).

21. But for groundbreaking explorations of this problem, see Brown and Morgan, *Arming Slaves*; Allen Isaacman and Barbara Isaacman, *Slavery and Beyond: The Making of Men and Chikunda Ethnic Identities in the Unstable World of South-Central Africa, 1750–1920* (Portsmouth, NH: Heinemann, 2004).

22. Douglas H. Johnson, "The Structure of a Legacy: Military Slavery in Northeast Africa," *Ethnohistory* 36, no. 1 (1989): 72–88.

23. Juhani Koponen, *Development for Exploitation: German Colonial Policies in Mainland Tanzania, 1884–1914* (Hamburg: LIT, 1994), 570.

24. See Michelle Moyd, "'All people were barbarians to the *askari*': Askari Identity and Honor in the Maji Maji War, 1905–1907," in *Maji Maji: Lifting the Fog of War*, ed. James Giblin and Jamie Monson (Leiden: Brill, 2010), 149–80.

25. Michelle Moyd, "Becoming *Askari*: African Soldiers and Everyday Colonialism in German East Africa, 1850–1918" (PhD diss., Cornell University, 2008).

26. Anthony H. M. Kirk-Greene, "'Damnosa hereditas': Ethnic Ranking and the Martial Races Imperative in Africa," *Ethnic and Racial Studies* 3, no. 4 (1980): 393–414; David E. Omissi, *The Sepoy and the Raj: The Indian Army, 1860–1940* (London: Macmillan, 1994); Heather Streets, *Martial Races: The Military, Race, and Masculinity in British Imperial Culture, 1857–1914* (Manchester: Manchester University Press, 2004). On martial races in African colonial armies, see Hal Brands, "Wartime Recruiting Practices, Martial Identity and Post–World War II Demobilization in Colonial Kenya," *Journal of African History* 46, no. 1 (2005): 103–25; Parsons, "'Wakamba warriors are soldiers of the queen': The Evolution of the Kamba as a Martial Race, 1890–1970," *Ethnohistory* 46, no. 4 (1999): 671–701; Joe Lunn, "'Les races guerrières': Racial Preconceptions in the French Military about West African Soldiers during the First World War," *Journal of Contemporary History* 34, no. 4 (1999): 517–36; Risto Marjomaa, "The Martial Spirit: Yao Soldiers in British Service in Nyasaland (Malawi), 1895–1939," *Journal of African History* 44, no. 3 (2003): 413–32.

27. Kirk-Green, "Damnosa hereditas,'" 402.

28. Michael Von Herff, "'They walk through the fire like the blondest German': African Soldiers Serving the Kaiser in German East Africa (1888–1914)" (MA thesis, McGill University, 1991), 56.

29. Cf. Lionel Caplan, "'Bravest of the Brave': Representations of 'the Gurkha' in British Military Writings," *Modern Asian Studies* 25, no. 3 (1991): 571–97.

30. Kirk-Green, "Damnosa hereditas,'" 406–7. Cf. Titunik, "The Myth of the Macho Military," *Polity* 40, no. 2 (2008): 150–51.

31. Kirk-Green, "Damnosa hereditas,'" 406–7.

32. *Anleitung zum Felddienst in Deutsch-Ostafrika* (Dar es Salaam: Deutsch-Ostafrikanische Rundschau, 1911), 4. But see Nigmann, *Geschichte der Kaiserlichen Schutztruppe*, 70–71, where he claims that most Hehe recruits were disappointing soldiers. See also Morlang, "Wahehe." On dependence and the recruitment of defeated soldiers as "martial races," see Cynthia Enloe, *Ethnic Soldiers: State Security in Divided Societies* (Athens: University of Georgia Press, 1980), 27. See also Harold E. Raugh Jr., *The Victorians at War, 1815–1914: An Encyclopedia of Military History* (Santa Barbara: ABC-CLIO, 2004), 156.

33. *Anleitung zum Felddienst*, 6.

34. Enloe, *Ethnic Soldiers*, 28.

35. Ibid., 27. See also Holly Elisabeth Hanson, *Landed Obligation: The Practice of Power in Buganda* (Portsmouth, NH: Heinemann, 2003), 15; Sean Stilwell, *Paradoxes of Power: The Kano "Mamluks" and Male Royal Slavery in the Sokoto Caliphate, 1804–1903* (Portsmouth, NH: Heinemann, 2004), 117–18.

36. Ali Effendi Gifoon, "Memoirs of a Soudanese Soldier (Ali Effendi Gifoon)," trans. Percy Machell, *Cornhill Magazine*, n.s. 1 (1896): 31.

37. Omissi, *Sepoy and the Raj*.

38. Cf. Max Weber's description of the patrimonial army as an agent of "prebureaucratic" domination." Weber, *Economy and Society: An Outline of Interpretive Sociology*, 3 vols. (New York: Bedminster Press, 1968), 3:1019.

39. See Isaacman and Isaacman, *Slavery and Beyond*; Stilwell, *Paradoxes of Power*; Christopher Leslie Brown and Philip D. Morgan, eds., *Arming Slaves: From Classical Times to the Modern Age* (New Haven: Yale University Press, 2006).

40. Johnson, "The Structure of a Legacy," 144.

41. Douglas H. Johnson, "Sudanese Military Slavery from the Eighteenth to the Twentieth Century," in *Slavery and Other Forms of Unfree Labour*, ed. Leonie J. Archer (London: Routledge, 1988), 145.

42. B. R. Mitford, "Extracts from the Diary of a Subaltern on the Nile in the Eighties and Nineties," *Sudan Notes and Records* 18, no. 2 (1935): 103.

43. Allan R. Millett, "Professionalism," in *The Reader's Companion to Military History*, ed. Robert Cowley and Geoffrey Parker (New York: Houghton Mifflin, 1996), 370–71.

44. Richard Leslie Hill and Peter C. Hogg, *A Black Corps d'Élite: An Egyptian Sudanese Conscript Battalion with the French Army in Mexico, 1863–1867, and in Subsequent African History* (East Lansing: Michigan State University Press, 1995), 13.

45. Johnson, "Sudanese Military Slavery from the Eighteenth to the Twentieth Century,"145. See also Hill and Hogg, *Black Corps d'Élite*, 13.

46. For German cases of indiscipline that bordered on mutiny, see chapter 3, note 43. For comparison to the Turco-Egyptian and Anglo-Egyptian contexts, see Ahmad Alawad Sikainga, "Comrades in Arms or Captives in Bondage: Sudanese Slaves in the Turco-Egyptian Army, 1821–1865," in *Slave Elites in the Middle East and Africa: A Comparative Study*, ed. Miura Toru and John Edward Philips (London: Kegan Paul International, 2000), 197–214; R. W. Beachey, "Macdonald's Expedition and the Uganda Mutiny, 1897–98," *Historical Journal* 10, no. 2 (1967)): 237–54. For an overview of military indiscipline in modern African history, see Timothy Parsons, *The 1964 Army Mutinies and the Making of Modern East Africa* (Portsmouth, NH: Heinemann, 2003), 1–30.

47. For detailed information on how many ex-askari resided in each district and how many might be willing to return to service in the event of war, see *Militärisches Orientierungsheft für Deutsch-Ostafrika* (Dar es Salaam: Deutsch-Ostafrikanische Rundschau, 1911).

48. RM 2/1846, BArch. Thanks to Bernhard Gissibl for this reference. See also Marine-Oberingenieur Bockmann, "Berichte über Deutsch-Ostafrika," RM 8/368, pp. 160–61, BArch; Thomas Morlang, *Askari und Fitafita: "Farbige" Söldner in den deutschen Kolonien* (Berlin: Links, 2008), 93–96.

49. *Anleitung zum Felddienst*, 8.

50. See, e.g., "Nguru," *Deutsche Kolonialzeitung* 22, no. 6 (9 February 1905), which recounts the punishment of a Sudanese askari for sleeping at his post.

51. *Anleitung zum Felddienst*, 3. African soldiers' poor accuracy in firing their weapons frustrated German officers. The Turco-Egyptian and Anglo-Egyptian armies provided their troops only limited access to firearms and ammunition supplies for training purposes. They conducted extensive training on bayonet charges but gave little attention to marksmanship. E. Mann, *Mikono ya damu*, 76.

52. Jane L. Parpart and Marianne Rostgaard, eds., *The Practical Imperialist: Letters from a Danish Planter in German East Africa 1888–1906* (Leiden: Brill, 2006), 223.

53. Magdalene von Prince, *Eine deutsche Frau im innern Deutsch-Ostafrikas* (Berlin: Mittler und Sohn, 1903), 81.

54. Georg Maercker, *Unsere Schutztruppe in Ostafrika* (Berlin: Karl Siegismund, 1893), 41.

55. Nigmann, *Geschichte der Kaiserlichen Schutztruppe*, 24.

56. "black lansquenets": Friedrich Fülleborn, *Das deutsche Njassa- und Rowuma-Gebiet, Land und Leute, nebst Bemerkungen über die Schire-Länder* (Berlin: Dietrich Reimer [Ernst Vohsen], 1906), 8; "men who perceived": Dennis Showalter, "Gunpowder and Regional Military Systems," in *The Military and Conflict between Cultures: Soldiers at the Interface*, ed. James C. Bradford (College Station: Texas A&M University Press, 1997), 72.

57. Karen Hagemann, "German Heroes: The Cult of Death for the Fatherland in Nineteenth-Century Germany," in *Masculinities in Politics and War: Gendering Modern History*, ed. Stefan Dudink, Hagemann, and John Tosh (Manchester: Manchester University Press, 2004), 116–34.

58. NL von Prittwitz und Gaffron, box 245, typescript, p. 89 (dated 19 September 1897), LIL. *Shaush* was equivalent to the rank of *Unteroffizier* in the Prussian military. Cf. J. A. Meldon, "Notes on the Sudanese in Uganda," *Journal of the Royal African Society* 7, no. 26 (1908): 144.

59. Rockel, *Carriers of Culture*, 188–89. Cf. A. J. Mountenay Jephson, *The Diary of A. J. Mountenay Jephson: Emin Pasha Relief Expedition, 1887–1889*, ed. Dorothy Middleton and Maurice Denham Jephson (London: Cambridge University Press, 1969), 260.

60. "apex:" Herff, "'They walk through the fire,'" 56. See also Hans Paasche, *Im Morgenlicht: Kriegs-, Jagd-, und Reise-Erlebnisse in Ostafrika* (Berlin: C. U. Schwetschke und Sohn, 1907), 130.

61. Marianne Bechhaus-Gerst, *Treu bis in den Tod: Von Deutsch-Ostafrika nach Sachsenhausen: Eine Lebensgeschichte.* 1st ed. (Berlin: Links, 2007), 19–27.

62. Nigmann, *Geschichte der Kaiserlichen Schutztruppe*, 72. See also Mark Leopold, "Legacies of Slavery in North-West Uganda: The Story of the 'One-Elevens,'" in *Slavery in the Great Lakes Region of East Africa*, ed. Henri Médard and Shane Doyle, 180–99 (Athens: Ohio University Press, 2007), 180–99.

63. Cf. Johnson, "Structure of a Legacy," 77–78. See also Mitford, "Diary of a Subaltern," 181–82.

64. Douglas H. Johnson, "Recruitment and Entrapment in Private Slave Armies: The Structure of the *Zara'ib* in the Southern Sudan," *Slavery and Abolition* 13, no. 1 (1992): 166.

65. Local Egyptian administrators sometimes also "forcibly enrolled" boys into the army as punishment for provoking disputes with neighboring peoples. Such was the case with Faraj Sadik, who grew up in southern Darfur in the 1860s. See A. C. Hope, "The Adventurous Life of Faraj Sadik," *Sudan Notes and Records* 32, no. 1 (1951): 154.

66. Francis Mading Deng, *The Dinka of the Sudan* (New York: Holt, Rinehart and Winston, 1972), 7. See also Deng, *Dinka Cosmology* (London: Ithaca Press, 1980), 76.

67. Deng, *Dinka of the Sudan*, 137. See also Deng, *Dinka Cosmology*, 68–87. Gérard Prunier, "Military Slavery in the Sudan during the Turkiyya, 1820–1885," in *The Human Commodity: Perspectives on the Trans-Saharan Slave Trade*, ed. E. Savage (London: Frank Cass, 1992), 134–35; Ali Effendi Gifoon, "Memoirs of a Soudanese Soldier," 40; F. R. Wingate, *Mahdism and the Egyptian Sudan: Being an Account of the Rise and Progress of Mahdism, and of Subsequent Events in the Sudan to the Present Time* (London: Macmillan, 1891), 490.

68. Gunboys accompanied their masters into battle, maintaining, carrying, and loading the soldier's weapon for him. In German East Africa, askariboys did the same work for their askari "fathers" (*babas*). On gunboys in Sudan, see Johnson, "Structure of a Legacy," 77–78; Salim Wilson, *I Was a Slave* (London: Stanley Paul, 1960), 156, 174. On *askariboys* in German East Africa, see Bechhaus-Gerst, *Treu bis in den Tod*, 29–38; Fülleborn, *Deutsche Njassa- und Rowuma-Gebiet*, 8; August Hauer, "'Watoto,' die Kleinsten der Lettow-Truppe," in *Die deutschen Kolonien in Wort und Bild*, ed. H. Zache (Augsburg: Bechtermünz, 2003), 460–63.

69. The Dinka, along with the group Wilson described as their "sister-tribe," the Shilluk, lived in the southern regions of present-day Sudan, including Bahr-el-Ghazal, Upper Nile, and parts of Kordofan Provinces. S. Wilson, *I Was a Slave*, 9.

70. Ali Effendi Gifoon, "Memoirs of a Soudanese Soldier," 30–40, 175–87, 326–38, 484–92; Richard Gray, *A History of the Southern Sudan, 1839–1889* (London: Oxford University Press, 1961), 12; Lamothe, *Slaves of Fortune*, 19–34.

71. Salim Wilson was a Christian convert who, after his emancipation, took employment with a British missionary and eventually ended up living in northern England until his death, in 1946. His self-promoting evaluation of relative levels of "civilization" among Dinka peoples suggests that his story reflects an attempt to position himself in his British Christian world. It also undoubtedly reflects the perspectives of British ghostwriters and editors. See Douglas H. Johnson, "Salim Wilson: The Black Evangelist of the North," *Journal of Religion in Africa* 21, no. 1 (1991): 38; Eve M. Troutt Powell, "Translating Slavery," *International Journal of Middle Eastern Studies* 39 (2007): 165–67.

72. Richard Reid, "Arms and Adolescence: Male Youth, Warfare, and Statehood in Nineteenth-Century Eastern Africa," in *Generations Past: Youth in East African History*, ed. Andrew Burton and Hélène Charton-Bigot (Athens: Ohio University Press, 2010), 26.

73. The socialization experiences and gendering processes described by Wilson and Gifoon resemble those of pastoralist societies in eastern Africa such as the Maasai. The Sudanese Schutztruppe soldiers' masculinities thus might be fruitfully analyzed as an analog to eastern African pastoralist masculinities that placed the Sudanse askari in a kind of insider-outsider position within German East Africa. This positioning might help us better explain the awkward representational position they occupy in the source materials, in which they are lauded as ideal troops but also described as aloof and stoic. I thank an anonymous reviewer for this insight. For more on the gendered world of the Maasai, see Dorothy Hodgson, *Once Intrepid Warriors: Gender, Ethnicity, and the Cultural Politics of Maasai Development* (Bloomington: Indiana University Press, 2001), 22–36.

74. Ali Effendi Gifoon, "Memoirs of a Soudanese Soldier," 332, 333.

75. Ernst Nigmann, *Felddienstübungen für farbige (ostafrikanische) Truppen* (Dar es Salaam: Deutsch-Ostafrikanische Zeitung, 1910).

76. Tore Nordenstam, *Sudanese Ethics* (Uppsala: Scandinavian Institute of African Studies, 1968), 77–78.

77. Ahmad Alawad Sikainga, *The Western Bahr al-Ghazal under British Rule: 1898–1956* (Athens: Ohio University Center for International Studies, 1991), 37. The Habbaniyya are a subgroup of the Baggara, who are all known to be "nomadic cattle-herding people[s]." They were also active supporters of the Mahdiyya. Carolyn Fluehr-Lobban, Richard A. Lobban Jr., and John Obert Voll, eds., *Historical Dictionary of the Sudan*, 2nd ed. (Metuchen, NJ: Scarecrow Press, 1992), 30.

78. For an Egyptian soldier's perspective on the Sudanese and their need for "cultural and social development," see Eve Troutt Powell, *A Different Shade of Colonialism: Egypt, Great Britain, and the Mastery of the Sudan* (Berkeley: University of California Press, 2003), 127–28.

79. Leue, *Dar-es-Salaam*, 144.

80. Farrag's first military trial by fire in the Egyptian army came in 1881 during the 'Urabi Revolt. To protect British interests in the Suez and to bolster the khedive's authority, the British sent an expeditionary force to Egypt in summer 1882, and a brief war against 'Urabi Pasha's army followed. The British, led by General Sir Garnet Wolseley, finally destroyed 'Urabi's army in the Battle of Tel el-Kebir, in September 1882. Raugh, *Victorians at War*, 17; Powell, *Different Shade of Colonialism*, 5.

81. The Mahdi proclaimed jihad against the Egyptian government in late August 1881. The Mahdi's army, having already met and defeated Egyptian forces at Fashoda in June 1882, set about consolidating territory, further undermining Egyptian authority in the region.

82. See Callwell, *Small Wars*, 256–85. Many of Callwell's examples are drawn from colonial Sudan's history.

83. Ibid. *Bana mkuba* (or *bwana mkubwa*) translates to Mr. Big or Big Man in Kiswahili.

84. See Bror Urme MacDonell, *Mzee Ali: The Biography of an African Slave-Raider Turned Askari and Scout* (Johannesburg: 30° South Publishers, 2006).

85. Ibid., 100–101; *Anleitung zum Felddienst für Deutsch-Ostafrika* (Dar es Salaam: Deutsch-Ostafrikanische Rundschau, 1911); Nigmann, *Felddienstübungen*.

86. Leue, *Dar-es-Salaam*, 148.

87. Ibid.

88. Ibid., 150. Raugh notes that "news of the veritable annihilation of Hicks's army shocked Cairo and shattered complacency in London, where the nature of the Sudanese quagmire was finally realized." Raugh, *Victorians at War*, 166. For a Mahdist perspective on el-Obeid, see 'Ismat Hasan Zulfo, *Karari: The Sudanese Account of the Battle of Omdurman*, trans. Peter Clark (London: Frederick Warne, 1980), 15–17. See also "The Diary of Abbas Bey," *Sudan Notes and Records* 32, no. 2 (1951): 179–96.

89. Leue, *Dar-es-Salaam*, 149. Farrag's supposed use of the word *boma* to describe the enclosure is a perfect example of the difficulties of using this source. In Sudan such enclosures were called *zara'ib*. Farrag might have simply used the term that had become familiar to him in East Africa, or perhaps Leue simply replaced *zariba* with *boma* to simplify his text. Douglas H. Johnson, "Recruitment and Entrapment in Private Slave Armies: The Structure of the *Zara'ib* in the Southern Sudan," *Slavery and Abolition* 13, no. 1 (1992): 162–73.

90. Johnson, "Recruitment," 151. See also G. R. F. Bredin, "The Life-Story of Yuzbashi 'Abdullah Adlan," *Sudan Notes and Records* 42 (1961): 47.

91. Leue, *Dar-es-Salaam*, 151–52.

92. Ibid. The colorful patches on the *jibba* represented the Mahdists' commitment to an ascetic life. See also Bredin, "Yuzbashi 'Abdullah Adlan," 42.

93. Leue, *Dar-es-Salaam*, 152

94. Farrag's narrative also conveys his sense of wonder at the technology the British used in battle against 'Urabi, then the Ansar. For example, the fort that Farrag's regiment occupied "flew into the air during the [British] bombardment [of Alexandria]." Although a bitter engagement with 'Urabi's forces forced the British to withdraw, Farrag was awed by British weaponry, observing with astonishment a British artillery piece so large it could be moved only by rail. Leue, *Dar-es-Salaam*, 144.

95. "cattle nomad": Sikainga, *Western Bahr al-Ghazal*, 37. On the importance of cattle wealth among northeastern Sudanese peoples, see Ian Cunnison, *Baggara Arabs: Power and the Lineage in a Sudanese Nomad Tribe* (Oxford: Clarendon Press, 1966), 28–30.

96. Leue, *Dar-es-Salaam*, 153.

97. Ibid.

98. Wilson Chacko Jacob, "The Masculine Subject of Colonialism: The Egyptian Loss of the Sudan," in *African Masculinities: Men in Africa from the Late Nineteenth Century to the Present*, ed. Lahoucine Ouzgane and Robert Morrell, eds. (New York: Palgrave, 2005), 154. Jacob analyzes the memoir of Ibrahim Fawzi Pasha, an Egyptian army officer who spent some thirty years in Sudan as a minor officer and prisoner of the Mahdi. Jacob also uses a life history to show how colonialism helped create a particular masculine subjectivity.

99. Leue, *Dar-es-Salaam*, 153–54. The Mahdi's forces besieged Khartoum beginning in March 1884. Although a relief expedition under Wolseley was finally authorized by Parliament and sent out in October 1884, it did not arrive in time to save Gordon and his men from the Mahdi's devastating attack on Khartoum at the end of January 1885. In fact, the *Mahdi* decided to launch the final attack on Khartoum when he found out about the approach of the relief expedition "to avoid being caught between two fires." See Zulfo, *Karari*, 20. Gordon's death at Khartoum, elevated to heroic proportions, became the rallying cry thirteen years later for a new British expedition to defeat the Mahdiyya once and for all.

100. General Gordon, whose reputation as a great leader of "native" troops peppers many military histories, received Farrag the next day. He praised Farrag's loyalty and questioned him about the strengths and capabilities of the Ansar siege troops. He also asked him the details of the defeat of the Hicks Pasha expedition, and Farrag had an opportunity to demonstrate his skills as an observer. Both Farrag and Leue had reason to include the meeting with Gordon as an element of the story. For Farrag, it marked the highest recognition of his loyalty to the Anglo-Egyptian army and allowed him to position himself as a loyal soldier to the Germans. For Leue, it does the same thing, with the added benefit of embedding the narrative in the widely circulated story of the siege of Khartoum and the heroic death of Gordon while defending it against the Ansar. Leue easily used Gordon as a stand-in for his own notion of what qualities made a good *Schutztruppe* officer-patron.

101. Leue, *Dar-es-Salaam*, 155.

102. On the governmental and military missteps that led to the ultimate failure of the Gordon relief expedition, see Garnet Joseph Wolseley, *In Relief of Gordon: Lord Wolseley's Campaign Journal of the Khartoum Relief Expedition, 1884–1885*, ed. Adrian Preston (London: Hutchinson, 1967).

103. Leue, *Dar-es-Salaam*, 158.

104. Ibid. In the penultimate paragraph of the chapter "Kismet," Leue described how his column encountered a cemetery where "several soldiers who had fallen in battle at Unyangwira were buried." He continued, "This lonely burial place, which lay on an uninhabited [*menschenleer*] steppe, made a deep impression on me and moved me, particularly [because] as

a result of the portrayal of the soldier [Farrag] my imagination was still full of pictures of war and conflict, of adversity and death. —Was not the soil of our colony also fertilized with blood?" On the German "cult of the fallen soldier," see Hagemann, "German Heroes"; George Mosse, *Fallen Soldiers: Reshaping the Memory of the World Wars* (New York: Oxford University Press, 1990), 83–93.

105. Nigmann, *Geschichte der Kaiserlichen Schutztruppe*, 2.

106. Maercker, *Unsere Schutztruppe*, 38.

107. W. H. Besant, "The Early Days of the Egyptian Army, 1883–1892," *Journal of the Royal African Society* 33, no. 131 (1934): 167.

108. Hagemann, "German Heroes," 127.

109. Jacob, "Masculine Subject of Colonialism," 154.

110. Frank Gunderson, *Sukuma Labor Songs from Western Tanzania* (Leiden: Brill, 2010), 73–111; MacDonell, *Mzee Ali*, 34–39; Rockel, *Carriers of Culture*, 56–61. On the Manyema, see Melvin Page, "The Manyema Hordes of Tippu Tip: A Case Study in Social Stratification and the Slave Trade in Eastern Africa," *International Journal of African Historical Studies* 7, no. 1 (1974): 69–84; and Ruth Rempel, "'No Better than a Slave or Outcast': Skill, Identity, and Power among the Porters of the Emin Pasha Relief Expedition, 1887–1890,'" *International Journal of African Historical Studies* 43, no. 2 (2010): 279–318.

111. Morlang, *Askari und Fitafita*, 10, 18–19.

112. This is an area in need of much further research, which I cannot undertake here. See Patrick Harries, "Slavery, Social Incorporation and Surplus Extraction: The Nature of Free and Unfree Labour in South-East Africa," *Journal of African History* 22, no. 3 (1981): 309–30; Gerhard Liesegang, "Nguni Migrations between Delagoa Bay and the Zambezi, 1821–1839," *African Historical Studies* 3, no. 2 (1970): 317–37.

113. Maercker, *Unsere Schutztruppe*, 51.

114. Morlang, *Askari und Fitafita*, 18.

115. Ibid., 50–51. I return to the Zelewski expedition's effects on troop morale in chapter 3.

116. See G. Richelmann, *Meine Erlebnisse in der Wissmann-Truppe* (Magdeburg: Creutz'sche Verlagsbuchhandlung, 1892) 17–19.

117. "pure nature children": Richelmann, *Meine Erlebnisse*, 17; "pettishness" and "sense of honor": Hans-Joachim Rafalski, "Die Unteroffiziere in den Kolonialtruppen," unpublished manuscript, MSg 2/984, p. 164, BArch; Maercker, *Unsere Schutztruppe*, 51. See also Wilhelm Langheld, *Zwanzig Jahre in deutschen Kolonien* (Berlin: Wilhelm Weicher, 1909), 4.

118. Tom von Prince, "Tembenkämpfe," cited in Werner von Langsdorff, *Deutsche Flagge über Sand und Palmen: 53 Kolonialkrieger erzählen* (Gütersloh: C. Bertelsmann, 1942), 76–77.

119. T. O. Ranger, *Dance and Society in Eastern Africa, 1890–1970: The Beni Ngoma* (Berkeley: University of California Press, 1975), 58. See also

Morlang, *Askari und Fitafita*, 76; Mohamed Said, *The Life and Times of Abdulwahid Sykes (1924–1968): The Untold Story of the Muslim Struggle against British Colonialism in Tanganyika* (London: Minerva, 1998), 29–40.

120. Said, *Abdulwahid Sykes*, 39.

121. Maercker, *Unsere Schutztruppe*, 48.

122. Ibid., 42, 46–48.

123. For a contemporary assessment of Tabora's importance to German East Africa, see Paul Reichard, "Die Bedeutung von Tabora für Deutsch-Ostafrika," *Deutsche Kolonialzeitung* 2, no. 6 (1890): 67–68.

124. MacDonell, *Mzee Ali*, 83.

125. Ibid., 85. See also Koponen, *Development for Exploitation*, 118.

126. MacDonell, *Mzee Ali*, 85.

127. Jan-Georg Deutsch, *Emancipation without Abolition in German East Africa, c. 1884–1914.* Oxford: James Currey, 2006, 170.

128. Rockel, *Carriers of Culture*, 235–36.

129. On sisal plantations and migration, see Hanan Sabea, "Mastering the Landscape? Sisal Plantations, Land, and Labor in Tanga Region, 1893–1980s," *International Journal of African Historical Studies* 41, no. 3 (2008): 419–22.

130. Nigmann, *Geschichte der Kaiserlichen Schutztruppe*, 70; Alon Peled, *A Question of Loyalty: Military Manpower Policy in Multiethnic States* (Ithaca: Cornell University Press, 1998), 1.

131. Nigmann, *Geschichte der Kaiserlichen Schutztruppe*, 70. See also Humann to Reichskolonialamt (hereafter, RKA), 19 July 1912, R1001/725, p. 64, BArch.

132. Humann to Gouverneur, "Festnahme und Tod des letzten Rebellenführers aus dem Aufstande 1905," 19 July 1912, R1001/725, p. 64, BArch.

133. Cf. Rockel, *Carriers of Culture*, 42–43.

134. Juhani Koponen, *People and Production in Late Precolonial Tanzania: History and Structures* (Helsinki: Finnish Society for Development Studies, 1988), 123–24.

135. John Iliffe, *A Modern History of Tanganyika*, (Cambridge: Cambridge University Press, 1979), 132.

136. Iliffe, *Modern History*, 133. See also Koponen, *Development for Exploitation*, 219.

137. The complicated effects of intensifying cash economies on intergenerational and gender relationships in African social history have been extensively studied. See, for example, James Leonard Giblin with Blandina Kaduma Giblin, *A History of the Excluded: Making Family a Refuge from State in Twentieth-Century Tanzania* (Oxford: James Currey, 2005), 61–62; Iliffe, *Modern History*, 299–300; John Iliffe, *Honour in African History* (Cambridge: Cambridge University Press, 2005), 267–70; Elizabeth Schmidt, *Peasants, Traders, and Wives: Shona Women in the History of Zimbabwe, 1870–1939* (Portsmouth, NH: Heinemann, 1992), 113–15. On bridewealth in precolonial Tanzania, see Koponen, *People and Production*, 311–16.

138. Koponen, *Development for Exploitation*, 118. Christian missions provided an alternative path to respectability. Iliffe, *Honour*, 246–61.

139. Nigmann, *Geschichte der Kaiserlichen Schutztruppe*, 70–71.

140. Ibid., 70.

141. See "Wanjamwesi," in *Deutsches Kolonial-Lexikon*, ed. Heinrich Schnee (Leipzig: Quelle und Meyer, 1920), 3:672. See also Richard Burton, *The Lake Regions of Central Africa: A Picture of Exploration*, 2 vols. (1860; repr., New York: Horizon Press, 1961), 2:339.

142. Norman Robert Bennett, *Mirambo of Tanzania, 1840?-1884* (New York: Oxford University Press, 1971); Aylward Shorter, "Nyungu-ya-Mawe and the 'Empire of the Ruga-Rugas,'" *Journal of African History* 9, no. 2 (1968); E. Mann, *Mikono ya damu*.

143. According to Andrew Roberts, "When the first traders from the far western hinterland arrived on the east coast, they were called 'people of the moon' (*wanyamwezi*), because the new moon is first seen in the west." Andrew Roberts, "The Nyamwezi," in *Tanzania before 1900*, ed. Roberts (Nairobi: East African Publishing House, 1968), 117. See also Rockel, *Carriers of Culture*, 40; Fritz Spellig, "Die Wanjamwesi: Ein Beitrag zur Völkerkunde Ostafrikas." *Zeitschrift für Ethnologie* 59, no. 3/6 (1927): 202.

144. Roberts, "Nyamwezi," 117.

145. Ibid.

146. A. C. Unomah, *Mirambo of Tanzania* (London: Heinemann Educational, 1977), 5–6.

147. Ibid., 6–7.

148. Ibid., 7; Rockel, *Carriers of Culture*, 45.

149. Unomah, *Mirambo*, 7–8; Rockel, *Carriers of Culture*, 41.

150. Rockel, *Carriers of Culture*, 54.

151. Abdul Sheriff, *Slaves, Spices and Ivory in Zanzibar: Integration of an East African Commercial Empire in the World Economy, 1770–1873* (London: James Currey, 1987), 181. Sheriff labels the vbandevba "a new agrico-commercial bourgeoisie."

152. Glassman, *Feasts and Riot*, 62.

153. Ibid. See also Page, "Manyema Hordes," 70–71.

154. Jonathon Glassman, *Feasts and Riot: Revelry, Rebellion, and Popular Consciousness on the Swahili Coast, 1856–1888* (Portsmouth, NH: Heinemann, 1995), 56. See also Rockel, *Carriers of Culture*, 43–56.

155. Glassman, *Feasts and Riot*, 56.

156. "patricians": ibid., 67; Unomah, *Mirambo*, 9; MacDonell, *Mzee Ali*, 20.

157. Unomah, *Mirambo*, 9. See also Page, "Manyema Hordes."

158. Rockel, *Carriers of Culture*, 173–74.

159. Ibid., 69; Spellig, "Wanjamwesi," 219.

160. Rockel, *Carriers of Culture*, 70–74.

161. Ibid., 228.

162. Ibid., 75, 83.

163. "war games": Paul Reichard, "Die Wanjamuesi," *Zeitschrift der Gesellschaft für Erdkunde zu Berlin* 24 (1889): 259; "lion attacks": MacDonell, *Mzee Ali*, 20. See also R. Reid, "Arms and Adolescence," 31–32.

164. Reichard, "Wanjamuesi," 259.

165. Ibid., 308. See also Spellig, "Wanjamwesi," 206. For more on why young people sometimes choose to become soldiers, see Rachel Brett and Irma Specht, *Young Soldiers: Why They Choose to Fight* (Boulder: Lynne Rienner, 2004), 29–32.

166. Thaddeus Sunseri, *Vilimani: Labor Migration and Rural Change in Early Colonial Tanzania* (Portsmouth, NH: Heinemann, 2002), 59.

167. Bennett, *Mirambo of Tanzania*, 34.

168. MacDonell, *Mzee Ali*, 20. The *Schutztruppe* concluded its conquest of Unyanyembe in 1895. Ali became an askari some time thereafter. See pp. 81-85. For relevant dates in the conquest of Unyanyembe, see also E. Mann, *Mikono ya damu*, 155–98. See also Paul Groeschel, *Amelye. Ein Lebensbild aus dem Benavolk in Deutsch-Ostafrika* (Berlin: Berlin Missionsgesellschaft, 1911), 9, which describes how Bena boys learned to use various weapons as part of learning to be men. See also R. Reid, "Arms and Adolescence," 35–36, for wider African history context for understanding the relationship between manhood and learning to handle weapons.

169. MacDonell, *Mzee Ali*, 20–21. For descriptions of another famous slave raider's first safari, cf. Heinrich Brode, *Tippoo Tib: The Story of His Career in Central Africa*, trans. H. Havelock (London: Edward Arnold, 1907), 16–18, 24–36.

170. MacDonell, *Mzee Ali*, 71–72.

171. Ibid., 45–47.

172. Ibid., 63–66.

173. Michael Pesek, *Koloniale Herrschaft in Deutsch-Ostafrika: Expeditionen, Militär und Verwaltung seit 1880* (Frankfurt: Campus, 2005), 95.

174. Rockel, *Carriers of Culture*, 70; Andrew Roberts, "Nyamwezi Trade," in *Pre-Colonial African Trade: Essays on Trade in Central and Eastern Africa before 1900*, ed. R. Gray and D. Birmingham (London: Oxford University Press, 1970), 71; Beachey, "Arms Trade," 451–67.

175. MacDonell, *Mzee Ali*, 77. See also E. S. Atieno Odhiambo, "The Movement of Ideas: A Case Study of Intellectual Responses to Colonialism among the Liganua Peasants," in *Hadith 6: History and Social Change in East Africa*, ed. Bethwell Ogot (Nairobi: East African Literanture Bureau, 1976), 175–76.

176. Pesek, *Koloniale Herrschaft*, 97.

177. Rockel, *Carriers of Culture*, 78.

178. Iliffe, *Honour*, 248.

179. Rockel, *Carriers of Culture*, 68.

180. See Brode, *Tippoo Tib*, 18–23.

181. Shorter maintains that "the Arabs enthroned [Mkasiwa] as their puppet." Shorter, "Nyungu-ya-Mawe," 239.

182. On Unyanyembe's history between 1860 and 1865, see Unomah, *Mirambo of Tanzania*, 10–12; Roberts, "Nyamwezi," 131–34; Aylward Shorter, *Chiefship in Western Tanzania: A Political History of the Kimbu* (Oxford: Clarendon Press, 1972), 264–66; Iliffe, *Modern History*, 61–62.

183. Unomah, *Mirambo*, 12.

184. Shorter, "Nyungu-ya-Mawe," 235; Aylward Shorter, *Nyungu-ya-Mawe: Leadership in Nineteenth Century Tanzania* (Nairobi: East African Publishing House, 1969), 8; Bennett, *Mirambo*, 33; Unomah, *Mirambo*, 33.

185. Unomah, *Mirambo*, 17; Shorter, *Nyungu-ya-Mawe*, 11. For more on succession and customary practices around the batemi, see Bennett, *Mirambo*, 9–10.

186. Shorter, "Nyungu-ya-Mawe," 11.

187. Unomah, *Mirambo*, 22.

188. *Mirambo* means corpses. *Nyungu-ya-Mawe* means pot of stone (lit.,the pot that cannot break.) Bennett, *Mirambo*, 37; Shorter, "Nyungu-ya-Mawe," 240.

189. R. Reid, "Arms and Adolescence," 36–37.

190. John Roscoe, *Twenty-Five Years in East Africa* (1921; repr., New York: Negro Universities Press, 1969), 48–50.

191. Paul Reichard, "Vorschläge zu einer Reiseausrüstung für Ost- und Centralafrika," *Zeitschrift der Gesellschaft für Erdkunde* 24, no. 1 (1889): 78.

192. See William Stairs, *African Exploits: The Diaries of William Stairs, 1887–1892*, ed. Roy MacLaren (Montreal: McGill-Queen's University Press, 1998), 95, 111, 235, 236, 241, 242. Stairs's column also had a number of regular soldiers, who were mostly Sudanese.

193. Ibid., 235.

194. See, for example, Edward Coode Hore, *Missionary to Tanganyika, 1877–1888: The Writings of Edward Coode Hore, Master Mariner*, ed. James B. Wolf (London: Frank Cass, 1971), 51. Hore, writing in 1878 about his journey through Mirambo's territory (Urambo) defines *ruga-ruga* as "robbers" in a diary entry in which he describes a raid on his caravan porters. See also Lionel Declé, *Three Years in Savage Africa* (1900; repr., Bulawayo: Books of Rhodesia, 1974), 372; C. T. Wilson, "A Journey from Kagéi to Tabora and Back," *Proceedings of the Royal Geographical Society and Monthly Record of Geography*, n.s., 2, no. 10 (1880): 618–19. Wilson wrote, "The district between the Monungu and Masimbo is jungle, and haunted by Ruga-Ruga, not, however, Mirambo's renowned warriors, Ruga-Ruga being a name for all highway robbers."

195. Shorter, "Nyungu-ya-Mawe," 239. The mgunda mkali, which required about ten days to march across, stretched from Ugogo to Unyamwezi. Its inhospitable conditions and sparse settlement patterns made passing caravans vulnerable to thirst, hunger, and attack from ruga-ruga. For more on the mgunda mkali, see Paul Reichard, *Deutsch-Ostafrika: Das Land und seine Bewohner, seine politische und wirtschaftliche Entwickelung* (Leipzig: Otto

Spamer, 1892), 332–33; and Alfred Tucker, *Eighteen Years in Uganda and East Africa* (London: Edward Arnold, 1908), 66–68.

196. Ibid., 242.

197. Ibid., 240.

198. Ibid., 242.

199. Unomah, *Mirambo*, 17. Iselamagazi means "streams of blood" in Kinyamwezi. See Spellig, "Wanjamwesi," 205.

200. Unomah, *Mirambo*, 24.

201. Bennett, *Mirambo*, 35. On Wangoni methods of warfare and their roots in Zulu military history, see Thomas T. Spear, *Zwangendaba's Ngoni, 1821–1890: A Political and Social History of a Migration* (Madison: University of Wisconsin, African Studies Program, 1972), 35; Carl Wiese, *Expedition in East-Central Africa, 1888–1891: A Report*, ed. Harry W. Langworthy, trans. Donald Ramos (Norman: University of Oklahoma Press, 1983), 28–30, 153–56, 179–81; Donald Fraser, *Winning a Primitive People: Sixteen Years' Work among the Warlike Tribe of the Ngoni and the Senga and Tumbuka Peoples of Central Africa* (1914; repr., Westport, CT: Negro Universities Press, 1970), 34–40; P. Elzear Ebner, "Die Wangoni—einst Krieger, heute friedliche Bauern," in *Der fünfarmige Leuchter: Beiträge zum Werden und Wirken der Benediktinerkongregation von St. Ottilien*, ed. F. Renner (St. Ottilien: Eos, 1971). 181–97. On the Ngoni, see Margaret Read, "Tradition and Prestige among the Ngoni," *Africa: Journal of the International African Institute* 9, no. 4 (1936): 453–84; Read, "The Moral Code of the Ngoni and Their Former Military State," *Africa: Journal of the International African Institute* 11, no. 1 (1938): 1–24.

202. Spellig, "Wanjamwesi," 206.

203. Roberts, "Nyamwezi," 133.

204. Unomah, *Mirambo*, 22.

205. Achim Gottberg, *Unyamwesi: Quellensammlung und Geschichte* (Berlin: Akademie-Verlag, 1971), 127. Spellig, "Wanjamwesi," 202–3. See also Shorter, "Nyungu-ya-Mawe," 258. Page notes a similar development among the *waungwana*, who spoke a Swahili form known as *kiungwana*. Page, "Manyema Hordes," 71. Cf. Mungai Mutonya and Timothy Parsons, "KiKAR: A Swahili Variety in Kenya's Colonial Army," *Journal of African Languages and Linguistics* 25 (2004): 111–25.

206. Bennett, *Mirambo*, 39.

207. Spellig, "Wanjamwesi," 214.

208. Wilhelm Blohm, *Die Nyamwezi: Gesellschaft und Weltbild* (Hamburg: Friederichsen, De Gruyter, 1933), 63. For similar observations about the Sukuma, see Hans Cory, *The Ntemi: The Traditional Rites in Connection with the Burial, Election, Enthronement and Magic Powers of a Sukuma Chief* (London: Macmillan, 1951), 67.

209. John Lamphear, "'The rage of ancestors who died in ancient wars': The Military Background to the Maji Maji Rebellion," unpublished manuscript, University of Texas, Austin 26; emphasis in original. Used with author's permission.

210. On East African weaponry during this time, cf. Christopher Spring, *African Arms and Armor* (Washington, DC: Smithsonian Institution Press, 1993), 94–138.

211. Shorter, *Chiefship in Western Tanzania*, 277.

212. "long hanks of hair": Shorter, "Nyungu-ya-Mawe," 241; "charms": Blohm, *Nyamwezi: Gesellschaft*, 88.

213. Ibid., 88. See also Burton, *Lake Regions*, 2:350–36.

214. Blohm, *Nyamwezi: Gesellschaft*, 63 (see also p. 87).

215. Shorter, "Nyungu-ya-Mawe," 241. Such materials must be placed within the larger critical literature on rumors of cannibalistic acts in African history. See William Arens, *The Man-Eating Myth: Anthropology and Anthropophagy* (New York: Oxford University Press, 1979); Beatrix Heintze, "Propaganda Concerning 'Man-Eaters' in West-Central Africa in the Second Half of the Nineteenth Century," *Paideuma* 49 (2003). For reported instances of Schutztruppe askari engaging in cannibalistic practices associated with warfare, see Hans Cory, "The Ingredients of Magic Medicines," *Africa: Journal of the International African Institute* 19, no. 1 (1949): 26; Thomas Morlang, "'Ich habe die Sache satt hier, herzlich satt': Briefe des Kolonialoffiziers Rudolf von Hirsch aus Deutsch-Ostafrika, 1905–1907," *Militärgeschichtliche Zeitschrift* 61 (2002): 511.

216. Norman Etherington, "Barbarians Ancient and Modern," *American Historical Review* 116, no. 1 (2011): 33.

217. Ibid.

218. Ibid., 35. There has been extensive scholarly debate on Shaka and the Zulu military, particularly regarding their place at the center of the massive upheaval of the early 1800s referred to as the *mfecane*, or the crushing. See Carolyn Hamilton, *Terrific Majesty: The Powers of Shaka Zulu and the Limits of Historical Invention* (Cambridge, MA: Harvard University Press, 1998). See also Peter Geschiere, "Shaka and the Limits of Colonial Invention," *African Studies Review* 44, no. 2 (2001): 167–76; Richard Reid, *Warfare in African History* (Cambridge: Cambridge University Press, 2012), 121–22; Timothy J. Stapleton, *A Military History of South Africa* (Santa Barbara: Praeger, 2010), 12–15.

219. C. Wilson, "Journey from Kagéi," 617–18.

220. Ibid., 617–19.

221. Reichard, "Wanjamuesi," 323.

222. Blohm, *Nyamwezi*, 62. See also A. T. Culwick and G. M. Culwick, *Ubena of the Rivers* (London: Allen and Unwin, 1935), 204.

223. Blohm, *Nyamwezi*, 62.

224. Cory, *Ntemi*, 67–68. For more recent examples of rehabilitative rituals after war, see Carolyn Nordstrom, *A Different Kind of War Story* (Philadelphia: University of Pennsylvania Press, 1997), 145–47.

225. Shorter, "Nyungu-ya-Mawe," 241. See also Pesek, *Koloniale Herrschaft*, 313; J. B. Kabeya, *King Mirambo: One of the Heroes of Tanzania* (Kampala:

East African Literature Bureau, 1976), 12–13. On banghi smoking and its effects on Wanyamwezi ruga-ruga and porters, see Reichard, "Wanjamuesi," 328–31. See also Johannes Fabian, *Out of Our Minds: Reason and Madness in the Exploration of Central Africa* (Berkeley: University of California Press, 2000), 151–79; R. Reid, "Arms and Adolescence," 36–37.

226. *Militärischer Suaheli-Sprachführer für Deutsch-Ostafrika* (Dar es Salaam: Deutsch-Ostafrikanische Rundschau, 1911), 21.

227. Fabian, *Out of Our Minds*, 3.

228. Ibid. See also Warwick Anderson, "The Trespass Speaks: White Masculinity and Colonial Breakdown," *American Historical Review* 102, no. 5 (1997): 1343–70.

229. For a general discussion of how intoxication, charms, magic, and prayer aid in soldiers' "fear management," see William Ian Miller, *The Mystery of Courage* (Cambridge, MA: Harvard University Press, 2000), 201–31.

230. Bennett, *Mirambo*, 40.

231. Blohm, *Nyamwezi*, 63.

232. Shorter, *Chiefship*, 277.

233. Blohm, *Nyamwezi*, 63.

234. Bennett, *Mirambo*, 41; Blohm, *Nyamwezi*, 63, 64.

235. Shorter, *Chiefship*, 296.

236. Ibid.

237. Ibid.

238. Ibid.

239. E. Mann, *Mikono ya damu*, 166.

240. Ibid., 167; Roberts, "Nyamwezi," 140.

241. Emin Pasha, *Emin Pasha: His Life and Work*, comp. Georg Schweitzer, 2 vols. (New York: Negro Universities Press, 1969), 2:77–78.

242. Iliffe, *Modern History*, 103.

243. E. Mann, *Mikono ya damu*, 169.

244. Ibid., 170.

245. Ibid., 172. See also A. C. Unomah, "African Collaboration with the Germans in the Conquest of Isike of Unyanyembe, 1890–1893," unpublished manuscript, Makerere University, Kampala, 1970, 11–14.

246. Gustav Adolf, Graf von Götzen, *Durch Afrika von Ost nach West: Resultate und Begebenheiten einer Reise von der deutsch-ostafrikanischen Küste bis zur Kongomündung in den Jahren 1893/94* (Berlin: Dietrich Reimer, 1899), 256.

247. H. F. von Behr, *Kriegsbilder aus dem Araberaufstand in Deutsch-Ostafrika* (Leipzig: Brockhaus, 1891), 65. See also Paul Reichard, *Deutsch-Ostafrika: Das Land und seine Bewohner, seine politische und wirtschaftliche Entwicklung* (Leipzig: Otto Spamer, 1891), which recounts this scene almost verbatim. Reichard probably lifted this account from Behr's, since Behr was an officer in the Wissmanntruppe during the coastal war. Reichard, on the other hand, was not involved in the war. See Schnee, *Deutsches Kolonial-Lexikon*, 1:159, 3:146.

248. Reichard, *Deutsch-Ostafrika*, 173.

249. E. Mann, *Mikono ya damu*, 77.

250. Richard Kandt, *Caput Nili: Eine empfindsame Reise zu den Quellen des Nils*, 5th ed. (Berlin: Dietrich Reimer, 1921), 65.

251. For another case of askari taking German surnames as their own, see Götzen, *Durch Afrika*, 7. Askari also named themselves after famous African chiefs and military men. For example, an ombasha named Mirambo served under Lieutenant Correck during the Maji Maji war. *Ombasha* Mirambo had a particular reputation for brutality. See NL Correck, entry for 21.3.06, Handschriftensammlung HS 908, Abteilung 4, Kriegsarchiv, Bayerisches Hauptstaatsarchiv (hereafter, BHA), Munich. Paul Reichard observed that Wanyamwezi often took on new names when they became porters or ruga-ruga. They also changed these nicknames frequently, which "made it very difficult to learn people's correct names." Reichard, "Wanjamuesi," 258. See also Sunseri, *Vilimani*, 144.

252. Blohm, *Nyamwezi: Gesellschaft*, plate 10, pictures 134, 135, 136, 140, 142; Blohm, *Die Nyamwezi: Land und Wirtschaft* (Hamburg: Friederichsen, De Gruyter, 1931), iii.

253. MacDonell, *Mzee Ali*, 125, 155.

254. Mlolwa Nkuli, "Notes on Nyamwezi Utani," in *Utani Relationships in Tanzania*, ed. Stephen A. Lucas, 7 vols. (Dar es Salaam: University of Dar es Salaam, 1975), 4:1–9.

255. Gottberg, *Unyamwesi*, 398.

CHAPTER 2: MAKING ASKARI WAYS OF WAR

1. Mwalimu Mbaraka bin Shomari, "Shairi la Bwana Mkubwa," in *Kala Shairi: German East Africa in Swahili Poems*, ed. Gudrun Miehe, Katrin Bromber, Said Khamis, and Ralf Grosserhode (Cologne: Köppe, 2002), 400.

2. "glue": Don M. Snider, "An Uninformed Debate on Military Culture," *Orbis* 43, no. 1 (1999): 14. See also José Arturo Saavedra Casco, *Utenzi, War Poems, and the German Conquest of East Africa: Swahili Poetry as Historical Source* (Trenton: Africa World Press, 2007), 227.

3. Cf. Frederick Cooper, "Conflict and Connection: Rethinking Colonial African History," *American Historical Review* 99, no. 5 (1994): 1534.

4. For details on the many "punitive expeditions" undertaken by the Schutztruppe, see Ernst Nigmann, *Geschichte der Kaiserlichen Schutztruppe für Deutsch-Ostafrika* (Berlin: Mittler und Sohn, 1911), 149–57; Kirsten Zirkel, "Military Power in German Colonial Policy: The *Schutztruppen* and Their Leaders in East and South-West Africa, 1888–1918," in Killingray and Omissi, *Guardians of Empire*, 97.

5. Scott Hughes Myerly, *British Military Spectacle: From the Napoleonic Wars through the Crimea* (Cambridge, MA: Harvard University Press, 1996), 12.

6. Ibid., 75–77.

7. James Burk, "Military Culture," in *Encyclopedia of Violence, Peace, and Conflict*, ed. Lester Kurtz, 2nd ed. (San Diego: Academic Press, 2008), 1242–56. On the central role of training in the maintenance of soldiers' morale, see Hew Strachan, "Training, Morale, and Modern War," *Journal of Contemporary History* 41, no. 2 (2006): 215–27.

8. Admiralty War Staff, Intelligence Division, *A Handbook of German East Africa* (London: HMSO, 1916), 203; and *Anleitung zum Felddienst in Deutsch-Ostafrika* (Dar es Salaam: Deutsch-Ostafrikanische Rundschau, 1911), 8, 18.

9. Bror Urme MacDonell, *Mzee Ali: The Biography of an African Slave-Raider Turned Askari and Scout* (Johannesburg: 30° South Publishers, 2006), 169.

10. NL Correck, diary, 19 June 1906, and 29 June 1906, BHA.

11. See NL Correck, diary, 30 August 1906, BHA. See also entries for 18 July 1906, 21 August 1906, and 25 August 1906.. On East African nicknaming practices for Europeans, see Miehe et al., *Kala Shairi*, 44–47; Rudolf Wagner and E. Buchmann, *Wir Schutztruppler: Die deutsche Wehrmacht übersee* (Berlin: Buntdruck, 1913), 110–11.

12. NL Correck, diary, 29 August 1906, BHA.

13. Paul Fussell, *Wartime: Understanding and Behavior in the Second World War* (Oxford: Oxford University Press, 1989), 80.

14. See MacDonell, *Mzee Ali*, 176.

15. Ibid., 190–91; Leonard Mosley, *Duel for Kilimanjaro: An Account of the East African Campaign, 1914–18* (London: Weidenfeld and Nicolson, 1963), 12–13.

16. Marine-Oberingenieur Bockmann, "Berichte über Deutsch-Ostafrika," RM 8/368, p. 157, BArch. On askari's coercive practices in everyday colonial life, see G. C. K. Gwassa and John Iliffe, *Records of the Maji Maji Rising* (Nairobi: East African Publishing House, 1969).

17. Moyd, "'We don't want to die for nothing': Askari at War in German East Africa, 1914–1918," in *Race, Empire and First World War Writing*, ed. Santanu Das (Cambridge: Cambridge University Press, 2011), 102.

18. Zirkel, "Military Power," 97.

19. MacDonell, *Mzee Ali*, 169, 172. Cf. E. B. Sledge, *With the Old Breed: At Peleliu and Okinawa* (Oxford: Oxford University Press, 1990), 22.

20. Sledge, *Old Breed*, 11.

21. Prussian War Ministry, *Exerzir-Reglement für die Infanterie* (Berlin: Mittler und Sohn, 1889), 1.

22. Dr. Paur, "Die Psychologie in der militärischen Erziehung," *Jahrbücher für die deutsche Armee und Marine* 97 (1895): 98–104; Erich Weniger, *Die Erziehung des deutschen Soldaten* (Berlin: Mittler und Sohn, 1944), 20–21.

23. Myerly, *British Military Spectacle*, 9–10.

24. Burkhard Vieweg, *Macho Porini—die Augen im Busch: Kautschukpflanzer Karl Vieweg in Deutsch-Ostafrika: Authentische Berichte 1910–1919* (Weikersheim: Margraf, 1996), 277.

25. Ibid.

26. *Anleitung zum Felddienst,* 8; Bockmann, "Berichte," p. 157, BArch; Bernhard Gissibl, "Die 'Treue' der Askari: Mythos, Ehre und Gewalt im Kontext des deutschen Kolonialismus in Ostafrika," in *Treue: Politische Loyalität und militärische Gefolgschaft in der Moderne,* ed. Nikolaus Buschmann and Karl Borromäus Murr (Göttingen: Vandenhoeck und Ruprecht, 2008), 242; Thomas Morlang, *Askari und Fitafita: "Farbige" Söldner in den deutschen Kolonien* (Berlin: Links, 2008), 315.

27. D. C. Dorward, "Ethnography and Administration: A Study of Anglo-Tiv 'Working Misunderstanding,'" *Journal of African History* 15, no. 3 (1974): 457–77.

28. Erick J. Mann, *Mikono ya damu: "Hands of Blood": African Mercenaries and the Politics of Conflict in German East Africa, 1888–1904* (Frankfurt: Peter Lang, 2002), 46.

29. Robert Doughty and Ira Gruber et al., *Warfare in the Western World: Military Operations from 1600 to 1871* (Lexington, MA: D. C. Heath, 1996), 70.

30. Ibid.

31. Steven D. Jackman, "Shoulder to Shoulder: Close Control and 'Old Prussian Drill' in German Offensive Infantry Tactics, 1871–1914," *Journal of Military History* 68, no. 1 (2004): 73–104. See also Paur, "Psychologie," 104; Paul von Schmidt, *Die Erziehung des Soldaten* (Berlin: Verlag der Liebelschen Buchhandlung, 1894), 60.

32. Doughty and Gruber, *Warfare,* 475.

33. Isabel V. Hull, *Absolute Destruction: Military Culture and the Practices of War in Imperial Germany* (Ithaca: Cornell University Press, 2005), 117.

34. C. E. Callwell, *Small Wars: Their Principles and Practice,* 3rd ed. (1896; Lincoln: University of Nebraska Press, 1996). See also Hermann von Wissmann, *Afrika. Schilderungen und Rathschläge zur Vorbereitung für den Aufenthalt und den Dienst in den deutschen Schutzgebieten* (Berlin: Mittler und Sohn, 1903); Bertrand Taithe, *The Killer Trail: A Colonial Scandal in the Heart of Africa* (Oxford: Oxford University Press, 2009), 65.

35. See, for example, "Übersetzung des Exerzierreglements für den belgischen Kongo," G 1/153, 21.2.1916, TNA; various excerpts on the French colonial army from German newspapers of 1899, R 1001/7245, BArch.

36. Kommando-Befehl no. 5, 31 May 1909, R 1003 FC 1136, BArch.

37. Ibid.

38. NL Alfred Reuss, diary entry 21.11.1910, KlE 857, Bundesarchiv Koblenz (hereafter, BK); NL von Prittwitz und Gaffron, diary entry 12.10.97, box 245, folder 1/245, LIL.

39. On the Seminar for Oriental Languages, which opened in 1887, see Ludger Wimmelbücker, *Mtoro bin Mwinyi Bakari: Swahili Lecturer and Author in Germany* (Dar es Salaam: Mkuki na Nyota, 2009), 27–40. On Schutztruppe officers' fluency in Kiswahili, see Hermann von Bengerstorf, *Unter der Tropensonne Afrikas: Ernstes und Heiteres* (Hamburg: Fr. W. Thaden, 1914), 185. On early experiences with training African recruits, see Wagner and Buchmann, *Wir Schutztruppler,* 105–12.

40. NL Correck, diary, 6 March 1906, BHA. See also diary entries for 10 and 11 January 1906, 4 February 1906, and 1 May 1906.

41. See E. Mann, *Mikono ya damu*, 47–50.

42. G. Richelmann, *Meine Erlebnisse in der Wissmann-Truppe* (Magdeburg: Creutz'sche Verlagsbuchhandlung, 1892), 13, 17; "Vorschriften über die Handhabung des Dienstbetriebes auf den Stationen der Schutztruppe für Ost-Afrika," *DKB*, 2, no. 3 (1891): 56. Jane L. Parpart and Marianne Rostgaard, eds., *The Practical Imperialist: Letters from a Danish Planter in German East Africa 1888–1906* (Leiden: Brill, 2006), 85.

43. Richelmann, *Meine Erlebnisse*, 17. On language in the initial stages of forming the *Wissmanntruppe*, see also Hans-Joachim Rafalski, "Die Unteroffiziere in den Kolonialtruppen," unpublished manuscript, MSg 2/984, p. 169, BArch.

44. Richelmann, *Meine Erlebnisse*, 17.

45. Wagner and Buchman, *Wir Schutztruppler*, 109–10.

46. *Militärischer Suaheli-Sprachführer für Deutsch-Ostafrika* (Dar es Salaam: Deutsch-Ostafrikanische Rundschau, 1911).

47. F. Hildebrandt, "Warnke's Tod," *Deutsch-Ostafrikanische Zeitung*, 3 June 1905; Maercker, *Unsere Schutztruppe*, 66–67.

48. Karl Weule, *Native Life in East Africa: The Results of an Ethnological Research Expedition*, trans. Alice Werner (Westport, CT: Negro Universities Press, 1970), 30–34.

49. Heinrich Fonck, *Deutsch-Ost-Afrika: Eine Schilderung deutscher Tropen nach 10 Wanderjahren* (Berlin: Vossische Buchhandlung, 1910), 73; Hans Paasche, *Im Morgenlicht: Kriegs-, Jagd-, und Reise-Erlebnisse in Ostafrika* (Berlin: C. U. Schwetschke und Sohn, 1907), 340.

50. See, for example, "Koloniale Scherzecke," *UP*, 14 April 1906. In King's African Rifles (KAR), askari spoke a "simplified Swahili variety" known as KiKAR. See Mungai Mutonya and Timothy Parsons, "KiKAR: A Swahili Variety in Kenya's Colonial Army," *Journal of African Languages and Linguistics* 25 (2004): 111. Similarly, "Nubi" colonial soldiers in Uganda and Kenya came to speak a language variety known as KiNubi, which linguists have described as a "pidgin Arabic." See Alan S. Kaye and Mauro Tosco, "Early East African Pidgin Arabic," *Sprache und Geschichte in Afrika* 14 (1993): 271, 301.

51. Schleinitz to Gouvernement, 12 June 1904, G 9/56, p. 131, TNA.

52. Fonck, *Deutsch-Ost-Afrika*, 44; Kommando-Befehl Nr. 7, 31 July 1909, R 1003 FC 1136, BArch; letter from Götzen, 31 July 1903, G 9/1, p. 149, TNA.

53. C. Waldemar Werther, *Die mittleren Hochländer des nördlichen Deutsch-Ost-Afrika. Wissenschaftliche Ergebnisse der Irangi-Expedition 1896–1897 nebst kurzer Reisebeschreibung* (Berlin: Hermann Paetel, 1898), 6–7.

54. Fonck, *Deutsch-Ost-Afrika*, 45. For official training expectations and uniform wear in the first years of the Schutztruppe, see "Vorschriften über die Handhabung des Dienstbetriebes." See also *Deutschlands koloniale Wehrmacht in ihrer gegenwärtigen Organisation und Schlagfähigkeit* (Berlin: R. v. Decker, 1906), 13–14; Dar es Salaam to all police units, 22 June 1912, R 1003 FC 1136, BArch.

55. Admiralty War Staff: Intelligence Division, A *Handbook of German East Africa* (London: HMSO, 1916), 203; Prussian War Ministry, *Exerzir-Reglement für die Infanterie* (Berlin: Mittler und Sohn, 1889); Freiherr von Freytag-Loringhoven, *Das Exerzier-Reglement für die Infanterie vom 29. Mai 1906 kriegsgeschichtlich erläutert* (Berlin: Mittler und Sohn, 1907).

56. "Vom Exerzierplatz in Daressalam," *Kolonie und Heimat* 1, no. 4 (10 November 1907), 8–9.

57. Fonck, *Deutsch-Ost-Afrika*, 74.

58. Ibid.

59. *Deutschlands koloniale Wehrmacht*, 15–16.

60. Gustav Adolf, Graf von Götzen, *Durch Afrika von Ost nach West: Resultate und Begebenheiten einer Reise von der deutsch-ostafrikanischen Küste bis zur Kongomündung in den Jahren 1893/94*, 2nd ed. (Berlin: Dietrich Reimer, 1899).

61. Ernst Nigmann, *Felddienstübungen für farbige (ostafrikanische) Truppen* (Dar es Salaam: Deutsch-Ostafrikanische Zeitung, 1910).

62. Ibid., 1, 3, 4.

63. "dependable, long-serving": Nigmann, *Felddienstübungen*, x. See also Wagner and Buchmann, *Wir Schutztruppler*, 112.

64. "Lokales," *Usambara Post*, 14 April 1906.

65. Nigmann, *Felddienstübungen*, ix–x.

66. *Anleitung zum Felddienst*, 11.

67. Nigmann, *Felddienstübungen*, ix.

68. Ibid.

69. Fonck, *Deutsch-Ost-Afrika*, 75.

70. "Lokales," *Usambara Post*, 14 April 1906.

71. "exploratory purposes": Gideon von Grawert, "Die militärische Lage im Schutzgebiet Deutsch-Ostafrika im Jahre 1908/09," in *Jahrbuch über die deutschen Kolonien*, ed. Karl Schneider (Essen: Baedeker, 1911), 3:110.

72. "Übungsmarsch und gefechtsmässiges Schiessen der 5. Kompagnie," *Deutsch-Ostafrikanische Zeitung* (hereafter, *DOAZ*), 6, no. 27 (1904).

73. "Zu dem Übungsmarsch der 5. Kompagnie," *DOAZ*, 6, no. 29 (1904).

74. "Aus Daressalam und Umgegend," *DOAZ*, 6, no. 29 (1904).

75. Cf. Rechenberg to all district offices, residencies, and military stations, 4 July 1910, R 1001/6879, p. 60, BArch.

76. Rafalski, "Unteroffiziere," MSg 2/984, p. 188, BArch.

77. Wagner and Buchmann, *Wir Schutztruppler*, 109.

78. Ernst Nigmann, *Schwarze Schwänke: Fröhliche Geschichten aus unserem schönen alten Deutsch-Ostafrika* (Berlin: Safari, 1922), 147–48. See also Berit Elisabeth Dencker, "Popular Gymnastics and the Military Spirit in Germany, 1848–1871," *Central European History* 34, no. 4 (2001): 503–30. For comparisons to British and French colonial militaries' efforts at physical fitness training, see Anthony Clayton, "Sport and African Soldiers: The Military Diffusion of Western Sport throughout Sub-Saharan Africa," in *Sport in*

Africa: Essays in Social History, ed. William J. Baker and James A. Mangan (New York: African Publishing, 1987), 114–36.

79. Fonck, Deutsch-Ost-Afrika, 74. Lieutenant Correck lamented in his diary his own deteriorating abilities in gymnastics: "Attempt at gymnastics on the trapeze failed totally. Old age is coming." NL Correck, diary, 18 November 1907, BHA.

80. Fonck, Deutsch-Ost-Afrika, 48–51; Wagner and Buchmann, Wir Schutztruppler, 112–13; Nigmann, Geschichte der Kaiserlichen Schutztruppe, 127; von Grawert to all district offices, 30 May 1912, R 1003 FC 1136, BArch; "Runderlass," 29 August 1911, R 1003 FC 1136, BArch. On detailed training goals for shooting, see Deutschlands koloniale Wehrmacht, 16–18; Gouverneur to all police units, 22 June 1912, R 1003 FC 1136, BArch. On awards for sharpshooting, see Gouverneur's circular to all districts, 29 August 1911, R 1003 FC 1136, BArch. For an example of how German commands became fodder for Kiswahili wordplay during firearms training, see "Koloniale Scherzecke," UP, 14 April 1906.

81. Wagner und Buchmann, Wir Schutztruppler, 100; "Aus Daressalam und Umgegend: Preisschiessen." DOAZ, 16 April 1904. See also "Aus Daressalam und Umgegend," DOAZ, 11 June 1904, 18 June 1904.

82. On askari involvement in smallpox vaccination campaigns, see enclosure 9, 1 June 1911, G 1/7, TNA.

83. MacDonell, Mzee Ali, 85.

84. Cf. Sledge, Old Breed, 27, 33.

85. Fonck, Deutsch-Ost-Afrika, 49; Paasche, Morgenlicht, 130; Dar es Salaam to all police units, 22 June 1912, R 1003 FC 1136, BArch.

86. MacDonell, Mzee Ali, 20.

87. Sledge, Old Breed, 22.

88. MacDonell, Mzee Ali, 20.

89. Fonck, Deutsch-Ost-Afrika, 74.

90. For an overview of firearms use in East African warfare during the German colonial period, see Reinhard Klein-Arendt, "'Bautz! Schuß durch den Ast und durch den Kerl . . .': Der Einsatz moderner Infanteriewaffen gegen afrikanische Widerstandsbewegungen in Deutsch-Ostafrika," in Die (koloniale) Begegnung: AfrikanerInnen in Deutschland (1880–1945) — Deutsche in Afrika (1880–1945), ed. Marianne Bechhaus-Gerst and Reinhard Klein-Arendt (Frankfurt: Peter Lang, 2003), 171–91.

91. Fonck, Deutsch-Ostafrika, 48. See examples of askari pay books in G 14/3, TNA. On soldiers' decorations, see Thomas Morlang, Askari und Fitafita: "Farbige" Söldner in den deutschen Kolonien (Berlin: Links, 2008), 38–41.

92. Mitteilung Gitega to Residenturnebenstelle Usumbura, 16 June 1914, R 1003 FC/1156, BArch.

93. David Killingray, Fighting for Britain: African Soldiers in the Second World War (Woodbridge, Suffolk: James Currey, 2010), 84.

94. Kommandobefehl no. 1, 1 January 1904, G 9/56, TNA. See also Killingray, Fighting for Britain, 84; Timothy Parsons, The African Rank-and-File:

Social Implications of Colonial Military Service in the King's African Rifles,
1902–1964 (Portsmouth, NH: Heinemann, 1999), 111; Keletso E. Atkins, *The*
Moon Is Dead! Give Us Our Money! The Cultural Origins of an African Work
Ethic, Natal, South Africa, 1843–1900 (Portsmouth, NH: Heinemann, 1993),
78–99.

95. "Kasuistik," in *Medizinal-Berichte über die deutschen Schutzgebiete*
1903/4 (Berlin: Mittler und Sohn, 1905), 31; Juhani Koponen, *Development*
for Exploitation: German Colonial Policies in Mainland Tanzania, 1884–1914
(Hamburg: LIT, 1994), 469.

96. "Kasuistik," 17–19; *Anleitung zum Felddienst,* 156–62.

97. *Anleitung zum Felddienst,* 165–66.

98. Otto Peiper, *Pocken und Pockenbekämpfung in Deutsch-Ostafrika*
(Berlin: Richard Schoetz, 1925), 7.

99. "Löhnungs- und Verpflegungsordnung für die farbigen Soldaten der
Schutztruppe und der Polizeitruppe des ostafrikanischen Schutzgebietes,"
1 January 1904, R 1001/9587, BArch.

100. Ibid., n.p.

101. Bernd Arnold, *Steuer- und Lohnarbeit im Südwesten von Deutsch-*
Ostafrika, 1891–1916 (Münster: LIT, 1994), 197; Koponen, *Development for*
Exploitation, 493; "Venerische Krankheiten," in *Medizinal-Berichte über die*
Deutschen Schutzgebiete 1903/04 (Berlin: Mittler und Sohn, 1905), 72. See
also "Bericht über die hygienischen Massnahmen im Bezirk Morogoro in der
Zeit vom 1.4.08 bis 31.3.09, Section IV. Geschlechtskrankheiten," 31 March
1909, G 1/5, n.p., TNA.

102. Arnold, *Steuer- und Lohnarbeit,* 197.

103. "Venerische Krankheiten," 72.

104. Some evidence suggests that outsiders also read and incorporated
insignia into their own bodily adornment practices. A Schutztruppe doctor
working in the Kilwa area reported seeing a tattoo on a woman's arm that
resembled the rank of sol, the highest possible rank for an askari in German
East Africa. Otto Peiper, "Ethnographische Beobachtungen aus dem Bezirke
Kilwa, Deutsch-Ostafrika." *Baessler Archiv: Beiträge zur Völkerkunde* (Berlin:
Dietrich Reimer), 1926.

105. Janet Andrewes, *Bodywork: Dress as Cultural Tool: Dress and De-*
meanour in the South of Senegal (Leiden: Brill, 2005), 29–30; Carol Burke,
Camp All-American, Hanoi Jane, and the High-and-Tight: Gender, Folklore,
and Changing Military Culture (Boston: Beacon Press, 2004), 82–83. For
background on askari uniforms as part of a wider history of imperial soldiering, see Thomas S. Abler, *Hinterland Warriors and Military Dress: European*
Empires and Exotic Uniforms (Oxford: Berg, 1999), 127–28.

106. *Militärischer Suaheli-Sprachführer,* 49.

107. Jennifer Craik, *Uniforms Exposed: From Conformity to Transgression*
(Oxford: Berg, 2005), 4.

108. See, for example, Michels, *Schwarze deutsche Kolonialsoldaten,* 51.

109. Paul Fussell, *Uniforms: Why We Are What We Wear* (Boston: Houghton Mifflin, 2002), 5; emphasis in original.

110. *Militärischer Suaheli-Sprachführer*, 9, 22, 38.

111. Similar responses to askari sightings appear in various kinds of sources. For one vivid example, see "Nachrichten aus Myambani: Quartalbericht von Miss. Augustus (4. Quartal 1904)," *Evangelisch-Lutherisches Missionsblatt* (*ELM*) 60, no. 7 (1905): 165–66.

112. For an example from the early British period in Tanganyika, see "Proclamation No. 11 of 1919, Impersonation of Askari, Etc.," *Occupied Territory of German East Africa, Official Gazette* (Dar es Salaam): 1, no. 4 (30 September 1919), n.p.

113. Fonck to all police units, 24 February 1908, R1003 FC/1140, BArch.

114. F. J. Sassen, *Deutsches Kolonial-Militärrecht* (Rastatt: H. Greiser, 1911), 97–98; NL Correck, diary, 6 November 1907, BHA. For cases brought against, and punishments administered to, individual askari, see G 14/1 and 14/2, TNA. For evidence of two former Sudanese askari being exiled from German East Africa or certain districts of the colony see Heinrich Schnee, "Bekanntmachung," *Amtlicher Anzeiger für Deutsch-Ostafrika* 14, no. 40 (1913): 107–9.

115. Cf. David Killingray, "The 'Rod of Empire': The Debate over Corporal Punishment in the British African Colonial Forces, 1888–1946," *Journal of African History* 35, no. 2 (1994): 201–16.

116. Götzen, *Durch Afrika*, 107; NL Correck, diary, 18 July, 21 August 1906; 21 March 1907, BHA.

117. Fonck, *Deutsch-Ost-Afrika*, 70. See also "Nguru," DOAZ, 11 August 1906; and Jane L. Parpart and Marianne Rostgaard, eds., *The Practical Imperialist: Letters from a Danish Planter in German East Africa 1888–1906* (Leiden: Brill, 2006), 86.

118. Fonck, *Deutsch-Ost-Afrika*, 70.

119. Wissmann, *Afrika*, 66.

120. Weinberger, Hauptbuch, p. 12, BHA.

121. Wissmann, *Afrika*, 66.

122. NL Correck, diary, 2 May 1906, BHA; Johannes Fabian, *Out of our Minds: Reason and Madness in the Exploration of Central Africa* (Berkeley: University of California Press, 2000), 60–63, 78; Tanja Bührer, *Die kaiserliche Schutztruppe für Deutsch-Ostafrika: Kolonial Sicherheitspolitik und transkulturelle Kriegführung, 1885 bis 1918* (Munich: Oldenbourg, 2011), 113–14.

123. Anna Crozier, "What Was Tropical about Tropical Neurasthenia? The Utility of the Diagnosis in the Management of British East Africa," *Journal of the History of Medicine and Allied Sciences* 64, no. 4 (2009): 518–48. See also Warwick Anderson, "The Trespass Speaks: White Masculinity and Colonial Breakdown," *American Historical Review* 102, no. 5 (1997): 1343–70; Eva Bischoff, "Tropenkoller: Male Self-Control and the Loss of Colonial Rule," in *Helpless Imperialists: Imperial Failure, Fear and Radicalization*, ed.

Maurus Reinkowski and Gregor Thum (Gottingen: Vandenhoeck and Ruprecht, 2013), 117–36; Dane Kennedy, "Diagnosing the Colonial Dilemma: Tropical Neurasthenia and the Alienated Briton," in *Decentering Empire: Britain, India, and the Transcolonial World*, ed. Kennedy and Durba Ghosh (Hyderabad: Orient Longman, 2006), 157–81.

124. Crozier, "Tropical Neurasthenia," 548.

125. Kommandeur der Schutztruppe, "Löhnungs- und Verpflegungsordnung für die farbigen Soldaten der Schutztruppe und der Polizeitruppe des ostafrikanisches Schutzgebietes," 1 January 1904, R 1001/9587, p. 4, BArch. For rules regarding "natural provisions" and various states of imprisonment, see p. 8.

126. Ibid., p. 4.

127. "Sammelerlass No. 2," 30 August 1912, G 1/106, TNA; "Sammelerlass No. 13," 8 October 1913, G 1/106, TNA; "Kommandobefehl No. 1," 1 January 1904, G 9/56, TNA.

128. "Sammelerlass No. 13," 8 October 1913, G1/106, TNA.

129. Ibid.

130. For more on tensions between non-Schutztruppe Europeans and askari, see Thomas Morlang, "'Prestige der Rasse' contra 'Prestige des Staates': Die Diskussionen über die Befugnisse farbiger Polizeisoldaten gegenüber Europäern in den deutschen Kolonien," *Zeitschrift für Geschichtswissenschaft* 49, no. 6 (2001): 498–509. Cf. Erica Wald, "Health, Discipline and Appropriate Behaviour: The Body of the Soldier and Space of the Cantonment," *Modern Asian Studies* 46, no. 4 (2012): 815–56.

131. Maercker, *Unsere Schutztruppe*, 65.

132. Ibid., 42; Josef Weinberger aus Tölz: Ein bayerischer Unteroffizier als Sergeant bei der Kaiserlichen Schutztruppe in Deutsch-Ostafrika, 1891–1896, M200, pt. 1, sec. 14, BHA.

133. In 1905, Governor von Götzen recruited a contingent of Sudanese reinforcements from Massaua, Eritrea, which was under Italian colonial authority.

134. R 1001/1026, pp. 107, 117, BArch.

135. Bührer, *Kaiserliche Schutztruppe*, 63.

136. Nigmann, *Geschichte der Kaiserlichen Schutztruppe*, 73.

137. Fonck, *Deutsch-Ost-Afrika*, 53.

138. Nigmann, *Geschichte der Kaiserlichen Schutztruppe*, 73.

139. Ibid., 70–71.

140. The Maasai experienced a series of animal disease epidemics beginning in the early 1880s that devastated their livestock herds through 1891. That was followed by a smallpox epidemic in 1892. In addition, colonial punitive expeditions and confinement on a reserve beginning in 1905 gave the Maasai little reason to want to cooperate with the Germans. Dorothy Hodgson, *Once Intrepid Warriors: Gender, Ethnicity, and the Cultural Politics of Maasai Development* (Bloomington: Indiana University Press, 2001), 38–39; Koponen,

Development for Exploitation, 647–48. Cf. Timothy Parsons, "'Wakamba warriors are soldiers of the queen': The Evolution of the Kamba as a Martial Race, 1890–1970." *Ethnohistory* 46, no. 4 (1999): 679. Parsons argues that in contrast to other groups like the Wakamba and Samburu whose economic fortunes drew them into KAR service between 1918 and 1939, the Maasai "remained aloof from the [KAR]" because "their precolonial pastoral economy remained largely intact." See also John Lamphear, "Brothers in Arms: Military Aspects of East African Age-Class Systems in Historical Perspective," in *Conflict, Age, and Power in Northeast Africa: Age Systems in Transition*, ed. Eisei Kurimoto and Simon Simonse (Athens: Ohio University Press, 1998), 86–89. On the Hehe, see Alison Redmayne, "Mkwawa and the Hehe Wars," *Journal of African History* 9, no. 3 (1968): 434–35.

141. Tom von Prince, *Gegen Araber und Wahehe: Erinnerungen aus meiner ostafrikanischen Leutnantszeit 1890–1895* (Berlin: Ernst Siegfried Mittler und Sohn, 1914), 292.

142. Karen Hagemann, "German Heroes: The Cult of Death for the Fatherland in Nineteenth-Century Germany," in *Masculinities in Politics and War: Gendering Modern History*, ed. Stefan Dudink, Hagemann, and John Tosh (Manchester: Manchester University Press, 2004), 116–34; Sandra Mass, *Weisse Helden, schwarze Krieger: Zur Geschichte kolonialer Männlichkeit in Deutschland, 1918–1964* (Cologne: Böhlau, 2006).

143. Parsons, "'Wakamba warriors,'" 674–93.

CHAPTER 3: THE ASKARI WAY OF WAR

1. On the number of German colonial military expeditions conducted from 1889 to 1911, see Ernst Nigmann, *Geschichte der Kaiserlichen Schutztruppe für Deutsch-Ostafrika* (Berlin: Mittler und Sohn, 1911), 149–57; Kirsten Zirkel, "Military Power in German Colonial Policy: The *Schutztruppen* and Their Leaders in East and South-West Africa, 1888–1918," in *Guardians of Empire: The Armed Forces of the Colonial Powers c. 1700–1964*, ed. D. Killingray and D. Omissi (New York: Manchester University Press, 1999), 97. For a discussion of "pacification," see Trutz von Trotha, "'The Fellows Can Just Starve': On Wars of 'Pacification' in the African Colonies of Imperial Germany and the Concept of 'Total War,'" in *Anticipating Total War: The German and American Experience, 1871–1914*, ed. Manfred F. Boemeke, Roger Chickering, and Stig Förster (Cambridge: Cambridge University Press, 1999), 415–35.

2. "soldiers' culture": Wayne E. Lee, "Warfare and Culture," in *Warfare and Culture in World History*, ed. Lee (New York: New York University Press, 2011), 7; Peter H. Wilson, "Defining Military Culture," *Journal of Military History* 72, no. 1 (2008): 18; "logical products": Robert M. Citino, "The German Way of War Revisited," *Historically Speaking* 11, no. 5 (2010): 21.

3. Isabel V. Hull, *Absolute Destruction: Military Culture and the Practices of War in Imperial Germany* (Ithaca: Cornell University Press, 2005), 2. See also Lee, "Warfare and Culture," 2–8.

4. Citino, "German Way of War," 20.

5. G. C. K. Gwassa and John Iliffe, *Records of the Maji Maji Rising* (Dar es Salaam: East African Publishing House, 1969), 8. See also p. 23.

6. For Maji Maji, most recently, see Felicitas Becker and Jigal Beez, eds., *Der Maji Maji Krieg in Deutsch-Ostafrika* (Berlin: Links, 2005); James Giblin and Jamie Monson, eds., *Maji Maji: Lifting the Fog of War* (Leiden: Brill, 2010). For World War I, see Tanja Bührer, *Die kaiserliche Schutztruppe für Deutsch-Ostafrika: Kolonial Sicherheitspolitik und transkulturelle Kriegführung, 1885 bis 1918* (Munich: Oldenbourg, 2011); Eckard Michels, *"Der Held von Deutsch-Ostafrika": Paul von Lettow-Vorbeck: Ein preussischer Kolonialoffizier* (Paderborn: Ferdinand Schöningh, 2008); Michael Pesek, *Das Ende eines Kolonialreiches: Ostafrika im Ersten Weltkrieg* (Frankfurt: Campus, 2010); Hew Strachan, *The First World War in Africa* (Oxford: Oxford University Press, 2004).

7. For an example of the handover of a military post, its soldiers, equipment, ammunition, and livestock from a German NCO to an askari, see Ishangi to Kaiserliche Residentur Ruanda, 11 October 1906, R 1003 FC/1162, BArch.

8. Schnee's objective was different, inasmuch as he hoped that Germany would retain its colonial territories. He therefore wanted the colony preserved for the postwar period. He and Lettow-Vorbeck fought bitterly over this issue during the war, but Lettow-Vorbeck's will prevailed.

9. Callwell, *Small Wars*.

10. "organized armies": ibid., 21; "shirked": ibid., 31.

11. Ibid., 21.

12. Ibid., 24. Cf. Wissmann, *Afrika: Schilderungen und Rathschläge, zur Vorbereitung für den Aufenthalt und den Dienst in den deutschen Schutzgebieten* (Berlin: Mittler und Sohn, 1903), 8–10.

13. Callwell, *Small Wars*, 145.

14. Ibid., 21.

15. Ibid., 118. See also pp. 135–36. For a similar German perspective, see Wissmann, *Afrika*, 26–35. Cf. Bührer, *Kaiserliche Schutztruppe*, 235–45; Susanne Kuss, *Deutsches Militär auf kolonialien Kriegsschauplätzen: Eskalation von Gewalt zu Beginn des 20. Jahrhunderts* (Berlin: Links, 2010), 113–18.

16. Wolfgang Hubach, "Josef Weinberger aus Tölz: Ein bayerischer Unteroffizier als Sergeant bei der Kaiserlichen Schutztruppe in Deutsch-Ostafrika, 1891–1896," typescript, M200, p. 4a, BHA. The term *mafiti* was used as a collective name for "all predatory bands, that burst out of the interior in the 1890s, and [who] were armed in the Zulu style." See Schnee, *Deutsches Kolonial-Lexikon*, 2:474.

17. Hubach, "Josef Weinberger," 8–9.

18. Ibid., 13a.

19. Ibid., 11a, 15a. According to Weinberger, Lieutenant Johannes suffered from an advanced case of syphilis.

20. Cf. NL Correck, diary, 3 September 1907, BHA.

21. See also Paasche, *Im Morgenlicht: Kriegs-, Jagd-, und Reise-Erlebnisse in Ostafrika.* (Berlin: C. U. Schwetschke und Sohn, 1907), 100.

22. David M. Keithly, "Khaki Foxes: The East Afrika Korps," *Small Wars and Insurgencies* 12, no. 1 (2001): 167.

23. Eduard von Liebert, *Neunzig Tage im Zelt: Meine Reise nach Uhehe, Juni bis September 1897* (Berlin: Mittler und Sohn, 1898), 33.

24. "The Maji Maji Rising in Majimahuu," Maji Maji Research Project (hereafter, MMRP), no. 6/68/1/1.

25. For examples from the 1890s, see Hubach, *Josef Weinberger,* "Ostafrikabelege," 33; "Das Hauptbuch," 9; "Das Notizheft," 4. For Maji Maji, see Admiralstab der Marine, *Die Tätigkeit der Marine während der Niederwerfung des Eingeborenen-Aufstandes in Ostafrika 1905/6* (Berlin: Mittler und Sohn, 1907), 44; NL Correck, diary, 6 June 1906, BHA; Paasche, *Morgenlicht,* 289. For World War I, see Ludwig Deppe, *Mit Lettow-Vorbeck durch Afrika* (Berlin: August Scherl, 1919), 393.

26. "Aus dem Bericht des Regierungsrats Chrapkowski über seine Expedition vom Viktoria-Njansa (Bukoba) zum Tanganyika (Usumbura)," *Deutsches Kolonialblatt* 16, no. 20 (1905): 601.

27. Hubach, *Josef Weinberger,* "Ostafrikabelege," 23a; Paasche, *Morgenlicht,* 336; Buluda Itandala, "African Response to German Colonialism in East Africa: The Case of Usukuma, 1890–1918," *Ufahamu* 20, no. 1 (1992): 9–11; "The Maji Maji Rising in Majimahuu," MMRP 6/68/1/1; Aidan K. Kalembo, "An Account of the Maji Maji Rising in the Lukuledi Valley," MMRP 7/68/1/1.

28. Schmidt, "(Re)negotiating Marginality: The Maji Maji War and Its Aftermath in Southwestern Tanzania, ca. 1905–1916," *International Journal of African Historical Studies* 43, no. 1 (2010): 49; Jamie Monson, "Relocating Maji Maji: The Politics of Alliance and Authority in the Southern Highlands of Tanzania, 1870–1918," *Journal of African History* 39, no. 1 (1998): 96; MMRP 5/68/1/3/9.

29. NL von Prittwitz und Gaffron, diary, 26 June 1897, box 245, folder 1, p. 183, LIL.

30. "campaign community": John A. Lynn II, *Women, Armies, and Warfare in Early Modern Europe* (New York: Cambridge University Press, 2008), 18.

31. Michelle Moyd, "Making the Household, Making the State: Colonial Military Communities and Labor in German East Africa," *International Labor and Working-Class History* 80, no. 1 (2011): 53–76.

32. Gustav Adolf, Graf von Götzen, *Durch Afrika von Ost nach West: Resultate und Begebenheiten einer Reise von der deutsch-ostafrikanischen Küste bis zur Kongomündung in den Jahren 1893/94* (Berlin: Dietrich Reimer, 1899), 8. See also NL Correck, diary, May 3, 1906, BHA; NL von Prittwitz und Gaffron, diary, August 6, 1898, box 248, folder 6/248, LIL; Heinrich Fonck, *Deutsch-Ost-Afrika: Eine Schilderung deutscher Tropen nach 10 Wanderjahren* (Berlin: Vossische Buchhandlung, 1910), 65; Paasche, *Morgenlicht,* 300.

33. For comparative perspectives on African colonial soldiers' wives and women dependents, see Stefanie Michels, "Soldatische Frauenwelten," in *Frauen in den deutschen Kolonien*, ed. Marianne Bechhaus-Gerst and Mechthild Leutner (Berlin: Links, 2009), 122–30; Sarah Zimmerman, "*Mesdames Tirailleurs* and Indirect Clients: West African Women and the French Colonial Army, 1908–1918," *International Journal of African Historical Studies* 44, no. 2 (2011): 299–322.

34. Paul von Lettow-Vorbeck, *Heia Safari! Deutschlands Kampf in Ostafrika* (Leipzig: Koehler, 1920), 147–48. Cf. Ascan Roderich Lutteroth, *Tunakwenda: Auf Kriegssafari in Deutsch-Ostafrika* (Hamburg: Broschek, 1938), 156.

35. Cf. NL Correck, diary, 4 May, 5 July 1906, BHA. Cf. Paasche, *Morgenlicht*, 297–98.

36. NL von Prittwitz und Gaffron, diary, 12 January 1899, box 248, folder 6/248, p. 46, LIL.

37. NL Correck, diary, 4 February, 28 April 1906, BHA.

38. "comforts of home": Luise White, *The Comforts of Home: Prostitution in Colonial Nairobi* (Chicago: University of Chicago Press, 1990).

39. NL Correck, diary, 30 September 1906, BHA.

40. Marine-Oberingenieur Bockmann, "Berichte über Deutsch-Ostafrika," RM 8/368, p. 160, BArch.

41. Hubach, *Josef Weinberger*, "Das Hauptbuch," 19.

42. Allen Isaacman and Barbara Isaacman, *Slavery and Beyond: The Making of Men and Chikunda Ethnic Identities in the Unstable World of South-Central Africa, 1750–1920* (Portsmouth, NH: Heinemann, 2004), 15.

43. NL Correck, diary, 30 April 1906, BHA. See also Schmidt, "(Re)Negotiating Marginality," 51–56, for analysis of the particular ways colonial violence during Maji Maji affected women.

44. Hubach, *Josef Weinberger*, "Hauptbuch," 14 (entries for 28 July and 16 August 1894).

45. Ibid., 17 (entry for 10 August 1894). Entries for 15, 18, 19, and 24 August 1894 all note incidents in which women were shot or hanged. See also "Acta des Kaiserlichen Gouvernment von Deutsch-Ostafrika betreffend Irangi-Gesellschaft—Lieutenant Werther," unpublished typescript transcription (Basel: Basler Afrika Bibliographien, 1995), 20–21.

46. Hubach, *Josef Weinberger*, "Hauptbuch," p. 17, p. 15 (entry for 1 August 1894).

47. See NL von Prittwitz und Gaffron, diary, 22 January 1898, box 245, folder 1, p. 182, LIL.

48. NL Correck, diary, 3, 4 May 1906, BHA.

49. Stephen J. Rockel, "Enterprising Partners: Caravan Women in Nineteenth Century Tanzania," *Canadian Journal of African Studies* 34, no. 3 (2000): 748–78. For comparative military contexts, see Ronald M. Lamothe, *Slaves of Fortune: Sudanese Soldiers and the River War, 1896–1898* (Woodbridge, Suffolk: James Currey, 2011), 78–89; O. W. Furley, "The Sudanese Troops in Uganda," *African Affairs* 58, no. 233 (1959): 325.

50. Cf. Rockel, *Carriers of Culture*, 126.

51. NL Correck, diary, 28 April 1906, BHA.

52. Rockel, *Carriers of Culture*, 128.

53. For syntheses of the current state of scholarly knowledge on the ruga-ruga, see Michael Pesek, *Koloniale Herrschaft in Deutsch-Ostafrika: Expeditionen, Militär und Verwaltung seit 1880* (Frankfurt: Campus, 2005), 312–15; Pesek, *Ende eines Kolonialreiches*, 187–96.

54. Lutteroth, *Tunakwenda*, 33; T.W. Turuka, "Maji Maji Rebellion in Njelu," MMRP No. 6/68/3/1.

55. Gustav Adolf, Graf von Götzen, *Deutsch-Ostafrika im Aufstand 1905/06* (Berlin: Dietrich Reimer, 1909), 133.

56. Pesek, *Ende eines Kolonialreiches*, 191.

57. NL von Prittwitz und Gaffron, diary, 26 June 1897, box 245, folder 1, p. 20, LIL.

58. For an early vision of using African irregulars as "a replacement for cavalry" in colonial military operations, see Wissmann, *Afrika*, 32. See also Admiralty War Staff, *German East Africa*, 223. For sample column configurations and numbers, see NL Correck, diary, 2 July, 21 July 1906, BHA; *Deutsch-Ostafrikanische Zeitung* 8, no. 24 (16 June 1906); Lutteroth, *Tunakwenda*, 30; *Militärisches Orientierungsheft für Deutsch-Ostafrika* (Dar es Salaam: Deutsch-Ostafrikanische Rundschau, 1911), which provides numbers of available ruga-ruga around each Schutztruppe station.

59. NL Correck, diary, 8, 9 July, 8 September 1906, BHA; Wilhelm Langheld, *Zwanzig Jahre in deutschen Kolonien* (Berlin: Wilhelm Weicher, 1909), 246; "Das Massaireservat," *Deutsch-Ostafrikanische Zeitung* 8, no. 30 (28 July 1908).

60. Detlef Bald, "Afrikanischer Kampf gegen koloniale Herrschaft: Der Maji-Maji-Aufstand in Ostafrika," *Militärgeschichtliche Mitteilungen* 19, no. 1 (1976): 43; T. W. Turuka, "Maji Maji Rebellion in Njelu," MMRP 6/68/3/1.

61. Götzen, *Deutsch-Ostafrika*, 132–33; Wissmann, *Afrika*, 32.

62. Pesek, *Koloniale Herrschaft*, 312; Richard Wenig, *Kriegs-Safari: Erlebnisse und Eindrücke auf den Zügen Lettow-Vorbecks durch das östliche Afrika* (Berlin: August Scherl, 1920), 108.

63. Hubach, *Josef Weinberger*, "Ostafrikabelege," 21a. See also Thomas Morlang, "'Ich habe die Sache satt hier, herzlich satt': Briefe des Kolonialoffiziers Rudolf von Hirsch aus Deutsch-Ostafrika, 1905–1907," *Militärgeschichtliche Zeitschrift* 61, no. 2 (2002): 511; Paasche, *Morgenlicht*, 340.

64. Boris Barth and Jürgen Osterhammel, foreword to *Zivilisierungsmissionen: Imperialen Weltverbesserung seit dem 18. Jahrhundert*, ed. Barth and Osterhammel (Konstanz: UVK Verlagsgesellschaft, 2005), 9–10.

65. Erick J. Mann, *Mikono ya damu: "Hands of Blood": African Mercenaries and the Politics of Conflict in German East Africa, 1888–1904* (Frankfurt: Peter Lang, 2002), 18–20.

66. Callwell, *Small Wars*, 23–24.

67. Ibid.; R. W. Beachey, "The Arms Trade in East Africa in the Late Nineteenth Century," *Journal of African History* 3, no. 3 (1962); Richard Reid,

War in Pre-colonial Eastern Africa: The Patterns and Meanings of State-Level Conflict in the Nineteenth Century (Athens: Ohio University Press, 2007), 45–46, 50–51.

68. Callwell, *Small Wars*, 90.

69. For explanations of weapons deployments that occurred in the late-nineteenth-century colonial wars, see John Ellis, *The Social History of the Machine Gun* (Baltimore: Johns Hopkins University Press, 1975); Daniel R. Headrick, *The Tools of Empire: Technology and European Imperialism in the Nineteenth Century* (New York: Oxford University Press, 1981), 100–103, 115–24; Howard Whitehouse, *Battle in Africa, 1879–1914* (Camberley, UK: Field Books, 1987), 32–35.

70. There were exceptions. Most notably, Menelik's Ethiopian army, which defeated the Italian colonial army in 1896 at Adowa, had breechloaders, machine guns, and field artillery. See Headrick, *Tools of Empire*, 100; Bruce Vandervort, *Wars of Imperial Conquest in Africa, 1830–1914* (Bloomington: Indiana University Press, 1998), 160.

71. Headrick, *Tools of Empire*, 100. Maxim guns and other heavy equipment were transported by porters who marched in the columns with the askari companies.

72. For the 1890s, see Hubach, *Josef Weinberger*, "Hauptbuch," 14, 17, and "Notizheft," 4. For Maji Maji, see Admiralstab der Marine, *Die Tätigkeit der Marine während der Niederwerfung des Eingeborenen-Aufstandes in Ostafrika, 1905/6* (Berlin: Mittler und Sohn, 1907), 36, 41; Götzen, *Deutsch-Ostafrika*, 125; Gilbert Gwassa, *The Outbreak and Development of the Maji Maji War 1905–1907*, ed. Wolfgang Apelt (Cologne: Rüdiger Köppe, 2005), 173; Gwassa and Iliffe, *Maji Maji Rising*, 21. On using firearms as part of the spectacle of power, see also Johannes Fabian, *Out of Our Minds: Reason and Madness in the Exploration of Central Africa* (Berkeley: University of California Press, 2000), 144–50; Michael Pesek, "Colonial Conquest and the Struggle for the Presence of the Colonial State in German East Africa, 1885–1903," in *Inventing Collateral Damage: Civilian Casualties, War, and Empire*, ed. Stephen J. Rockel and Rick Halpern (Toronto: Between the Lines, 2009), 165–66, 168; Gudrun Miehe, Katrin Bromber, Said Khamis, and Ralf Grosserhode, eds., *Kala Shairi: German East Africa in Swahili Poems* (Cologne: Köppe, 2002), 245, 330, 332, 333; Hubach, *Josef Weinberger*, "Notizbuch," 5.

73. Gwassa and Iliffe, *Maji Maji Rising*, 8; Pesek, "Colonial Conquest," 166. On African racial constructions of other Africans, see Glassman, *War of Words, War of Stones: Racial Thought and Violence in Colonial Zanzibar* (Bloomington: Indiana University Press, 2011); Bruce Hall, *A History of Race in Muslim West Africa, 1600–1960* (Cambridge: Cambridge University Press, 2011).

74. MMRP, no. 2/68/1/4/4.

75. Hubach, *Josef Weinberger*, "Notizheft," 6 (emphasis in original).

76. On matembe, see Heinrich Schnee, ed., *Deutsches Koloniallexikon*, 3 vols. (Leipzig: Quelle und Mayer, 1920), 3:474. On machine guns being used

to cut a path through thick vegetation to allow a column to continue march-ing, see "Matschemba Expedition," *DKB* 10, no. 20 (1899): 692.

77. Wissmann, *Afrika*, 15. For a historical analysis of one style of fortifi-cation used in northeastern Tanzania before the German period, see H. A. Fosbrooke, "Chagga Forts and Boltholes," *Tanganyika Notes and Records* 37 (July 1954): 115–29. For an overview of Schutztruppe approaches to assaulting maboma see Bührer, *Kaiserliche Schutztruppe*, 246–56.

78. Wissmann, *Afrika*, 22; E. Mann, *Mikono ya damu*, 66; R. Jackson, "Resistance to the German Invasion of the Tanganyikan Coast, 1888–1891," in *Protest and Power in Black Africa*, ed. R. I. Rotberg and A. Mazrui (New York: Oxford University Press, 1970), 67.

79. Wissmann, *Afrika*, 23.

80. Ibid., 24.

81. Ibid.

82. Ibid. Cf. Callwell, *Small Wars*, 40–41. For related analysis of how different U.S. military actors have approached the "culture" question in the recent war in Iraq, see Keith Brown, "'All they understand is force': Debat-ing Culture in Operation Iraqi Freedom," *American Anthropologist* 110, no. 4 (2008): 443–53.

83. R. Reid, *War in Pre-colonial Eastern Africa*, 61.

84. Ibid.

85. Ibid., 63.

86. Ibid., 61.

87. Bührer, *Kaiserliche Schutztruppe*; Jan-Bart Gewald, "Colonial War-fare: Hehe and World War One, the Wars besides Maji Maji in south-western Tanzania," African Studies Centre Working Paper 63 (Leiden: ASC, 2005); E. Mann, *Mikono ya damu*; Pesek, *Koloniale Herrschaft*; Pesek, *Ende eines Kolonialreiches*; David Pizzo, "'To devour the land of Mkwawa': Colonial Vio-lence and the Hehe War in East Africa, ca. 1884–1914" (PhD diss., University of North Carolina, Chapel Hill, 2007).

88. Martin Baer and Olaf Schröter, *Eine Kopfjagd: Deutsche in Ostafrika* (Berlin: Links, 2001); Bührer, *Kaiserliche Schutztruppe*, 162–66, 242–45; E. Mann, *Mikono ya damu*, 135–37; Thomas Morlang, 'Die Kerls haben ja nicht mal Gewehre': Der Untergang der Zelewski-Expedition in Deutsch-Ostafrika im August 1891," *Militärgeschichte: Zeitschrift für historische Bildung* 11, no. 2 (2001): 22–28; Pizzo, "'Devour the land,'" 76–104. See also Alison Redmayne, "Mkwawa and the Hehe Wars," *Journal of African History* 9, no. 3 (1968): 409–36.

89. For later observations on the speed and effectiveness of Hehe scouts in reporting to Mkwawa on askari movements, see NL von Prittwitz und Gaffron, diary, 25 January 1898, box 245, p. 187, LIL.

90. E. Mann, *Mikono ya damu*, 136. Abdulcher Farrag, whose life story appears in chapter 1, was supposedly among the sixty-two askari survivors.

91. Pizzo, "'Devour the Land,'" 106.

92. Ibid., 76; Thomas Paul Ansorge von Prince, *Gegen Araber und Wahehe Erinnerungen aus meiner ostafrikanischen Leutnantszeit 1890–1895* (Berlin: Mittler und Sohn, 1914), 88.

93. T. Prince, *Araber und Wahehe*, 88.

94. E. Mann, *Mikono ya damu*, 137.

95. T. Prince, *Araber und Wahehe*, 97.

96. Ibid., 96.

97. Ibid., 157.

98. Ibid., 159.

99. Ibid.

100. Ibid., 75–77, 81.

101. Wissmann, *Afrika*, 58–69.

102. Bührer, *Kaiserliche Schutztruppe*, 143; Hubach, *Josef Weinberger,* "Hauptbuch," 29–30.

103. Bührer, *Kaiserliche Schutztruppe*, 143.

104. Hubach, *Josef Weinberger*, "Hauptbuch," 29–30.

105. Ibid., 32; "ringleaders": Bührer, *Kaiserliche Schutztruppe*, 143. For another example of four Sudanese soldiers complaining against a *Schutztruppe* officer, ultimately forcing him out of command, see Bührer, *Kaiserliche Schutztruppe*, 144. For more analysis of African soldiers' strikes against German colonial officers across the empire, see Thomas Morlang, *Askari und Fitafita: "Farbige" Söldner in den deutschen Kolonien* (Berlin: Links, 2008), 93–96.

106. Nigmann, *Geschichte der Kaiserlichen Schutztruppe*, 153.

107. For a succinct overview of the causes and course of the war, see Giblin and Monson, *Maji Maji*, 1–9.

108. Figures for how many died during Maji Maji range from Governor von Götzen's contemporary estimate of seventy-five thousand, to Tanzanian historian Gilbert Gwassa's estimate of two hundred fifty to three hundred thousand deaths. For a discussion of the demographic disaster caused by the *Schutztruppe*'s actions during Maji Maji, see Ludger Wimmelbücker, "Verbrannte Erde: Zu den Bevölkerungsverlusten als Folge des Maji-Maji-Krieges," in *Der Maji-Maji-Krieg in Deutsch-Ostafrika, 1905–1907*, ed. Felicitas Becker and Jigal Beez (Berlin: Links, 2005), 87–99. Following his suggestion, I use the higher number to indicate the degree to which the askari way of war targeted East Africans' abilities to rebuild following disaster. See also Gwassa and Iliffe, *Records of the Maji Maji Rising*, 27–28; and O. B. Mapunda and G. P. Mpangara, *The Maji Maji War in Ungoni* (Nairobi: East African Publishing House, 1969), 26–29.

109. See Marcia Wright, "Maji Maji: Prophecy and Historiography," in *Revealing Prophets: Prophecy in Eastern African History*, ed. David M. Anderson and Douglas H. Johnson (London: James Currey, 1995), 124–42. See also Felicitas Becker, "Traders, 'Big Men' and Prophets: Political Continuity and Crisis in the Maji Maji Rebellion in Southeast Tanzania," *Journal of African*

History 45, no. 1 (2004): 1–22; Jamie Monson, "Relocating Maji Maji: The Politics of Alliance and Authority in the Southern Highlands of Tanzania, 1870–1918," *Journal of African History* 39, no. 1 (1998): 95–120; Thaddeus Sunseri, "Famine and Wild Pigs: Gender Struggles and the Outbreak of Maji Maji in Uzaramo (Tanzania)," *Journal of African History* 38, no. 2 (1997): 235–59.

110. Sunseri, "Famine and Wild Pigs," 242.

111. On *maji* and its "message," see Jamie Monson, "War of Words: The Narrative Efficacy of Medicine in the Maji Maji War," in *Maji Maji: Lifting the Fog of War* (Leiden: Brill, 2010), 33–71. See also Wright, "Maji Maji," 124–42.

112. Bald, "Afrikanischer Kampf," 39; G. C. K. Gwassa, "African Methods of Warfare during the Maji Maji War 1905–1907," in *War and Society in Africa*, ed. Bethwell Ogot (London: Routledge, 1970), 143.

113. Götzen, *Deutsch-Ostafrika*, 132,149. See also Bald, "Afrikanischer Kampf," 37, 41.

114. Gwassa, *The Outbreak and Development of the Maji Maji War*, 171–72; John Iliffe, *A Modern History of Tanganyika* (Cambridge: Cambridge University Press, 1979), 197.

115. Paasche, *Morgenlicht*, 94.

116. Gwassa, "African Methods," 143–44. For a comparison to similar processes of "brutalization from below" in German Southwest Africa, see Matthias Häussler and Trutz von Trotha, "Brutalisierung 'von unten': Kleiner Krieg, Entgrenzung der Gewalt und Genozid im kolonialien Deutsch-Südwestafrika," *Mittelweg* 36, no. 3 (2012): 57–89.

117. Paul Gröschel, *Zehn Jahre christlicher Kulturarbeit in Deutsch-Ostafrika: Dargestellt in Briefen aus den Jahren 1898–1908* (Berlin: Berliner ev. Missionsgesellschaft, 1911), 189. See Joanna Bourke, *An Intimate History of Killing: Face-to-Face Killing in Twentieth-Century Warfare* (New York: Basic Books, 1999), 127–58; Karl Marlantes, *What It Is Like to Go to War* (New York: Atlantic Monthly Press, 2011), 36–42, for comparative reflections on soldiers' psychological responses to the fear of losing comrades in combat.

118. Paasche diary entries for 4 and 5 November 1905, RM 121/I/452, BArch; G 9/4, pp. 3, 23–64, TNA; NL Correck, diary, 7 July, 14 August, 8 September 1906, BHA; diary entry 7 February 1906, Kigonsera Chronicle, typescript, Peramiho Abbey, Peramiho, Tanzania, p. 67; Götzen, *Deutsch-Ostafrika*, 133. For further analysis of the Schutztruppe's capture of women during Maji Maji, see James Leonard Giblin, *A History of the Excluded: Making Family a Refuge from State in Twentieth-Century Tanzania* (Oxford: James Currey, 2005), 28–42; Monson, "Relocating Maji Maji," 115–16; Moyd, "'All people were barbarians to the *askari*': Askari Identity and Honor in the Maji Maji War, 1905–1907," in *Maji Maji: Lifting the Fog of War*, ed. James Giblin and Jamie Monson (Leiden: Brill, 2010), 169–70; H. Schmidt, "(Re)Negotiating Marginality," 50–55.

119. Cf. NL von Prittwitz und Gaffron, diary, 22 January 1898, box 245, pp. 182–83; 8 August 1897, p. 64, LIL.

120. Gröschel, *Christlicher Kulturarbeit*, 189; Jahresberichte 1908 Tsongea, Tabora, Mahenge, 1 April 1909, G 1/6, p. 12, TNA; Morlang, "'Ich habe die Sache satt hier,'" 513.

121. G 3/70, pp. 129–31, TNA.

122. Ibid., 129–31; G 3/72, p. 56, TNA; Songea to Gouvernement, 10 August 1909, G 3/77, n.p., TNA.

123. G 3/70, p. 41, TNA.

124. G 3/70, pp. 59–60, TNA; G 3/71, pp. 69–76, TNA.

125. Gwassa and Iliffe, *Maji Maji Rising*, 28.

126. Paul von Lettow-Vorbeck, *My Reminiscences of East Africa* (1920; Nashville: Battery Classics, 1991), 177; Lutteroth, *Tunakwenda*, 156; Wenig, *Kriegs-Safari*, 99–100.

127. German embassy, Dar es Salaam, to Auswärtiges Amt, 21 February 1962, Auswärtiges Amt, Politisches Archiv (PA AA), B 34, bd. 366; Bechhaus-Gerst, *Treu bis in den Tod: Von Deutsch-Ostafrika nach Sachsenhausen: Eine Lebensgeschichte*, 1st ed. (Berlin: Links, 2007); Bror Urme MacDonell, *Mzee Ali: The Biography of an African Slave-Raider Turned Askari and Scout* (Johannesburg: 30° South Publishers, 2006); Stefanie Michels, "'Reichsadler und Giraffe': Askari am Grab von Lettow-Vorbeck," in *Koloniale und postkoloniale Konstruktionen von Afrika und Menschen afrikanischer Herkunft in der deutschen Alltagskultur*, ed. Marianne Bechhaus-Gerst and Sunna Gieseke (Frankfurt: Peter Lang, 2007), 315–37.

128. See esp. Bechhaus-Gerst, *Treu bis in den Tod*.

CHAPTER 4: STATION LIFE

1. Juhani Koponen, *Development for Exploitation: German Colonial Policies in Mainland Tanzania, 1884–1914* (Hamburg: LIT, 1994), 619.

2. "enacted and reenacted": David Studdert, *Conceptualising Community: Beyond the State and Individual* (New York: Palgrave Macmillan, 2005), 161. For a graphic representation of a typical district station, see Dr. Kohlschütter, "Situationsplan der Halbinsel Langenburg," *Deutsches Kolonialblatt* (*DKB*) 10, no. 23 (1899): n.p.

3. Studdert, *Conceptualising Community*, 161. See also Thomas T. Spear, "Neo-Traditionalism and the Limits of Invention in British Colonial Africa" *Journal of African History* 44, no. 1 (2003): 26–27.

4. Alexander Becker, "Die Niederwerfung des Aufstandes im Süden," in *Hermann von Wissman: Deutschlands grösster Afrikaner: Sein leben und Wirken unter Benutzung des Nachlasses*, ed. Becker and C. v. Perbandt (Berlin: Alfred Schall, 1907), 325.

5. Ibid., 326. See also Alison Redmayne, "Mkwawa and the Hehe Wars," *Journal of African History* 9, no. 3 (1968): 409–36.

6. Erick J. Mann, *Mikono ya Damu: "Hands of Blood": African Mercenaries and the Politics of Conflict in German East Africa, 1888–1904* (Frankfurt: Peter Lang, 2002), 78; Thomas T. Spear, *Mountain Farmers: Moral Economies*

of Land and Agricultural Development in Arusha and Meru (Oxford: James Currey, 1997), 78–80.

7. Kirsten Zirkel, "Military Power in German Colonial Policy: The *Schutztruppen* and Their Leaders in East and South-West Africa, 1888–1918," in Killingray and Omissi, *Guardians of Empire*, 103. In the aftermath of Maji Maji and the Herero-Nama war in Southwest Africa, and public outrage over colonial abuses, Colonial Office Secretary Bernhard Dernburg tried to reform German colonial administration and economies to emphasize a more "scientific" approach to Germany's colonial projects. A pillar of his plan for reform included minimizing the military presence in colonial governance, but in fact, very little real change in this area took place in German East Africa. A useful overview of the "Dernburg Reforms" appears in Bradley Naranch, "'Colonized Body,' 'Oriental Machine': Debating Race, Railroads, and the Politics of Reconstruction in Germany and East Africa, 1906–1910," *Central European History* 33, no. 3 (2000): 299–302.

8. Herrman von Wissmann, *Afrika: Schilderungen und Rathschläge zur Vorbereitung für den Aufenthalt und den Dienst in den deutschen Schutzgebieten* (Berlin: Mittler und Sohn, 1903), 46.

9. Ibid.; Thomas Paul Ansorge von Prince, *Gegen Araber und Wahehe: Erinnerungen aus meiner ostafrikanischen Leutnantszeit 1890–1895* (Berlin: Mittler und Sohn, 1914), 113–14.

10. T. Prince, *Araber und Wahehe*, 114. See also Sperling to Gouvernement, 1 March 1911, G 7/42, n.p., TNA.

11. Michael Pesek, *Koloniale Herrschaft in Deutsch-Ostafrika: Expeditionen, Militär und Verwaltung seit 1880* (Frankfurt: Campus, 2005), 245.

12. Hans Poeschel, *Bwana Hakimu: Richterfahrten in Deutsch-Ostafrika* (Leipzig: Koehler und Voigtländer, 1940), 70.

13. Heinrich Schnee, ed., *Deutsches Kolonial-Lexikon*, 3 vols. (Leipzig: Quelle und Meyer, 1920), 1:229. Ethnographer Karl Weule echoes this definition of the boma. Karl Weule, *Der Krieg in den Tiefen der Menschheit* (Stuttgart: Kosmos, Gesellschaft der Naturfreunde, 1916), 135–36. For an extensive description of East African boma styles, see Paul Reichard, *Deutsch-Ostafrika: Das Land und seine Bewohner, seine politische und wirtschaftliche Entwickelung* (Leipzig: Otto Spamer, 1891), 167–70.

14. See Wissmann, *Afrika*, 15–22; H. A. Fosbrooke, "Chagga Forts and Bolt Holes," *Tanganyika Notes and Records* 37 (1954): 118–20. Cf. Douglas H. Johnson, "Recruitment and Entrapment in Private Slave Armies: The Structure of the *Zara'ib* in the Southern Sudan," *Slavery and Abolition* 13, no. 1 (1992): 163.

15. Schnee, *Kolonial-Lexikon*, 1:154.

16. "Skizze des Brandes des Utffz. Postens Mkalama aus 7.8.01," Acta des Kaiserlichen Gouvernements von Deutsch-Ostafrika betreffend Verwaltungs-Angelegenheiten, Mpapua, fol. 26, Basel Afrika Bibliografien.

17. Schnee, *Kolonial-Lexikon*, 1:229; Poeschel, *Bwana Hakimu*, 71.

18. Poeschel, *Bwana Hakimu*, 70.

19. Schnee, *Kolonial-Lexikon*, 1:154.

20. Ibid. For a more detailed description of the ideal colonial fortress, see *Anleitung zum Felddienst für Deutsch-Ostafrika* (Dar es Salaam: Deutsch-Ostafrikanische Rundschau, 1911), 65–76, 65–76. For a comparative case, see Alison K. Hoagland, "Village Constructions: U.S. Army Forts on the Plains, 1848–1890," *Winterthur Portfolio* 34, no. 4 (1999): 217–18.

21. Hermann von Bengerstorf, *Unter der Tropensonne Afrikas: Ernstes und Heiteres* (Hamburg: Fr. W. Thaden, 1914), 15.

22. Ibid., 14–15.

23. Ibid., 16.

24. Ibid., 16. But see G 32/5, 2/8 1912 and 10/8/1912, TNA, which contains two brief descriptions of askari using kibokos to beat women working on chain gangs.

25. Bengerstorf, *Unter der Tropensonne*, 16.

26. See also Ernst Nigmann, *Schwarze Schwänke: Fröhliche Geschichten aus unserem schönen alten Deutsch Ostafrika* (Berlin: Safari, 1922); Otto Stollowsky, *Jambo Sana! Lustige Geschichten, Plaudereien und Schnurren aus dem Leben in Deutsch-Ost-Afrika* (Leipzig-Anger: Walther Dachsel, 1935).

27. On this question, my thinking has been influenced by Cynthia Enloe's work on gender and global militarization. See, for instance, Enloe, *Maneuvers: The International Politics of Militarizing Women's Lives* (Berkeley: University of California Press, 2000). See also Rachel Woodward, *Military Geographies* (Oxford: Blackwell, 2004).

28. G 3/70, n.d., n.p., TNA; Usumbura to Ishangi, 22 June 1904, R 1003 FC/1162, BArch. See also Moyd, "'All people were barbarians,'" 170–71.

29. Usumbura to Ishangi, 22 June 1904, R 1003 FC/1162, BArch.

30. Götzen circular, ca. October 1905, n.p., G 3/70, TNA.

31. Marcia Wright, *Strategies of Slaves and Women: Life Stories from East/Central Africa* (New York: Lilian Barber, 1993), 207. See also Nigmann, *Schwarze Schwänke*, 163.

32. G 21/592, Strafsache Miersen, TNA.

33. Both Luise and Susanna signed their names to their statements. Neither Abdallah nor Habiba signed their statements, and the document notes that Habiba was " illiterate." A court scribe named Chalife recorded the statements and translated them from Kiswahili into German for the records.

34. *Bibi* means woman or wife in Kiswahili. Here, Miersen is referring to African women living with European men as companions and sexual partners who also handled household chores. See also references throughout Weinberger's diaries to mabibi with whom he had sexual relations.

35. *Mchumba* means either boyfriend or girlfriend in Kiswahili. The German word used is *Geliebte*. *Mchumba* is difficult to translate directly into English without losing its connotations, which include marriagelike practices such as living together as sexual and household partners, perhaps with the intent of formally marrying at some point.

36. In this case, Miersen presumably asked for the native judge to evaluate Habiba's reliability based on his "expert" perspective from previous experiences in hearing cases among Africans. See Harald Sippel, "Verwaltung und Recht in Deutsch-Ostafrika," in *Kolonisierung des Rechts. Zur kolonialen Rechts- und Verwaltungsordnung*, ed. Rüdiger Voigt and Peter Sack (Baden-Baden: Nomos, 2001), 285–86.

37. Both Treuge and "the oldest Dangaroni [*sic*] woman," Hongahonga, did not believe, based on their experience, that Habiba had hit Miersen after he supposedly refused her proposition. "Dangoro" is a Kiswahili word for brothel, and *dangoroni* means in or at the brothel. The current standard Kiswahili spelling of this word is *danguroni*, but *dangoroni* appears in Carl Velten, *Prosa und Poesie der Suaheli* (Berlin: Carl Velten, 1907), 165.

38. Treuge used the term *Mädchenjäger* (girl chaser; lit., girl-hunter) instead of the more common *Schurzenjäger* (skirt chaser, womanizer) to describe Miersen. Treuge could have meant this in two ways. First, since Habiba was a young African woman, referring to her as a girl may have been representative of the paternalism inherent in his role as a native judge. Second, he seemed to have been referring to Miersen's predilection for "girls" as sexual partners. The documents lend themselves to either of these readings, and may have both influenced how the case was recorded.

39. The district court that heard the case against Miersen included a district judge, two businessmen who served as observers, and a district official. All were Germans. For a brief description of the district courts, see Schnee, *Kolonial-Lexikon*, 1:198.

40. Another witness, Tembo, was judged untrustworthy because it was determined that she drank, smoked hashish, and chewed muscat nuts (nutmeg), which have a narcotic effect.

41. See note 37 above. On danguroni in Nairobi in the 1930s, see Luise White, *The Comforts of Home: Prostitution in Colonial Nairobi* (Chicago: University of Chicago Press, 1990), 86–102.

42. For a useful introduction to the historical dynamics affecting women during colonialism, see Dorothy Hodgson and Sheryl McCurdy, "Wayward Wives, Misfit Mothers, and Disobedient Daughters: 'Wicked' Women and the Reconfiguration of Gender in Africa," *Canadian Journal of African Studies* 30, no. 1 (1996): 1–9.

43. Cynthia Enloe has argued extensively in her body of work that military communities constitute more than just what is behind the checkpoints, walls, and barbed wire that define the boundaries of the "base," "post," "camp," or in this case, boma. The military sphere of influence spills out of its visible confines, influencing local gendered economies and social relations in numerous obvious and less obvious ways. Militaries are more integrated into and dependent on civilian contexts than many—especially military officials—would like to acknowledge. Boundaries between "civil" and "military" are porous and fluid, not least in the ways that soldiers participate in everyday local economies

and sociabilities. See Enloe, *Bananas, Beaches, and Bases: Making Feminist Sense of International Politics*, 1st U.S. ed. (Berkeley: University of California Press, 1990), 65–92. In German East Africa such crossing of civil and military geographies was the norm, because askari women or askariboys performed many of the routine services required by Schutztruppe personnel.

44. In a short piece entitled "Kazi ya askari wa polis [Work of the police-askari]," Kiswahili linguist Carl Velten presents an example of "daily" conversation for students of the language to study. "Ten askari are on town patrol duty. Four askari pass through the Indian street, four pass through the Swahili street, two stop at dangoroni." Velten, *Prosa und Poesie*, 165.

45. White, *Comforts of Home*, 16. White's study also explains Nairobi prostitutes' self-understandings, especially in terms of the concept of heshima (dignity, respect). See p. 23. For a discussion of prostitution in the King's African Rifles in British East Africa for a later period, see Timothy Parsons, "'All askaris are family men': Sex, Domesticity and Discipline in the King's African Rifles, 1902–1964," in *Guardians of Empire: The Armed Forces of the Colonial Powers c. 1700–1964*, ed. D. Killingray and D. E. Omissi (New York: Manchester University Press, 1999), 161–66; Parsons, *The African Rank-and-File: Social Implications of Colonial Military Service in the King's African Rifles, 1902–1964* (Portsmouth, NH: Heinemann, 1999), 158–66.

46. This rich—if problematic—source is open to much more detailed analysis and interpretation than can be offered here. For more detailed context, see Michelle Moyd, "Becoming *Askari*: African Soldiers and Everyday Colonialism in German East Africa, 1850–1918" (PhD diss., Cornell University, 2008), 202–30.

47. For more on tembe, see Schnee, *Kolonial-Lexikon*, 3:474.

48. F. Hildebrandt, *Eine deutsche Militärstation im innern Afrikas* (Wolfenbüttel: Heckners, 1905), 6.

49. Cf. Hoagland, "Village Constructions," 234–35.

50. Missionsinspektor Weishaupt, "Überblick über unsere Missionsstationen in Ostafrika. (Fortsetzung.) 4. Moschi," *Evangelisches-Lutherisches Missionsblatt* (hereafter, *ELM*) 67, no. 9 (1912): 206. For more examples of German maboma designs and arrangements, and how the maboma related to the development of towns, see H. A. Fosbrooke, "Arusha Boma," *Tanganyika Notes and Records* 38 (1955): 51–52; Robert B. Munson, "The Landscape of German Colonialism: Mt. Kilimanjaro and Mt. Meru, ca. 1890–1916" (PhD diss., Boston University, 2005), 66–197; Rona Elayne Peligal, "Spatial Planning and Social Fluidity: The Shifting Boundaries of Ethnicity, Gender, and Class in Arusha, Tanzania, 1920–1967" (PhD diss., Columbia University, 1999), 38–70.

51. Fritz Spellig, "Die Wanjamwesi: Ein Beitrag zur Völkerkunde Ostafrikas," *Zeitschrift für Ethnologie* 59, no. 3/4 (1927): 218–19.

52. Bezirksamt Bagamoyo to Kaiserliche Gouvernement, 22 August 1907, G 7/134, TNA. Thanks to Steven Fabian for sharing this reference with me.

53. Ibid.

54. Poeschel, *Bwana Hakimu*, 23.

55. Weishaupt, "Missionsstationen in Ostafrika," 206. See also Hildebrandt, *Deutsche Militärstation*, 60.

56. "Intergroup joking partnerships were especially concentrated along the main trade routes, and the most commercially active peoples, especially the Nyamwezi, had a complex network of recognized joking partners, potentially including members of virtually all ethnic or other sociocultural groups they encountered while engaged in caravan travel." Stephen J. Rockel, *Carriers of Culture: Labor on the Road in Nineteenth-Century East Africa*, Social History of Africa (Portsmouth, NH: Heinemann, 2006), 202. See esp. Mlolwa Nkuli, "Notes on Nyamwezi Utani," in *Utani Relationships in Tanzania*, ed. Stephen A. Lucas, 7 vols. (Dar es Salaam: University of Dar es Salaam, 1974–76), 4:5–6.

57. See also Michael Pesek, "The Boma and the Peripatetic Ruler: Mapping Colonial Rule in German East Africa, 1889–1903," *Western Folklore* 66, nos. 3–4 (2007): 233–57.

58. Diana Taylor, "Translating Performance," *Profession* (2002): 48. Emphasis in original.

59. Pesek, *Koloniale Herrschaft*, 191.

60. Otto Peiper, *Pocken und Pockenbekämpfung in Deutsch-Ostafrika* (Berlin: Richard Schoetz, 1925), 7; see also p. 9.

61. Ibid. See also Brian Siegel, "Bomas, Missions, and Mines: The Making of Centers on the Zambian Copperbelt," *African Studies Review* 31, no. 3 (1988): 61.

62. "islands of rule": Pesek, *Koloniale Herrschaft*, 244–59.

63. For detailed information on the kinds of markets and goods available within the districts, see *Militärisches Orientierungsheft für Deutsch-Ostafrika* (Dar es Salaam: Deutsch-Ostafrikanische Rundschau, 1911). The handbook is organized by district, with details about a wide range of everyday concerns provided for each one. On "compulsory" market halls and monetization, see Koponen, *Development for Exploitation*, 186.

64. Wright, *Strategies of Slaves* 185–87.

65. Stollowsky, *Jambo Sana!*, 123. See also Wright, *Strategies of Slaves*, 179–223. On gardening, see Hildebrandt, *Deutsche Militärstation*, 12.

66. Hildebrandt, *Deutsche Militärstation*, 23.

67. Ibid., 23.

68. T. Prince, *Araber und Wahehe*, 114. On African work ethics, see Keletso E. Atkins, *The Moon Is Dead! Give Us Our Money! The Cultural Origins of an African Work Ethic, Natal, South Africa, 1843–1900* (Portsmouth, NH: Heinemann, 1993); Thaddeus Sunseri, *Vilimani: Labor Migration and Rural Change in Early Colonial Tanzania* (Portsmouth, NH: Heinemann, 2002). On the German obsession with "education for work [Erziehung zur Arbeit]" see Sebastian Conrad, *Globalisierung und Nation im deutschen Kaiserreich* (Munich: C. H. Beck, 2006).

69. Hildebrandt, *Deutsche Militärstation*, 20.

70. Ibid., 20.

71. "tax-laborers": ibid., 19–20.

72. Sperling to Gouvernement, 1 March 1911, G 7/42, n.p., TNA. See also G 7/12, p. 66, TNA.

73. Wright, *Strategies of Slaves*, 200.

74. Weishaupt, "Missionsstationen in Ostafrika," 207. See also Carl J. Hellberg, *Missions on a Colonial Frontier West of Lake Victoria: Evangelical Missions in North-West Tanganyika to 1932* (Lund: Gleerups, 1965), 67–68; and Georg Volkens, "Reise des Dr. G. Volkens nach Moschi," *DKB* 5, no. 14 (1894): 308.

75. See Heinrich Fonck, *Deutsch Ost-Afrika: Eine Schilderung deutscher Tropen nach 10 Wanderjahren* (Berlin: Vossische Buchhandlung, 1910), 63–64.

76. See G 32/4, Bauangelegenheiten; G 7/133; G 7/134, TNA.

77. See Mwanza, January 1902, Bukoba, 3 March 1902, G 7/10, TNA.

78. *Anleitung zum Felddienst*, 85. The Schutztruppe had not recruited troops from outside German East Africa for at least five years when this handbook was written. Further details on the varieties of askari housing at different stations can be found in G 7/10, G 7/11, G 7/12, G 7/13, TNA. On fires in askari villages, see "Bericht betreffend den Brand des Askaridorfes am 1 December 1902," G 1/91, TNA; "Skizze des Brandes des Utffz. Postens Mkalama aus 7.8.01," Acta des Kaiserlichen Gouvernements von Deutsch-Ostafrika betreffend Verwaltungs-Angelegenheiten, Mpapua, fol. 26., Basel Afrika Bibliografien.

79. *Anleitung zum Felddienst*, 85.

80. Fonck, *Deutsch Ost-Afrika*, 64.

81. On sanitation concerns in the askari village and caravanserai at Mpwapwa, see "Bericht über sanitäre Massnahmen in Bezirk Mpapua in Etatsjahr 1909/10," 31 March 1909, G 1/9, TNA.

82. G 7/12, p. 66, TNA.

83. Stollowsky, *Jambo Sana*, 125–27.

84. August Leue, *Dar-es-Salaam: Bilder aus dem Kolonialleben* (Berlin: Wilhelm Süsserott, 1903), 191–92.

85. "Veränderungs-Nachweisung in der Nachweisung der zur Militärstation Kilimatinde gehörigen Gebäude und Grundstücke," 1 January 1904, G 7/12, p. 53, TNA.

86. Leue, *Dar-es-Salaam*, 180–81. The askari's "boy" lived nearby with his parents.

87. "Bericht betreffend den Brand des Askaridorfes am 1 December 1901," 1 April 1902, G 1/91, TNA.

88. Leue, *Dar-es-Salaam*, 191–92.

89. Hildebrandt, *Deutsche Militärstation*, 7.

90. Weishaupt, "Missionsstationen in Ostafrika," 207.

91. *Anleitung zum Felddienst*, 86.

92. Hildebrandt, *Deutsche Militärstation*, 7.

93. Ibid., 7–8.

94. Poeschel, *Bwana Hakimu*, 72–73; Weishaupt, "Missionsstationen in Ostafrika," 207; Reuss journal, 23 November 1910, KlE 857/1 (Alfred Reuss), BArch.

95. Marianne Bechhaus-Gerst, *Treu bis in den Tod: Von Deutsch-Ostafrika nach Sachsenhausen: Eine Lebensgeschichte*, 1st ed. (Berlin: Links, 2007); Reuss journal, 23 November 1910, KlE 857, BArch.

96. Schnee, *Deutsches Kolonial-Lexikon*, 2:68.

97. Michael S. Neiberg, *Soldiers' Lives through History: The Nineteenth Century* (Westport, CT: Greenwood, 2006), 64.

98. Fonck, *Deutsch Ost-Afrika*, 67–68. On the effects of militarization on women's lives, see Cynthia H. Enloe, *Does Khaki Become You? The Militarisation of Women's Lives* (London: Pandora, 1988).

99. Stollowsky, *Jambo Sana*, 125. See also Reichard, "Wanjamuesi," 324.

100. See for example Apostolic Vicar, Dar es Salaam to Gouvernement, 31 July 1912, p. 3, G9/4, TNA.

101. See also J. Spencer Trimingham, *Islam in East Africa* (Oxford: Clarendon Press, 1964), 43–44, 49–50.

102. Weishaupt, "Missionsstationen in Ostafrika," 207.

103. "Missionschronik: Aus unserer Mission," *ELM* 67, no. 22 (1912): 510.

104. "Reisebriefe unseres Missionsdirektors. 7. In Dar-es-Salaam," *ELM* 68, no. 4 (1913): 76.

105. Schachschneider to Collegium das Evangelisch-Lutherisches Mission, Leipzig, 1 May 1912, fiche 70 (no. 2), Leipzig Mission Archives.

106. Graf v. Götzen, 31 July 1903, G 9/1, p. 149, TNA.

107. Ibid.

108. G 9/30, TNA; *Militärisches Orientierungsheft*, sec. 7—Bezirk Langenburg (no page numbers). See also R 1003 FC/1156, BArch. An annual report for Urundi in 1913 noted that eleven Christian askari served as a "counterweight" to the predominantly Muslim government employees in the district.

109. Sammelerlass no. 3/1914, 9 March 1914, R 1003 FC/1156, BArch. See also Apostolic Vicar, Dar es Salaam to Gouvernement, 31 July 1912, G 9/4, TNA.

110. Schnee to Reichskolonialamt, 31 December, 1913, R 1001/923, pp. 172–74, BArch, cited in Thomas Morlang, "'Ich habe die Sache satt hier, herzlich satt': Briefe des Kolonialoffiziers Rudolf von Hirsch aus Deutsch-Ostafrika, 1905–1907," *Militärgeschichtliche Zeitschrift* 61 (2002): 501.

111. "Dschagga-Konferenz in Moschi: Bericht von Miss. Fokken—Aruscha," *ELM* 59, no. 24 (1904): 592.

112. Morlang, "'Ich habe die Sache,'" 516, 519–20.

113. "follow the example": Dr. Schippel, "Von Islam im westlichen Teile von Deutsch-Ostafrika," *Die Welt des Islams* 2, no. 1 (1914): 10; askari-boys: Apostolic Vicar, Dar es Salaam to Gouvernement, 31 July 1912, G 9/4, p. 3, TNA.

114. John Iliffe, *A Modern History of Tanganyika* (Cambridge: Cambridge University Press, 1979), 190.

115. Bradford G. Martin, "Muslim Politics and Resistance to Colonial Rule: Shaykh Uways B. Muhammad al-Bārawī and the Qādirīya Brotherhood in East Africa," *Journal of African History* 10, no. 3 (1969): 477, 478, 482.

116. Bagamoyo to RKA Berlin, 21 August 1908; Mahenge to RKA, 31 August 1908, G 9/46, pp. 40–41, TNA.

117. Michael Pesek, "Islam und Politik in Deutsch-Ostafrika," in *Alles unter Kontrolle: Disziplinierungsprozesse im kolonialen Tansania (1850–1960)*, ed. Albert Wirz, Andreas Eckert, and Katrin Bromber (Cologne: Köppe, 2003), 109.

118. Ibid. On Effendi Plantan, see also p. 120.

119. Ibid., 114–17.

120. Elpons to Gouvernement, Langenburg, 31 October 1898, G 9/27, pp. 65–84, TNA, cited in Hans-Joachim Niesel, "Kolonialverwaltung und Missionen in Deutsch Ostafrika 1890–1914" (PhD diss., Freie Universität, Berlin, 1971), 201.

121. "Nachrichten aus Moschi," *ELM* 57, no. 6 (1902): 128.

122. Ibid.

123. Ibid.

124. "Überblick über unsere Missionsstationen," 207.

125. See also G 9/56, pp. 131–32, TNA.

126. Missionary Wärthl, "Durch Busch und Wald im Innern Afrikas," *ELM* 67, no. 17 (1912): 389–90.

127. See also Paul von Lettow-Vorbeck, *Afrika wie ich es wiedersah* (Munich: J. F. Lehmann, 1955); Eckard Michels, "Deutschlands bekanntester 'Kolonialheld' und seine 'Askari': Paul von Lettow-Vorbeck und der Feldzug in Ostafrika im Ersten Weltkrieg," *Revue d'Allemagne et pays de langue allemande* 38, no. 4 (2006): 541–54.

128. Lambrecht to Gouvernement, 12 January 1901, R 1001/224, p. 12, BArch.

129. Ibid., p. 15.

130. Schleinitz to Gouvernement, 10 June 1903, R 1001/224, p. 28, BArch.

131. Section 11, Bezirksamt Morogoro, *Militärisches Orientierungsheft für Deutsch-Ostafrika*, 8.

132. By way of comparison, rank-and-file askari earned 20 rupees per month in salary. The German pound [*Pfund*] was used to measure the weight of the sacks described here. A Pfund equaled 500 grams. See "Angaben über Masse und Gewichte," *Militärisches Orientierungsheft für Deutsch-Ostafrika*, n.p.

133. Heinrich Dauber, ed., *"Nicht als Abentheurer bin ich hierherhergekommen": 100 Jahre Entwicklungshilfe; Tagebücher und Briefe aus Deutsch-Ostafrika 1896–1902* (Frankfurt: Verlag für Interkulturelle Kommunikation, 1991), 176.

134. Schleinitz to Gouvernement, 10 June 1903, R 1001/224, p. 28, BArch.

135. "Aus der Kolonie," *DOAZ* 7, no. 23 (1905).

136. Ibid.

137. Ibid.

138. "Tolles Vorgehen farbiger Polizeisoldaten," *UP*, 31 August 1912, suppl. 1, pp. 11, 35.

139. Ibid.

140. Wärthl, "Busch und Wald," 360.

141. "Unsere schwarze Polizei," *UP*, suppl. 1, 27 July 1912, pp. 11, 30.

142. Koponen, *Development for Exploitation*, 291, 628–30.

143. The grants were divided into five "classes," of 150, 125, 100, 75, or 50 "crop-bearing" palms. Methner to Bezirksamt Bagamoyo, 23/3/1911, G 8/65, TNA.

144. On the process of tapping palms, see Justin Willis, *Potent Brews: A Social History of Alcohol in East Africa, 1850–1999* (London: James Currey, 2002), 31–32.

145. Weber to Gouvernement, Dar es Salaam, 26 August 1911, G 8/65, TNA.

146. Ibid.

147. Ibid.; Schmidt to Gouvernement, 28 December 1911, G 8/65, TNA.

148. Bezirksamt Bagamoyo to Gouvernement, Dar es Salaam, 28 December 1911, G 8/65, TNA.

149. Ibid.

150. Ibid.

151. Pesek, "Boma and the Peripatetic Ruler," 253.

CHAPTER 5: ASKARI AS AGENTS OF EVERYDAY COLONIALISM

1. "Nachrichten aus Myambani: Quartalbericht von Miss. Augustus (4. Quartal 1904)," *ELM* 60, no. 7 (1905): 165–66.

2. See also P. Joh. Haefliger, 12 October 1901, "Chronik von Kigonsera," unpublished typescript, Peramiho Abbey, Tanzania.

3. Albinus, "Dienstreise im Bezirk Ssongea," 15 November 1904, R 1001/234, pp. 15–16, BArch; Heinrich Dauber, ed., *"Nicht als Abentheurer bin ich hierhergekommen": 100 Jahre Entwicklungs-"Hilfe": Tagebücher und Briefe aus Deutsch-Ostafrika, 1896–1902* (Frankfurt: Verlag für Interkulturelle Kommunikation, 1991), 176.

4. Albinus to Gouvernement, 15 November 1904, R 1001/234, pp. 17–18, BArch.

5. *Akidas* were part of a layered administrative structure and hierarchy of titled, salaried offices that the Germans adopted from previous Zanzibari administrative practices. "After putting down the coastal resistance the Germans allied with some Arab and Swahili notables. In towns some of these notables were appointed to the highest subordinate positions called *liwali*. In the countryside small chiefs called *jumbe* were included in larger administrative units headed by [nonwhite] officials termed *akida*." Juhani Koponen, *Development for Exploitation: German Colonial Policies in Mainland Tanzania, 1884–1914* (Hamburg: LIT, 1994), 119; see also pp. 121–29. In the colonial context, these

functionaries worked for the German station chiefs, carrying out a wide range of tasks of governance the station chiefs delegated to them.

6. Michels to Gouverneur, 20 July 1914, G 9/23, p. 148, TNA.

7. Ibid.

8. Lorne E. Larson, "A History of the Mahenge (Ulanga) District, ca. 1860–1957" (PhD diss., University of Dar es Salaam, 1976), 109.

9. Jan-Georg Deutsch, "Celebrating Power in Everyday Life: The Administration of Law and the Public Sphere in Colonial Tanzania, 1890–1914," *Journal of African Cultural Studies* 14, no. 1 (2002): 96. For examples of cases heard in *shauris* in Tanga in 1906, see "Shaurihalle," *UP*, 14 April 1906, 5, 23. See also Michael Pesek, *Koloniale Herrschaft in Deutsch-Ostafrika: Expeditionen, Militär und Verwaltung seit 1880* (Frankfurt: Campus, 2005), 277–83.

10. Hans Poeschel, *Bwana Hakimu: Richterfahrten in Deutsch-Ostafrika* (Leipzig: Koehler und Voigtländer, 1940), 58. See also Thomas Paul Ansorge von Prince, *Gegen Araber und Wahehe: Erinnerungen aus meiner ostafrikanischen Leutnantszeit 1890–1895* (Berlin: Mittler und Sohn, 1914), 115–16; F. Hildebrandt, *Eine deutsche Militärstation im innern Afrikas* (Wolfenbüttel: Heckners, 1905), 53.

11. Weishaupt, "Überblick über unsere Missionsstationen in Ostafrika," *ELM* 67, no. 9 (1912): 206.

12. Charisius to Rechenberg, 16 January 1907, R 1001/227, p. 5, BArch. Charisius's report covered a "district trip" he undertook between 19 October and 3 December 1906.

13. T. Prince, *Araber und Wahehe*, 115.

14. NL von Prittwitz und Gaffron, 16–24 June 1898, folder 6, box 248, LIL.

15. See, for example, Major v. Prittwitz und Gaffron, Tabora Annual Report, G 1/6, pp. 29–32, TNA. Prittwitz's report offers an extended description of the district officers' excessive workload, which is exacerbated by ever increasing numbers of Africans attending *mashauri*. See also Reuss to parents, 19 May 1909, KlE 857/1 (Alfred Reuss), BArch.

16. David D. Kim, "Scandals of Translation: Cannibalism and the Limits of Colonial Authority in the Trial of Iringa," *German Studies Review* 34, no. 1 (2011): 130.

17. Poeschel, *Bwana Hakimu*, 169.

18. Burkhard Vieweg, *Macho Porini — die Augen im Busch: Kautschuk-pflanzer Karl Vieweg in Deutsch-Ostafrika: Authentische Berichte, 1910–1919* (Weikersheim: Margraf, 1996), 144. See also Hildebrandt, *Deutsche Militärstation*, 3, 54–55.

19. See Hauptmann Puder, "Bericht über die Shirambo-Expedition," *DKB* 10, no. 14 (1899): 473. This report describes a situation in which a local leader's decision to flee into the bush instead of reporting for a shauri led Schutztruppe captain Puder to send an askari patrol to find and arrest him. Puder then punished him for his "open rebellion and his disobedience."

20. T. Prince, *Araber und Wahehe*, 115. In cases between Africans, German officials tended to favor plaintiffs. As Tom von Prince put it, plaintiffs

were right "nine out of ten times" because they would only risk an encounter with the state "if [they] were genuinely seeking protection and amends" for a wrong done to them (see p. 116). See also Déclé, *Three Years in Savage Africa* (1900; Bulawayo: Books of Rhodesia, 1974), 386–87.

21. The askari's name, Kasi Moto [*kazi moto*], means hot work in Kiswahili. Willmann to Schanz, G 9/31, Leipziger Missions-Gesellschaft, p. 115, TNA. Msaba, or Mshabaa, was an associate of Marealle, an important Chagga ally of the Germans. On Marealle, see Kathleen Mary Stahl, *History of the Chagga People of Kilimanjaro* (London: Mouton, 1964), 308–36.

22. Willmann to Schanz, 11 April 1905, G 9/31, p. 117, TNA.

23. G 55/23, n.p., TNA.

24. Found in Gillmann papers, Mss. Afr. S. 1175 (1), 11 January 1906, Rhodes House, Oxford (hereafter, RH).

25. Pesek, *Koloniale Herrschaft*, 191; Johannes Fabian, *Out of our Minds: Reason and Madness in the Exploration of Central Africa* (Berkeley: University of California Press, 2000), 102–27.

26. "Nachrichten aus Myambani," *ELM* 60, no. 7 (1905): 165–66.

27. Gillman papers, Mss. Afr. S. 1175 (1), 10 January 1906, Rhodes House (emphasis in original). See also Karl Weule, *Negerleben in Ostafrika: Ergebnisse einer ethnologischen Forschungsreise* (Leipzig: F .A. Brockhaus, 1908), 42.

28. Gillman papers, Mss. Afr. S. 1175 (1), 25 January 1906, RH.

29. See also Bror Urme MacDonell, *Mzee Ali: The Biography of an African Slave-Raider Turned Askari and Scout* (Johannesburg: 30° South Publishers, 2006), 123–42. On railway labor forces, see Thaddeus Sunseri, *Vilimani: Labor Migration and Rural Change in Early Colonial Tanzania* (Portsmouth, NH: Heinemann, 2002), 167–71.

30. Freiherr v. Ledebur, 1 August 1902, R 1001/1030, p. 103, BArch. See also Pesek, *Koloniale Herrschaft*, 217.

31. Freiherr v. Ledebur, R 1001/1030, p. 101, BArch.

32. Ibid., p. 102.

33. Cf. MacDonnell, *Mzee Ali*, 106–8.

34. Freiherr v. Ledebur, R 1001/1030, p. 102, BArch.

35. Ibid.

36. Timothy Mitchell, "The Limits of the State: Beyond Statist Approaches and Their Critics," *American Political Science Review* 85, no. 1 (1991): 91.

37. Erving Goffman, *The Presentation of Self in Everyday Life*, 1st ed. (New York: Anchor, 1959), 75–76.

38. Ibid.

39. Mitchell, "Limits of the State," 95.

40. James Ferguson and Akhil Gupta, "Spatializing States: Toward an Ethnography of Neoliberal Governmentality," *American Ethnologist* 29, no. 4 (2002): 981–1002.

41. Ibid.

42. Timothy Mitchell, "Everyday Metaphors of Power," *Theory and Society* 19, no. 5 (1990): 566.

43. NL Correck, diary, 22 October 1907, BHA (see descriptions of similar occasions in entries for 1 July 1906, 27 January 1908); Poeschel, *Bwana Hakimu*, 47.

44. These dance associations were also mutual-aid societies and sometimes were arranged around generational age-sets. Men and women sometimes had separate ngoma, but most associations seem to have incorporated both men and women in prescribed roles. The classic historical work on the *beni* form of ngoma, is T. O. Ranger, *Dance and Society in Eastern Africa, 1890–1970: The Beni Ngoma* (Berkeley: University of California Press, 1975).

45. Jonathon Glassman draws on Marcel Mauss to argue that settings like ngoma constituted "total social phenomena," where it was impossible to distinguish between different forms of authority and where "all kinds of institutions [were] given expression at one and the same time—religious, juridical, and moral, which relate to both politics and the family; likewise economic ones, which suppose special forms of production and consumption, or rather of performing total services of distribution. This is not to take into account the aesthetic phenomena to which these facts [led], and the contours of the phenomena that these institutions manifest[ed]." Jonathon Glassman, *Feasts and Riot: Revelry, Rebellion, and Popular Consciousness on the Swahili Coast, 1856–1888* (Portsmouth, NH: Heinemann, 1995), 146. See also Marcel Mauss, *The Gift: Forms and Functions of Exchange in Archaic Societies*, trans. W. D. Halls (Abingdon, UK: Routledge, 1990), 3–4.

46. See the exchange on the subject in various issues of *Anzeigen für Tanga (Stadt und Bezirk)*, May–July 1903. On drinking and sociability in East Africa, see Justin Willis, *Potent Brews: A Social History of Alcohol in East Africa, 1850–1999* (Oxford: James Currey, 2002), 9–10.

47. Dance arenas were called maboma in some contexts. James G. Ellison, "Competitive Dance and Social Identity: Converging Histories in Southwest Tanzania," in *Mashindano! Competitive Music Performance in East Africa*, ed. Frank Gunderson and Gregory Barz (Dar es Salaam: Mkuki na Nyota, 2000), 204, 228; Christopher F. Kamlongera, "An Example of Syncretic Drama from Malawi: Malipenga,"*Research in African Literatures* 17, no. 2 (1986): 202.

48. Scott Hughes Myerly, "'The eye must entrap the mind': Army Spectacle and Paradigm in Nineteenth-Century Britain," *Journal of Social History* 26, no. 1 (1992): 114–15.

49. For a discussion of intermediaries as a social category and historical frame, see Benjamin N. Lawrance, Emily Lynn Osborn, and Richard L. Roberts, "African Intermediaries and the 'Bargain' of Collaboration," introduction to *Intermediaries, Interpreters, and Clerks: African Employees in the Making of Colonial Africa, Africa and the Diaspora*, ed. Lawrance, Osborn, and Roberts (Madison: University of Wisconsin Press, 2006), 5–7.

50. William McNeill, *Keeping Together in Time: Dance and Drill in Human History* (Cambridge, MA: Harvard University Press, 1995).

51. "mesmerizing": Myerly, "'Eye must entrap,'" 113.

52. "Lokales": *Anzeigen für Tanga (Stadt und Bezirk)*, 24 October 1903.

53. Tempelhof (in Berlin) was perhaps the oldest and most famous military parade field in Prussia. "Was Prinz Adalbert in Tanga gesehen hat. Bilder vom Prinzenbesuch am 13. Februar," *UP*, suppl., 18 February 1905. See also"Eröffnung der Usambara-Eisenbahn in Neu-Moschi am 7. Februar 1912," *ELM* 67, no. 9 (1912): 208–9.

54. "Eröffnung der Usambara-Eisenbahn."

55. "Gouvernement Befehl," 8 October 1891; Schmidt to Soden, 24 October 1891, G 1/4, TNA.

56. Pesek, *Koloniale Herrschaft*, 262–63. See also Simbo Janira, *Kleiner grosser schwarzer Mann: Lebenserinnerungen eines Buschnegers* (Eisenach: Erich Röth, 1956), 119.

57. Ranger, *Dance and Society*, 5.

58. Ibid.

59. Ibid., 35.

60. Ibid., 40.

61. Ibid., 53. Ranger contends that a "polarization" in the competitive identities of these two societies occurred during World War I, when *arinoti* members asserted themselves against *marini* efforts to monopolize the glory of the Schutztruppe's initial successes against Allied forces in East Africa in 1914 (see pp. 53–55).

62. Walter Rehfeldt, *Bilder vom Kriege in Deutsch-Ostafrika nach Aquarellen* (Hamburg: Charles Fuchs, 1920), 12, found in NL Schnee, no. 86, Geheimes Staatsarchiv-Preussisches Kulturbesitz, Berlin-Dahlem; Ascan Roderich Lutteroth, *Tunakwenda: Auf Kriegssafari in Deutsch-Ostafrika* (Hamburg: Broschek, 1938), 295–97.

63. NL von Prittwitz und Gaffron, diary, 4 June 1898, box 248, folder 6, p. 8, LIL. See also entry for 10 July 1897, box 245, folder 1, p. 10, which describes the reception of the Gouverneur at Iringa in July 1897, during which a "war-dance" and a "peace dance" (ngoma) were performed. See also Lothar von Trotha, *Meine Bereisung von Deutsch-Ostafrika* (Berlin: Verlag von B. Brigl, 1897), 43. On the physiological effects of dance and drill, see Judith Lynne Hanna, "African Dance and the Warrior Tradition," in *The Warrior Tradition in Modern Africa*, ed. Ali A. Mazrui (Leiden: Brill, 1977), 113–23; McNeill, *Keeping Together*, 1–11.

64. Pesek, *Koloniale Herrschaft*, 262–63. On "theatricality," see Diana Taylor, "Translating Performance," *Profession* (2002).

65. For more on the parallel activities set up for Europeans to participate in after the formal celebration ended, see Poeschel, *Bwana Hakimu*, 49–50.

66. Ranger, *Dance and Society*, 19.

67. "Gouvernement Befehl," 8 October 1891; Schmidt to Soden, 24/10/1891, G 1/4, TNA; "mock fighting": "The Beni Society of Tanganyika Territory," *Primitive Man* 11, nos. 3–4 (1938): 79; Ellison, "Competitive Dance," 210, 216–18; Ranger, *Dance and Society*, 59.

68. Stephen Martin describes the "pan-ethnic character" of beni ngoma as "somewhat analogous to the development of East Africa's lingua franca, Kiswahili, i.e. *beni* was a 'musical lingua franca.'" Martin, "Brass Bands and the Beni Phenomenon in Urban East Africa," *African Music* 7, no. 1 (1991): 79.

69. August Leue, *Dar-es-Salaam: Bilder aus dem Kolonialleben* (Berlin: Wilhelm Süsserott, 1903), 187–89.

70. Ibid., 187. On *banji* (*kibanji*), see Ranger, *Dance and Society*, 36–37. *Kimrima* comes from *mrima*, a term for the Kiswahili-speaking coast of East Africa. *Kiunguya* (*kiunguja*) comes from the Kiswahili term for the island of Zanzibar (Unguja).

71. Ranger, *Dance and Society*, 19.

72. *Heimat* means home or homeland, but also conveys more complex ideas and sentiments. Celia Applegate describes it as "the effort, for better or for worse, to maintain 'community' against the economic, political, and cultural forces that would scatter it." Celia Applegate, *A Nation of Provincials: The German Idea of Heimat* (Berkeley: University of California Press, 1990), 6. See also Jeremy DeWaal, "The Reinvention of Tradition: Form, Meaning, and Local Identity in Modern Cologne Carnival," *Central European History* 46, no. 3 (2013): 495–532.

73. Sebastian Conrad, *Globalisierung und Nation im Deutschen Kaiserreich* (Munich: C. H. Beck, 2006), 79–83.

74. Pesek, *Koloniale Herrschaft*, 262.

75. Glassman, *Feasts and Riot*, 245–46. See also Jane L. Parpart and Marianne Rostgaard, eds., *The Practical Imperialist: Letters from a Danish Planter in German East Africa 1888–1906* (Leiden: Brill, 2006), 160.

76. Parpart and Rostgaard, *Practical Imperialist*, 160.

77. Glassman, *Feasts and Riot*, 164.

78. Parpart and Rostgaard, *Practical Imperialist*, 151.

79. Poeschel, *Bwana Hakimu*, 72–73; "Überblick über unsere Missionsstationen in Ostafrika," *ELM* 67, no. 9 (1912): 207; diary entry for 23 November 1910, KlE 857/1 (Alfred Reuss), BArch.

80. Magdalena von Prince, cited in Michael Von Herff, "'They walk through the fire like the blondest German': African Soldiers Serving the Kaiser in German East Africa (1888–1914)'" (MA thesis, McGill University, 1991), 85.

81. Leue, *Dar-es-Salaam*, 188–89.

82. Von Herff, "'Walk through the fire,'" 85.

83. "Aus Tanga und Umgegend," *UP*, 14 November 1908; "Runderlass an alle Bezirksämter, Residenturen, Militärstationen," 25 June 1913, TNA; R 1001/1047, pp. 138–39, BArch.

84. Rehfeldt, *Bilder vom Kriege*, 12.

85. Leue, *Dar-es-Salaam*, 188–89.

86. Ibid., 191–92, 224–26.

87. Ibid., 226.

CONCLUSION: MAKING ASKARI MYTHS

1. See Van Deventer to War Office, 20 November 1918, CO 691/19, p. 617, NAK (see also pp. 578–618).

2. See Ascan Roderich Lutteroth, *Tunakwenda: Auf Kriegssafari in Deutsch-Ostafrika* (Hamburg: Broschek, 1938), 169. See also Sandra Mass, *Weisse Helden, Schwarze Krieger: Zur Geschichte kolonialer Männlichkeit in Deutschland, 1918–1964* (Cologne: Böhlau, 2006), 67.

3. See I. K. Katoke and P. Rwehumbiza, "The Administrator: Francis Lwamugira"; Daisy Sykes Buruku, "The Townsman: Kleist Sykes"; A. L. Sakafu, "The Pastor," all in *Modern Tanzanians: A Volume of Biographies*, ed. John Iliffe (Nairobi: East African Publishing House, 1973).

4. Marianne Bechhaus-Gerst, *Treu bis in den Tod: Von Deutsch-Ostafrika nach Sachsenhausen: Eine Lebensgeschichte*, 1st ed. (Berlin: Links, 2007), 29–38, 68–71, 78–81, 110–25. For further reflections on the place of Mahjub bin Adam Mohamed in African history, see E. S. Atieno Odhiambo, "The Landscapes of Memory in Twentieth-Century Africa," in *In Search of a Nation: Histories of Authority and Dissidence in Tanzania*, ed. Gregory H. Maddox and James L. Giblin (Oxford: James Currey, 2005), 114–27. Odhiambo refers to him as Mohammed Hussein Bayume, a name that he adopted later in life.

5. Ibid., 143–50.

6. For references to ex-askari who settled in the Kilimanjaro region, see William Arens, *On the Frontier of Change: Mto wa Mbu, Tanzania* (Ann Arbor: University of Michigan Press, 1979), 33–34, 126–27, 128. On an ex-askari settlement in Dar es Salaam, see J. A. K. Leslie, *A Survey of Dar es Salaam* (London: Oxford University Press, 1963), 47–50. On ex-askari living in Portuguese East Africa, see Orde-Brown to Secretary to the Administration, Dar es Salaam, 8 February 1919, CO 691/21, p. 257, NAK. See also John Iliffe, *Modern History of Tanganyika* (Cambridge: Cambridge University Press, 1979), 248.

7. F. J. Bagshawe, "Annual Report: 1919/20: Mkalama," 11 June 1920, Secretariat 1733/15, AB 4, pp. 12–13, TNA.

8. Ralph D. Hult, "Annual Report of the Work of the Mashame Mission Station during the period, February 1923–June 1924," Evangelisch-Lutherisches Missionswerk Leipzig, Afrika II., 32.2a Machame 1893–1905, Frankesche Stiftungen zu Halle, Germany.

9. For a summary of what became of Germany's ex-colonial soldiers across the former German empire, see Thomas Morlang, *Askari und Fitafita: "Farbige" Söldner in den deutschen Kolonien* (Berlin: Links, 2008), 147–62. On German government and humanitarian efforts to take care of ex-askari in Tanzania after 1918, see Stephanie Michels, *Schwarze deutsche Kolonialsoldaten: Mehrdeutige Repräsentationsräume und früher Kosmopolitismus in Afrika* (Bielefeld: Transcript, 2009), 133–51.

10. John Iliffe, *Modern History of Tanganyika*, 248.

11. Bror Urme MacDonell, *Mzee Ali: The Biography of an African Slave-Raider Turned Askari and Scout* (Johannesburg: 30° South Publishers, 2006), 213. Cf. Joe Lunn "Male Identity and Martial Codes of Honor: A Comparison of the War Memoirs of Robert Graves, Ernst Jünger, and Kande Kamara," *Journal of Military History* 69, no. 3 (2005): 724.

12. For more on this topic, see Bechhaus-Gerst, *Treu bis in den Tod*, 39–50; Susann Lewerenz, "'Loyal Askari' and 'Black Rapist' — Two Images in the German Discourse on National Identity and Their Impact on the Lives of Black People in Germany, 1918–1945," in *German Colonialism and National Identity*, ed. Michael Perraudin und Jürgen Zimmerer (New York: Routledge, 2011), 173–83; Stephanie Michels, "Askari — treu bis in den Tod? Vom Umgang der Deutschen mit ihren schwarzen Soldaten," in *Afrikanerinnen in Deutschland und schwarze Deutsche — Geschichte und Gegenwart*, ed. Marianne Bechhaus-Gerst and Reinhard Klein-Arendt (Münster: LIT, 2004), 171–86; Michelle Moyd,"Becoming *Askari*: African Soldiers and Everyday Colonialism in German East Africa, 1850–1918" (PhD diss., Cornell University, 2008), 267–302.

13. Roland Barthes, *Mythologies*, trans. Annette Lavers (New York: Noonday Press, 1972), 151.

14. The seminal work on this topic is Susanne Zantop, *Colonial Fantasies: Conquest, Family, and Nation in Precolonial Germany, 1770–1870* (Durham, NC: Duke University Press, 1997). See also Zantop, "Colonial Legends, Postcolonial Legacies," in *A User's Guide to German Cultural Studies*, ed. S. Denham, I. Kacandes, and J. Petropoulos (Ann Arbor: University of Michigan Press, 1997), 189–205.

15. For a feminist reinterpretation of the German propaganda campaign against the use of francophone African occupation troops in the Rheinland, see Julia Roos, "Women's Rights, Nationalist Anxiety, and the 'Moral' Agenda in the Early Weimar Republic: Revisiting the 'Black Horror' Campaign against France's African Occupation Troops," *Central European History* 42, no. 3 (2009): 473–508.

16. See Gisela Graichen and Horst Gründer, *Deutsche Kolonien: Traum und Trauma* (Berlin: Ullstein, 2005), 380; Wolfe W. Schmokel, *Dream of Empire: German Colonialism, 1919–1945* (New Haven: Yale University Press, 1964), 16. On the cultural reverberations of colonial revisionist activities through print and performance culture, see Katharine Kennedy, "African Heimat: German Colonies in Wilhelmine and Weimar Reading Books," *Internationale Schulbuchforschung* 24 (2002): 7–26; Lewerenz, *Deutsche Afrika-Schau*.

17. But see B34/527, 1964 Auswärtiges Amt Politisches Archiv (AA), Berlin, for examples of correspondence between former askari, the German Embassy in Tanzania, and interested parties in Germany, regarding the veterans' need for financial aid.

18. See "Kaiser's Geburtstag," 27 January 1977, MSG 2/2121, BArch, for three brief notes written in German by an eighty-one-year-old former

Schutztruppe askari (M. Amandzi) praising the Kaiser and the Fatherland. For experiences of African veterans of other European colonial armies, see Joe Lunn, *Memoirs of the Maelstrom: A Senegalese Oral History of the First World War* (Portsmouth, NH: Heinemann, 1999), 187–222, 228–36; Gregory Mann, *Native Sons: West African Veterans and France in the Twentieth Century* (Durham, NC: Duke University Press, 2006), 63–107, 108–45; Timothy Parsons, *The African Rank-and-File: Social Implications of Colonial Military Service in the King's African Rifles, 1902–1964* (Portsmouth, NH: Heinemann, 1999), 224–69.

Glossary

akida. A local African colonial administrator; plural *maakida* (Kiswahili).

amri ya mungu. God's will (Kiswahili).

Ansar. The Mahdist army in Sudan (Arabic).

askari. An African soldier of the German colonial army in East Africa; plural *askari* (Kiswahili; Arabic).

askariboy. A servant or gunboy to an askari (German).

Askaridorf. An askari village (German).

baba. A father, patron; plural *baba* (Kiswahili).

banghi. Hemp (Kiswahili).

batemi. Plural of *mtemi* (Unyamwezi); local rulers (Kinyamwezi).

beni. A competitive dance form in East Africa (Kiswahili).

beshaush. A sergeant (Turkish).

bibi. A woman, wife; plural *mabibi* (Kiswahili).

boma. An enclosure, fortress, military outpost; plural *maboma* (Kiswahili).

butemi. Small polity in Unyamwezi, ruled by an *mtemi* (Kinyamwezi).

bwana. A man, Mister (Kiswahili).

bwana mdogo. A little man, Mister Small (Kiswahili).

bwana mkubwa. A big man, Mister Big (Kiswahili).

danguroni. In or at the city quarter where prostitution took place (Kiswahili).

Deutsch-Ostafrika Gesellschaft (DOAG). German East Africa Company (German).

effendi. An officer (Turkish, Arabic).

Exerzierplatz (pl., *Exerzierplätze*). Training or parade ground (German).

Gouvernement. Colonial government headquarters in German East Africa; office of the Gouverneur (governor) (German).

hamsa ishirini. Twenty-five lashes with a whip; a standard punishment in German East Africa (lit., twenty-five) (Kiswahili).

Hauptmann. A captain (German).

heshima. Respect, dignity (Kiswahili).

jumbe. A chief, local African administrator; plural *majumbe* (Kiswahili).

Kaiserreich. Empire (German).

kiboko. A hippopotamus- or rhinoceros-hide whip (Kiswahili).

King's African Rifles (KAR). The British colonial army in East Africa (English).

Kiswahili. The Swahili language (Kiswahili).

Leutnant. A lieutenant (German).

maboma. Plural of *boma* (Kiswahili).

Mahdi. Title taken by the Rightly Guided One, a messianic Muslim leader (Arabic).

Mahdiyya. The state founded by the Rightly Guided One (Mahdi) in Sudan, 1881–98 (Arabic).

mashauri. Plural of *shauri* (Kiswahili).

matembe. Plural of *tembe* (Kiswahili).

mchumba. A girlfriend, boyfriend (Kiswahili).

Mnyamwezi. An individual from the Unyamwezi region of west-central Tanzania (Kiswahili).

mshenzi. A barbarian, bumpkin, uncivilized person (Kiswahili).

mtama. Sorghum (Kiswahili).

mtemi. A local ruler in Unyamwezi; plural *batemi*; see *butemi* (Kinyamwezi).

mutini. An unripe fig (Kinyamwezi).

mutwaale. The trusted military captain of a Nyamwezi leader (Kinyamwezi).

mwalimu. Teacher (Kiswahili).

mwungwana. An urban gentleperson (Kiswahili).

mzee. An elderly person; respectful title given to an elder (Kiswahili).

ngoma. Drum, dance, party, dance association; a festive occasion where dancing takes place; plural *ngoma* (Kiswahili).

nguvu. Strength, hardness (Kiswahili).

Nyamwezi. People from Unyamwezi in west-central Tanzania (Kiswahili).

ombasha. A lance corporal (Turkish).

pombe. Beer, local brew (Kiswahili).

ruga-ruga. A caravan guard; soldiers in armies of west-central Tanzania in nineteenth-century; German military auxiliaries (Kinyamwezi, Kiswahili).

safari. A journey; esp. for eastern Africa, a caravan hunting or trading expedition; a military expedition (Kiswahili, Arabic).

Schaurizettel. A German colonial document used to summon someone to a *shauri* (German).

Schutztruppe. The German colonial army (German).

shauri. An all-purpose community meeting for the resolution of disputes, legal proceedings, and discussion of issues; see *mashauri* (Kiswahili).

shaush. A corporal (Turkish).

sol. A master sergeant (Turkish).

tembe. A rectangular structure with a curved roof, prevalent in west-central Tanzania (Kiswahili).

tembo. Palm wine (Kiswahili).

Unyamwezi. A region in west-central Tanzania; home to the Nyamwezi (Kiswahili).

vatwaale. Plural of *mutwaale* (Kinyamwezi).

vbandevba. The cattle-owning, farming, and merchant class in Unyamwezi (Kinyamwezi).

waganga. Local healers or ritual practitioners (Kiswahili).

washenzi. Plural of *mshenzi* (Kiswahili).

waungwana. Plural of *mwungwana* (Kiswahili).

Wissmantruppe. The precursor to the Schutztruppe, named after founder Hermann von Wissmann (German).

zariba. A thorn enclosure in Sudan (Arabic).

Bibliography

ARCHIVES

Auswärtiges Amt Politisches Archiv (AA)
Basel Afrika Bibliografien, Basel
Bayerisches Hauptstaatsarchiv, Munich (BHA)
Bundesarchiv (BArch)
Geheimes Staatsarchiv, Preussischer Kulturbesitz, Berlin-Dahlem (GSA)
Leibniz-Institut für Länderkunde, Leipzig (LIL)
National Archives, Kew (London) (NAK)
Peramiho Abbey, Songea
Rhodes House, Oxford (RH)
Tanzania National Archives (TNA)

NEWSPAPERS

Amtlicher Anzeiger für Deutsch-Ostafrika
Anzeigen für Tanga (Stadt und Bezirk)
Deutsches Kolonialblatt (DKB)
Deutsche Kolonialzeitung (DKZ)
Deutsch-Ostafrikanische Zeitung (DOAZ)
Evangelisches-Lutherisches Missionsblatt (ELM)
Kolonie und Heimat
Usambara Post (UP)

BOOKS AND ARTICLES

Abler, Thomas S. *Hinterland Warriors and Military Dress: European Empires and Exotic Uniforms.* Oxford: Berg, 1999.
Abbott, Peter. *Armies in East Africa, 1914–18* Oxford: Osprey, 2002.
Admiralstab der Marine. *Die Tätigkeit der Marine während der Niederwerfung des Eingeborenen-Aufstandes in Ostafrika, 1905/6.* Berlin: Mittler und Sohn, 1907.
Admiralty War Staff. Intelligence Division. A *Handbook of German East Africa.* London: HMSO, 1916.
Alpers, Edward. "The Story of Swema: Female Vulnerability in Nineteenth-Century East Africa." In *Women and Slavery in Africa,* edited by C. C.

Robertson and M. A. Klein, 185–99. Madison: University of Wisconsin Press, 1983.

Anderson, David M. "Massacre at Ribo Post: Expansion and Expediency on the Colonial Frontier in East Africa." *International Journal of African Historical Studies* 37, no. 1 (2004): 33–54.

Anderson, Ross. *The Forgotten Front: The East African Campaign, 1914–1918.* Stroud, Gloucestershire: Tempus, 2004.

Anderson, Warwick. "The Trespass Speaks: White Masculinity and Colonial Breakdown." *American Historical Review* 102, no. 5 (1997): 1343–70.

Andrewes, Janet. *Bodywork: Dress as Cultural Tool: Dress and Demeanour in the South of Senegal.* Leiden: Brill, 2005.

Anleitung zum Felddienst für Deutsch-Ostafrika. Dar es Salaam: Deutsch-Ostafrikanische Rundschau, 1911.

Applegate, Celia. *A Nation of Provincials: The German Idea of Heimat.* Berkeley: University of California Press, 1990.

Arens, William. *The Man-Eating Myth: Anthropology and Anthropophagy.* New York: Oxford University Press, 1979.

———. *On the Frontier of Change: Mto Wa Mbu, Tanzania.* Ann Arbor: University of Michigan Press, 1979.

Arnold, Bernd. *Steuer- und Lohnarbeit im Südwesten von Deutsch-Ostafrika, 1891–1916.* Münster: LIT, 1994.

Atkins, Keletso E. *The Moon Is Dead! Give Us Our Money! The Cultural Origins of an African Work Ethic, Natal, South Africa, 1843–1900.* Portsmouth, NH: Heinemann, 1993.

"Aus Daressalam und Umgegend." *DOAZ,* 11 June, 18 June, and 16 July 1904.

"Aus Daressalam und Umgegend: Preissschiessen." *DOAZ,* 16 April 1904.

"Aus dem Bericht des Regierungsrats Chrapkowski über seine Expedition vom Viktoria-Njansa (Bukoba) zum Tanganyika (Usumbura)." *DKB* 16, no. 20 (1905).

"Aus der Kolonie." *DOAZ* 7, no. 23 (10 June 1905).

"Aus Tanga und Umgegend." *UP* 14 (November 1908).

Austen, Ralph. "Colonialism from the Middle: African Clerks as Historical Actors and Discursive Subjects." *History in Africa* 38 (2011): 21–33.

———. *Northwest Tanzania under German and British Rule.* New Haven: Yale University Press, 1968.

Baer, Martin, and Olaf Schröter, eds. *Eine Kopfjagd: Deutsche in Ostafrika.* Berlin: Links, 2001.

Bald, Detlef. "Afrikanischer Kampf gegen koloniale Herrschaft: Der Maji-Maji-Aufstand in Ostafrika." *Militärgeschichtliche Mitteilungen* 19, no. 1 (1976): 23–50.

Barbour, Bernard, and Michelle Jacobs. "The Mi'raj: A Legal Treatise on Slavery by Ahmad Baba." In *Slaves and Slavery in Muslim Africa,* edited by J. R. Willis, 125–59. London: Frank Cass, 1991.

Barth, Boris, and Jürgen Osterhammel. Foreword to *Zivilisierungsmissionen: Imperialen Weltverbesserung seit dem 18. Jahrhundert*, edited by Barth and Osterhammel, 7–11. Konstanz: UVK Verlagsgesellschaft, 2005.

Barthes, Roland. *Mythologies*. Translated by Annette Lavers. New York: Noonday Press, 1972.

Bartov, Omer. *Hitler's Army: Soldiers, Nazis, and War in the Third Reich*. New York: Oxford University Press, 1991.

Bayart, Jean-François. *The Illusion of Cultural Identity*. Chicago: University of Chicago Press, 2005.

Beachey, R. W. "The Arms Trade in East Africa in the Late Nineteenth Century." *Journal of African History* 3, no. 3 (1962): 451–67.

———. "Macdonald's Expedition and the Uganda Mutiny, 1897–98." *Historical Journal* 10, no. 2 (1967): 237–54.

Bechhaus-Gerst, Marianne. *Treu bis in den Tod: Von Deutsch-Ostafrika nach Sachsenhausen: Eine Lebensgeschichte*. 1st ed. Berlin: Links, 2007.

Becker, Alexander. "Die Niederwerfung des Aufstandes im Süden." In *Hermann von Wissmann, Deutschlands grösster Afrikaner: Sein Leben und Wirken unter Benutzung des Nachlasses*, edited by Becker and C. von Perbandt, 316–38. Berlin: Alfred Schall, 1907.

Becker, Felicitas. "Netzwerke vs. Gesamtgesellschaft: Ein Gegensatz? Anregungen für Verflechtungsgeschichte." *Geschichte und Gesellschaft* 30, no. 2 (2004): 314–24.

———. "Traders, 'Big Men' and Prophets: Political Continuity and Crisis in the Maji Maji Rebellion in Southeast Tanzania." *Journal of African History* 45, no. 1 (2004): 1–22.

Becker, Felicitas, and Jigal Beez, eds. *Der Maji-Maji-Krieg in Deutsch-Ostafrika, 1905–1907*. Berlin: Links, 2005.

Behr, H. F. von. *Kriegsbilder aus dem Araberaufstand in Deutsch-Ostafrika*. Leipzig: Brockhaus, 1891.

Behrend, Heike. *Alice Lakwena and the Holy Spirits: War in Northern Uganda*. Oxford: James Currey, 1999.

Bengerstorf, Hermann von. *Unter der Tropensonne Afrikas: Ernstes und Heiteres*. Hamburg: Fr. W. Thaden, 1914.

"Beni Society of Tanganyika Territory, The." *Primitive Man* 11, nos. 3–4 (1938): 74–81.

Bennett, Norman Robert. *Mirambo of Tanzania, 1840?–1884*. New York: Oxford University Press, 1971.

Besant, W. H. "The Early Days of the Egyptian Army, 1883–1892." *Journal of the Royal African Society* 33, no. 131 (1934): 160–68.

Bischoff, Eva. "Tropenkoller: Male Self-Control and the Loss of Colonial Rule." In *Helpless Imperialists: Imperial Failure, Fear and Radicalization*, edited by Maurus Reinkowski and Gregor Thum, 117–36. Gottingen: Vandenhoeck and Ruprecht, 2013.

Blohm, Wilhelm. *Die Nyamwezi: Gesellschaft und Weltbild*. Hamburg: Friederichsen, De Gruyter, 1933.
———. *Die Nyamwezi: Land und Wirtschaft*. Hamburg: Friederichsen, De Gruyter, 1931.
Boell, Ludwig. *Die Operationen in Ostafrika, Weltkrieg 1914–1918*. Hamburg: W. Dachert, 1951.
Bourke, Joanna. *An Intimate History of Killing: Face-to-Face Killing in Twentieth-Century Warfare*. New York: Basic Books, 1999.
Boyd, William. *An Ice-Cream War*. New York: Vintage International, 1999.
Branch, Daniel. *Defeating Mau Mau, Creating Kenya*. Cambridge: Cambridge University Press, 2009.
———. "The Enemy Within: Loyalists and the War against Mau Mau in Kenya." *Journal of African History* 48, no. 2 (2007): 291–315.
Brands, Hal. "Wartime Recruiting Practices, Martial Identity and Post–World War II Demobilization in Colonial Kenya." *Journal of African History* 46, no. 1: (2005): 103–25.
Bredin, G. R. F. "The Life-Story of Yuzbashi 'Abdullah Adlan." *Sudan Notes and Records* 42 (1961): 37–52.
Brett, Rachel, and Irma Specht. *Young Soldiers: Why They Choose to Fight*. Boulder: Lynne Rienner, 2004.
Brinkmann, Inge. *A War for People: Civilians, Mobility, and Legitimacy in South-East Angola during the MPLA's War for Independence*. Cologne: Köppe, 2005.
Brode, Heinrich. *Tippoo Tib, the Story of His Career in Central Africa*. Translated by H. Havelock. London: Arnold, 1907.
Brower, Benjamin. *A Desert Named Peace: The Violence of France's Empire in the Algerian Sahara, 1844–1902*. New York: Columbia University Press, 2009.
Brown, Christopher Leslie, and Philip D. Morgan, eds. *Arming Slaves: From Classical Times to the Modern Age*. New Haven: Yale University Press, 2006.
Brown, Keith. "'All they understand is force': Debating Culture in Operation Iraqi Freedom." *American Anthropologist* 110, no. 4 (2008): 443–53.
Brown, Kevin K. "The Military and Social Change in Colonial Tanganyika, 1919–1964." PhD diss., Michigan State University, 2001.
Brunschwig, Henri. "French Expansion and Local Reactions in Black Africa in the Time of Imperialism." In *Expansion and Reaction: Essays on European Expansion and Reaction in Asia and Africa*, edited by H. L. Wesseling. Leiden: Leiden University Press, 1978: 116–40.
Bührer, Tanja. *Die kaiserliche Schutztruppe für Deutsch-Ostafrika: Kolonial Sicherheitspolitik und transkulturelle Kriegführung, 1885 bis 1918*. Munich: Oldenbourg, 2011.
———. "Ein 'Parlamentsheer' ohne 'preussische Erbstücke'? Die zivilmilitärischen Konflikte um die Führungsorganisation der Kaiserlichen Schutztruppen." *Militärgeschichtliche Zeitschrift* 71, no. 1 (2012): 1–24.

Burk, James. "Military Culture." In *Encyclopedia of Violence, Peace, and Conflict*, edited by Lester Kurtz, 1242–56. 2nd ed. San Diego: Academic Press, 2008.

Burke, Carol. *Camp All-American, Hanoi Jane, and the High-and-Tight: Gender, Folklore, and Changing Military Culture*. Boston: Beacon Press, 2004.

Burton, Richard Francis. *The Lake Regions of Central Africa: A Picture of Exploration*. 2 vols. New York: Horizon Press, 1961.

Buruku, Daisy Sykes. "The Townsman: Kleist Sykes." In *Modern Tanzanians: A Volume of Biographies*, edited by John Iliffe, 95–114. Nairobi: East African Publishing House, 1973.

Callwell, C. E. *Small Wars: Their Principles and Practice*. 1896. 3rd ed. Lincoln: University of Nebraska Press, 1996.

Caplan, Lionel. "'Bravest of the Brave': Representations of 'the Gurkha' in British Military Writings." *Modern Asian Studies* 25, no. 3 (1991): 571–97.

Ciarlo, David M. "Rasse konsumieren: Von der exotischen zur kolonialen Imagination in der Bildreklame des Wilhelminischen Kaiserreichs." In *Phantasiereiche: Zur Kulturgeschichte des deutschen Kolonialismus*, edited by Birthe Kundrus, 135–79. Frankfurt am Main: Campus, 2003.

Citino, Robert M. "The German Way of War Revisited." *Historically Speaking* 11, no. 5 (2010): 20–21.

———. "Military Histories Old and New: A Reintroduction." *American Historical Review* 112, no. 4 (2007): 1070–90.

Citino, Robert M., Brian McAllister Linn, Peter Lorge, and James Jay Carafano. "Comparative Ways of War: A Roundtable." *Historically Speaking* 11, no. 5 (2010): 20–26.

Clayton, Anthony. "Sport and African Soldiers: The Military Diffusion of Western Sport throughout Sub-Saharan Africa." In *Sport in Africa: Essays in Social History*, edited by William J. Baker and James A. Mangan, 114–37. New York: African Publishing, 1987.

Clayton, Anthony, and David Killingray. *Khaki and Blue: Military and Police in British Colonial Africa*. Athens: Ohio University, Center for International Studies, 1989.

Cocks, C. J. *Fireforce: One Man's War in the Rhodesian Light Infantry*. Roodeport, South Africa: Covos Books, 1997.

———. *Survival Course*. Weltevreden Park, South Africa: Covos Books, 1999.

Cohen, David William, Stephan F. Miescher, and Luise White. "Voices, Words, and African History." In *African Words, African Voices: Critical Practices in Oral History*, edited by Cohen, Miescher, and White, 4–10. Bloomington: Indiana University Press, 2001.

Conrad, Sebastian. *German Colonialism: A Short History*. Cambridge: Cambridge University Press, 2012.

———. *Globalisierung und Nation im deutschen Kaiserreich*. Munich: C. H. Beck, 2006.

Cooper, Frederick. *Colonialism in Question: Theory, Knowledge, History.* Berkeley: University of California Press, 2005.

———. "Conflict and Connection: Rethinking Colonial African History." *American Historical Review* 99, no. 5 (1994): 1516–45.

———. "Islam and Cultural Hegemony: The Ideology of Slaveowners on the East African Coast." In *The Ideology of Slavery in Africa,* edited by Paul E. Lovejoy, 271–307. Beverly Hills: Sage, 1981.

Cooper, Frederick, with Rogers Brubaker. "Identity." In *Colonialism in Question: Theory, Knowledge, History,* 59–90. Berkeley: University of California Press, 2005.

Cooper, Frederick, and Ann Laura Stoler. "Between Metropole and Colony: Rethinking a Research Agenda." In *Tensions of Empire: Colonial Cultures in a Bourgeois World,* edited by Cooper and Stoler, 1–58. Berkeley: University of California Press, 1997.

———, eds. *Tensions of Empire: Colonial Cultures in a Bourgeois World.* Berkeley: University of California Press, 1997.

Cooper, Randolf G. S. "Culture, Combat, and Colonialism in Eighteenth- and Nineteenth-Century India." *International History Review* 27, no. 3 (2005): 534–49

Cory, Hans. "The Ingredients of Magic Medicines." *Africa: Journal of the International African Institute* 19, no. 1 (1949): 13–32.

———. *The Ntemi: The Traditional Rites in Connection with the Burial, Election, Enthronement and Magic Powers of a Sukuma Chief.* London: Macmillan, 1951.

Craik, Jennifer. *Uniforms Exposed: From Conformity to Transgression.* Oxford: Berg, 2005.

Crais, Clifton. "Chiefs and Bureaucrats in the Making of Empire: A Drama from the Transkei, South Africa, October 1880." *American Historical Review* 108, no. 4 (2003): 1034–56.

Crozier, Anna. "What Was Tropical about Tropical Neurasthenia? The Utility of the Diagnosis in the Management of British East Africa." *Journal of the History of Medicine and Allied Sciences* 64, no. 4 (2009): 518–48.

Culwick, A. T., and G. M. Culwick. *Ubena of the Rivers.* London: Allen and Unwin, 1935.

Cunnison, Ian. *Baggara Arabs: Power and the Lineage in a Sudanese Nomad Tribe.* Oxford: Clarendon Press, 1966.

Dachs, Anthony J. "Politics of Collaboration—Imperialism in Practice." In *The Early History of Malawi,* edited by Bridglal Pachai, 283–89. London: Longman, 1972.

Das, Santanu, ed. *Race, Empire, and First World War Writing.* Cambridge: Cambridge University Press, 2011.

Dauber, Heinrich. *"Nicht als Abentheurer bin ich hierhergekommen": 100 Jahre Entwicklungs-"Hilfe": Tagebücher und Briefe aus Deutsch-Ostafrika, 1896–1902.* Frankfurt: Verlag für Interkulturelle Kommunikation, 1991.

Declé, Lionel. *Three Years in Savage Africa.* 1900. Reprint, Bulawayo: Books of Rhodesia, 1974.

Dencker, Berit Elisabeth. "Popular Gymnastics and the Military Spirit in Germany, 1848–1871." *Central European History* 34, no. 4 (2001): 503–30.

Deng, Francis Mading. *Dinka Cosmology.* London: Ithaca Press, 1980.

———. *The Dinka of the Sudan.* New York: Holt, Rinehart and Winston, 1972.

Deppe, Ludwig. *Mit Lettow-Vorbeck durch Afrika.* Berlin: August Scherl, 1919.

Deutsch, Jan-Georg. "Celebrating Power in Everyday Life: The Administration of Law and the Public Sphere in Colonial Tanzania, 1890–1914." *Journal of African Cultural Studies* 15, no. 1 (2002): 93–103.

———. *Emancipation without Abolition in German East Africa, c. 1884–1914.* Oxford: James Currey, 2006.

Deutschlands koloniale Wehrmacht: In ihrer gegenwärtigen Organisation und Schlagfähigkeit. Berlin: R. v. Decker, 1906.

DeWaal, Jeremy. "The Reinvention of Tradition: Form, Meaning, and Local Identity in Modern Cologne Carnival." *Central European History* 46, no. 3 (2013): 495–532.

"The Diary of Abbas Bey." *Sudan Notes and Records* 32, no. 2 (1951): 179–96.

Dorward, D. C. "Ethnography and Administration: A Study of Anglo-Tiv 'Working Misunderstanding.'" *Journal of African History* 15, no. 3 (1974): 457–77.

Doughty, Robert, and Ira Gruber, et al. *Warfare in the Western World: Military Operations from 1600 to 1871.* Lexington, MA: D. C. Heath, 1996.

"Dschagga-Konferenz in Moschi: Bericht von Miss. Fokken—Aruscha." *ELM* 59, no. 24 (1904): 592–95.

Ebner, P. Elzear. "Die Wangoni—einst Krieger, heute friedliche Bauern." In *Der fünfarmige Leuchter: Beiträge zum Werden und Wirken der Benediktinerkongregation von St. Ottilien,* edited by F. Renner. 181–97. St. Ottilien: Eos, 1971.

Echenberg, Myron. *Colonial Conscripts: The* Tirailleurs Sénégalais *in French West Africa, 1857–1960.* Portsmouth, NH: Heinemann, 1991.

Eckert, Andreas, and Adam Jones. "Historical Writing about Everyday Life." *Journal of African Cultural Studies* 15, no. 1 (2002): 5–16.

Eksteins, Modris. *Rites of Spring: The Great War and the Birth of the Modern Age.* Boston: Houghton Mifflin, 2000.

Ellis, John. *The Social History of the Machine Gun.* Baltimore: Johns Hopkins University Press, 1975.

Ellis, Stephen. *The Mask of Anarchy: The Destruction of Liberia and the Religious Dimension of an African Civil War.* 2nd ed. New York: NYU Press, 2007.

Ellison, James. "Competitive Dance and Social Identity: Converging Histories in Southwest Tanzania." In *Mashindano! Competitive Music Performance in East Africa,* edited by Frank Gunderson and Gregory Barz, 199–231. Dar es Salaam: Mkuki na Nyota, 2000.

Emin Pasha. *Emin Pasha: His Life and Work.* Compiled by Georg Schweitzer. 2 vols. New York: Negro Universities Press, 1969.

Enloe, Cynthia. *Bananas, Beaches, and Bases: Making Feminist Sense of International Politics.* 1st U.S. ed. Berkeley: University of California Press, 1990.

———. *Does Khaki Become You? The Militarisation of Women's Lives.* London: Pandora, 1988.

———. *Ethnic Soldiers: State Security in Divided Societies.* Athens: University of Georgia Press, 1980.

———. *Maneuvers: The International Politics of Militarizing Women's Lives.* Berkeley: University of California Press, 2000.

Etherington, Norman. "Barbarians Ancient and Modern." *American Historical Review* 116, no. 1 (2011): 31–57.

Fabian, Johannes. *Out of our Minds: Reason and Madness in the Exploration of Central Africa.* Berkeley: University of California Press, 2000.

Fahmy, Khaled. *All the Pasha's Men: Mehmed Ali, His Army, and the Making of Modern Egypt.* Cairo: American University in Cairo Press, 2002.

Fair, Laura. *Pastimes and Politics: Culture, Community, and Identity in Post-Abolition Urban Zanzibar, 1890–1945.* Athens: Ohio University Press, 2001.

Farrell, Brian P. "Mind and Matter: The Practice of Military History with Reference to Britain and Southeast Asia." *Journal of American History* 93, no. 4 (2007): 1146–50.

Farwell, Byron. *The Great War in Africa, 1914–1918.* New York: Norton, 1989.

Ferguson, James, and Akhil Gupta. "Spatializing States: Toward an Ethnography of Neoliberal Governmentality." *American Ethnologist* 29, no. 4 (2002): 981–1002.

Finnström, Sverker. *Living with Bad Surroundings: War, History, and Everyday Moments in Northern Uganda.* Durham, NC: Duke University Press, 2008.

Fitzpatrick, Matthew. "Narrating Empire: *Die Gartenlaube* and Germany's Nineteenth-Century Liberal Expansionism." *German Studies Review* 30, no. 1 (2007): 97–120.

Fluehr-Lobban, Carolyn, Richard A. Lobban Jr., and John Obert Voll, eds. *Historical Dictionary of the Sudan.* 2nd ed. Metuchen, NJ: Scarecrow Press, 1992.

Foden, Giles. *Mimi and Toutou's Big Adventure: The Bizarre Battle of Lake Tanganyika.* New York: Vintage, 2006.

Fonck, Heinrich. *Deutsch-Ost-Afrika: Eine Schilderung deutscher Tropen nach 10 Wanderjahren.* Berlin: Vossische Buchhandlung, 1910.

Förster, Stig, Wolfgang J. Mommsen, and Ronald Edward Robinson, eds. 1988. *Bismarck, Europe, and Africa: The Berlin Africa Conference 1884–1885 and the Onset of Partition.* Oxford: Oxford University Press.

Fosbrooke, H. A. "Arusha Boma." *Tanganyika Notes and Records* 38 (1955): 51–52.

———. "Chagga Forts and Bolt Holes." *Tanganyika Notes and Records* 37 (1954): 115–29.

Fraser, Donald. *Winning a Primitive People: Sixteen Years' Work among the Warlike Tribe of the Ngoni and the Senga and Tumbuka Peoples of Central Africa.* 1914. Reprint, Westport, CT: Negro Universities Press, 1970.

Freytag-Loringhoven, Freiherr von. *Das Exerzier-Reglement für die Infanterie vom 29. Mai 1906 kriegsgeschichtlich erläutert.* Berlin: Mittler und Sohn, 1907.

Friedrichsmeyer, Sara, Sara Lennox, and Susanne Zantop. *The Imperialist Imagination: German Colonialism and Its Legacy.* Ann Arbor: University of Michigan Press, 1998.

Fülleborn, Friedrich. *Das deutsche Njassa- und Rowuma-Gebiet, Land und Leute, nebst Bemerkungen über die Schire-Länder.* Berlin: Dietrich Reimer (Ernst Vohsen), 1906.

Furley, O. W. "The Sudanese Troops in Uganda." *African Affairs* 58, no. 233 (1959): 311–28.

Fussell, Paul. *Uniforms: Why We Are What We Wear.* Boston: Houghton Mifflin, 2002.

———. *Wartime: Understanding and Behavior in the Second World War.* Oxford: Oxford University Press, 1989.

Gardner, Brian. *German East: The Story of the First World War in East Africa.* London: Cassell, 1963.

Geertz, Clifford. *The Interpretation of Culture.* New York: Basic Books, 1973.

———. "'From the Native's Point of View': On the Nature of Anthropological Understanding." *Bulletin of the American Academy of Arts and Sciences* 28, no. 1 (1974): 26–45.

———. *Local Knowledge: Further Essays in Interpretive Anthropology.* 3rd ed. New York: Basic Books, 2000.

Geschiere, Peter. "Shaka and the Limits of Colonial Invention." *African Studies Review* 44, no. 2 (2001): 167–76.

Gewald, Jan-Bart. "Colonial Warfare: Hehe and World War One, the Wars besides Maji Maji in South-western Tanzania." African Studies Centre Working Paper 63, Leiden: ASC, 2005.

Giblin, James Leonard, with Blandina Kaduma Giblin. *A History of the Excluded: Making Family a Refuge from State in Twentieth-Century Tanzania.* Oxford: James Currey, 2005.

Giblin, James, and Jamie Monson, eds. *Maji Maji: Lifting the Fog of War.* Leiden: Brill, 2010.

Gifoon, Ali Effendi. "Memoirs of a Soudanese Soldier (Ali Effendi Gifoon)." Translated by Percy Machell. *Cornhill Magazine,* n.s. 1 (1896): 30–40, 175–87, 326–38, 484–92.

Gissibl, Bernhard. "Die 'Treue' der Askari: Mythos, Ehre und Gewalt im Kontext des deutschen Kolonialismus in Ostafrika." In *Treue: Politische Loyalität und militärische Gefolgschaft in der Moderne,* edited by Nikolaus

Buschmann and Karl Borromäus Murr, 214–52. Göttingen: Vandenhoeck und Ruprecht, 2008.

Glassman, Jonathon. *Feasts and Riot: Revelry, Rebellion, and Popular Consciousness on the Swahili Coast, 1856–1888.* Portsmouth, NH: Heinemann, 1995.

——. *War of Words, War of Stones: Racial Thought and Violence in Colonial Zanzibar.* Bloomington: Indiana University Press, 2011.

Goffman, Erving. *The Presentation of Self in Everyday Life,* 1st ed. New York: Anchor, 1959.

Götzen, Gustav Adolf, Graf von. *Deutsch-Ostafrika im Aufstand 1905/06.* Berlin: D. Reimer, 1909.

——. *Durch Afrika von Ost nach West: Resultate und Begebenheiten einer Reise von der deutsch-ostafrikanischen Küste bis zur Kongomündung in den Jahren 1893/94.* Berlin: Dietrich Reimer, 1899.

Gottberg, Achim. *Unyamwesi: Quellensammlung und Geschichte.* Berlin: Akademie-Verlag, 1971.

Graichen, Gisela, and Horst Gründer. *Deutsche Kolonien: Traum und Trauma.* Berlin: Ullstein, 2005.

Grawert, von, Gideon. "Die militärische Lage im Schutzgebiet Deutsch-Ostafrika im Jahre 1908/9." In *Jahrbuch über die deutschen Kolonien,* edited by Karl Schneider. Vol 3. Essen: Baedeker, 1911.

Gray, Richard. *A History of the Southern Sudan, 1839–1889.* London: Oxford University Press, 1961.

Gray, Richard, and David Birmingham, eds. *Pre-Colonial African Trade: Essays on Trade in Central and Eastern Africa before 1900.* London: Oxford University Press, 1970.

Greene, Sandra. *West African Narratives of Slavery: Texts from Late Nineteenth- and Early Twentieth-Century Ghana.* Bloomington: Indiana University Press, 2011.

Grimsley, Mark. "In Not So Dubious Battle: The Motivations of American Civil War Soldiers." *Journal of Military History* 62, no. 1 (1998): 175–88.

Groeschel, Paul. *Amelye. Ein Lebensbild aus dem Benavolk in Deutsch-Ostafrika.* Berlin: Berlin Missionsgesellschaft, 1911.

——. *Zehn Jahre christlicher Kulturarbeit in Deutsch-Ostafrika: Dargestellt in Briefen aus den Jahren 1898–1908.* Berlin: Berliner ev. Missionsgesellschaft, 1911.

Gurnah, Abdulrazak. *Paradise.* London: Hamish Hamilton, 1994.

Gunderson, Frank. *Sukuma Labor Songs from Western Tanzania.* Leiden: Brill, 2010.

Gwassa, G. C. K. "African Methods of Warfare during the Maji Maji War 1905–1907." In *War and Society in Africa,* edited by Bethwell Ogot, 123–48. London: Routledge, 1970.

——. "The German Intervention and African Resistance in Tanzania." In *A History of Tanzania,* edited by I. N. Kimambo and A. J. Temu, 85–122. Nairobi: East African Publishing House, 1969.

——. *The Outbreak and Development of the Maji Maji War, 1905–1907*. Edited by Wolfgang Apelt. Cologne: Rüdiger Köppe, 2005.

Gwassa, G. C. K., and John Iliffe, eds. *Records of the Maji Maji Rising*. Dar es Salaam: East African Publishing House, 1969.

Haefliger, P. Joh. 12 October 1901. "Chronik von Kigonsera," unpublished typescript, Peramiho Abbey, Tanzania.

Hagemann, Karen. "German Heroes: The Cult of Death for the Fatherland in Nineteenth-Century Germany." In *Masculinities in Politics and War: Gendering Modern History*, edited by Stefan Dudink, Hagemann, and John Tosh, 116–34. Manchester: Manchester University Press, 2004.

Haggard, Andrew. *Under Crescent and Star*. Edinburgh: William Blackwood and Sons, 1895.

Hajivayanis, G. G., A. C. Motowa, and J. Iliffe. "The Politicians: Ali Ponda and Hassan Suleiman." In *Modern Tanzanians: A Volume of Biographies*, edited by Iliffe, 227–53. Nairobi: East African Publishing House, 1973.

Hall, Bruce. *A History of Race in Muslim West Africa, 1600–1960*. Cambridge: Cambridge University Press, 2011.

Hamilton, Carolyn. *Terrific Majesty: The Powers of Shaka Zulu and the Limits of Historical Invention*. Cambridge, MA: Harvard University Press, 1998.

Hanna, Judith Lynne. "African Dance and the Warrior Tradition." In *The Warrior Tradition in Modern Africa*, edited by A. Mazrui, 111–33. Leiden: Brill, 1977.

Hanson, Holly Elisabeth. *Landed Obligation: The Practice of Power in Buganda*. Portsmouth, NH: Heinemann, 2003.

Harries, Patrick. "Slavery, Social Incorporation and Surplus Extraction: The Nature of Free and Unfree Labour in South-East Africa." *Journal of African History* 22, no. 3 (1981): 309–30.

Hauer, August. *Kumbuke: Erlebnisse eines Arztes in Deutsch-Ostafrika*. Berlin: Reimar Hobbing, 1923.

——. "'Watoto,' die Kleinsten der Lettow-Truppe." In *Die deutschen Kolonien in Wort und Bild*, edited by H. Zache, 460–63. 1926. Reprint, Augsburg: Bechtermünz, 2003.

Häussler, Matthias, and Trutz von Trotha. "Brutalisierung 'von unten': Kleiner Krieg, Entgrenzung der Gewalt und Genozid im kolonialien Deutsch-Südwestafrika." *Mittelweg* 36, no. 3 (2012): 57–89.

Headrick, Daniel R. *The Tools of Empire: Technology and European Imperialism in the Nineteenth Century*. New York: Oxford University Press, 1981.

Hebbert, G. C. K. "The Bandala of the Bahr el-Ghazal." *Sudan Notes and Records* 8 (1925): 187–94.

Hedges, Chris. *War Is a Force That Gives Us Meaning*. 1st ed. New York: Public Affairs, 2002.

Heintze, Beatrix. "Propaganda Concerning 'Man-Eaters' in West-Central Africa in the Second Half of the Nineteenth Century." *Paideuma* 49 (2003): 125–35.

Hellberg, Carl J. *Missions on a Colonial Frontier West of Lake Victoria: Evangelical Missions in North-West Tanganyika to 1932*. Lund: Gleerups, 1965.

Highmore, Ben. *Everyday Life and Cultural Theory: An Introduction*. London: Routledge, 2002.

Hildebrandt, F. *Eine deutsche Militärstation im innern Afrikas*. Wolfenbüttel: Heckners, 1905.

———. "Warnke's Tod." *Deutsch-Ostafrikanische Zeitung*, 3 June 1905.

Hill, Richard Leslie, and Peter C. Hogg. *A Black Corps d'Élite: An Egyptian Sudanese Conscript Battalion with the French Army in Mexico, 1863–1867, and in Subsequent African History*. East Lansing: Michigan State University Press, 1995.

Hiskett, M. "Enslavement, Slavery and Attitudes towards the Legally Enslavable in Hausa Islamic Literature." In *Slaves and Slavery in Muslim Africa*, edited by J. R. Willis, 106–24. London: Frank Cass, 1985.

Hoagland, Alison K. "Village Constructions: U.S. Army Forts on the Plains, 1848–1890." *Winterthur Portfolio* 34, no. 4 (1999): 215–37.

Hodges, Geoffrey. "African Manpower Statistics for the British Forces in East Africa, 1914–1918." *Journal of African History* 19, no. 1 (1978): 101–16.

———. *Kariokor: The Carrier Corps*. Nairobi: Nairobi University Press, 1999.

Hodgson, Dorothy. *Once Intrepid Warriors: Gender, Ethnicity, and the Cultural Politics of Maasai Development*. Bloomington: Indiana University Press, 2001.

Hodgson, Dorothy, and Sheryl McCurdy. "Wayward Wives, Misfit Mothers, and Disobedient Daughters: 'Wicked' Women and the Reconfiguration of Gender in Africa." *Canadian Journal of African Studies* 30, no. 1 (1996): 1–9.

Hope, A. C. "The Adventurous Life of Faraj Sadik." *Sudan Notes and Records* 32, no. 1 (1951): 154–58.

Hordern, Charles, and H. Fitz M. Stacke. *Military Operations, East Africa*. Nashville: Battery Press, 1990.

Hore, Edward Coode. *Missionary to Tanganyika, 1877–1888: The Writings of Edward Coode Hore, Master Mariner*. Edited by James B. Wolf. London: Frank Cass, 1971.

Hoyle, B. S. *Gillman of Tanganyika, 1882–1946: The Life and Work of a Pioneer Geographer*. Aldershot: Avebury, 1987.

Hull, Isabel V. *Absolute Destruction: Military Culture and the Practices of War in Imperial Germany*. Ithaca: Cornell University Press, 2005.

Humphrey J. *Slavery in the History of Muslim Black Africa*. New York: New York University Press, 2001.

Iliffe, John. *Honour in African History*. Cambridge: Cambridge University Press, 2005.

———. *Maji Maji Research Project, Collected Papers*. Dar es Salaam: University College, 1968.

———. *A Modern History of Tanganyika*. Cambridge: Cambridge University Press, 1979.

——. *Modern Tanzanians: A Volume of Biographies.* Nairobi: East African Publishing House, 1973.

——. *Tanganyika under German Rule, 1905–1912.* Cambridge: Cambridge University Press, 1969.

Isaacman, Allen, and Barbara Isaacman. "Resistance and Collaboration in Southern Central Africa, c. 1850–1920." *International Journal of African Historical Studies* 10, no. 7 (1977): 31–62.

——. *Slavery and Beyond: The Making of Men and Chikunda Ethnic Identities in the Unstable World of South-Central Africa, 1750–1920.* Portsmouth, NH: Heinemann, 2004.

Itandala, Buluda. "African Response to German Colonialism in East Africa: The Case of Usukuma, 1890–1918." *Ufahamu* 20, no. 1 (1992): 3–29.

Jackman, Steven D. "Shoulder to Shoulder: Close Control and 'Old Prussian Drill' in German Offensive Infantry Tactics, 1871–1914." *Journal of Military History* 68, no. 1 (2004): 73–104.

Jackson, Aaron P. "Expanding the Scope and Accessibility of Non-Western Military History." *Journal of Military History* 75, no. 2 (2011): 603–13.

Jackson, Robert D. "Resistance to the German Invasion of the Tanganyikan Coast, 1888–1891." In *Protest and Power in Black Africa*, edited by R. I. Rotberg and A. Mazrui, 37–79. New York: Oxford University Press, 1970.

Jacob, Wilson Chacko. "The Masculine Subject of Colonialism: The Egyptian Loss of the Sudan." In *African Masculinities: Men in Africa from the Late Nineteenth Century to the Present*, edited by Lahoucine Ouzgane and Robert Morrell, 153–69. New York: Palgrave, 2005.

Janira, Simbo. *Kleiner grosser schwarzer Mann: Lebenserinnerungen eines Buschnegers.* Eisenach: Erich Röth, 1956.

Jephson, A. J. Mounteney. *The Diary of A. J. Mounteney Jephson: Emin Pasha Relief Expedition, 1887–1889.* Edited by Dorothy Middleton and Maurice Denham Jephson. London: Cambridge University Press, 1969.

Johnson, Douglas H. "Recruitment and Entrapment in Private Slave Armies: The Structure of the *Zara'ib* in the Southern Sudan." *Slavery and Abolition* 13, no. 1 (1992): 162–73.

——. "Salim Wilson: The Black Evangelist of the North." *Journal of Religion in Africa* 21, no. 1 (1991): 26–41.

——. "The Structure of a Legacy: Military Slavery in Northeast Africa." *Ethnohistory* 36, no. 1 (1989): 72–88.

——. "Sudanese Military Slavery from the Eighteenth to the Twentieth Century." In *Slavery and Other Forms of Unfree Labour*, edited by L. J. Archer, 142–56. London: Routledge, 1988.

Jones, Ben. *Beyond the State in Rural Uganda.* Edinburgh: Edinburgh University Press, 2009.

Kabeya, J. B. *King Mirambo: One of the Heroes of Tanzania.* Kampala: East African Literature Bureau, 1976.

Kamlongera, Christopher. "An Example of Syncretic Drama from Malawi: Malipenga." *Research in African Literatures* 17, no. 2 (1986): 197–210.

Kandt, Richard. *Caput Nili: Eine empfindsame Reise zu den Quellen des Nils.* 5th ed. Berlin: Dietrich Reimer, 1921.

"Kasuistik." In *Medizinal-Berichte über die deutschen Schutzgebiete 1903/4.* Berlin: Mittler und Sohn, 1905.

Katoke, I. K., and P. Rwehumbiza. "The Administrator: Francis Lwamugira." In *Modern Tanzanians: A Volume of Biographies*, edited by John Iliffe, 43–65. Nairobi: East African Publishing House, 1973.

Kaye, Alan S., and Mauro Tosco. "Early East African Pidgin Arabic." *Sprache und Geschichte in Afrika* 14 (1993): 269–306.

Keithly, David M. "Khaki Foxes: The East Afrika Korps." *Small Wars and Insurgencies* 12, no. 1 (2001): 166–85.

Kennedy, Dane. "Diagnosing the Colonial Dilemma: Tropical Neurasthenia and the 'Alienated Briton." In *Decentering Empire: Britain, India, and the Transcolonial World*, edited by Kennedy and Durba Ghosh, 157–81. Hyderabad: Orient Longman, 2006.

Kennedy, Katharine. "African Heimat: German Colonies in Wilhelmine and Weimar Reading Books." *Internationale Schulbuchforschung* 24 (2002): 7–26.

Kieran, J. A. "Abushiri and the Germans." In *Hadith 2*, edited by B. Ogot, 157–201. Nairobi: East Africa Publishing House, 1970.

Killingray, David. *Fighting for Britain: African Soldiers in the Second World War.* Woodbridge, Suffolk: James Currey, 2010.

———. "Gender Issues and African Colonial Armies." In *Guardians of Empire: The Armed Forces of the Colonial Powers c. 1700–1964*, edited by Killingray and David E. Omissi, 221–48. Studies in Imperialism. New York: Manchester University Press, 1999.

———. "The Maintenance of Law and Order in British Colonial Africa." *African Affairs* 85, no. 340 (1986): 411–37.

———. "The Mutiny of the West African Regiment in the Gold Coast, 1939–50." *International Journal of African History Studies* 16, no. 3 (1983): 523–34.

———. "'The Rod of Empire': The Debate over Corporal Punishment in the British African Colonial Forces, 1888–1946." *Journal of African History* 35, no. 2 (1994): 201–16.

———. "The War in Africa." In *The Oxford Illustrated History of the First World War*, edited by Hew Strachan, 92–103. Oxford: Oxford University Press, 1998.

Killingray, David, and David E. Omissi, eds. 1999. *Guardians of Empire: The Armed Forces of the Colonial Powers c. 1700–1964, Studies in Imperialism.* New York: Manchester University Press.

Kim, David D. "Scandals of Translation: Cannibalism and the Limits of Colonial Authority in the Trial of Iringa." *German Studies Review* 34, no. 1 (2011): 125–42.

Kirk, R. "The Sudanese in Mexico." *Sudan Notes and Records* 24 (1941): 113–30.

Kirk-Greene, Anthony H. M. "'Damnosa Hereditas': Ethnic Ranking and the Martial Races Imperative in Africa." *Ethnic and Racial Studies* 3, no. 4 (1980): 393–414.

———. "The Thin White Line: The Size of the British Colonial Service in Africa." *African Affairs* 79, no. 314 (1980): 25–44.

Klein, Martin. *Slavery and Colonial Rule in French West Africa.* Cambridge: Cambridge University Press, 1998.

Klein-Arendt, Reinhard. "'Bautz! Schuß durch den Ast und durch den Kerl . . .': Der Einsatz moderner Infanteriewaffen gegen afrikanische Widerstandsbewegungen in Deutsch-Ostafrika. In *Die (koloniale) Begegnung: Afrikanerinnen in Deutschland (1880–1918)—Deutsche in Afrika (1880–1918)*, edited by Marianne Bechhaus-Gerst and Reinhard Klein-Arendt, 171–91. Frankfurt: Peter Lang, 2003.

Knight, Ian. *The Anatomy of the Zulu Army from Shaka to Cetshwayo, 1818–1879.* London: Greenhill Books, 1995.

Kohlschütter, Dr. "Situationsplan der Halbinsel Langenburg." *Deutsches Kolonialblatt* 10, no. 23 (1899): n.p.

"Koloniale Scherzecke." *Usambara Post*, 14 April 1906.

Koponen, Juhani. *Development for Exploitation: German Colonial Policies in Mainland Tanzania, 1884–1914.* Hamburg: LIT, 1994.

———. *People and Production in Late Precolonial Tanzania: History and Structures.* Helsinki: Finnish Society for Development Studies, 1988.

Kühne, Thomas. "Comradeship: Gender Confusion and Gender Order in the German Military, 1918–1945." In *Home/Front: The Military, War, and Gender in Twentieth-Century Germany*, edited by K. Hagemann and S. Schueler-Springorum, 233–54. Oxford: Berg, 2002.

Kuss, Susanne. *Deutsches Militär auf kolonialen Kriegsschauplätzen: Eskalation von Gewalt zu Beginn des 20. Jahrhunderts.* Berlin: Links, 2010.

Lamothe, Ronald M. *Slaves of Fortune: Sudanese Soldiers and the River War, 1896–1898.* Woodbridge, Suffolk: James Currey, 2011.

Lamphear, John, ed. *African Military History.* Aldershot, UK: Ashgate, 2007.

———. "Brothers in Arms: Military Aspects of East African Age-Class Systems in Historical Perspective." In *Conflict, Age, and Power in Northeast Africa: Age Systems in Transition*, edited by Eisei Kurimoto and Simon Simonse. Athens: Ohio University Press, 1998: 79–97.

———. "'The rage of ancestors who died in ancient wars': The Military Background to the Maji Maji Rebellion." Unpublished manuscript. University of Texas–Austin.

Langbehn, Volker, and Mohammad Salama, eds. *German Colonialism: Race, the Holocaust, and Postwar Germany.* New York: Columbia University Press, 2011.

Langheld, Wilhelm. *Zwanzig Jahre in deutschen Kolonien.* Berlin: Wilhelm Weicher, 1909.

Langsdorff, Werner von. *Deutsche Flagge über Sand und Palmen: 53 Kolonialkrieger erzählen.* Gütersloh, Germany: C. Bertelsmann, 1942.

Larson, Lorne E. "A History of the Mahenge (Ulanga) District, ca. 1860–1957." PhD diss., University of Dar es Salaam, 1976.

Launay, Robert. *Beyond the Stream: Islam and Society in a West African Town.* Berkeley: University of California Press, 1992.

Lawler, Nancy Ellen. *Soldiers of Misfortune: Ivoirien Tirailleurs of World War II.* Athens: Ohio University Press, 1992.

Lawrance, Benjamin. *Locality, Mobility and "Nation": Periurban Colonialism in Togo's Eweland, 1900–1960.* Rochester, NY: University of Rochester Press, 2007.

Lawrance, Benjamin N., Emily Lynn Osborn, and Richard L. Roberts, eds. *Intermediaries, Interpreters, and Clerks: African Employees in the Making of Colonial Africa, Africa and the Diaspora.* Madison: University of Wisconsin Press, 2006.

Lee, Wayne. "A Final Word." *Journal of American History* 93, no. 4 (2007): 1161–62

———. "Mind and Matter—Cultural Analysis in American Military History: A Look at the State of the Field." *Journal of American History* 93, no. 4 (2007): 1116–42.

———. "Warfare and Culture." In *Warfare and Culture in World History,* edited by Lee. New York: NYU Press, 2011.

Leopold, Mark. "Legacies of Slavery in North West Uganda: The Story of the 'One-Elevens.'" In *Slavery in the Great Lakes Region of East Africa,* edited by Henri Médard and Shane Doyle, 180–99. Athens: Ohio University Press, 2007.

Leslie, J. A. K. *A Survey of Dar es Salaam.* London: Oxford University Press, 1963.

Lettow-Vorbeck, Paul von. *Afrika wie ich es wiedersah.* Munich: J. F. Lehmann, 1955.

———. *Heia Safari! Deutschlands Kampf in Ostafrika.* Leipzig: Koehler, 1920.

———. *Meine Erinnerungen aus Ostafrika.* Leipzig: Koehler, 1920.

———. *My Reminiscences of East Africa.* 1920. Reprint, Nashville: Battery Classics, 1991.

Lettow-Vorbeck, Paul von, and Ursula von Lettow-Vorbeck. *Mein Leben.* Biberach, Germany: Koehler, 1957.

Leue, August. *Dar-es-Salaam: Bilder aus dem Kolonialleben.* Berlin: Wilhelm Süsserott, 1903.

Lewerenz, Susann. *Die deutsche Afrika-Schau (1935–1940): Rassismus, Kolonialrevisionismus und postkoloniale Auseinandersetzungen im nationalsozialistischen Deutschland.* Frankfurt: Peter Lang, 2006.

———. "'Loyal Askari' and 'Black Rapist'—Two Images in the German Discourse on National Identity and Their Impact on the Lives of Black People in Germany, 1918–1945." In *German Colonialism and National Identity,* edited by Michael Perraudin und Jürgen Zimmerer, 173–83. New York: Routledge, 2011.

Liebert, Eduard von. *Neunzig Tage im Zelt: Meine Reise nach Uhehe, Juni bis September 1897*. Berlin: Mittler und Sohn, 1898).

Liesegang, Gerhard. "Nguni Migrations between Delagoa Bay and the Zambezi, 1821–1839." *African Historical Studies* 3, no. 2 (1970): 317–37.

Lindsay, Lisa, and Stephan F. Miescher. "Men and Masculinities in Modern African History." Introduction to *Men and Masculinities in Modern Africa*, edited by Lindsay and Miescher. Portsmouth, NH: Heinemann, 2003.

"Lokales." *Anzeigen für Tanga (Stadt und Bezirk)*, 24 October 1903.

"Lokales." *Usambara Post*. 14 April 1906.

Lonsdale, John. "Agency in Tight Corners: Narrative and Initiative in African History." *Journal of African Cultural Studies* 13, no. 1 (2000): 5–16.

Lubkemann, Stephen. *Culture in Chaos: An Anthropology of the Social Condition in War*. Chicago: University of Chicago Press, 2008.

Lucassen, Jan, and Erik Jan Zürcher. "Conscription as Military Labour: The Historical Context." *International Review of Social History* 43, no. 3 (1998): 405–19.

Lüdtke, Alf. "People Working: Everyday Life and German Fascism." *History Workshop Journal* 50 (2000): 74–92.

———. "What Is the History of Everyday Life and Who Are Its Practitioners?" Introduction to *The History of Everyday Life*, edited by Lüdtke, 3–40. Princeton: Princeton University Press, 1995.

Lunn, Joe. "Male Identity and Martial Codes of Honor: A Comparison of the War Memoirs of Robert Graves, Ernst Jünger, and Kande Kamara." *Journal of Military History* 69, no. 3 (2005): 713–35.

———. *Memoirs of the Maelstrom: A Senegalese Oral History of the First World War*. Portsmouth, NH: Heinemann, 1999.

———. "'Les races guerrières': Racial Preconceptions in the French Military about West African Soldiers during the First World War." *Journal of Contemporary History* 34, no. 4 (1999): 517–36.

Lutteroth, Ascan Roderich. *Tunakwenda: Auf Kriegssafari in Deutsch-Ostafrika*. Hamburg: Broschek, 1938.

Lynn, John A., II. *Battle: A History of Combat and Culture*. New York: Westview, 2003.

———. *The Bayonets of the Republic: Motivation and Tactics in the Army of Revolutionary France, 1791–94*. Urbana: University of Illinois Press, 1984.

———. *Women, Armies, and Warfare in Early Modern Europe*. New York: Cambridge University Press, 2008.

MacDonell, Bror Urme. *Mzee Ali: The Biography of an African Slave-Raider Turned Askari and Scout*. Johannesburg: 30° South Publishers, 2006.

Maddox, Gregory H. "Mtunya: Famine in Central Tanzania, 1917–20." *Journal of African History* 31, no. 2 (1990): 181–97.

Mader, Friedrich Wilhelm. *Die rätselhafte Boma: Erzählung aus den Kämpfen der deutschen Schutztruppe in Ostafrika im Sommer 1918*. Kolonial-Bücherei, vol. 84. Berlin: Steiniger, 1942.

Maercker, Georg. *Unsere Schutztruppe in Ostafrika*. Berlin: Karl Siegismund, 1893.

Mann, Erick J. *Mikono ya damu: "Hands of Blood": African Mercenaries and the Politics of Conflict in German East Africa, 1888–1904*. Frankfurt: Peter Lang, 2002.

Mann, Gregory. "Locating Colonial Histories: Between France and West Africa." *American Historical Review* 110, no. 2 (2005): 409–34.

——. *Native Sons: West African Veterans and France in the Twentieth Century*. Durham, NC: Duke University Press, 2006.

——. "What Was the *Indigénat*? The 'Empire of Law' in French West Africa." *Journal of African History* 50, no. 3 (2009): 331–53.

Mapunda, O. B., and G. P. Mpangara. *The Maji Maji War in Ungoni*. Dar es Salaam: East African Publishing House, 1969.

Marjomaa, Risto. "The Martial Spirit: Yao Soldiers in British Service in Nyasaland (Malawi), 1895–1939." *Journal of African History* 44, no. 3 (2003): 413–32.

Marlantes, Karl. *What It Is Like to Go to War*. New York: Atlantic Monthly Press, 2011.

Martin, Bradford G. *Muslim Brotherhoods in Nineteenth-Century Africa*. Cambridge: Cambridge University Press, 1976.

——. "Muslim Politics and Resistance to Colonial Rule: Shaykh Uways B. Muhammad al-Bārawī and the Qādirīya Brotherhood in East Africa." *Journal of African History* 10, no. 3 (1969): 471–86.

Martin, Peter. *Schwarze Teufel, edle Mohren: Afrikaner in Geschichte und Bewusstsein der Deutschen*. Hamburg: Hamburger Edition, 2001.

Martin, Stephen H. "Brass Bands and the Beni Phenomenon in Urban East Africa." *African Music* 7, no. 1 (1991): 72–81.

Marvin, David K. "The Boma at Masoko—Rungwe District." *Tanganyika Notes and Records* 57 (1961): 216–25.

Mass, Sandra. "Das Trauma des weissen Mannes: Afrikanische Kolonialsoldaten in propagandistischen Texten, 1914–1923." *L'homme* 12, no. 1 (2001): 11–33.

——. *Weisse Helden, schwarze Krieger: Zur Geschichte kolonialer Männlichkeit in Deutschland, 1918–1964*. Cologne: Böhlau, 2006.

"Matschemba Expedition." *DKB* 10, no. 20 (1899): 692.

Mauss, Marcel. *The Gift: Forms and Functions of Exchange in Archaic Societies*. Translated by W. D. Halls. Abingdon, UK: Routledge, 1990.

McBride, Dwight. *Impossible Witnesses: Truth, Abolitionism, and Slave Testimony*. New York: New York University Press, 2001.

McCracken, John. "Coercion and Control in Nyasaland: Aspects of the History of a Colonial Police Force." *Journal of African History* 27, no. 1 (1986): 127–47.

McIntosh, Janet. *The Edge of Islam: Power, Personhood, and Ethnoreligious Boundaries on the Kenya Coast*. Durham, NC: Duke University Press, 2009.

McLaughlin, Peter. "Victims as Defenders: African Troops in the Rhodesian Defence System, 1890–1980." *Small Wars and Insurgencies* 2, no. 2 (1991): 240–75.

McNeill, William Hardy. *Keeping Together in Time: Dance and Drill in Human History*. Cambridge, MA: Harvard University Press, 1995.

Médard, Henri, and Shane Doyle, eds. *Slavery in the Great Lakes Region of East Africa*. Oxford, James Currey, 2007.

Meinertzhagen, Richard. *Army Diary, 1899–1926*. Edinburgh: Oliver and Boyd, 1960.

Meldon, J. A. "Notes on the Sudanese in Uganda." *Journal of the Royal African Society* 7, no. 26 (1908): 123–46.

Mercer, Patricia. "Shilluk Trade and Politics from the Mid-Seventeenth Century to 1861." *Journal of African History* 12, no. 3 (1971): 407–26.

Methfessel, Christian. "Spreading the European Model by Military Means? The Legitimization of Colonial Wars and Imperialist Interventions in Great Britain and German around 1900." *Comparativ* 22, no. 6 (2012): 42–60.

Michels, Eckard. "Deutschlands bekanntester 'Kolonialheld' und seine 'Askari': Paul von Lettow-Vorbeck und der Feldzug in Ostafrika im Ersten Weltkrieg." *Revue d'Allemagne et pays de langue allemande* 38, no. 4 (2006): 541–54.

———. "Ein Feldzug—zwei Perspektiven? Paul von Lettow-Vorbeck und Heinrich Schnee über den Ersten Weltkrieg in Ostafrika." In *Militärische Erinnerungskultur: Soldaten im Spiegel von Biographien, Memoiren und Selbstzeugnissen*, edited by M. Epkenhans, S. Förster, and K. Hagemann, 152–68. Paderborn: Ferdinand Schöningh, 2006.

———. *"Der Held von Deutsch-Ostafrika": Paul von Lettow-Vorbeck: Ein preussischer Kolonialoffizier*. Paderborn: Ferdinand Schöningh, 2008.

Michels, Stefanie. "Askari—treu bis in den Tod? Vom Umgang der Deutschen mit ihren schwarzen Soldaten." In *AfrikanerInnen in Deutschland und schwarze Deutsche—Geschichte und Gegenwart*, edited by Marianne Bechhaus-Gerst and Reinhard Klein-Arendt, 171–86. Münster: LIT, 2004.

———. "Macht der Bilder: Herrschaftspose, Hetzbild, AnklageStreit um eine Kolonialfotografie." In *"Macht und Anteil an der Weltherrschaft": Berlin und der deutsche Kolonialismus*, edited by Ulrich van der Heyden and Joachim Zeller, 185–90. Münster: Unrast, 2005.

———. "'Reichsadler und Giraffe'—Askari am Grab von Lettow-Vorbeck." In *Koloniale und postkoloniale Konstruktion von Afrika und Menschen afrikanischer Herkunft in der deutschen Alltagskultur*, edited by Marianne Bechhaus-Gerst and Sunna Gieseke, 315–38. Frankfurt am Main: Lang, 2007.

———. *Schwarze deutsche Kolonialsoldaten: Mehrdeutige Repräsentationsräume und früher Kosmopolitismus in Afrika*. Bielefeld: Transcript, 2009.

———. "Soldatische Frauenwelten." In *Frauen in den deutschen Kolonien*, edited by Marianne Bechhaus-Gerst and Mechthild Leutner, 162–93. Berlin: Links, 2009.

Miehe, Gudrun, Katrin Bromber, Said Khamis, and Ralf Grosserhode, eds. *Kala Shairi: German East Africa in Swahili Poems*. Cologne: Köppe, 2002.

Miescher, Stephan F. "The Life Histories of Boakye Yiadom (Akasease Kofi of Abetifi, Kwawu): Exploring the Subjectivity and 'Voices' of a Teacher-Catechist in Colonial Ghana." In *African Words, African Voices: Critical Practices in Oral History*, edited by Luise White, Miescher, and David William Cohen, 162–93. Bloomington: Indiana University Press, 2001.

Militärischer Suaheli-Sprachführer für Deutsch-Ostafrika. Dar es Salaam: Deutsch-Ostafrikanische Rundschau, 1911.

Militärisches Orientierungsheft für Deutsch-Ostafrika. Dar es Salaam: Deutsch-Ostafrikanische Rundschau, 1911.

Miller, Charles. *Battle for the Bundu: The First World War in East Africa*. London: Macdonald and Jane's, 1974.

Miller, Joseph. "The Imbangala and the Chronology of Early Central African History." *Journal of African History* 13, no. 4 (1972): 549–74.

Miller, William Ian. *The Mystery of Courage*. Cambridge, MA: Harvard University Press, 2000.

Millett, Allan R. "Professionalism." In *The Reader's Companion to Military History*, edited by Robert Cowley and Geoffrey Parker, 370–71. New York: Houghton Mifflin, 1996.

"Missionschronik: Aus unserer Mission." *ELM* 67, no. 22 (1912): 509–11.

Mitchell, Timothy. "Everyday Metaphors of Power." *Theory and Society* 19, no. 5 (1990): 545–77.

———. "The Limits of the State: Beyond Statist Approaches and Their Critics." *American Political Science Review* 85, no. 1 (1991): 77–96.

Mitford, B. R. "Extracts from the Diary of a Subaltern on the Nile in the Eighties and Nineties." *Sudan Notes and Records* 18, no. 2 (1935): 167–93.

Miura, Toru, and John Edward Philips, eds. *Slave Elites in the Middle East and Africa: A Comparative Study*. London: Kegan Paul International, 2000.

Moesta, K. "Die Einwirkungen des Krieges auf die Eingeborenenbevölkerung in Deutsch-Ostafrika." *Koloniale Rundschau* 1/3 (1919): 5–25.

Monson, Jamie. "Relocating Maji Maji: The Politics of Alliance and Authority in the Southern Highlands of Tanzania, 1870–1918." *Journal of African History* 39, no. 1 (1998): 95–120.

———. "War of Words: The Narrative Efficacy of Medicine in the Maji Maji War." In *Maji Maji: Lifting the Fog of War*, edited by James Giblin and Jamie Monson, 33–69. Leiden: Brill, 2010.

Moore, Sally Falk. *Social Facts and Fabrications: "Customary" Law on Kilimanjaro, 1880–1980*. Cambridge: Cambridge University Press, 1986.

Morlang, Thomas. *Askari und Fitafita: "Farbige" Söldner in den deutschen Kolonien*. Berlin: Links, 2008.

———. "Die farbigen Soldaten und Hilfskrieger der deutschen Kolonialtruppen." MA thesis, Westfälischen Wilhelms-Universität zu Münster, 1990.

———. "'Die Kerls haben ja nicht mal Gewehre': Der Untergang der Zelewski-Expedition in Deutsch-Ostafrika im August 1891." *Militärgeschichte: Zeitschrift für historische Bildung* 11, no. 2 (2001): 22–28.

———. "'Ich habe die Sache satt hier, herzlich satt': Briefe des Kolonialoffiziers Rudolf von Hirsch aus Deutsch-Ostafrika, 1905–1907." *Militärgeschichtliche Zeitschrift* 61 (2002): 489–521.

———. "'Prestige der Rasse' contra 'Prestige des Staates': Die Diskussionen über die Befugnisse farbiger Polizeisoldaten gegenüber Europäern in den deutschen Kolonien." *Zeitschrift für Geschichtswissenschaft* 49, no. 6 (2001): 498–509.

———. "'Die Wahehe haben ihre Vernichtung gewollt': Der Krieg der 'Kaiserlichen Schutztruppe' gegen die Hehe in Deutsch-Ostafrika (1890–1898)." In *Kolonialkriege: Militärische Gewalt im Zeichen des Imperialismus*, edited by Thoralf Klein and Frank Schumacher, 80–108. Hamburg: Hamburger Edition, 2006.

Mosley, Leonard. *Duel for Kilimanjaro: An Account of the East African Campaign, 1914–18*. London: Weidenfeld and Nicolson, 1963.

Mosse, George L. *Fallen Soldiers: Reshaping the Memory of the World Wars*. New York: Oxford University Press, 1990.

Moyd, Michelle. "'All people were barbarians to the *askari*': Askari Identity and Honor in the Maji Maji War, 1905–1907." In *Maji Maji: Lifting the Fog of War*, edited by James Giblin and Jamie Monson, 149–80. Leiden: Brill, 2010.

———. "Becoming *Askari*: African Soldiers and Everyday Colonialism in German East Africa, 1850–1918." PhD diss., Cornell University, 2008.

———. "Bomani: African Soldiers as Colonial Intermediaries in German East Africa, 1890–1914." In *German Colonialism Revisited: African, Asian, and Oceanic Experiences*, edited by Nina Berman, Klaus Mühlhahn, and Patrice Nganang, 101–13. Ann Arbor: University of Michigan Press, 2014.

———. "Language and Power: Africans, Europeans, and Language Policy in German Colonial Tanganyika." Master's thesis, University of Florida, Gainesville, 1996.

———. "Making the Household, Making the State: Colonial Military Communities and Labor in German East Africa." *International Labor and Working-Class History* 80, no. 1 (2011): 53–76.

———. "'We don't want to die for nothing': Askari at War in German East Africa, 1914–1918." In *Race, Empire and First World War Writing*, edited by Santanu Das, 90–107. Cambridge: Cambridge University Press, 2011.

Müller, Fritz Ferdinand. *Deutschland, Zanzibar, Ostafrika: Geschichte einer deutschen Kolonialeroberung, 1884–1890*. Berlin: Rütten and Loening, 1959.

———. *Kolonien unter der Peitsche: Eine Dokumentation*. Berlin: Rütten und Loening, 1962.

Munson, Robert B. "The Landscape of German Colonialism: Mt. Kiliman-jaro and Mt. Meru, ca. 1890–1916." PhD diss., Boston University, 2005.

Murray, Williamson. "Does Military Culture Matter?" Orbis 43, no. 1 (1999): 134–51.

Muschalek, Marie. "Policing Colonial Africa: Rethinking a Research Agenda." Unpublished seminar paper, History Department, Cornell University, 2009.

———. "Everyday Violence and the Production of Colonial Order: The Police in German Southwest Africa, 1905–1915." PhD diss., Cornell University, 2014.

Mutonya, Mungai, and Timothy Parsons. "KiKAR: A Swahili Variety in Kenya's Colonial Army." Journal of African Languages and Linguistics 25 (2004): 111–25.

Myerly, Scott Hughes. British Military Spectacle: From the Napoleonic Wars through the Crimea. Cambridge, MA: Harvard University Press, 1996.

———. "'The eye must entrap the mind': Army Spectacle and Paradigm in Nineteenth-Century Britain." Journal of Social History 26, no. 1 (1992): 105–31.

"Nachrichten aus Moschi." ELM 57, no. 6 (1902): 128–31.

"Nachrichten aus Myambani: Quartalbericht von Miss. Augustus (4. Quartal 1904)." Evangelisch-Lutherisches Missionsblatt 60, no. 7 (1905).

Naranch, Bradley. "'Colonized Body,' 'Oriental Machine': Debating Race, Railroads, and the Politics of Reconstruction in Germany and East Africa, 1906–1910." Central European History 33, no. 3 (2000): 299–338.

Neiberg, Michael. Soldiers' Lives through History: The Nineteenth Century. Westport, CT: Greenwood, 2006.

Newbury, C. W., and A. S. Kanya-Forstner. "French Policy and the Origins of the Scramble for West Africa." Journal of African History 10, no. 2 (1969): 253–76.

"Nguru." DOAZ, 11 August 1906.

Niesel, Hans-Joachim. "Kolonialverwaltung und Missionen in Deutsch-Os-tafrika 1890–1914." PhD diss., Freie Universität, Berlin, 1971.

Nigmann, Ernst. Felddienstübungen für farbige (ostafrikanische) Truppen. Dar es Salaam: Deutsch-Ostafrikanische Zeitung, 1910.

———. German Schutztruppe in East Africa: History of the Imperial Protec-torate Force, 1889–1911. Translated by R. E. Dohrenwend. 1911. Reprint, Nashville: Battery Press, 2005.

———. Geschichte der kaiserlichen Schutztruppe für Deutsch-Ostafrika. Berlin: Mittler und Sohn, 1911.

———. Schwarze Schwänke: Fröhliche Geschichten aus unserem schönen alten Deutsch Ostafrika. Berlin: Safari, 1922.

Nkuli, Mlolwa. "Notes on Nyamwezi Utani." In Utani Relationships in Tan-zania, edited by Stephen A. Lucas, 4:1–9. 7 vols. Dar es Salaam: Univer-sity of Dar es Salaam, 1975.

Nordenstam, Tore. "Descriptive Ethics in the Sudan: An Example." *Sudan Notes and Records* 48 (1967): 90–98.

———. *Sudanese Ethics*. Uppsala: Scandinavian Institute of African Studies, 1968.

Nordstrom, Carolyn. *A Different Kind of War Story*. Philadelphia: University of Pennsylvania Press, 1997.

Ochonu, Moses E. *Colonialism by Proxy: Hausa Imperial Agents and Middle Belt Consciousness in Nigeria*. Bloomington: Indiana University Press, 2014.

Odhiambo, E. S. Atieno. "The Movement of Ideas: A Case Study of Intellectual Responses to Colonialism among the Liganua Peasants." In *Hadith*, vol. 6, *History and Social Change in East Africa*, edited by Bethwell Ogot, 163–80. Nairobi: East African Literature Bureau, 1976.

———. "The Landscapes of Memory in Twentieth-Century Africa." In *In Search of a Nation: Histories of Authority and Dissidence in Tanzania*, edited by Gregory H. Maddox and James L. Giblin, 114–27. Oxford: James Currey, 2005.

Omissi, David E. *The Sepoy and the Raj: The Indian Army, 1860–1940*. London: Macmillan, 1994.

Ortner, Sherry. *Anthropology and Social Theory: Culture, Power, and the Acting Subject*. Durham, NC: Duke University Press, 2006.

———. "Resistance and the Problem of Ethnographic Refusal." *Comparative Studies in Society and History* 37, no. 1 (1995): 173–93.

Osborn, Emily Lynn. "'Circle of Iron': African Colonial Employees and the Interpretation of Colonial Rule in French West Africa." *Journal of African History* 44, no. 1 (2003): 29–50.

———. *Our New Husbands are Here: Households, Gender, and Politics in a West African State from the Slave Trade to Colonial Rule*. Athens: Ohio University Press, 2011.

Osterhammel, Jürgen. 2005. *Colonialism: A Theoretical Overview*. 2nd ed. Princeton: Markus Wiener.

Paasche, Hans. *Im Morgenlicht: Kriegs-, Jagd-, und Reise-Erlebnisse in Ostafrika*. Berlin: C. U. Schwetschke und Sohn, 1907.

Page, Melvin E. "Black Men in a White Man's War." Introduction to *Africa and the First World War*, edited by M. E. Page. New York: St. Martin's, 1987.

———. *The Chiwaya War: Malawians and the First World War*. Boulder: Westview, 2000.

———. "The Manyema Hordes of Tippu Tip: A Case Study in Social Stratification and the Slave Trade in Eastern Africa." *International Journal of African Historical Studies* 7, no. 1 (1974): 69–84.

———. "The War of Thangata: Nyasaland and The East African Campaign, 1914–1918." *Journal of African History* 19, no. 1 (1978): 87–100.

Paice, Edward. *Tip and Run: The Untold Tragedy of the Great War in Africa*. London: Weidenfeld and Nicolson, 2007.

Parpart, Jane L., and Marianne Rostgaard, eds. *The Practical Imperialist: Letters from a Danish Planter in German East Africa 1888–1906*. Leiden: Brill, 2006.

Parsons, Timothy. *The African Rank-and-File: Social Implications of Colonial Military Service in the King's African Rifles, 1902–1964*. Portsmouth, NH: Heinemann, 1999.

——. "'All *askaris* are family men': Sex, Domesticity and Discipline in the King's African Rifles, 1902–1964." In *Guardians of Empire: The Armed Forces of the Colonial Powers c. 1700–1964*, edited by D. Killingray and D. E. Omissi, 157–78. New York: Manchester University Press, 1999.

——. "'Kibra is our blood': The Sudanese Military Legacy in Nairobi's Kibera Location, 1902–1968." *International Journal of African Historical Studies* 30, no. 1 (1997): 87–122.

——. *The 1964 Army Mutinies and the Making of Modern East Africa*. Portsmouth, NH: Heinemann, 2003.

——. "'Wakamba warriors are soldiers of the queen': The Evolution of the Kamba as a Martial Race, 1890–1970." *Ethnohistory* 46, no. 4 (1999): 671–701.

Paur, Dr. "Die Psychologie in der militärischen Erziehung." *Jahrbücher für die deutsche Armee und Marine* 97 (1895): 98–104.

Peiper, Otto. "Ethnographische Beobachtungen aus dem Bezirke Kilwa, Deutsch-Ostafrika." *Baessler Archiv: Beiträge zur Völkerkunde*, vol. 10. Berlin: Dietrich Reimer, 1926.

——. *Pocken und Pockenbekämpfung in Deutsch-Ostafrika*. Berlin: Richard Schoetz, 1925.

Peligal, Rona Elayne. "Spatial Planning and Social Fluidity: The Shifting Boundaries of Ethnicity, Gender, and Class in Arusha, Tanzania, 1920–1967." PhD diss., Columbia University, 1999.

Peled, Alon. 1998. *A Question of Loyalty: Military Manpower Policy in Multiethnic States*. Ithaca: Cornell University Press.

Perras, Arne. "Colonial Agitation and the Bismarckian State." In *Wilhelminism and Its Legacies: German Modernities, Imperialism, and the Meanings of Reform, 1890–1930: Essays for Hartmut Pogge von Strandmann*, edited by Geoff Eley and James N. Retallack, 154–70. New York: Berghahn Books, 2003.

Pesek, Michael. "The Boma and the Peripatetic Rule: Mapping Colonial Rule in German East Africa, 1889–1903." *Western Folklore* 66, nos. 3–4, (2007): 233–57.

——. "Colonial Conquest and the Struggle for the Presence of the Colonial State in German East Africa, 1885–1903." In *Inventing Collateral Damage: Civilian Casualties, War, and Empire*, edited by Stephen J. Rockel and Rick Halpern, 161–82. Toronto: Between the Lines, 2009.

——. *Das Ende eines Kolonialreiches: Ostafrika im Ersten Weltkrieg*. Frankfurt: Campus, 2010.

——."Islam und Politik in Deutsch-Ostafrika." In *Alles unter Kontrolle: Disziplinierungsprozesse im kolonialen Tansania (1850–1960)*, edited by Albert Wirz, Andreas Eckert, and Katrin Bromber, 99–140. Cologne: Köppe, 2003.

——. *Koloniale Herrschaft in Deutsch-Ostafrika: Expeditionen, Militär und Verwaltung seit 1880*. Frankfurt am Main: Campus, 2005.

——. "*Ruga-ruga*: The History of an African Profession, 1820–1918." In *German Colonialism Revisited: African, Asian, and Oceanic Experiences*, edited by Nina Berman, Klaus Mühlhahn, and Patrice Nganang, 85–100. Ann Arbor: University of Michigan Press, 2014.

——. *Tänze der Hoffnung, Tänze der Macht: Koloniale Erfahrung und ästhethischer Ausdruck im östlichen Afrika*. Sozialanthropologische Arbeitspapiere, no. 72. Berlin: Das Arabische Buch, 1997.

Pizzo, David. "'To devour the land of Mkwawa': Colonial Violence and the Hehe War in East Africa, ca. 1884–1914." PhD diss., University of North Carolina, Chapel Hill, 2007.

Poeschel, Hans. *Bwana Hakimu: Richterfahrten in Deutsch-Ostafrika*. Leipzig: Koehler und Voigtländer, 1940.

Pouwels, Randall Lee. *Horn and Crescent: Cultural Change and Traditional Islam on the East African Coast, 800–1900*. Cambridge: Cambridge University Press, 1987.

Powell, Eve Troutt. *A Different Shade of Colonialism: Egypt, Great Britain, and the Mastery of the Sudan*. Berkeley: University of California Press, 2003.

——. "Translating Slavery." *International Journal of Middle Eastern Studies* 39 (2007): 165–67.

Prince, Magdalene von. *Eine deutsche Frau im innern Deutsch-Ostafrikas*. Berlin: Mittler und Sohn, 1903.

Prince, Thomas Paul Ansorge von. *Gegen Araber und Wahehe: Erinnerungen aus meiner ostafrikanischen Leutnantszeit 1890–1895*. Berlin: Mittler und Sohn, 1914.

Prunier, Gérard. "Military Slavery in the Sudan during the Turkiyya, 1820–1885." In *The Human Commodity: Perspectives on the Trans-Saharan Slave Trade*, edited by E. Savage, 129–39. London: Frank Cass, 1992.

Prussian War Ministry. *Exerzir-Reglement für die Infanterie*. Berlin: Mittler und Sohn, 1889.

Puder, Hauptmann. "Bericht über die Shirambo-Expedition." *DKB* 10, no. 14 (1899): 473–75.

Ranger, T. O. *Dance and Society in Eastern Africa, 1890–1970: The Beni Ngoma*. Berkeley: University of California Press, 1975.

Raugh, Harold E., Jr. *The Victorians at War, 1815–1914: An Encyclopedia of Military History*. Santa Barbara: ABC-CLIO, 2004.

Raum, [Missionary] "Eröffnung der Usambara-Eisenbahn in Neu-Moschi am 7. Februar 1912." *ELM* 67, no. 9 (1912): 208–11.

Raum, Otto Friedrich. "German East Africa: Changes in African Life under German Administration, 1892–1914." In *History of East Africa*, edited by V. Harlow and E. M. Chilver, 163–207. Oxford: Clarendon Press, 1965.

Read, Margaret. "The Moral Code of the Ngoni and Their Former Military State." *Africa: Journal of the International African Institute* 11, no. 1 (1938): 1–24.

———. "Tradition and Prestige among the Ngoni." *Africa: Journal of the International African Institute* 9, no. 4 (1936): 453–84.

Redmayne, Alison. "Mkwawa and the Hehe Wars." *Journal of African History* 9, no. 3 (1968): 409–36.

Rehfeldt, Walter. *Bilder vom Kriege in Deutsch-Ostafrika nach Aquarellen.* Hamburg: Charles Fuchs, 1920.

Reichard, Paul. "Die Bedeutung von Tabora für Deutsch-Ostafrika." *Deutsche Kolonialzeitung* 2, no. 6 (1890): 67–68.

———. *Deutsch-Ostafrika: Das Land und seine Bewohner, seine politische und wirtschaftliche Entwickelung.* Leipzig: Otto Spamer, 1892

———. "Vorschläge zu einer Reiseausrüstung für Ost- und Centralafrika." *Zeitschrift der Gesellschaft für Erdkunde* 24 (1889): 1–80.

———. "Die Wanjamwuesi." *Zeitschrift der Gesellschaft für Erdkunde zu Berlin* 24 (1889): 246–60, 304–31.

Reid, Brian Holden. "American Military History: The Need for Comparative Analysis." *Journal of American History* 93, no. 4 (2007): 1154–57.

Reid, Richard. "Arms and Adolescence: Male Youth, Warfare, and Statehood in Nineteenth-Century Eastern Africa." In *Generations Past: Youth in East African History*, edited by Andrew Burton and Hélène Charton-Bigot. Athens: Ohio University Press, 2010: 25–46.

———. "Past and Presentism: The 'Precolonial' and the Foreshortening of African History." *Journal of African History* 52, no. 2 (2011): 135–55.

———. "Revisiting Primitive War: Perceptions of Violence and Race in History." *War and Society* 26, no. 2 (2007): 1–25.

———. "Warfare and the Military." In *The Oxford Handbook of Modern African History*, edited by John Parker and Richard Reid, 114–31. Oxford: Oxford University Press, 2013.

———. *Warfare in African History.* Cambridge: Cambridge University Press, 2012.

———. *War in Pre-colonial Eastern Africa: The Patterns and Meanings of State-level Conflict in the Nineteenth Century.* Athens: Ohio University Press, 2007.

"Reisebriefe unseres Missionsdirektors. 7. In Dar-es-Salaam." *ELM* 68, no. 4 (1913).

Rempel, Ruth. "'No Better than a Slave or Outcast': Skill, Identity, and Power among the Porters of the Emin Pasha Relief Expedition, 1887–1890.'" *International Journal of African Historical Studies* 43, no. 2 (2010): 279–318.

Richelmann, G. *Meine Erlebnisse in der Wissmann-Truppe.* Magdeburg: Creutz'sche Verlagsbuchhandlung, 1892.

Richards, Paul. *Fighting for the Rainforest: War, Youth and Resources in Sierra Leone.* Oxford. James Currey, 1996.

Roberts, Andrew. "Nyamwezi Trade." In *Pre-colonial African Trade: Essays on Trade in Central and Eastern Africa before 1900,* edited by R. Gray and D. Birmingham, 39–74. London: Oxford University Press, 1970.

——, ed. *Tanzania before 1900.* Nairobi: East African Publishing House, 1968.

Robinson, Ronald. "Non-European Foundations of European Imperialism: Sketch for a Theory of Collaboration." In *Studies in the Theory of Imperialism,* edited by Roger Owen and Bob Sutcliffe, 117–42. Bristol: Longman, 1972.

Rockel, Stephen J. *Carriers of Culture: Labor on the Road in Nineteenth-Century East Africa.* Social History of Africa. Portsmouth, NH: Heinemann, 2006.

——. "Enterprising Partners: Caravan Women in Nineteenth Century Tanzania." *Canadian Journal of African Studies* 34, no. 3 (2000): 784–78.

Rodgers, Thomas Earl. "Billy Yank and GI Joe: An Exploratory Essay on the Sociopolitical Dimensions of Soldier Motivation." *Journal of Military History* 69, no. 1 (2005): 93–121.

Roos, Julia. "Women's Rights, Nationalist Anxiety, and the 'Moral' Agenda in the Early Weimar Republic: Revisiting the 'Black Horror' Campaign against France's African Occupation Troops." *Central European History* 42, no. 3 (2009): 473–508.

Roscoe, John. *Twenty-Five Years in East Africa.* 1921. Reprint, New York: Negro Universities Press, 1969.

Rotberg, Robert I., and Ali Al'Amin Mazrui, eds. *Protest and Power in Black Africa.* New York: Oxford University Press, 1970.

Saavedra Casco, José Arturo. *Utenzi, War Poems, and the German Conquest of East Africa: Swahili Poetry as Historical Source.* Trenton: Africa World Press, 2007.

Sabea, Hanan. "Mastering the Landscape? Sisal Plantations, Land, and Labor in Tanga Region, 1893–1980s." *International Journal of African Historical Studies* 41, no. 3 (2008): 419–22.

Said, Mohamed. *The Life and Times of Abdulwahid Sykes (1924–1968): The Untold Story of the Muslim Struggle against British Colonialism in Tanganyika.* London: Minerva, 1998.

Sakafu, A. L. "The Pastor: Yohane Nyagava." In *Modern Tanzanians: A Volume of Biographies,* edited by John Iliffe. Nairobi: East African Publishing House, 1973.

Sassen, F. J. *Deutsches Kolonial-Militärrecht.* Rastatt: H. Greiser, 1911.

Scheper-Hughes, Nancy, and Philippe Bourgois. "Making Sense of Violence." Introduction to *Violence in War and Peace: An Anthology,* edited by Scheper-Hughes and Bourgois, 1–32. Oxford: Blackwell, 2004.

Schippel, Dr. "Von Islam im westlichen Teile von Deutsch-Ostafrika." *Die Welt des Islams* 2, no. 1 (1914): 6–10.

Schmidt, Elizabeth. *Peasants, Traders, and Wives: Shona Women in the History of Zimbabwe, 1870–1939*. Portsmouth, NH: Heinemann, 1992.

Schmidt, Heike. "(Re)negotiating Marginality: The Maji Maji War and Its Aftermath in Southwestern Tanzania, ca. 1905–1916." *International Journal of African Historical Studies* 43, no. 1 (2010): 27–62.

Schmidt, Paul von. *Die Erziehung des Soldaten*. Berlin: Verlag der Liebelschen Buchhandlung, 1894.

Schmokel, Wolfe W. *Dream of Empire: German Colonialism, 1919–1945*. New Haven: Yale University Press, 1964.

Schnee, Heinrich, ed. *Deutsches Kolonial-Lexikon*. 3 vols. Leipzig: Quelle und Meyer, 1920.

——. *Deutsch-Ostafrika im Weltkriege*. Leipzig: Quelle und Meyer,1919.

——. *Die koloniale Schuldlüge*. Berlin: Sachers und Kuschel, 1924.

Schnee, Heinrich, and William Harbutt Dawson. *German Colonization, Past and Future: The Truth about the German Colonies*. London: Allen and Unwin, 1926.

Scott, James C. *The Art of Not Being Governed: An Anarchist History of Upland Southeast Asia*. New Haven: Yale University Press, 2009.

Scott, Joan. "The Evidence of Experience." *Critical Inquiry* 17, no. 4 (1991): 773–97.

"Shaurihalle." *UP* 5, no. 23 (14 April 1906).

Sharkey, Heather J. "African Colonial States." In *The Oxford Handbook of Modern African History*, edited by John Parker and Richard Reid, 151–70. Oxford: Oxford University Press, 2013.

Shaw, Bryant P. "Force Publique, Force Unique: The Military in the Belgian Congo, 1914–1939." PhD diss., University of Wisconsin, 1984.

Sheriff, Abdul. *Slaves, Spices and Ivory in Zanzibar: Integration of an East African Commercial Empire into the World Economy, 1770–1873*. London: James Currey, 1987.

Shomari, Mwalimu Mbaraka bin. "Shairi la Bwana Mkubwa." In *Kala Shairi: German East Africa in Swahili Poems*, edited by Gudrun Miehe, Katrin Bromber, Said Khamis, and Ralf Grosserhode. Cologne: Köppe, 2002.

Shorter, Aylward. *Chiefship in Western Tanzania: A Political History of the Kimbu*. Oxford: Clarendon Press, 1972.

——. *Nyungu-ya-Mawe: Leadership in Nineteenth Century Tanzania*. Nairobi: East African Publishing House, 1969.

——. "Nyungu-ya-Mawe and the 'Empire of the Ruga-Rugas.'" *Journal of African History* 9, no. 2 (1968): 235–59.

Showalter, Dennis. "Gunpowder and Regional Military Systems." In *The Military and Conflict between Cultures: Soldiers at the Interface*, edited by James C. Bradford, 49–88. College Station: Texas A&M University Press, 1997.

Siegel, Brian. "Bomas, Missions, and Mines: The Making of Centers on the Zambian Copperbelt." *African Studies Review* 31, no. 3 (1988): 61–84.

Sikainga, Ahmad Alawad. "Comrades in Arms or Captives in Bondage: Sudanese Slaves in the Turco-Egyptian Army, 1821–1865." In *Slave Elites in the Middle East and Africa: A Comparative Study*, edited by Miura Toru and John Edward Philips, 197–214. London: Kegan Paul International, 2000.

——. "Military Slavery and the Emergence of a Southern Sudanese Diaspora in the Northern Sudan, 1884–1954." In *White Nile, Black Blood: War, Leadership, and Ethnicity from Khartoum to Kampala*, edited by J. Spaulding and S. Beswick, 23–38. Lawrenceville, NJ: Red Sea Press, 2001.

——. *The Western Bahr al-Ghazal under British Rule, 1898–1956*. Athens: Ohio University Center for International Studies, 1991.

Sippel, Harald. "Koloniale Begegnung im rechtsfreien Raum? Die Jurisdiktion der 'Eingeborenenrichter' in den afrikanischen Kolonien des deutschen Reiches." In *Die (koloniale) Begegnung*, edited by Marianne Bechhaus-Gerst and Reinhard Klein-Arendt, 297–98. Frankfurt: Peter Lang, 2003.

Sippel, Harald. "Verwaltung und Recht in Deutsch-Ostafrika." In *Kolonisierung des Rechts. Zur kolonialen Rechts- und Verwaltungsordnung*, edited by Rüdiger Voigt and Peter Sack, 271–92. Baden-Baden: Nomos, 2001.

Sledge, E. B. *With the Old Breed: At Peleliu and Okinawa*. Oxford: Oxford University Press, 1990.

Smedt, Johan de. "The Nubis of Kibera: A Social History of the Nubians and Kibera Slums." PhD diss., University of Leiden, 2011.

Snider, Don M. "An Uninformed Debate on Military Culture." *Orbis* 43, no. 1 (1999): 115–33.

Spear, Thomas T. *Mountain Farmers: Moral Economies of Land and Agricultural Development in Arusha and Meru*. Oxford: James Currey, 1997.

——. "Neo-Traditionalism and the Limits of Invention in British Colonial Africa." *Journal of African History* 44, no. 1 (2003): 3–27.

——. *Zwangendaba's Ngoni, 1821–1890: A Political and Social History of a Migration*. Madison: University of Wisconsin, African Studies Program, 1972.

Spellig, Fritz. "Die Wanjamwesi: Ein Beitrag zur Völkerkunde Ostafrikas." *Zeitschrift für Ethnologie* 59, no. 3/6 (1927): 201–52.

Spiller, Roger J. "Military History and Its Fictions." *Journal of Military History* 70, no. 4 (2006): 1081–97.

Spring, Christopher. *African Arms and Armor*. Washington, DC: Smithsonian Institution Press, 1993.

Stahl, Kathleen Mary. *History of the Chagga People of Kilimanjaro*. London: Mouton, 1964.

Stairs, William G. *African Exploits: The Diaries of William Stairs, 1887–1892*. Edited by Roy MacLaren. Montreal: McGill-Queen's University Press, 1998.

Stapleton, Timothy J. *African Police and Soldiers in Colonial Zimbabwe, 1923–80*. Rochester: University of Rochester Press, 2011.

——. "The Composition of the Rhodesia Native Regiment during the First World War: A Look at the Evidence." *History in Africa* 30 (2003): 283–95.

———. "The Impact of the First World War on African People." In *Daily Lives of Civilians in Wartime Africa: From Slavery Days to Rwandan Genocide*, edited John Laband, 113–37. Westport, CT: Greenwood, 2007.

———. *A Military History of South Africa*. Santa Barbara: Praeger, 2010.

———. *No Insignificant Part: The Rhodesia Native Regiment and the East Africa Campaign of the First World War*. Waterloo, ON: Wilfrid Laurier University Press, 2006.

Steege, Paul, Andrew Stewart Bergerson, Maureen Healy, and Pamela E. Swett. "The History of Everyday Life: A Second Chapter." *Journal of Modern History* 80, no. 2 (2008): 358–78.

Steinmetz, George. "'The Devil's Handwriting': Precolonial Discourse, Ethnographic Acuity, and Cross-Identification in German Colonialism." *Comparative Studies in Society and History* 45, no. 1 (2003): 41–95.

Stilwell, Sean Arnold. *Paradoxes of Power: The Kano "Mamluks" and Male Royal Slavery in the Sokoto Caliphate, 1804–1903. Social History of Africa.* Portsmouth, NH: Heinemann, 2004.

Stoecker, Helmut. "The Conquest of Colonies: The Establishment and Extension of German Colonial Rule." In *German Imperialism in Africa: From the Beginning until the Second World War*, edited by Stoecker. Translated by Bernd Zöller. London: C. Hurst, 1986.

Stoler, Ann. "Colonial Archives and the Arts of Governance." *Archival Science* 2, nos. 1–2 (2002): 87–109.

Stollowsky, Otto. *Jambo Sana! Lustige Geschichten, Plaudereien und Schnurren aus dem Leben in Deutsch-Ost-Afrika*. Leipzig-Anger: Walther Dachsel, 1935.

Strachan, Hew. *The First World War in Africa*. Oxford: Oxford University Press, 2004.

———. "Training, Morale, and Modern War." *Journal of Contemporary History* 41, no. 2 (2006): 211–27.

Streets, Heather. *Martial Races: The Military, Race, and Masculinity in British Imperial Culture, 1857–1914.* Manchester: Manchester University Press, 2004.

Studdert, David. *Conceptualising Community: Beyond the State and Individual*. New York: Palgrave Macmillan, 2005.

Sunseri, Thaddeus. "Famine and Wild Pigs: Gender Struggles and the Outbreak of Maji Maji in Uzaramo (Tanzania)." *Journal of African History* 38, no. 2 (1997): 235–59.

———. "Statist Narratives and Maji Maji Ellipses." *International Journal of African Historical Studies* 33, no. 3 (2000): 567–84.

———. *Vilimani: Labor Migration and Rural Change in Early Colonial Tanzania*. Portsmouth, NH: Heinemann, 2002.

Taithe, Bertrand. *The Killer Trail: A Colonial Scandal in the Heart of Africa*. Oxford: Oxford University Press, 2009.

Taylor, Diana. "Translating Performance." *Profession* (2002): 44–50.

Thompson, David G. "Villains, Victims, and Veterans: Buchheim's *Das Boot* and the Problem of the Hybrid Novel-Memoir as History." *Twentieth Century Literature* 39, no. 1 (1993): 59–78.

Thompson, J. Malcolm. "Colonial Policy and the Family Life of Black Troops in French West Africa, 1817–1904." *International Journal of African Historical Studies* 23, no. 3 (1990): 423–53.

Thompson, P. S. *Black Soldiers of the Queen: The Natal Native Contingent in the Anglo-Zulu War.* Tuscaloosa: University of Alabama Press, 2006.

Thorburn, D. Hay. "Sudanese Soldiers' Songs." *Journal of the Royal African Society* 24, no. 96 (1925): 314–21.

Thornton, John. "The Art of War in Angola, 1575–1680." *Comparative Studies in Society and History* 30, no. 2 (1988): 360–78.

———. *Warfare in Atlantic Africa, 1500–1800.* London: UCL Press, 1999.

Titunik, Regina. "The Myth of the Macho Military." *Polity* 40, no. 2 (2008): 137–63.

"Tolles Vorgehen farbiger Polizeisoldaten." *UP* 11, no. 35 (31 August 1912).

Trimingham, J. Spencer. *Islam in East Africa.* Oxford: Clarendon Press, 1964.

———. *Islam in the Sudan.* London: Frank Cass, 1965.

Trotha, Lothar von. *Meine Bereisung von Deutsch-Ostafrika.* Berlin: B. Brigl, 1897.

Trotha, Trutz von. "'One for Kaiser': Beobachtungen zur politischen Soziologie der Prügelstrafe am Beispiel des 'Schutzgebietes Togo.'" In *Studien zur Geschichte des deutschen Kolonialismus in Afrika*, edited by P. Heine and U. van der Heyden, 415–35. Pfaffenweiler: Centaurus, 1995.

———. "'The Fellows Can Just Starve': On Wars of 'Pacification' in the African Colonies of Imperial Germany and the Concept of 'Total War.'" In *Anticipating Total War: The German and American Experience, 1871–1914*, edited by Manfred F. Boemeke, Roger Chickering, and Stig Förster, 415–35. Cambridge: Cambridge University Press, 1999.

Tucker, Alfred. *Eighteen Years in Uganda and East Africa.* London: Edward Arnold, 1908.

"Übungsmarsch und gefechtsmässiges Schiessen der 5. Kompagnie." *DOAZ* 6, no. 27 (1904).

Unomah, A. C. "African Collaboration with the Germans in the Conquest of Isike of Unyanyembe, 1890–1893." Unpublished manuscript, Makerere University, Kampala, 1970.

———. 1977. *Mirambo of Tanzania.* London: Heinemann Educational.

"Unsere schwarze Polizei." *UP* 11, no. 30 (27 July 1912).

Van Onselen, Charles. "The Role of Collaborators in the Rhodesian Mining Industry, 1900–1935." *African Affairs* 72, no. 289 (1973): 401–18.

Vandervort, Bruce. *Wars of Imperial Conquest in Africa, 1830–1914.* Bloomington: Indiana University Press, 1998.

Vansina, Jan. *Paths in the Rainforest: Toward a History of Political Tradition in Equatorial Africa.* Madison: University of Wisconsin Press, 1990.

Velten, Carl. *Prosa und Poesie der Suaheli.* Berlin: Carl Velten, 1907.

Vieweg, Burkhard. *Macho Porini—die Augen im Busch: Kautschukpflan-zer Karl Vieweg in Deutsch-Ostafrika: Authentische Berichte, 1910–1919.* Weikersheim: Margraf, 1996.

Vogel, Jakob. "Military, Folklore, *Eigensinn:* Folkloric Militarism in Germany and France, 1871–1914." *Central European History* 33, no. 4 (2000): 487–504.

Volkens, Georg. "Reise des Dr. G. Volkens nach Moschi." *DKB* 5, no. 14 (1894): 308–16.

"Vom Exerzierplatz in Daressalam." *Kolonie und Heimat* 1, no. 4 (1907): 8–9.

Von Herff, Michael. "'They walk through the fire like the blondest German': African Soldiers Serving the Kaiser in German East Africa (1888–1914)." MA thesis, McGill University, 1991.

"Vorschriften über die Handhabung des Dienstbetriebes auf den Stationen der Schutztruppe für Ost-Afrika." *DKB* 2, no. 3 (1891): 55–59.

Wagner, Rudolf, and F. Buchmann. *Wir Schutztruppler: Die deutsche Wehrmacht übersee.* Berlin: Buntdruck, 1913.

Wald, Erica. "Health, Discipline and Appropriate Behaviour: The Body of the Soldier and Space of the Cantonment." *Modern Asian Studies* 46, no. 4 (2012): 815–56.

Wärthl, [Missionary]. "Durch Busch und Wald im innern Afrikas." *ELM* 67, no. 17 (1912): 389–92.

"Was Prinz Adalbert in Tanga gesehen hat: Bilder vom Prinzenbesuch am 13. Februar." *UP* 4, no. 15 (18 February 1905).

Weber, Max. *Economy and Society: An Outline of Interpretive Sociology.* 3 vols. New York: Bedminster Press, 1968.

Weishaupt, [missionary]. "Überblick über unsere Missionsstationen in Os-tafrika. (Fortsetzung.) 4. Moschi." *ELM* 67, no. 9 (1912): 204–8.

Wenig, Richard. *Kriegs-Safari: Erlebnisse und Eindrücke auf den Zügen Let-tow-Vorbecks durch das östliche Afrika.* Berlin: Scherl, 1920.

Weniger, Erich. *Die Erziehung des deutschen Soldaten.* Berlin: Mittler und Sohn, 1944.

Werther, C. Waldemar, ed. *Die mittleren Hochländer des nördlichen Deutsch-Ost-Afrika: Wissenschaftliche Ergebnisse der Irangi-Expedition 1896–1897 nebst kurzer Reisebeschreibung.* Berlin: Hermann Paetel, 1898.

Weule, Karl. *Der Krieg in den Tiefen der Menschheit.* Stuttgart: Kosmos, Ge-sellschaft der Naturfreunde, 1916.

———. *Native Life in East Africa: The Results of an Ethnological Research Expedition.* Translated by Alice Werner. London: Pitman and Sons, 1909. Reprint, Westport, CT: Negro Universities Press, 1970.

———. *Negerleben in Ostafrika: Ergebnisse einer ethnologischen Forschun-gsreise.* Leipzig: F. A. Brockhaus, 1908. Original edition of *Native Life in East Africa.*

———. "Ostafrikanische Eingeborenen-Zeichnungen: Psychologische Einblicke in die Künstlerseele des Negers." In *IPEK: Jahrbuch für prähistorische und ethnographische Kunst,* edited by H. Kühn. Leipzig: Klinkhardt und Biermann, 1926.

White, Luise. *The Assassination of Herbert Chitepo: Texts and Politics in Zimbabwe*. Bloomington: Indiana University Press, 2003.

——. *The Comforts of Home: Prostitution in Colonial Nairobi*. Chicago: University of Chicago Press, 1990.

Whitehouse, Howard. *Battle in Africa, 1879–1914*. Camberley, UK: Field Books, 1987.

Wiese, Carl. *Expedition in East-Central Africa, 1888–1891: A Report*. Edited by Harry W. Langworthy. Translated by Donald Ramos. 1st ed. Norman: University of Oklahoma Press, 1983.

Willis, Justin. *Potent Brews: A Social History of Alcohol in East Africa, 1850–1999*. London: James Currey, 2002.

Wilson, C. T. "A Journey from Kagéi to Tabora and Back." *Proceedings of the Royal Geographical Society and Monthly Record of Geography*, n.s., 2, no. 10 (1880): 616–20.

Wilson, Peter H. "Defining Military Culture." *Journal of Military History* 72, no. 1 (2008): 11–41.

Wilson, Salim. *I Was a Slave*. London: Stanley Paul, 1960.

Wimmelbücker, Ludger. *Mtoro bin Mwinyi Bakari: Swahili Lecturer and Author in Germany*. Dar es Salaam: Mkuki na Nyota, 2009.

——. "Verbrannte Erde: Zu den Bevölkerungsverlusten als Folge des Maji-Maji-Krieges." In *Der Maji-Maji-Krieg in Deutsch-Ostafrika, 1905–1907*, edited by Felicitas Becker and Jigal Beez, 87–99. Berlin: Links, 2005.

Wingate, F. R. *Mahdism and the Egyptian Sudan: Being an Account of the Rise and Progress of Mahdiism, and of Subsequent Events in the Sudan to the Present Time*. London: Macmillan, 1891.

Wissmann, Hermann von. *Afrika: Schilderungen und Rathschläge zur Vorbereitung für den Aufenthalt und den Dienst in den deutschen Schutzgebieten*. Berlin: Mittler und Sohn, 1903.

Wolseley, Garnet Joseph. *In Relief of Gordon: Lord Wolseley's Campaign Journal of the Khartoum Relief Expedition, 1884–1885*. Edited by Adrian Preston. London: Hutchinson, 1967.

Woodward, Rachel. *Military Geographies*. Oxford: Blackwell, 2004.

Wright, Marcia. "Local Roots of Policy in German East Africa." *Journal of African History* 9, no. 4 (1968): 621–30.

——. "Maji Maji: Prophecy and Historiography." In *Revealing Prophets: Prophecy in Eastern African History*, edited by David M. Anderson and Douglas H. Johnson, 124–42. London: James Currey, 1995.

——. *Strategies of Slaves and Women: Life Stories from East/Central Africa*. New York: Lilian Barber, 1993.

Zantop, Susanne. *Colonial Fantasies: Conquest, Family, and Nation in Precolonial Germany, 1770–1870*. Durham, NC: Duke University Press, 1997.

——. "Colonial Legends, Postcolonial Legacies." In *A User's Guide to German Cultural Studies*, edited by S. Denham, I. Kacandes, and J. Petropoulos. Ann Arbor: University of Michigan Press, 1997.

Zeller, Joachim. "Das Ende der deutschen Kolonialgeschichte—Der Einzug Lettow-Vorbecks und seiner 'Heldenschar' in Berlin." In *Kolonialmetropole Berlin: Eine Spurensuche*, edited by U. Van der Heyden and Zeller. Berlin: Berlin Edition, 2002.

Zimmerman, Sarah. "*Mesdames Tirailleurs* and Indirect Clients: West African Women and the French Colonial Army, 1908–1918." *International Journal of African Historical Studies* 44, no. 2 (2011): 299–322.

Zirkel, Kirsten. "Military Power in German Colonial Policy: The *Schutztruppen* and Their Leaders in East and South-West Africa, 1888–1918." In *Guardians of Empire: The Armed Forces of the Colonial Powers c. 1700–1964*, edited by D. Killingray and D. Omissi, 91–113. New York: Manchester University Press, 1999.

"Zu dem Übungsmarsch der 5. Kompagnie." *DOAZ* 6, no. 29 (16 July 1904).

Zulfo, 'Ismat Hasan. *Karari: The Sudanese Account of the Battle of Omdurman*. Translated by Peter Clark. London: Frederick Warne, 1980.

Index

Abercorn, 7, 209
Achmed, Mohamed, 53
Alexandria, 2, 238n94
amanuenses, 25–27
Anglo-Egyptian army, 27, 45, 59, 84,
113; Abdulcher Farrag and, 26, 39,
53–57, 59; Schutztruppe recruitment and, 37, 41, 46, 49–51, 61,
111–12
Anleitung zum Felddienst in Deutsch-
Ostafrika, 47
Ansar, 53, 54–58
Arusha, 2, 171
askariboys, 123, 124, 145, 164, 166, 171,
172, 208

Baden-Württemburg, 93
Bagamoyo: askari in, 137, 161–12, 167,
178–80, 184; Bushiri bin Salim and,
6, 36, 84; recruitment at, 97
Baggara, 50, 237 n. 77
banghi, 80–81, 194
Barthes, Roland, 209
batemi, 69, 73, 74–75, 76
Bavaria, 93
Belgian colonial army, 62, 143, 145
Belgian Congo, 32, 70
Bengerstorf, Hermann von, 154
beni, 14, 198
Bennett, Norman, 72
Berlin, 66, 95, 96
Berlin Conference, 16, 39
beshaush, 113, 120–21, 168, 184
Bezirksamt, 157, 169
Bezirksgericht, 156
"big men," 33, 46, 65, 72, 92, 135, 192;
officer-patrons and, 89, 110; status
and, 2, 4, 19, 27, 43, 106, 110, 125,
145–47; violence and, 5, 116, 132;
wealth and, 4, 18, 123

bin Abdallah, Juma, 156–60
bin Adam Mohamed, Mahjub, 208
bin Salim, Bushiri, 6, 36–37, 40, 84
bin Shomari, Mwalimu Mbaraka, 88
binti Mkondo, Habiba, 156–59
Bockmann, Marine-Oberingenieur,
1–2, 3
Boell, Ludwig, 7
boma. See maboma
Branch, Daniel, 34–35
British colonial army, 3, 11, 31, 37, 46,
50, 54, 58, 117–18, 143, 145. See also
King's African Rifles (KAR)
British East Africa, 3, 10–11, 17, 110, 147,
207–9
British War Office, 207
Bukoba, 167

Cairo, 27, 37, 41, 53, 58, 59, 60
Callwell, Charles E., 117–19, 130
campaign communities see Schutztruppe: campaign communities
caravan trading, 49, 61, 63; Ali Kalikilima and, 27; Bushiri bin
Salim, 6, 36; guards and, 41, 61,
65, 71–72; Nyamwezi and, 65,
69–76, 85; porters and, 41, 65,
70–71, 75, 164; trade routes, 41,
65, 104, 112, 150, 169, 175–77;
women and, 127
Chagga, 174, 187, 208
chain gangs, 21–22, 47, 98, 108, 110, 138,
158, 162, 166, 179, 185, 190
Christianity, 52, 157, 171–72, 184. See also
Lutherans; missionaries
cloth, 67, 70, 72, 73, 77–78, 106, 156,
168
coastal wars. See Wissmanntruppe:
coastal wars and
Cold War, 10

CPSIA information can be obtained at www.ICGtesting.com
Printed in the USA
LVOW08s1235091214

417978LV00004B/5/P